A Subtle Balance

Expertise, Evidence, and Democracy in Public Policy and Governance, 1970–2010

Edited by

EDWARD A. PARSON

McGill-Queen's University Press
Montreal & Kingston • London • Ithaca

ISBN 978-0-7735-4529-8 (cloth)
ISBN 978-0-7735-4530-4 (paper)
ISBN 978-0-7735-8382-5 (ePDF)
ISBN 978-0-7735-8387-0 (ePUB)

Legal deposit second quarter 2015
Bibliothèque nationale du Québec

Printed in Canada on acid-free paper that is 100% ancient forest free (100% post-consumer recycled), processed chlorine free

This book has been published with the help of a grant from the Canadian Federation for the Humanities and Social Sciences, through the Awards to Scholarly Publications Program, using funds provided by the Social Sciences and Humanities Research Council of Canada.

McGill-Queen's University Press acknowledges the support of the Canada Council for the Arts for our publishing program. We also acknowledge the financial support of the Government of Canada through the Canada Book Fund for our publishing activities.

Library and Archives Canada Cataloguing in Publication

A subtle balance : expertise, evidence, and democracy in public policy and governance, 1970–2010 / edited by Edward A. Parson.

This volume is inspired by the wide-ranging contributions to scholarship and practice of A.R. (Rod) Dobell.
Includes bibliographical references and index.
Issued in print and electronic formats.
ISBN 978-0-7735-4529-8 (bound). – ISBN 978-0-7735-4530-4 (pbk.). – ISBN 978-0-7735-8382-5 (ePDF). – ISBN 978-0-7735-8387-0 (ePUB)

1. Public administration – Canada – Decision making – History – 20th century. 2. Public administration – Canada – Decision making – History – 21st century. 3. Policy sciences – Canada – Decision making – History – 20th century. 4. Policy sciences – Canada – Decision making – History – 21st century. 5. Canada – Social policy – Decision making – History – 20th century. 6. Canada – Social policy – Decision making – History – 21st century. 7. Democracy – Canada. I. Parson, Edward A., 1954–, author, editor

JL86.D42S92 2015 352.3'30971 C2015-901248-1
C2015-901249-X

Typeset by Jay Tee Graphics Ltd. in 10.5/13 Sabon

Contents

Tables and Figures

TABLES

FIGURES

Acknowledgments

The completion of this project owes debts to many people who contributed in diverse ways. In addition to those who appear as chapter authors, the project benefited immeasurably from the thoughtful and substantive contributions of the additional symposium participants, who enriched the discussion and volume in more ways than I can identify. For this generosity and their insights I thank Emmanuel Brunet-Jailly, Ken Dobell, Peter Dobell, Martine Desbois, Brian Emmett, Liz Gilliland, Joy Illington, Bruce Kennedy, Robert Lapper, Evert Lindquist, Sharon Manson-Singer, Tom Pedersen, Sukumar Periwal, Ray Protti, Gordon Smith, Philip Steenkamp, and Joy Weismiller. In its initial conception the project benefited from enthusiastic support by Jamie Cassels, then provost (now president) of the University of Victoria. Project planning and oversight was handled by a steering committee including Lauren Dobell, John Langford, Justin Longo, Jodie Walsh, and Lyn Tait. Administration of the symposium and project was handled brilliantly by Jodie Walsh, ably assisted at the symposium by Jennifer Swift. Research assistance in completing the volume was provided by Behn Andersen at the University of Victoria, Laura Harlow and Janet Buchanan at the University of Michigan, and Susanna Pfeffer, John Bloom, and Amy Atchison at UCLA. Institutional support was provided by the President's Office and School of Public Administration of the University of Victoria, with financial support from the Social Sciences and Humanities Research Council of Canada under the Aid to Research Workshops and Conferences Programme, as well as the Institute for Research on Public Policy, CSCW Systems Corporation, Juniper Consulting, and Whitehall Policy Consulting. I am particularly grateful for all the support, including a congenial home for me during two summers preparing the volume, provided by the Centre for Global Studies at the University of Victoria under the leadership of its past and current directors, Gordon Smith and Oliver Schmidtke. For all these contributions, thank you.

A SUBTLE BALANCE

1

A Subtle Balance: Editor's Introduction

EDWARD A. PARSON

This volume presents a review and critical assessment of major trends and themes in public policy and governance in Canada over the past four decades. It is the culmination of a three-year project, centred on a symposium held at the University of Victoria in the summer of 2011. The symposium convened an intensive dialogue on policy and governance among thirty distinguished participants of two types: academics who conduct research on public policy and governance, and sophisticated practitioners with long experience dealing with policy and governance from the perspective of practical engagement in real, high-stakes decisions.

The project and volume are inspired by the intellectual legacy of A.R. (Rod) Dobell, whose career spans this period and tracks several of its trends and enduring challenges, as both participant and commentator. Straying some distance from his training in mathematics (UBC MA, 1961) and economics (MIT PhD, 1965), Dobell's career alternated periods of academic research and reflection on public policy and policy analysis with senior positions in government, international organizations, and independent research bodies. Highlights included being a founding faculty member in the Institute for Policy Analysis at the University of Toronto (1969–73), establishing the first full-time course in Quantitative Analysis for federal public servants (1971–73), serving as deputy secretary (planning) in the Treasury Board Secretariat (1973–76), directing the General Economics Branch of the OECD Secretariat (1976–78), directing the School of Public Administration at the University of Victoria (1978–84), and serving as president of the Institute for Research on Public Policy (IRPP) (1984–91). His academic home since 1976 has been the University of Victoria, where he held the inaugural Winspear Chair in Public Policy from 1991 to 1997.

The project uses Dobell and his contributions in several capacities. He has been, first, a prominent protagonist in the developments in policy, analysis, and governance that we examine; second, an exemplar of engaged thinking, both interdisciplinary and applied, speaking to a broad, non-specialist audience without losing rigour or precision, to which the project aspires; and third, a substantive contributor to the project. But while the project uses Dobell in these diverse ways, it is not primarily intended as a festschrift. The project aims to honour his contributions not through overt tribute or personal anecdote but through emulation of the engagement in enduring questions of high intellectual and practical importance, wide-ranging interests and enthusiasms, and goodwill that have consistently marked his contributions.

Our overall topic is public policy and governance over the past forty-odd years, mainly but not exclusively at the federal level in Canada. Over this period, what are the most prominent trends and the most enduring tensions and challenges? What are the main landmarks of progress and the major setbacks? What have we learned, and how can we do better? In posing these questions we speak of both public policy and governance, to recognize the fact that key public debates and decisions are not confined to, or exclusively determined within, the formal institutions of government. Indeed, one prominent trend of recent decades, noted by many scholars and elaborated by several contributions here, is a diffusion of influence over public debates and decisions among many institutions, both inside and outside government.

This topic presents a vast landscape, yet it has distinctive features. In particular, three prominent themes animated the papers and discussions at the symposium and are captured in this volume. They provide organizing principles that weave together many contributions of the volume but do not span the entire range of issues raised within them. For shorthand, we call them "expertise and democracy," "scales of authority," and "representation and participation."

The first is first among equals in the project – to the extent that it provides the volume subtitle, *Expertise, Evidence, and Democracy*. This theme concerns the persistent tension between two widely held aspirations for public decisions. On the one hand, we want them to be informed, even guided, by the best available knowledge, evidence, and analysis. This is an aspiration not for omniscience but merely for the knowledge that is available and relevant to be integrated into decisions in a justified and rational way. On the other hand, we also want decisions to be fully democratic and participatory, reflecting the will of citizens expressed directly or faithfully filtered through their elected representatives. The tension between these two aspirations has ancient roots, yet it is completely current; it manifests itself both in deep problems of political and social theory and in decisions raising heated controversy this month. It can be found in Plato, in Dewey, and in current debates as varied as those on climate change, genetically modified organisms, injection sites for drug addicts, military procurement, and public support for – and access to – scientific research and data collection.

While the ancient form of this tension was concerned with competing claims for aristocratic and popular rule based on supposed superior wisdom or virtue (Dahl 1991), its modern form mostly concerns specific expert knowledge of how the world works, whether the natural world, the social world, or the fabricated technological world. Such knowledge of facts and causal relations in the world informs understanding of the consequences of actions and is thus valuable for informing decisions made (at least partly) for instrumental purposes, to pursue desired consequences. The tension appears in modern political debate in various ways. Political actors who favor a choice for reasons other than evidence of its consequences may nevertheless try to deceive others (or themselves) that the evidence actually supports their preferred course. Advocates may try to build support for a preferred choice by selectively advancing scientific claims that favor it, even if these claims are eccentric, outweighed by better evidence, or simply wrong. For their part, experts may attempt to claim superior standing in public decisions by virtue of their scientific knowledge or status, when these can never be dispositive for decisions.

The tension is enduring, and admits no general resolution that cleanly divides authority between science and democracy or between evidence and political aims. Policy actors and institutions respond to it in diverse ways: with ambiguous terms like "policy-relevant" facts, used without looking too closely at what makes a fact policy-relevant, who decides, or what warrant for action "policy-relevant" implies; with liberal use of scientific claims and counterclaims in policy arguments; with a general, albeit uneven, commitment of public support to scientific research and data collection; and with diverse institutional designs to provide expert advice to decision makers that aim to jointly advance or balance the two aspirations. This muddling through succeeds to varying degrees on different issues. The tension often plays out, as multiple chapters here illustrate, within the labile, ambiguous concept of policy analysis – in continuing dispute over what policy analysis means, how to do it, and what its role is in legitimate public decisions. In particular, several chapters address the view, now common in Canadian policy circles, that the capacity to conduct high-quality policy analysis, and the availability of the data, tools, and institutional competencies it requires, have undergone a large and sustained decline over recent decades, and they examine the evidence for such a trend and its potential causes and consequences.

The second theme concerns spatial and institutional scale – the physical or structural scale at which policy issues manifest themselves and can most effectively be governed and the assignment of relevant authority across governing institutions or networks. Problems to be managed come at all scales from local to global, as do the capability and authority to address them. In practice, relevant legal authority and competency are often divided or ambiguously assigned, so solving problems requires coordination and negotiation among levels of government and between governments and other organizations, with many attendant opportunities for confusion and conflict. Like the expertise-democracy tension, questions of the proper allocation of authorities have old roots – in this case, based in concepts of sovereignty, international law, and federalism that have stabilized over several centuries – yet they also show current shifts and tensions.

While there have long been issues whose scale crossed levels of authority, the number and prominence of issues whose scale is mismatched to current authorities is increasing. Globalization is the most widely noted trend. The increasing intensity of interactions at a larger than national scale – economic, environmental, social, and political interactions – appears to call for coordinated governance at a corresponding large scale. Yet the substantive structure of many issues does not lie exclusively at one spatial scale. Even issues that look global can embed linkages and mutual influences that span multiple scales, from local to national to global. Climate change, a global process with linked effects at all scales down to the most local, is one clear example of complex cross-scale linkage, but by no means the only one. As issues shift in spatial scale or emerge at new scales, so also (to some degree) do needs for governance. Whether and how governance arrangements also shift is another matter, of course. Institutions do not easily give up power or status, and claims about the required scale to manage an issue are contestable, sometimes acting as proxies for conflict over how to manage it. Shifting issues thus require ongoing negotiation and accommodation among bodies with relevant authorities and capabilities to pursue new workable arrangements, however imperfect.

The third theme concerns the distribution of governance authority between different types of bodies and processes, particularly between those based on democratic representation and more direct participation by parties deemed to have special standing or concern in specific decisions. Starting with calls in the 1960s for "participatory democracy," recent decades have seen increasing demands to augment traditional representative processes with consultative and stakeholder-based processes that strengthen direct citizen involvement in decisions. In part, this trend can be viewed as a reaction to the increased strength and complexity of governments in modern nation-states. It may also reflect attempts to counterbalance trends related to the first two themes, because increased needs for expert input and international action move decisions away from citizens and raise concerns about a democratic deficit. The reality and importance of a trend to increased reliance on stakeholder processes is open to question, of course. It may represent a serious effort to redefine the relationship between representative and direct democratic processes. Alternatively, it may simply recast long-standing practices in modern language, or it may be more prominent in rhetorical enthusiasm than in real shifts of governance authority.

For each theme, we look over the interval since the late 1960s and ask the same questions. What are the main changes and trends over this period, and what are their causes? What are the main elements that endure, including persistent challenges and tensions, and what are their causes? And is there evidence of learning or progress – and how would we know? Our main focus is the federal level in Canada, which also provides most of the empirical material discussed in the chapters. But because similar trends and challenges have arisen over this period in multiple jurisdictions, notwithstanding differences in institutional and cultural contexts, the relevance of these themes and the insights we draw from them are broader, potentially including both sub-national jurisdictions within Canada and other national settings.

The volume is organized in clusters. Following this introduction, three chapters (2, 3, and 4) provide background and context. Zussman reviews the organization and management of policy analysis in the Canadian federal government from Prime Ministers Trudeau to Harper, providing a common historical and institutional background to inform subsequent contributions. A pair of short essays, by Ungerleider and Parson, then aim to show the current relevance of and controversy over the "expertise and democracy" theme, by taking two sides in a debate. Ungerleider cautions against the perils of technocracy, arguing that despite policy actors' desire for scientific evidence to support their positions, it is crucial to maintain enough separation between experts and democratic policymakers and to ensure the latter are on top. Parson presents a more sympathetic view of technical expertise in policy, laying out three conditions for issues where greater reliance on expertise is likely to be valuable and acceptable.

The next three chapters examine trends in the broad domain of social policy. Clark and Swain assess trends in policy and program evaluation in Aboriginal Affairs. Building on Zussman's large-scale history, they add rich institutional detail on how policy analysis and evaluation were integrated into the practices of one major federal department and how its aims and practices evolved over time under changing external conditions and pressures. Prince reviews reform of Canadian pension policy and its connection to broader political currents, focusing on three major episodes of reform between the 1960s and the 1990s. In contrast to scholarly accounts that highlight a shift from government to governance, he finds mixed trends in transparency and participation over this period and an overall tendency for governmental control over the process to increase – in terms of control over what options are considered, what decisions are reached, and framing the terms of the debate. Wolfson examines the use of analytic micro-simulation models in three major social-policy debates from the 1970s to the 1990s. His focus on a set of analytic tools and their use, rather than on political processes or outcomes, gives a unique perspective that rebuts several common critiques of formal policy analysis. In addition, he provides a striking account of the multiple ways models and analytic methods can enrich a policy debate, quite distinct from the simplistic view that they aim to provide a single recommended answer.

The next three chapters examine challenges related to environmental and natural resources policy. Van Eijndhoven reviews large-scale shifts in the character of environmental issues over the past five decades, highlighting two trends: a gradual shift toward global scale of processes, impacts, and required responses; and a shift in the role of science, from reactively interpreting observed environmental harms to identifying and characterizing long-term risks before they become clearly visible. Parson and Ernst examine the novel and potentially acute governance challenges posed by the emerging technological capability to engineer the global climate. Even more than the structural trends in environmental issues that van Eijndhoven identifies, these technologies – if ever deployed – appear to require a greater investment of authority in international-scale decision processes and in expert technical processes for real-time operational decisions if the grave risks the technologies pose are to be avoided. Turning from the global to the local scale, Bunton considers the 1990s conflict over land use and forest policy in British Columbia's Clayoquot Sound region and its resolution from the perspective of property rights, with particular focus on how structural conditions influenced the behaviour of the novel organization created to integrate multiple values in managing the region's forest resources.

While the previous two clusters of papers each examine a particular policy area, the third cluster considers issues related to methods, processes, and norms of policy-making and governance that cut across multiple policy areas. Culley and Horwitz extend and deepen a theme sketched by Bunton, the prospect of establishing novel forms of institutions as an alternative way to advance public purposes, instead of pursuing these aims by enacting regulations or other public policies. Examining current proposals for hybrid organizations that blend elements of private firms and not-for-profits, they express skepticism about this approach for several legal and policy reasons. Longo considers the rapid growth of computational capability and data, and identifies challenges and opportunities these capabilities pose for policy analysis and the networks of actors engaged in it – particularly in the possibility that open data and analytic platforms may facilitate increased or novel forms of citizen engagement in policy formation. Chapters by Langford and Carin add a normative dimension to the discussion, examining the responsibilities of policy analysts or others involved in policy development who are not the formally accountable decision makers. Langford notes and criticizes a common tendency for officials to deny personal moral responsibility for these acts, based on various rationalizations including an exaggerated Westminster model of ministerial (and only ministerial) accountability. Where Langford's analysis is based in moral philosophy, Carin examines the same problem from a practical perspective. Viewing the many pitfalls – cognitive, social, political, and economic – that obstruct both effective policy and policy analysis, he offers pragmatic guidelines for policy analysts who want to discharge these responsibilities honourably and well and still be effective.

In the first of two concluding essays Dobell provides his own five-decade overview of how he has understood the issues of the symposium and sought to guide constructive interventions, and how these have changed over time. Finally, I close the volume with a synthesis of common issues and insights that emerged from the multiple contributions and the rich commentary and discussion at the symposium.

2

Public Policy Analysis in Canada: A Forty-Year Overview

DAVID ZUSSMAN

INTRODUCTION

In September 2011 an offbeat sports movie with an improbable theme hit the silver screens across North America. The premise of the adaptation of Michael Lewis' 2003 book *Moneyball* was that the collected wisdom of baseball experts over the past century was subjective and often flawed. Long-established statistics concerning stolen bases, runs batted in, and batting averages, which had been used to gauge players' value since the early twentieth century, were relics of a time when data were scarce and better indicators were not available. Lewis argued that the Oakland Athletics, under General Manager Billy Beane, took advantage of better empirical measures of player performance to field a team that could compete successfully against much richer competitors. By re-evaluating strategies for player selection to better focus on wins on the field, the 2002 Oakland A's, with a salary budget of $41 million, quickly became competitive with teams like the New York Yankees, who spent over $125 million in salaries.

The movie was a hit because it told a compelling story that resonated with baseball fans and theatre-goers alike. Aside from great acting and storytelling, it reinforced the notion that data and analysis, if used correctly, provide an advantage over unwritten operating principles. *Moneyball* showed how rationality and analysis, based on relevant empirical evidence, provided better predictions and outcomes than tradition and preconceived ideas. While *Moneyball* is about the 2002 Athletics, the shift away from intuitive decision making in baseball started in the mid-1970s when Bill James, a Vietnam veteran and underemployed security guard, began to churn out in-depth analyses of whole baseball seasons. The timing of James' breakout work coincided with similar activities in most governments in developed economies, which became advocates of strategic planning, data collection, and the application of analysis to decision making. The storyline of evidence-based policy-making in Canada at first follows a trajectory similar to that in professional sports, with a steady adoption of new approaches, and then is later punctuated by disruptive events that shake up the landscape and leave recent progress ambiguous.

This chapter aims to give readers an appreciation of the major contributions of expertise and evidence to democratic policy and governance in Canada over the past forty years, which later chapters explore in detail. The chapter provides an overview of the evolution of policy-making since 1970, concluding with observations on the current policy environment. The focus is on the federal level, rather than including provinces, municipalities, or other organizations that practice policy analysis, for several reasons. Trends in the federal government have been extensively studied and are better documented. Policy work in other governments has varied widely in character and quality and so is difficult to characterize in general terms (Drummond 2011). And finally, it is mainly at the federal level that Rod Dobell, whose work has helped to animate and organize this project, made his major contributions to understanding and practice.

The chapter is divided into three sections. The first defines policy analysis and describes four major aspects of the political context for policy analysis in Canada. The second surveys key events and trends in policy analysis in Canada from 1970 to the present, divided into four periods coinciding with the tenure of different prime ministers. The chapter closes with a discussion of the policy environment today, highlighting major aspects of policy analysis that have been constant over the period and points of discontinuity that may signal major, perhaps permanent, changes in how policy analysis is done in Canada.

In addition to a review of the existing literature on policy-making in Canada, the chapter is based on evidence gleaned from two new strands of information. It draws on interviews with current and past policy leaders in the federal government. In addition, it draws on discussions at a roundtable session with a mixed group of academics and practitioners, held at the Centre on Public Management at the University of Ottawa in 2012.

POLICY ANALYSIS AND ITS POLITICAL CONTEXT IN CANADA

Of the many standard definitions of policy analysis, two are most relevant for our purposes. Radin (2000) argues that policy analysis seeks "to improve policy outcomes by applying systematic analytic methodologies to policy appraisal, assessment and evaluation." In contrast, Dobuzinskis, Howlett, and Laycock (2007) emphasize the role of multiple players in development of policy, observing that "policy analysis represents the efforts of actors inside and outside formal political decision-making processes to improve policy outcomes by applying systematic evaluative rationality to the development and implementation of policy options."

These two definitions offer three key insights regarding policy analysis and its place in decision making. First, both definitions stress that policy analysis explicitly aims at policy outcomes that improve the status quo. The goal is not simply to spend more tax dollars but to improve the current situation in any area of activity where government might have an interest. Second, both definitions emphasize that policy analysis relies on systematic use of a wide range of methods and disciplines – not just cost-benefit analysis, for example – thereby raising the question of what types of data or evidence are relevant and valid inputs to decision making. Third, the definitions remind us that policy analysis is concerned not only with developing options for decision makers, but also includes the process of defining the issue under consideration, the collection and analysis of relevant information, and the evaluation of outcomes. Simeon (1976, 550) captured the complexity and challenge of policy analysis when he argued that "policy-making is not, by and large, simply a matter of problem solving, of taking some common goal and seeking the 'best' or most cost effective 'solution.' It is rather a matter of choice in which resources are limited and in which goals and objectives differ and cannot easily be weighed against each other. Hence, policy-making is a matter of conflict."

Given the breadth of activities potentially included in these definitions, the professional role of policy analysis can, and has, varied

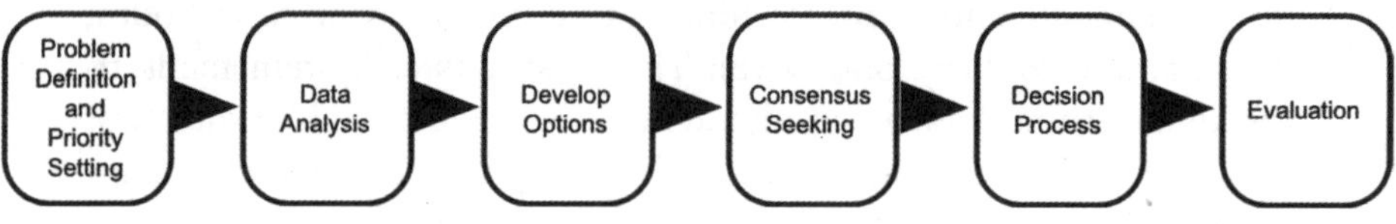

Figure 2.1 Elements of policy-making

widely depending on the agenda of the government, the demands of central agencies, and the requirements of individual ministers. Figure 2.1 provides a simplified representation of the six typical stages in policy-making and the various points where policy analysis can contribute to the decision-making process. Each stage can call on different skill sets, and different forms of interaction and consultation, between the political and public service side and between them and public or expert groups.

Policy decisions typically take a significant amount of time to move from problem definition to actual decision, although the process can be expedited for an emergency or a high government priority. Moreover, the time taken from the decision to adopt a policy to the evaluation of its outputs and outcomes can be many years. There are thus few instances where the same analysts are involved in a single policy from inception to evaluation. As a result, the policy process needs to be coordinated by senior officials who can manage the process and command the resources at the right time in the process.

Four enduring factors define the boundaries of policy analysis and development at the federal level in Canada. First, Canada is a federal state with constitutionally defined areas of federal and provincial responsibility, although both levels have moved on occasion into the others' areas in pursuit of policy objectives. Canadian federalism is further complicated by the particular role of Quebec, which has often sought to develop its own policies, including policies in areas that lie within federal jurisdiction (Brooks and Ménard 2013; Malcolmson and Myers 2012).

Second, Canada follows a Westminster system of government. The elements of that system are not precisely defined but typically include the need for a parliamentary majority in the lower house in order to govern, a fusion of executive and legislature, collective government decision making by cabinet, accountability of the government to parliament, and a professional career public service (Rhodes, Wanna, and Weller 2009, 232). The Westminster system tends to make government adversarial, a tendency strengthened by the "first past the post" electoral system with multiple parties, which "exaggerates voting majorities to cause regular changes of government and wholesale shifts in public policy" (Cairney 2012, 231). The Canadian version of Westminster gives particularly broad powers to the prime minister but still expects ministers to share collective responsibility for government decisions and be accountable to parliament for their own areas of responsibility. As a result – and despite the centralization of power in the Prime Minister's Office (Savoie 1999; Simpson 2001) – the policy-making mechanism still centres on the traditional Cabinet decision process, operating through approval of Memoranda to Cabinet sponsored by a responsible minister. Memoranda to Cabinet follow a fixed format that emphasizes analysis of policy options and program costs seen through a political lens.

Third, the advent of 24/7 news cycles and all-news networks representing a wide range of political ideologies has created a continuous demand for news, especially the kind that appeals to broad audiences by reporting on government failings and political pratfalls. As a result, the "drive for the 30-second sound bite diminishes the quality of the news" and has given the media unfiltered access to uninformed policy analysis (Cappe 2011). The effect of rapid news cycles on the policy community has been profound, since it has moved the nexus of policy discussions from policy units to communications offices, which exist to present the government's agenda in a favorable light. Tension between media and government communications officers has made the policy community less inclined to put their work before the public because they fear that the work will be misused or mischaracterized (Fallows 1996).

The fourth key contextual element for Canadian policy-making is the complex relationship between the public service and ministers (including the prime minister), which is central to a Westminster system of government. Alex Himelfarb, a recent secretary to the Cabinet, offered a clear characterization of this relationship when asked to explain it during the 2009 enquiry into the Sponsorship Program. He stated that the public service has two primary responsibilities to its political masters. First, it is obliged to offer fearless advice to ministers, informed by evidence-based analysis, even when it is not welcome (Wildavsky 1979). Second, it is obliged to loyally implement lawful decisions taken by the government, even when it believes the decisions are wrong.

These two responsibilities are the cornerstones of a professional, non-partisan, merit-based public service. They explain why governments have built protective walls like the Public Service Employment Act around the public service to guard it against political interference in appointments and promotions. Fearless advice and loyal implementation define the traditional – but no longer guaranteed – arrangement between the public service and ministers. In return, the public service has expected to be able to work anonymously and without direct accountability to the public, the media, or parliament, relying on its ministers to be publicly accountable for acts within their areas of responsibility. This relationship has recently changed significantly, first in the United Kingdom and Australia and then in Canada under the newly elected Conservative government in 2006 (Savoie 2003). With its first piece of legislation, the Federal Accountability Act (FAA), the new government assigned personal accountability to deputy ministers. Senior public servants could no longer operate as anonymous "fonctionnaires" shielded from public scrutiny by ministerial responsibility. At the same time, the government also signalled that the senior public service would no longer enjoy a privileged position in providing policy advice to ministers.

ANALYSIS AND EVIDENCE IN CANADIAN POLICY-MAKING, 1970–2010

This section reviews the development of policy analysis as a defined public service competency, from the Trudeau to the Harper governments. The review is necessarily schematic but aims at a minimum to capture key innovations and major changes. Since prime ministers are so influential in shaping the policy agenda and the way policy is developed, the section is divided by the terms of prime ministers since Trudeau. While the periods are delineated by sustained turnovers of governing party and long-serving prime ministers, prime ministers who served only briefly also affected the policy-making process significantly. John Turner, who served as prime minister for only two months and seventeen days in 1984, made major changes in the policy process when he eliminated the two coordinating Cabinet committees for social and economic development and abolished previous efforts to coordinate policy centrally. Similarly,

Kim Campbell shook the foundations of the public service in June 1993 when she implemented the de Cotret report (Canada 1992), restructured Cabinet decision making, and shrunk the Cabinet. The analysis of each period considers policy developments from three perspectives: that of significant external factors that affected federal policy-making, of organizational changes to the policy process, and of new developments in methods and analytical techniques. In addition to the narrative accounts, table 2.1 (p. 24) highlights the most significant changes of each period.

TRUDEAU/TURNER PERIOD, 1968–84 (INCLUDING CLARK, 1979–80)

The early Trudeau years were marked by widespread enthusiasm for rationalizing planning and decision making, which was evident in many decisions throughout government. In Cabinet, a system of standing committees was established to consider policy and program initiatives. Ministers were required to submit items in advance through Memoranda to Cabinet in forms that would support informed debate, with the process and submission criteria overseen by the Privy Council Office (PCO) (French 1984, 3). At the same time, new methods of applied micro-based policy analysis and evaluation were being promoted throughout the government, including novel integrated budget and planning systems such as the Planning, Programming Budgeting System (PPBS) recently developed in the United States Defense Department under Secretary Robert McNamara (Savoie 1999, 37–40). Promotion of these methods followed one major thrust of a 1962 Royal Commission on Government Organization.[1]

The main responsibility for these new analytic methods initially resided in the Planning Branch of the Treasury Board Secretariat (TBS), established in 1969 under the leadership of Al Johnson (secretary of the TBS) and Doug Hartle (deputy secretary of the Planning Branch). The TBS itself had been separated from Finance just three years before, with responsibility for government management and the expenditure budget. The rationale for deploying these methods and situating them in the TBS, as explained by Johnson, was that departmental spending proposals could only be reconciled with the government's overall fiscal framework only in the light of evaluations of program effectiveness and efficiency (Johnson 1971, 347).

The Planning Branch set out to explain, develop, and promote these methods through multiple initiatives, including a full-year training course in quantitative analysis (which Hartle brought Rod Dobell from the University of Toronto in 1970 to lead) and conducting a set of exemplary evaluations of important and problematic programs – including high-profile "Cabinet evaluation studies" overseen by committees of deputy ministers, with terms of reference approved by Cabinet committee. At the same time, ministries began establishing their own branches for policy, planning, and evaluation, many led by new positions of assistant deputy minister (ADM) for policy. The first of these were established in 1971, and nearly all ministries had them by the time a 1977 TBS directive required the functions (Johnson 1992, 85).

The broad mission of rationalizing government decision making – if the aim was ever in fact this expansive – faced significant challenges from the outset, both political and conceptual. Parallel areas of central authority in Finance and the PCO, albeit with less comprehensive and explicit intellectual foundations, limited the ambit of the TBS planning and evaluation system (French 1984, 35). Moreover, the formal methods being promoted were criticized for intellectual foundations too weak to support their expansive aspirations, for naiveté about bureaucratic and political incentives, and for ineffectiveness in persuading ministers to make hard choices – although these limits were also recognized and articulately discussed, starting early, by the proponents themselves (French 1984; Dobell 1999; Clark 2008).

Through the late 1970s, the highest ambitions for policy analysis were progressively eroded, even as its methods and processes were disseminating laterally both inside and outside the government – particularly the "evaluation" function, which quickly spread throughout the bureaucracy and into multiple new policy research institutes, as well as spawning a new market segment of private consulting firms. While TBS training, guidance, and provision of knowledgeble alumni stoked this growth in policy analysis capability, the Planning Branch itself faded in influence and was abolished in a budget-cutting move in 1978. Government-wide responsibility for evaluation was moved to the newly established controller-general (Auditor-General of Canada 1975), and its ambition was contracted. Following several years' experience of evaluations that aimed too far beyond political will or aimed at too many things, evaluations increasingly sought to support internal management and control rather than large-scale resource allocation and planning, with their target audiences shifted from ministers and Cabinet to deputy ministers and the TBS. To the extent that a government-wide mandate for policy analysis and planning remained it also went to the controller-general, but the abandonment of flagship studies, the targeting of internal clients, and the co-location of responsibility for evaluation and audit all signaled a shrinkage in the scale of the enterprise and its ambition to support forward-looking planning.

But there remained, as ever, a practical need to prioritize, coordinate activities, and allocate resources across programs and ministries, and a continuing aspiration that these large-scale activities draw on some rational planning and analytic capability. In the early 1980s, these coordination responsibilities were placed in new cabinet committees for Economic and Regional Development, and Social Development, each responsible for managing a broad policy area and expenditure envelope. The committees were supported by two small but technically expert Ministries of State (MSERD and MSSD), which operated like central agencies within their policy areas – including managing the agendas of their respective Cabinet committees. Both were abolished in 1984 during the brief Turner government, as part of a movement away from big government intended to dramatize differences from the Trudeau governments (Oberlander and Fallick 1987).

At the political level, the move to professionalize Parliament developed at a rapid pace during this period to match the growing interest in policy analysis. For example, members of Parliament received extra funds to bolster their administrative and research capacity, Parliamentary committees were given more responsibility to delve into legislation and more research staff to support this work, and the major political parties added research bureaus to their House of Commons staff.

Spurred by increasing interest in government accountability worldwide, in 1983 Canada became the thirteenth country to pass access to information and privacy acts. After this initial burst of enthusiasm for open government, however, subsequent governments have resisted all attempts to broaden the Access to Information Act or empower the information commissioner to direct the government to release information.

THE MULRONEY/CAMPBELL PERIOD, 1984–93

On taking office, the Mulroney government conducted a comprehensive program review aiming to identify opportunities to make government operations more efficient and effective. The new government also promised to empower ministers relative to officials and to relax central controls – a commitment symbolized by the creation of chief of staff positions at the ADM level in ministers' offices, by a series of statements by the prime minister that he would give "pink slips and running shoes" to the public service once his government was elected (Zussman 1986), and by a series of initiatives in government reorganization and management improvement.[2] The aims were couched in the newly fashionable language of New Public Management – a movement promoting the adoption of private-sector management techniques in government such as outsourcing, performance pay, and privatization – but they also conformed with periodic exhortations to relax central controls and "let the managers manage" dating back to the 1962 Glassco Commission (Savoie 1999, 208–9). Although these exercises had limited direct impact on the management performance of the government, they increased the scepticism about government's ability to manage major public issues and inadvertently encouraged more debate among interest groups and think tanks about the public service's ability to develop workable policies.

As the foregoing suggests, the early years of Mulroney's governments were marked by general stoking of hostility toward government and public servants, in part reflecting the prime minister's belief that government executives were liberal partisans working in the guise of neutral, professional public servants. This stance generated two internal reactions. First, there was an increase in concern with probity, accountability, and fiscal discipline, which resulted in increased emphasis on audit and control processes – thus further diverting attention and resources away from analytic work in support of major policy decisions or new initiatives. Second, this increased political oversight made government executives more risk-averse, since they were keen to not find themselves in the crosshairs of the media, the auditor general, or the PMO. In time, Paul Tellier's exhortation to his deputy minister colleagues to be "error-free" clashed totally with the general management rhetoric emanating from the TBS and the Canadian Centre for Management Development about the need for decentralization, empowerment of line managers, and more risk-taking in program delivery.

From his starting point of substantial hostility and suspicion toward the public service, Mulroney gradually changed his view. In time, the prime minister began to rely more and more on the public service for policy advice and promoted a number of key public servants into his own office to professionalize its activities when his political fortunes were slipping. Moreover, it was during Mulroney's first term that the Royal Commission on the Economic Union and Development Prospects for Canada (the Macdonald Commission) reported its findings. For the policy community, the Macdonald Commission report represented a high water mark since public servants provided most of the analysis and were deeply involved in framing the recommendations. While Trudeau initiated the commission in 1982 in recognition of the dramatic changes taking place in the global economy, the commission's work spanned two governments and served as the major policy agenda for Mulroney for the rest of his term as prime minister.

Perhaps in part owing to the close working relationships created in preparing the Macdonald Commission report, the hostility between politicians and public servants that characterized the early Mulroney years slowly dissipated, to the point that high levels of trust were established throughout the public service by the start of the second Mulroney term in 1988.

By the early 1990s, however, a recession and a series of tight budgets increasingly squeezed across the government, and staff functions such as planning and analysis were particularly vulnerable. Cuts fell especially sharply on independent research, analytic, and advisory bodies within the federal system – bodies such as the Science Council and Economic Council, which had no official role in policy-making and so were able to make more independent and long-range contributions to policy debates. Forty-one such advisory bodies were abolished in the 1992 budget, including both the Economic and Science Councils, and eight more in 1993.

A further contraction occurred in response to the 1992 de Cotret task force on government reorganization, which recommended a substantial shrinkage in Cabinet and in the number of departments, as well as revised roles for central agencies (Paquet and Shepherd 1996). In contrast to the previous few reorganization efforts, this one achieved a strong impact thanks to the transition to the brief Campbell government in 1993. Acting on the first recommendation, Campbell eliminated and consolidated nine departments (reducing the total from thirty-two to twenty-three) and eliminated six cabinet committees, including the formerly central Priorities and Planning Committee. She did not, however, follow the second recommendation to change the roles of central agencies.

THE CHRÉTIEN/MARTIN PERIOD, 1993–2005

The 1993 election brought the Chrétien government into office during a recession, in an environment of strong fiscal pressure and warnings from the financial community that the fiscal situation was not sustainable. A major program review was first organized around six broad questions, which addressed public interest, effectiveness, and the role of government, in addition to efficiency and affordability (Pacquet and Shepherd 1996, table 1). But the review, like much of the government's agenda, was overtaken by the paramount importance of budget cutting, in order to respond to pressure from international capital markets, including two credit downgrades and a *Wall Street Journal* editorial suggesting Canada was about to follow Mexico into financial crisis. In the end, the desired cuts were achieved mainly through large reductions in federal-provincial transfers and entitlement programs, not through precise targeting of programmatic cuts based on evidence of effectiveness, as was originally intended.

As successive waves of budget cutting and increased focus on narrowly drawn control and evaluation processes took their toll on capacity for planning and policy analysis, concern mounted about diminished capacity for long-range planning and coordination. In 1995 the clerk of the Privy Council asked Ivan Fellegi, chief statistician of Canada, to lead a task force to address these issues (Canadian Centre for Management Development 1996). The report noted that officials' preoccupation with urgent and short-term issues had weakened the capacity to address long-term and cross-cutting issues. Following the task force's recommendation, a Policy Research Secretariat was established in the PCO in 1996 with a mandate to foster collaboration across the public service and identify key issues relating to the government's policy agenda. The secretariat was subsequently replaced by a Policy Research Initiative (PRI) in 2000, then moved into Human Resources Canada under a steering committee of deputy ministers in 2006, then subsequently reconstituted as Policy Horizons Canada in 2011 – each step corresponding to an increasing focus on constructing collaborative networks inside and outside government, an increasing focus on foresight and exploration of long-term issues, and a further distancing from actual policy or managerial authority.

In addition to strengthening the policy capacity within the federal government, the improved fiscal situation in the late 1990s injected a heightened sense of optimism into the public service that created an atmosphere of experimentation that mirrored some of the changes taking place in other Westminster systems. For example, public engagement and consultation was championed, alternative service delivery was encouraged, and the government passed the Public Service Modernization Act in 2003 as a way of streamlining the recruitment process, increasing the role of deputy ministers in human resource management, and remedying the problems with staffing and appeals.

HARPER PERIOD, 2005 TO THE PRESENT

The Harper era has seen the continuance of several long-term trends evident in earlier periods, such as the weakening of policy analysis and planning capacity inside government, the parallel growth in the influence of outside organizations, and a shift of internal analytic functions toward compliance, control, and accountability, rather than forward-looking planning and analysis. All these actions are consistent with a government that has a limited policy agenda and continues to value the policy input from its political staff and from interest groups.

There have been no major reorganizations directed to policy-making, and no major decisions of the Harper era have explicitly targeted planning, policy analysis, or evaluation, although the new government's first major legislation, the Federal Accountability Act, further increased reporting and compliance responsibilities of senior officials and thus further reduced their ability to engage in larger-scale planning or analysis. Rather, activity related to evidence and analysis relevant to public decisions and informed debate, and the associated controversy, largely shifted to the related issues of provision and accessibility of government-funded scientific research and statistical data.

Table 2.1
Major policy developments in Canada, 1970–2010

Prime Minister	*Significant policy-related events*
Pierre Trudeau	Elaborate policy-making processes Expansion of policy units in departments Expansionist government programs
John Turner	Retrenchment of policy machinery
Brian Mulroney	Increased role for political staff Macdonald Commission reports New Public Management
Kim Campbell	Major reorganization of central agencies
Jean Chrétien	Program Review Alternative service delivery Government online Citizen engagement Public Service Modernization Act
Paul Martin	Expansion of decision-making processes
Stephen Harper	Federal Accountability Act (FAA) Deficit Reduction Action Plan (DRAP) Significant role for exempt staff Ideological government

Significant landmarks included restrictions on communications outside government by federal environmental and fisheries scientists; elimination of the required long-form census in 2010; elimination of more research and analytic bodies, including the National Roundtable on the Environment and Economy; and funding cuts that reduced or eliminated multiple programs in environmental and earth sciences research and monitoring. Furthermore, the government's battles with the Parliamentary Budget Office (PBO) and the Office of the Information Commission highlight ongoing government efforts to control the message and limit the public profile of those who disagree with the government.

Table 2.1 summarizes the major landmarks of policy development reviewed in this section. The table shows a highly active policy community in the federal government over a thirty-five-year period that ended with the arrival of the new Conservative government in 2006. During these decades, policy units came and went, new institutions were created to provide more oversight and information to decision makers, and efforts were made to rebuild the policy capacity of the public service to respond to the changing environment. A more careful inspection of these changes reveals several key points about the trajectory of policy analysis in the federal public service. First, successive prime ministers organized their governments, particularly the prime minister's office, to increase central power over the policy agenda and the machinery of government (Savoie 1999; Aucoin 1986; Heintzman 2013; Simpson 2001). This trend parallels developments in other Westminster systems such as the United Kingdom, Australia, and New Zealand.

In addition to this overall narrowing of the power structure in Ottawa, each period has also seen significant adjustments, retrenchments, and central agency and departmental reorganizations of the policy community. While each change was motivated by different circumstances, some reflected the view that prior innovations had produced less effective and efficient government. This would explain the demise of the Planning Branch, the Ministries of State, and various policy committees of Cabinet. Another reason for some for the more dramatic reorganizations is that playing with policy machinery was seen as a politically savvy way to signal to voters that the government has a serious policy agenda by making major changes in the structure of government without incurring significant financial costs.

Even this abbreviated analysis shows that until recently there was considerable innovation in policy-making in Canada over the previous forty years. While it is difficult to be definitive, most observers would agree that at various times over the period, especially in the 1970s and 1980s, Canada was a world leader in policy analytical capacity and decision-making processes. Innovation does not necessarily turn on who is in power in Ottawa. The data suggest that policy analysis has had great support during both Liberal and Conservative eras. In fact, some of the most dramatic reorganizations were led by prime ministers who succeeded prime ministers from the same political party. Campbell, Turner, and Martin all made dramatic changes to the machinery of government when they took over the reins of power from their same party leaders.

Another key driver of innovativeness in policy analysis has been, not surprisingly, the fiscal situation. Governments that are prepared to spend taxpayers' money are more likely to look for new processes to generate policy ideas and examine options. Hence, citizen engagement and alternative service delivery came into vogue when the

Chrétien government was building large surpluses. Similarly, with an eye to enlarging the state role in the early 1980s, Trudeau borrowed the Clark government's tentative efforts to modernize policy-making when he beefed up Ministries of State, creating two massive policy agencies to provide rational social and economic policies.

A further factor in policy innovation has been international influence. Many changes in the Canadian policy arena were stimulated by developments in other countries, notably the United Kingdom, Australia, New Zealand, and the United States. Examples of such innovations that diffused to Canada were elements of New Public Management, performance measurement and the creation of the UK Prime Minister's Delivery Unit, public consultation, citizen engagement and deliberative techniques, privatization and contracting out of government services, the differentiation of "steering and rowing" government activities, behavioural economics applied to public policy, and the increased role of policy advisors in the office of the prime minister.

THE POLICY ENVIRONMENT TODAY

The evidence suggests there has been a steady tinkering with the policy function in the federal government for more than forty years since policy units were first created and systematic analysis was first introduced into the Privy Council office and the Treasury Board Secretariat in the early 1970s. Over this period, the policy community has adapted to changing political environments and absorbed practices from other countries, to keep up with international developments and serve the government of the day. The policy environment looks very different today than in earlier periods, although there remain strong threads of continuity throughout the time period.

The constants can be summarized in the following way. First, despite decades of economic growth and innovation, there are still too many problems for governments to solve and too few resources available to be able to address them all. Within this reality, the majority of citizens in developed countries maintain the belief that government continues to makes a pivotal difference in determining quality of life and that strategic public policy decisions continue to make a difference to their own condition (Mulgan 2009). Moreover, Mulgan also argues that knowledge and power persistently continue to define the policy process and that the set of policy instruments available to solve society's problems has remained constant over the years. What has changed over this period is the degree to which certain policy instruments are preferred by different governments to reflect their view on the effectiveness of government as a service provider. Thus, conservative governments in Canada have traditionally viewed the private sector as more effective (and efficient) at delivering on government objectives, while the more left-of-centre governments have had more confidence in the public sector's ability to deliver the government's agenda.

Canadian public policy over the past twenty years has mostly been incremental and modest in its aspirations after a period of activist government that started in the early 1960s and continued to the early 1990s (Dobuzinskis, Howlett, and Laycock 2007).[3] Since then, successive governments have been cautious in their choice of policy agendas, with a few notable exceptions when circumstances forced them to action.[4] Several factors account for this general stability. First, policy processes exhibit "bounded rationality," because policy-makers have limited ability to consider all possible options and tend to be biased in favour of the status quo. Second, policy-makers can pay attention only to a small number of issues at a time and are also constrained by limitations of their own cognitive styles (Baumgartner and Jones 2009). Moreover, newly elected governments inherit previous government's commitments, operate in complex and multi-layered policy-making systems, and are constrained by economic and regulatory conditions. In view of all these factors, the high level of continuity in the policy arena is not surprising (Cairney 2012).

While many aspects of the current policy-making process may resemble the system developed during the Trudeau years,[5] the policy landscape beneath the process has dramatically and profoundly changed. Our roundtable participants, a mix of experienced practitioners and academics, concluded that the policy environment today would be largely unrecognizable to veteran policy experts of a few decades ago. They identified two major developments that have radically restructured the environment. The first is a general decline in the Canadian public's trust in public institutions, particularly the federal government and its elected officials. It is hard to pinpoint exactly when this trend began, but a good estimate would be the mid 1970s, when the scale of government spending and waste became a public issue, the role of the auditor general was expanded to ensure more government accountability, and new notions of access to information encouraged the media and academics to question the effectiveness of government programs. As trust declined, so too did public optimism about governments' ability to solve society's complex problems (Zussman 1987), a trend broadly mirrored in most democratic countries. Celebrated government failures, increased prosecutions of political wrongdoing, greater reporting of government waste by oversight organizations, and the growing sophistication of third-party observers, also contributed to these trends (Mulgan 2009; Zussman 2010). Declining public trust limited the policy ambitions of government, increased demands for public participation in decisions, and encouraged political leaders to demand "risk-free" government in order to avoid criticisms of mismanagement. This might explain why Paul Tellier, as secretary to the Cabinet in the mid 1980s, would challenge his deputy ministers to deliver "error-free administration" (Savoie 1999, 333).

Declining public trust and optimism have encouraged public devaluation of the validity of government intervention and of policy analysis within government (John 1998, 23–33). Mulgan has argued that declining trust and the increased complexity of policy solutions together doomed big government and led to a shift beyond command and control. Government thus increasingly became "less a closed system with a monopoly of power, and more an open system engaged in negotiation with other parties, a nexus of multiple or distributed connections rather than a bureaucratic monolith" (Mulgan 1998, 193–4; Kooiman 1993; Amin and Hausner 1997). This in turn created a policy environment that "is more complex and potentially unstable, populated by more fragmented governments and many participants with different values, perceptions and preferences" (Sabatier 2007, 3). Low trust in public institutions also spawned the creation of the Reform Party in Canada and the Tea Party in the United States, both established to promote smaller government, less interventionist policies, and lower taxes.

The growing emphasis on smaller government has brought several significant changes in the policy arena. Governments face increasing limits to their ability to enforce implementation of their policy choices regardless of their formal authority and so must increasingly consult, negotiate, and share power. Multi-level governance in Canada's federal system has dispersed power from the national level to other governments and to non-governmental actors. The old "clubby days" of politics have increasingly moved to a more open and competitive system with more participants in which it is difficult to monopolize or insulate decision making. In this increasingly complex environment, government policy analysts must compete with many others for policy-makers' attention (Cairney 2012).

PUBLIC SERVANTS AND THE NEW PLAYERS

The changing role of exempt political staff in Ottawa has had a profound impact on the policy-making community.[6] Since the 1980s, as the involvement of political staff in policy development, communications, and ministerial outreach has increased; they have become both more professional and more powerful. The parallel centralization of power in prime ministers' offices has created a new decision environment, in which the senior exempt staffer sits beside the minister at the apex of departmental policy-making, and the public servant policy analyst needs an invitation to join the conversation (Eichbaum and Shaw 2010; Heintzman 2013; Zussman 2009). The formal addition of exempt staff to the process has had a profound impact on policy development. As veteran *Toronto Star* political journalist Jim Travers observed, "the policy role of public servants is less about securing an intimate knowledge of the relevant sector and offering policy options and more about finding empirical justification for what the elected politicians have decided to do" (Travers 2006, A17). A senior public servant recently characterized the current environment similarly: "when I first joined the federal government more than 20 years ago, we worked on 'evidence-based policy-making.' Now, I work for a system that is 'policy-based evidence-making.'"[7]

Donald Savoie, who has studied the Ottawa policy environment for more than thirty years, has written extensively on the concentration of power in prime ministers' offices. He argues that as a result of this shift two policy-making processes now operate at the federal level. The first process, led by the prime minister and his advisors, requires that public servants who wish to participate must be responsive to their wishes. The second process includes many policy actors, and the role of public servants is "to network, to find common ground, and to strike partnership agreements" (Savoie 1999, 180). This is a far cry from the traditional model, where the deputy minister sat at the pinnacle of the departmental policy process.

As Paul Tellier, cabinet secretary in the Mulroney era, recounted in 2006, in this system "a deputy minister has to be able to put his foot down and say, I don't think the government should do this."[8] It is hard to imagine this perspective having any currency in today's public service.

Since 1993, all political parties have provided detailed election platforms, which a study by Greg Flynn found exhibit "a high degree of policy making capacity and ... the ability both to advance and implement fairly detailed plans for governing" (2011). This increase of policy capacity in political parties has further contributed to the influence of exempt staff and the diminution of policy expertise in the career public service (Hood, Lodge, and Clifford 2002). This shift has led a number of well-informed former senior public servants to raise concerns about the current state of the public service. In a recent Tansley lecture, Mel Cappe, former cabinet secretary, noted that politicians are increasingly ignoring evidence and analysis, basing decisions instead on their biases, ideologies, and preconceptions (2011). Don Drummond, former associate deputy minister of finance, stated that "historically, there was a critical mass of analytical thinking going on in the government because we would see the evidence of it, we could feel it, we could touch it, we could participate in it and, perhaps most importantly, we could question it. I think that this has not been the case in recent years." Calling the current state of policy analysis capacity in Canada "dismal," Drummond concludes that "there is precious little evidence of public policy analysis from the federal government in the public domain" (2011, 342). Andrew Griffith, a former senior official in Citizenship and Immigration Canada, describes the impact on the public service: "working with a government decidedly breaking with policy continuity poses a major challenge for public servants. Given the complexity of social policy issues, and thus the requirement for expert knowledge, advice, and expertise, such a challenge of the public-service role starts off by being demoralizing and even traumatic" (2013, 96).

Perhaps the harshest criticism of the recent decline in analytic capacity comes from Allan Gregg, a former Conservative pollster with a passion for public policy. Criticizing the elimination of the long form census, Gregg accused the government of intentionally weakening federal data collection: "This was no random act of downsizing, but a deliberate attempt to obliterate certain activities that were previously viewed as a legitimate part of government decision-making – namely, using research, science and evidence as the basis to make policy decisions. It also amounted to an attempt to eliminate anyone who might use science, facts and evidence to challenge government policies" (2012).

These concerns are exacerbated by the rapid growth since the mid-1980s of policy groups outside government, including industry associations and think tanks, which have developed both expertise in policy analysis and effective skills at disseminating their message, both to decision makers and to the public through the media (Dobuzinskis, Howlett, and Laycock 2007). All these developments have led Savoie to observe that "It's not too much of an exaggeration to write that the public advisory role of public servants in Anglo-American democracies has been turned on its head. Multiple sources of information and evidence-based policy advice no longer matter as they once did. Today, if policymaking in a post positivism world is a matter of opinion, where 2+2 = 5, then Google searches, focus groups, public opinion surveys in a well-connected lobbyist can provide any policy answer the politicians wish to hear" (Savoie 2013).

CONCLUSIONS

As the movie *Moneyball* recounted, Bill James' introduction of new data and analysis to baseball in the 1970s revolutionized thinking about the power of evidence in successful decision making. For the first time, it was possible to rely on hard data rather than intuition and experience to assess players and predict outcomes. Over the last forty years, Canadian policy analysts have aspired to finding the same success in assessing policy options by digging deeper into the data. In the federal government, this desire led to the creation of policy units with comprehensive policy approval processes, the broadening of sources of information and data to be analyzed, the creation of the Policy Research Initiative (PRI), and the development and application of sophisticated analytical tools. While formal decision-making processes have remained essentially the same over these decades, recent changes in the political environment have had a significant impact on the development of public policy. As the world of analytics and big data has expanded well beyond the scenario described in *Moneyball*, the current policy scene in Ottawa has moved in quite a different direction. Instead of building on new analytic tools based on technological innovation and computer capacity, the Harper government has chosen to eschew data collection and analysis in favour of ideology and playing to the political base, leaving many in the policy community with a limited role to play.

Determining the best policy for the government to pursue still requires the same elements shown in figure 2.1: articulating clear goals, developing options to attain those goals based on relevant data and evidence, engaging the public, securing the input of experts, honestly assessing options, and evaluating outcomes of the chosen option. The context in which these activities are carried out has greatly changed since the 1970s, however. At that time, the public service had almost complete control over policy-making: it owned the expertise and largely managed the process. With virtually no challenge from outside the public service, the debate was between spenders and guardians, who all ultimately played for the same team (Good 2007). Central agencies, notably the PCO and Finance, might take responsibility for initiating policy-making, while much of the innovative thinking on implementation might take place in departments.

At the same time, senior policy analysts were sensitive to the need for political input from their ministers as they explored options and looked for alternative ways of delivering on new policies. From policy analysts earliest days, they were counseled that theirs was an advisory role not a decision-making one, since they were not the ones elected to represent the views of Canadians. In return for their non-partisan work, policy analysts expected to have a professional relationship with ministers and their staff and to be listened to respectfully in the course of their conversations.

Those who observe policy-making from a distance have often failed to see the continuous exchange of views and reactions that existed between ministers and the public service. The process has always been more collaborative and dynamic than is suggested by simple models in which the public service submits options and ministers pick one. Lord Hennessey, the preeminent expert on UK Cabinet government, noted that when governments make consequential decisions there is an established practice among ministers and public servants to "eschew the rational, the written, the planned or the strategic," in favour of "understated, pragmatic, occasionally inspired adhockery and last-minute improvisation" (Hennessey 1986, 14). This landscape began to change in Westminster countries in the

1980s, with the election of more ideological governments that did not believe the public servants who worked for them shared their values. These governments hired more political advisors to work directly in ministers' offices, many of them strong policy analysts with well-established networks of their own, who had developed their policy interests while working for a political party.

This is now the prevailing policy-making environment in Canada. The public service is no longer the main source of policy options, but is rather one among many advisory groups to the ministry – and is, moreover, limited in its ability to consult with expert and interest groups, owing to limits on travel and other restrictions. Many new players provide input: exempt staff play an important role, as do members of their political and policy networks. The relationship between ministers' offices and the public service is less collaborative, and the PMO now plays the leading role in policy-making in contrast to the more department-led model of the past.

At its core, policy-making is still based on research, evidence, and political input. What has changed is the relative importance of these components and the source and use of each input. The government now gives "evidence" a broader meaning than previously. Greater weight is given to the views of politicians and their staff, and this, along with the sophistication of stakeholder groups, has moved the public service to a more peripheral role. In assessing whether this new balance of research, evidence, and politics will provide better decision making, it is important to remember that policy-making is fundamentally a political activity. As Simeon has noted, "policy making is a matter of conflict" and "who gets what, how and when" remains the most crucial question (1976). Good policy work requires strong political input that mobilizes the government's support, reflects the public's desire for change, and can deal with challenges from the opposition parties; at the same time, it can benefit from the expertise of the public servant who applies the skills of a policy analyst. This arrangement works best when the political leadership is clear about their policy and political goals and is willing to engage in an honest conversation, which can sometimes be heated, on how to best meet these objectives.

Attempts to reform policy-making have often sought to impose an artificial rationality on the process and have thereby fallen victim to the pressures and the need for improvisation that operate in a political environment. Hallsworth and Rutter (2011, 10) observe that both former ministers and civil servants report dissatisfaction with progress made improving policy-making processes. They offer several possible explanations, but the most compelling is the failure of machinery planners to adequately account for the role of the minister and the political environment in which he or she operates. To regain their place at the decision table, policy analysts must rethink their role and find new ways to rebuild respectful and trusting relationships with ministers, recognizing they no longer anchor the policy discussions. In anticipation of better times, the public service should also bolster its own expertise by slowing down the rapid turnover in departments and rebuilding the policy capacity in all federal departments.

Looking forward, an obvious question is what would happen to policy analysis in the federal government if a new government were elected from among the opposition parties? First, it is important to note that there is no point in trying to persuade a new government to go back to an earlier policy world. As has been discussed earlier there has been a succession of major environmental changes in public policy-making a return to a previous system unworkable. Second, because policy-making will remain a part of the political process for any elected government regardless of policy orientation, in future years public servants engaged in policy-making will need to recognize that they will work in a more politically charged environment so that they will have to understand the political context in which they develop policy regardless of the political party in power.

One unintended consequence of the 1995 Program Review was the disappearance of any coordinating function for the policy community. As a result, there is now no entity in the federal government to provide leadership for policy analysis and development, as the Treasury Board Secretariat once did in providing training for policy shops and quality control over the outputs. With his strong sense of planning and objectivity, Rod Dobell would no doubt applaud the re-establishment of such an organization to provide more structure for policy-making, in the spirit of the 1970s Planning Branch or the 1990s Policy Research Initiative. Less clear is how he would view the current policy environment, with the PMO in the lead and the public service reduced to one of many sources of advice. Given Dobell's profound belief that stakeholder engagement strengthens policy analysis, however, I suspect he would be comfortable with the increased role of political advisors and external groups, provided they bring new perspectives and engage in respectful dialogue. What might trouble him more would be the dominance of ideology over evidence, particularly where there is a clear disregard for relevant facts. Relying on just ideology is unlikely to bring the best policy decisions, especially given the increase in information and computing capacity to analyze it (Ayres 2007). In the end, Dobell's participation in any debate about the legitimacy of the current approach to policy-making would be measured, polite, objective, and above all devoted to finding the best policy outcomes to serve the needs of Canadians. And his advice would be "fearless" in that proud tradition of the Canadian public service.

NOTES

In preparing this chapter I have benefited from sage advice provided by colleagues Jim Lahey, Greg Fyffe, Thomas Townsend, Barry Carin, and Ian Clark. In addition, I wish to acknowledge comments on an earlier draft from Edward Parson and research assistance by Behn S. Andersen. Finally, my colleagues Alan Freeman, Luc Juillet, and Richard Van Loon shared detailed observations on past and present policy-making in the federal government. I am grateful to all those who helped shape the chapter by their insights and suggestions.

1 The Diefenbaker government established the so-called Glassco Commission in 1960 to look into the organization and methods of departments of the federal government. The five-volume report was completed in 1962 and recommended the decentralization of power to departments and better coordination from the centre of government. The odd tension in the recommendations – exercise central strategic control through new methods of planning and analysis like PPBS, while also relaxing traditional central controls over line ministries and managers (its widely repeated tagline was to "let the managers manage") – mapped lines of tension in many subsequent shifts, both in the balance between central control and ministry autonomy and in the role of analysis, evaluation, and planning methods in mediating that tension.

2 For example: Increased Ministerial Authority and Accountability, Public Service 2000, and the creation of first Special Operating Agencies (SOAs).

3 Examples are the Free Trade Agreement, the Patriation of the Canadian Constitution, the Charter of Rights and Freedoms, the National Energy

Policy, the Charlottetown Accord referendum, and the Goods and Services Tax (GST).

4 Examples include the 1995 fiscal crisis and Program Review, the Quebec referendum, and passage of the Clarity Act.

5 For example, the Memorandum to Cabinet, formal briefing notes from departmental officials to ministers, the lead role played by ministers in Cabinet and Cabinet committees, and the challenge function provided by the Privy Council Office.

6 In Canada, political advisors are called exempt staff because their hirings are exempt from normal public service hiring procedures and requirements.

7 Private conversation with a senior official in a central agency, 18 September 2013.

8 Government of Canada press release, "Prime Minister Harper Establishes Advisory Committee on the Public Service." (Ottawa: Office of the Prime Minister, 2006).

3

Affairs of the Smart: Will Researchers and Decision-Makers "Hook Up"?

CHARLES UNGERLEIDER

With notable exceptions, most contemporary politicians invoke the phrases "evidence-informed" or "evidence-based decision making." Barack Obama is no exception. Not long after his inauguration, the US president proclaimed that the public must be able to trust the scientific process informing public policy decisions. In remarks designed to distinguish his administration from that of his predecessor, Obama opined that office-holders should neither suppress nor alter scientific findings or conclusions.[1]

Appeals for evidence-informed decisions did not of course begin with Obama. Ten years earlier, in a *fin de siècle* effort "to get better government – for a better Britain," the Blair government embarked on efforts to modernize government, calling, among other things, for "better use of evidence and research in policy making and better focus on policies that will deliver long-term goals." Blair's desire for the application of evidence to governmental decision making in Britain was the most recent expression of a question raised by C.P. Snow (1960) in *Science and Government* roughly forty years earlier. Snow had served various British governments over the course of a quarter century, including as parliamentary secretary to the minister of technology in the Wilson government.

Snow was what today we would call a public intellectual who, in addition to his career in government was an essayist and novelist, contributing to our lexicon the phrase "corridors of power," a phrase he had coined in an earlier work that became the title of one of his novels about government. In *Science and Government*, a series of lectures delivered at Harvard, Snow asked whether and how democratic governments can make use of science and scientists. In his introductory remarks, Snow makes clear that there are no easy answers to the question: "No one who has ever thought at all about the relations of science and government, much less anyone who has experienced them directly, is likely to think that positive conclusions are going to be firm or easy to come by. Most of the concepts that administrative theorists use are at best rationalizations, not guides to further thought; as a rule they are unrealistically remote from the workaday experience" (1960, 3). Though he does not elaborate on the point, Snow's critique of administrative theorists is likely based on the fact that most of them had not dirtied their hands with the muck of governmental decision making. Snow's treatise was a plea for scientists to be directly active at all levels of government. His belief was that their contribution to government would be to supply what "our kind of existential society is desperately short of: so short of, that it fails to recognize of what it is starved. That is foresight" (1960, 81).

Forty years after Snow's *Science and Government*, researchers and policy-makers, though not exactly cohabitants, were living beneath the same roof. The Blair Cabinet Office had become home to a Strategy Unit designed to provide strategy and policy advice to the prime minister based on a systematic and careful reading of the available evidence.

What kind of a relationship would politicians and researchers have and, most important, could such a relationship last? Even though policy-makers have made use of evidence when it served their interests to do so, their attitude toward research has generally been dismissive. Researchers and political decision-makers live in different worlds, respond to different norms, and speak different languages. In his seminal and lengthy 1999 volume, *Governing from the Centre: The Concentration of Power in Canadian Politics*, Donald Savoie makes the case that in the last century, governments in Canada, the United Kingdom, and the United States "would move to strengthen their centre to promote greater policy and program coordination, to generate policy advice, and to promote better management practices in government operations." It is revealing that the role of research is of such little consequence in these central government processes that it is absent from the book's twenty-seven page index that addresses topics from Aboriginal affairs to youth employment. Ben Levin, a former deputy minister in both Ontario and Manitoba, tells a story that reveals the distance between the worlds occupied by politicians and researchers. Levin informed a minister with whom he worked that a course of action under consideration was supported by research, to which the minister replied, "You know, Ben, I don't believe that research votes in my constituency."

I doubt that it is possible to bridge the chasm that divides decision-makers and researchers. Few, if any, of the decisions most people make are informed by the evidence available. People are often more susceptible to influence by authority and their own tenacity than by the evidence available. If people seek evidence for the practical decisions they make, it is often after the fact, and if evidence supports the course of action taken, it is used to affirm prior judgment. If it does not, people discount, dissemble, or rationalize. When I owned a fifteen-year-old, twelve-cylinder Jaguar, I was quick to point out that it consumed about the same amount of gasoline as an SUV – as if the comparison justified ownership of such a vehicle. The worlds in which decision-makers and researchers live are both tightly rational, but, as Levin's anecdote makes clear, the evidence and methods that govern the public policy decision-making process are quite different from those governing research.

Although dismissive of research at that moment, the minister in Levin's anecdote, had he been asked, would have said that he does pay attention to evidence. His reply to Levin points to one source of evidence politicians consult: the approval of one's constituency is typically the paramount source of evidence, but it is not the sole source. Others include ideological and value commitments, media, lobbyists and advocates, personal and anecdotal experience, and, yes, even scientific knowledge. Democracy is government by persuasion. Since those who rule depend on the compliance of those who are governed, they must secure consent through the selective use of information consonant with the beliefs and dispositions of the governed. The alternative to persuasion is coercion – the use or threat of force to get people to do what they otherwise would not do. Thus, in one sense, democracy is a system in which the governed persuade themselves and choose to comply.

Politicians are astutely aware that in democratic societies, ideas are the main instruments for obtaining and maintaining political power, and they are keenly aware that persuasion is the main resource at their disposal. As a consequence, propaganda (what we have come to call "spin") is a necessary, if insufficient, concomitant of the political process. There is no politics without spin. Politicians will use evidence selectively in securing support for the ideas and ideals they favour and ignore it completely when it conflicts with those ideas. Members of the public may deplore the instrumental use of evidence by politicians, but until and unless we prepare future generations of citizens to understand, appreciate, and demand a stronger role for science in decision making, politicians will continue their instrumental and rhetorical use of evidence.

In democracies, politics is the process of adjustment by which conflicts concerning different values (goods) are resolved. As Weiss put it, "politics is the system we have for attaching values to facts" (quoted in Hogwood and Gunn 1988, 113). Research will not resolve the conflicts that arise because of value differences or because of differing value priorities. Values are not empirical claims; they are statements of beliefs in, rather than beliefs about, things (I believe in X as opposed to I believe that X will produce Y). Societies need a commitment to a process for resolving value differences, and in democratic societies, such differences are resolved through a process of electoral politics in which each of the contending interests attempts to persuade the electorate that its values are preferable. In fact, the greater the value commitment of a particular regime, the less likely it is to consider evidence, even where the value claims are amenable to empirical analysis.

Democracy's calculus takes into account those politicians who ignore evidence. In the short term, the consequence of ignoring evidence about issues that the public holds central is electoral defeat. In the long term, the consequence is reputational. There is no similar calculus for scientists. When scientists advocate for a particular public policy based on evidence, they are operating beyond the limits of their data. Scientists who define an issue as sufficiently important to merit public policy and suggest a course of action from among the broader universe of alternatives are no different from politicians save, perhaps, for the relative emphasis they place on their reading of the evidence. Nevertheless, while a marriage of research and decision making is unlikely, long-term liaisons are becoming more frequent than one-night stands. Decision-makers, especially those occupying public office, increasingly decide to use research evidence along with a variety of other forms of evidence to inform the decisions they make.

If our educational efforts are successful and the citizenry becomes more disposed toward and understanding of the contributions of science to public policy-making, we will, in time, see incremental improvement in the use of evidence to inform public policy. We should not expect more rapid change or demand that policy decisions should be determined by research evidence alone unless we are prepared to substitute a technocracy for a democracy, and coercion for compliance.

NOTE

1 Obama subsequently expressed support for charter schools and for value-added teacher assessment despite evidence that neither policy was efficacious.

4

Expertise and Evidence in Public Policy: In Defence of (a Little) Technocracy

EDWARD A. PARSON

Professor Ungerleider has given a cogent summary of limits to the role of expert knowledge and evidence in public decision making, in both how much influence they can have and how much they should. He argues that there are acute practical limits to the ability of science and evidence to guide public decisions, because political actors, like all of us, use evidence selectively to rationalize decisions and because the meaning of both rationality and evidence are different in the realm of policy – including, for example, ideology and constituent preferences – than in the realm of research to understand the world. Moreover, if we consider the cost and risk of over-weighting expertise in public decisions, we may not even want it. Rather, in the complex relationship between expertise and democratic authorities, the two must not get too close, and the latter must be in charge of the relationship. To demand more is to substitute technocracy for democracy and government by coercion for government by persuasion.

Ungerleider's use of C.P. Snow's 1960 Godkin Lectures for his text shows how these problems are both old and new, ancient in origin yet utterly current, although the specific decisions and controversies that raise them change over time – from control of new weapons in Snow's time to today's debates over biomedical science and its implications for autonomy and equity, information technology and its implications for privacy and identity, and – perhaps first among current challenges – protecting the environment.

It falls to me to give a more positive view of the role of expertise in policy, both in terms of what is possible and what is desirable – and a caution about the risks of public decisions having too little of it.

To put boundaries on our disagreement and avoid dealing in straw men, however, I must first clarify that I also reject alienating ultimate, comprehensive governing authority away from democratic institutions to some group defined by supposed expertise. But while that choice is not and should not be on the agenda, a moment's reflection shows wide variation across areas of public decisions in how strongly expert knowledge guides action. In many areas, authority is routinely taken from democratically accountable bodies and given to expert bodies. This is done, indeed widely accepted as necessary, in areas as diverse as public health, monetary policy, transportation safety (from air traffic control to allocating funds for highway safety), and managing the electrical grid. In addition, many policy areas now appear to be badly managed, at least partly owing to too little influence of science or other expert knowledge – notably climate change and other areas of environmental policy.

To examine the expertise/democracy tension more concretely and specifically, I propose a simple typology of issues, based on three conditions that favour a stronger role for expert-based knowledge and evidence in public decisions – even at the cost of reduced democratic control. I call these three conditions expertise, stakes, and separability.

First, there must exist real expertise relevant to the decisions at hand. Someone must know how the systems affected by proposed decisions work, whether the relevant system is the atmosphere, the influenza virus and its transmission, or the money supply and its macroeconomic consequences. Their knowledge must be good enough to project the effects of alternative choices better than common-sense guesses by non-expert citizens or their representatives. Moreover, this knowledge must be held by some identifiable group of experts whose superior knowledge can be at least roughly verified, for example, through good methods of validation and error correction or a track record of correct predictions. This first condition might seem simple, but when policy areas are contested, it is not always easy to determine. Not all claims of expertise are correct and experts on a subject do not always agree, so we must worry about who really are experts, how to identify them, and how to interpret expert disagreement. Moreover, as knowledge advances some areas become subject to expert knowledge that previously were not. As a cautionary lesson we must keep in mind the analogy some scholars have drawn – only partly in mischief – between modern scientific risk assessment practices and ancient priests or shamans who claimed expertise at detecting witchcraft and casting protective spells. If no expert group has an operational understanding of the system better than citizens or their representatives, then there is no expectation of better foresight or better outcomes to justify moving away from purely democratic decisions.

The second condition is that the stakes must be high. The societal consequences of bad choices – or in some cases, of good choices made too slowly – must be severe enough to offset the general presumption in favour of democratic decision processes. This is not to say that expert knowledge can specify what the right choice is: it nearly never can. But sometimes expert knowledge can identify important risks or harms that would follow from particular choices, which most citizens would want to avoid. Decisions that deny, misunderstand, or ignore these consequences can fairly be called bad ones, without falling into the error of saying expert knowledge alone can specify what the decision should be. This condition begins to frame the choice of how much control to give expert-based processes in benefit-cost terms: it requires that the societal benefits of relying on available expertise and evidence be high enough to justify the costs, which include a reduction in democratic control.

The third condition is that the decisions to be made must be sufficiently separable from other areas of political conflict in which expert knowledge is not relevant. The decisions must not strongly implicate deeply contested values or ideologies. Nor can they be strongly connected to classic "political" issues of the distribution of political power or the benefits and burdens of state action: for example, who pays for the choices made, how benefits are shared, and who gets to decide? This condition excludes issues for which shifting control from democratic processes to expert ones would raise the most severe risks of illegitimately suppressing or misdirecting real political conflict. These second and third conditions are closely related, since they suggest a balancing between the intensity of broadly shared interests that can be informed by expert knowledge and the conflicting interests – whatever their origin – that lead policy actors to favor one choice or another, regardless of what some expert says.

All three conditions have fuzzy boundaries, yet I contend they are still useful. Granted that expertise cannot be determined beyond dispute, yet for practical purposes we recognize and rely on it in many domains. Granted that no public decision confers perfectly shared social value or has no connection at all to issues of distribution or contested principles – at a minimum, differences over the proper scope of state action – yet sometimes the latter are small relative to the former. And granted that "good" or "competent" decisions cannot be determined based only on expertise but must also refer to some basis for valuing choices and consequences. Yet in many cases this second, normative step is unproblematic: as an extreme but instructive example, if it were confidently known that some choice would very likely cause economic collapse, millions of deaths, or loss of most present ecosystems, we would not need much discussion of how to value these outcomes before agreeing to avoid this choice if at all possible.

These three conditions provide a structure that helps account for the widely varying position of expert knowledge across current decision domains, and also provides insight into institutional design and authority for new issues. It helps distinguish areas dominated by principled commitments, symbols, or large-scale politics, where expertise has little role to play, from other areas where citizens accept, indeed demand, nearly total delegation to expert bodies. It also helps account for persistently difficult and contentious areas, such as issues where strong expert knowledge about consequences exists but is overpowered by political commitments, ideologies, or symbols – for example, policies governing addictive and recreational drug use or regulation of the private ownership and use of firearms.

Environmental issues provide an instructive and challenging case to explore the value and limits of this scheme. While there is substantial variation among specific issues, environmental issues often meet the conditions of expertise and stakes, the first and second conditions, but not the third condition of separability. On all environmental issues of current policy concern – including climate change, air and water pollution, toxic chemicals, and biodiversity – there are vast bodies of relevant scientific knowledge and the capability to generate further advances through continued research and monitoring. On most environmental issues there have also been sustained, effective efforts to synthesize and translate knowledge in policy-relevant terms to inform decisions, including model projections of the future consequences of relevant choices.

This knowledge has limits, of course. Current environmental knowledge, like all science, is always incomplete and uncertain, even when its depth and validation support high (not absolute) confidence in certain practical conclusions: for example, the reality and human cause of climate change and the expectation of continuing changes that will significantly disrupt human activities and ecosystems. Non-experts cannot authoritatively verify expertise, however, so deciding to rely on expert knowledge requires deciding whose claims of expertise – whether from individuals, disciplinary communities, or institutions – to trust. The extent of scientific knowledge can thus easily be obscured by organized non-scientific attacks, which can both disrupt what would otherwise be a widely recognized knowledge basis for action and undermine trust in the scientific bodies that articulate this knowledge base – even if, as in the current climate denial campaign, actual experts recognize that every claim raised is obviously false or insignificant. This struggle shows the need to distinguish between normative and positive framings of my first condition, the level of expertise: even when expertise is well enough established that relying on it would be justified, the politically relevant trust in that expertise needed to put such reliance into practice is always vulnerable to sufficiently well-resourced attacks.

Environmental issues also meet the second condition, albeit also with qualifications. For major environmental issues now on the policy agenda, the high end of the uncertainty range of potential outcomes includes harms so grave to people, resources, and ecosystems that virtually everyone would wish to avoid them. But the linkage of these high stakes to actionable public and political concern is weakened by the long time-lags and uncertainties that characterize climate change and other environmental issues. Many environmental systems respond only slowly to changes in human-imposed stresses. For example, current cuts in greenhouse-gas emissions reduce climate-change risks only decades in the future. Even if these future harms are severe, people disagree on their importance based on how much they care about the future and how much they believe "something will turn up" (i.e., some currently unknown solution) in the interim to avoid the worst harms. Uncertainties in the precise nature and severity of future harms also interact with belief in high collective stakes. As environmental damages grow more severe, they generally also distribute harms more broadly. Yet under any given state of knowledge, the most severe projected harms are also the least likely to occur. People will thus perceive higher social stakes to the extent they are more risk-averse and care more about the future, so people who differ in these characteristics will also tend to disagree whether scientific evidence provides a strong basis for action. These interactions qualify and to some degree weaken the extent to which environmental issues meet the "stakes" condition.

Environmental issues often do not meet the third, "separability" condition, however. Environmental issues are notoriously hard to disentangle from other policy areas and tend to strongly penetrate both distributional issues and contested values. Deciding which environmental risks to prioritize and how strongly to address them is tied up with what people care about, what they fear, what conditions they are willing to endure, and what trade-offs they are willing to make. Responses to environmental problems also touch political hot buttons. They often require constraints or burdens on firms and citizens, despite earnest attempts to frame these as positive "incentives," and so involve strong political differences over the proper scope of collective decisions and state coercion. And they impose costs on identified groups, those whose activities are causing the environmental harm in question.

Moreover, environmental policies have a recurrent structural difficulty in how they impose costs. Environmental harms are usually recognized only belatedly, after they are already occurring, so managing them requires restricting ongoing activities that were previously thought benign. The interests that have grown up around these activities understandably resist these controls. These fights could to some extent be avoided by acting in advance, guided by prospective assessment of environmental impacts, but such anticipatory assessment and action remain an aspiration rarely achieved in practice. Environmental assessment is usually stuck playing catch-up, forced to make the case that ongoing productive activities are imposing harms severe enough to warrant regulatory action. Even as knowledge advances, there often remains enough uncertainty to put a defensible face on the favoured position of a strong constituency. Holling and his colleagues made this point thirty years ago for fisheries management (see, for example, Ludwig, Hilborn, and Walters 1993), but it applies to any issue marked by uncertain knowledge and strong interests – including most environmental and resource-management issues, as well as others such as pension policy in the face of demographic and economic uncertainties. Uncertainties (real or exaggerated) enable biased interpretations of evidence that aim to support continuing current practices, deny bad news, or shift responsibility and regulatory burden onto others. This is always an unequal fight, in which the scientists saying "Hang on, there's a problem here," are up against the big guns: the fisheries biologists against the fishing industry, the eutrophication scientists against the farm lobby, the climate scientists against the tar sands. It is no surprise who usually wins.

But usually is not always. Scientific evidence of environmental risks sometimes gains traction in policy-making, and environmental controls to limit widely shared risks sometimes prevail over the established interests that bear the control costs. This progress can be related to the fact that the three conditions are not static. Where any particular issue sits with respect to the conditions can shift over time, owing to both advancing knowledge and increasing environmental pressures. As a result, environmental harms that were formerly prospective and contested become more clearly evident and harder to deny. Evidence of current harms makes stakes appear higher and also tends to highlight shared risks over distributive costs. These trends can shift how much an issue is seen as a priority for action and an appropriate area for strong scientific input.

This dynamic character of environmental issues must be considered in assessing appropriate roles for expertise in guiding choice, because differences in how mature an issue is – in terms of both scientific understanding and prior political choices – suggest widely differing answers. When an issue first becomes ripe for policy attention, there is little room for expert processes to exercise regulatory authority. Rather, the main job for scientific expertise at this stage is to communicate and synthesize what is known about the issue and associated risks, to bring the issue into the public eye and onto the policy agenda. Doing this job does not require any authoritative role in policy, merely the freedom and resources for relevant expert groups to conduct research and monitoring, meet and deliberate, and publicize their findings. It does require these, however – which is why recent decisions cutting policy-relevant data, research, and monitoring in Canada and elsewhere are so destructive.

At the other extreme, when an issue is mature – i.e., scientifically well understood, with initial large-scale response decisions made and some agreement on criteria for further decisions – conditions become favorable for strong delegation to expert-based processes. Such delegation typically occurs in a regulatory agency with well-defined objectives and authority within a larger-scale structure of accountability. The strongest forms of such delegation follow the model of independent central banks: some expert body is given provisional authority to set the level or other details of policy – for example, the number of emission permits issued, the rate of an emission tax, the particular species or ecosystems to protect – subject to provisions for accountability (for example, transparency of supporting research and analysis) and the possibility of override by some democratically accountable body.

The most troublesome cases, however, come as an issue develops between these extremes, when knowledge and policy debate have advanced to the point that serious regulatory responses are under consideration and the first major decisions about the form and intensity of response must be made. This intermediate stage broadly describes the most contentious current environmental issues, such as cutting greenhouse gases and protecting biodiversity. For issues at this stage, my three conditions often yield stubbornly mixed results. The issues are thus not ripe for strong delegation to an expert or administrative body. They need political decisions, but with decision-makers somehow motivated to attend, seriously and honestly, to available scientific knowledge. They need expertise, they need democracy, and they need the two of them to get along.

How can this be achieved? We have a long record of wise but rather vague guidance, often expressed in metaphors that invoke careful communication, informal accommodation, respect for distinct areas of authority, and trust – from Price's (1965) notion of separate "estates," to Jasanoff's (1994) idea of issue-specific negotiated boundaries between science and democracy, to Ungerleider's analogies with intimate relationships. But while these images capture essential elements of the expert-democracy relationship when it is working well, they give little guidance on how to improve matters when it is working badly. Moreover, there are many recent signs – in Canada and elsewhere – that norms of informal accommodation are breaking down and expert advice is losing influence – and even autonomy and resources – just as the need for decisions to be well informed by science is increasing.

In this situation, exhortations to mutual accommodation and respect remain worthwhile, since these are always needed. But when these are insufficient, the menu of options to make legislative or other political processes more responsive to expertise and evidence – without courting the dangers of excessive or premature alienation of authority – is rather thin. The two main routes are increased resources and procedural defaults. With more resources and independence, scientific advisory and assessment bodies may be able to bring enough attention to an issue to move political opinions even with no formal authority. In some cases, with appropriate mandates and skilful leadership, assessment bodies may draw on both expertise and consultation to synthesize relevant knowledge and provide recommendations for action – a hybrid approach between that of conventional scientific assessments and royal commissions. Alternatively, for issues that are well enough defined, appropriately configured expert bodies may be empowered to draft findings or even action proposals that are given influence over policy action by tilting procedures in their favor. Possibilities can range from a requirement that the government formally respond to the proposal to a procedural default that the proposal is enacted unless the relevant political body decides otherwise. In the strongest form, proposals of the expert body can be given more force by procedural rules that make them hard for the political body to reverse – for example, deadlines for action, super-majority voting, or requirements for a single vote without amendments, as used in the US Congress for fast-track treaty ratification or military base closings. Even the strongest form of these proposals shifts authority toward the expert body by degrees, as rebuttable presumptions, while ultimate authority remains with democratic institutions. After democratic institutions have taken serious action steps, the space for legitimate delegation of authority to expert or technical bodies broadens.

These proposals to give more clout to expertise-based findings must walk a fine line – strong enough to make them hard to ignore but not so strong as to improperly alienate democratic authority. Getting this right depends on context, on nuance of process design, and on the skill and judgment of individuals on both sides. Consequently, fully codified solutions that work for all issues are unlikely, and none of these fully avoids dependence on the good sense of decision makers. It is for this reason that I characterize my thesis as a defence of *a little* technocracy – both because I hope that a little is enough and because I agree with Ungerleider that more than a little poses dangers beyond its benefits.

5

Program Evaluation and Aboriginal Affairs: A History and a Thought Experiment

IAN D. CLARK AND HARRY SWAIN

The evaluation function at the Department of Indian Affairs and Northern Development (DIAND)[1] is now working as well as any in the Canadian federal government, fully up to the demands of the central agencies. These standards are a pale but expensive shadow, however, of the ambitious age of High Modernism forty years ago. Rod Dobell's approach has matured since then, but in key respects he is still at odds with the degraded standards of the present system.

A THOUGHT EXPERIMENT

The present performance of the evaluation function at DIAND stems from the central agency pressure to embed evaluation in the policy and expenditure management system, which owes so much to Dobell and his colleagues at the Treasury Board forty years ago. It also owes much to the complexity and confusions of policy toward Canada's Aboriginal peoples.

Since leaving Ottawa in 1976 for Paris and then Victoria, Dobell has continued to think and write on a wide range of policy issues, including the philosophy and practice of evaluation and the relationship between Canadian governments and Aboriginal Canadians. To frame this essay on the evolution of program evaluation in Aboriginal affairs, we pose the question, What if Rod Dobell had stayed in Ottawa?

Suppose Dobell had stayed on in the positions that we once held, secretary of the Treasury Board and deputy minister of Indian Affairs and Northern Development respectively. Although we acknowledge that Rod is intelligent enough to have done both our jobs at the same time, this would have been structurally inappropriate. Our experiment has Rod rotating every five years between 1978 and 2008 from deputy at Indian Affairs to Treasury Board secretary. He could thus periodically oversee the government-wide policy on evaluation, influence the resources devoted to evaluation, and actually use evaluation resources in a real department. In 2013, after seven five-year rotations, Rod would at last have earned the right to retire to Victoria.

Our point is not to imply that any particular individuals have failed in their duty but to illustrate how we think the worlds of evaluation and Aboriginal affairs might have been different if the federal government had had the benefit of the sustained contribution of senior officials who were as gifted in the theory, practice, and exposition of policy analysis and evaluation[2] as Rod Dobell.

One of the realistic elements in our experiment is that these matters – evaluation policy, overall evaluation resources, and the uses to which evaluations are put – are almost wholly in the hands of the mandarinate. All ministers we have worked with took these matters to be questions of management practice and were comfortable leaving the details to their officials. If deputy ministers decide that evaluation is important, it is relatively easy to cast the function in a way that fits the ideological mold of whichever party is in power. We would assert that the current strengths and weaknesses of the evaluation function in the federal government today are almost solely attributable to the decisions and actions of officials rather than politicians.

HIGH MODERNISM IN OTTAWA

Summarizing Zussman's detailed history above, the new Trudeau government established a Planning Branch in the Treasury Board Secretariat in 1969, where Al Johnson became secretary. Johnson recruited Douglas Hartle from the Political Economy Department at the University of Toronto to head the branch, and Hartle recruited many others, Dobell senior among them, to systematically apply the ideas of rational budgeting and evaluation of policy alternatives that had been developed in the 1950s and 1960s in the United States.[3] The central thought was that the costs of government actions could be measured against the outcomes of those actions, allowing rational re-design, a choice of different means, or a ranking of different action-outcome sets. This optimistic belief underlies any number of specific programs with acronyms like PPBS, MBO, and PEMS.

In retrospect, the Ottawa of Hartle and Dobell can be considered the apogee of what Moran, Rein, and Goodin (2006) refer to as the "high modernism" stage of policy analysis, with its "technocratic hubris, married to a sense of mission to make a better world" and "an overwhelming confidence in our ability to measure and monitor that world." They conclude that "high modernism is an anachronism." In a similar vein, Dobuzinskis, Howlett, and Laycock (2007) describe the divergence that has emerged between the "positivist" approach to policy analysis – rooted in microeconomics and based on mastery of a number of formal analytical techniques with the intent of "speaking truth to power" – and a newer "post-positivist" approach focusing more on process-related techniques for affecting policy discourse, ideas, and arguments. Van Loon summarizes the fate of the Treasury Board planning system centred in the Hartle/Dobell Planning Branch:

> Reams of material ha[ve] been produced on the difficulties encountered by microeconomic and evaluation-based planning processes. Indeed, a significant quantity of that material has been produced by Hartle himself who quickly grew disenchanted with the potential for introducing the particular definition of rationality he had espoused into political decision-making unless the rules of the game and the incentives and behaviour patterns of politicians and bureaucrats could be drastically altered. Suffice it to say here that the Planning Branch planning system never took hold in Ottawa, nor even managed to dominate its own agency, the Treasury Board. Thus, although some excellent technical work was done by its evaluators and some very interesting findings emerged, the high tide of the Planning Branch system ebbed quickly. The Planning Branch itself disappeared in an austerity move in 1978 and the evaluation function was shifted to the Office of the Comptroller General. (1981, 197)

Both Hartle and Dobell were brilliant, fearless, and analytically rigorous. Their intellectual journey, portrayed in writings about what they had learned from the Planning Branch's limited success in applying political-economic logic to real government settings, has been insightfully described in Dobell's contribution to the book written in tribute to Hartle (Dobell 1999). He calls the 1968–78 period the culture of BOISE – Bold Inference and Social Engineering. This was the era of cabinet evaluation studies, where major government expenditure programs whose economic outcomes were radically lower than stated expectations – such as the dairy program, investments in atomic energy, regional development incentives programs, and the Cape Breton Development Corporation – were examined with modern microeconomic techniques, with the explicit object of trying to improve their effectiveness through changes in the program design. Dobell succeeded Hartle as head (deputy secretary) of the Planning Branch in 1973. Although the branch was wound up soon after Dobell moved to the OECD, the underlying idea had the power of persistence. After a period of confusion in the late 1970s and early 1980s, the idea of program evaluation as a more modest and more routine part of governance began to be widely accepted. Dobell describes how BOISE evolved into the more prosaic ROME – Results-Oriented Management and Evaluation – in the decade from 1988 to 1998 (Dobell 1999).

The notion of routine program evaluation became institutionalized in the expectations that central agencies (especially the board) had for line departments and in departmental structures. Large-scale expenditure reviews in 1985 and 1995 created a demand for evaluation studies and the loss-of-control scandals of the 1997–2007 period multiplied central rules. Crucial to the government's current central control system, the Management Accountability Framework (Treasury Board Secretariat 2012), is the idea of universal, periodic and ostensibly risk-based audit and evaluation, with attendant performance measurement apparatus.

RATIONALISM AND REJECTION IN ABORIGINAL AFFAIRS

The rationalism of the old Planning Branch was echoed in odd ways in the world of Indian Affairs. Until 1970, policy was unabashedly assimilationist. Under the Indian Act the federal government acted as the benevolent ward of indigenous peoples, whose innocence of modern ways, it was thought, was so severe that they had to be protected from European settlers. Indian agents controlled every minute facet of community life on the reserves to which they had been consigned. Escape from these prisons of paternalism required assimilation and the casting aside of traditional languages and ways of life. In 1969 Prime Minister Trudeau and his young Indian Affairs minister, Jean Chrétien, appalled at the human consequences of this policy (Hawthorn 1966–67), published a White Paper that proposed to end at a stroke Canada's internal colonialism. Race-based discrimination (as well as entitlements) stemming from the obsolete and unequal treaties of the nineteenth century would end, and we would all be Canadians together. But Indians objected. If the conditions of their lives were to be changed, they wanted a hand in the design. Harold Cardinal's Red Paper of 1970 put paid to Trudeau's Enlightenment rationalism.

The second great blow to assimilationist policy, quickly following Cardinal, came from the Supreme Court, which was unable to conclude in *Calder* (1973) that aboriginal rights had been extinguished in those parts of the country, like Chief Calder's Nisga'a territory, not covered by treaties. Suddenly Indians had important (and after 1982, constitutionally protected) land rights. And their circumstances were straining the country's conscience.

Federal policy leapt into an entirely new dimension. Expenditures increased greatly, though not as rapidly as the respect (and subventions) granted such organizations as the National Indian Brotherhood (later the Assembly of First Nations) and the Inuit Tapirisat. In 1981–82, pressure from these newly empowered groups and progressive Canadians generally resulted in a section of the new Charter of Rights and Freedoms recognizing existing treaty and aboriginal rights, whatever they were. For the next thirty years the Supreme Court, with no further legislative guidance, began to flesh out the definition. Governments responded. By the late 1980s the negotiation of modern treaties no longer demanded the "extinguishment" of Aboriginal rights; by 1995 the government had recognized as one of those rights an "inherent right of self-government." The separate but unequal system of fiscal apartheid, through which Canada encouraged Indigenous peoples to stay in their traditional, often poorly endowed territories through large payments to Indian Act (rather than traditional) governments, was cemented in place. And in parallel with the re-recognition of these old rights the programming of the Department of Indian Affairs moved away from direct delivery – initially to devolution to band governments under annual, later multi-year, contribution agreements and then to transfer payments to new self-governing entities. Entirely aside from the pressure from the centre, DIAND developed an intense interest in knowing whether these new instrumentalities were effective. (Efficiency and economy claimed some rhetorical space but were distinctly secondary.)

EVALUATION AT INDIAN AFFAIRS AND NORTHERN DEVELOPMENT

By 1982 DIAND's evaluation practice was well established. The department had in fact anticipated TBS' 1977 direction by establishing the function as part of its own corporate policy in 1976. In keeping with the statement that the deputy minister was the primary client for program evaluations, only activities big enough (in several senses) to warrant that grandee's attention were to be covered. And since the deputy minister and, through him, the policy and expenditure management committees supporting the Cabinet were the primary audiences, there was an emphasis on identifying factors relevant to policy change and resource allocation priorities. The director of the evaluation branch was invited to append recommended changes to policy or program design to the "objective" studies going to the deputy. The benefits and costs of alternative program delivery systems, as well as the continuing relevance of program objectives, were seen as "basic issues for evaluation," to be covered in every study. A forward-looking, policy development outlook flavoured the whole enterprise, reflecting the optimism of the Dobell Planning Branch. TBS and the comptroller general also received copies of completed work, and the board might demand evaluations relevant to TB submissions. The central agencies were copied on the rolling five-year plans for evaluation studies so they could be taken into account in the Policy and Expenditure Management System, and Multi-Year Operational Plans. Central evaluations might have disappeared, but evaluation directorates in the line departments were given substantial scope, including an invitation to recommend policy changes, and they were generally encouraged to fan the flame of high modernism. The demise of the Ministries of State during the short premiership of John Turner slackened demand for internal program evaluation.

The Mulroney government, elected in 1984, determined to reduce the Trudeau administration's bequest of alarming deficits and debt, undertook a system-wide expenditure review under deputy prime minister Erik Nielsen.[4] The volume on Aboriginal programs was entrusted mostly to strong-minded non-governmental theorists who had forgotten the lessons of 1970, however, and their recommendations gained no traction.

By the late 1980s the audit and evaluation functions in DIAND were overseen by a department-wide committee chaired by the associate deputy minister, and a steady stream of reports ensued, focussing on areas that were most problematic or were thought to be subject to imminent policy review. Methodologically the reports were not state-of-the-art, and performance indicators, while discussed, were not systematically developed. Senior management was all too aware of the fragility of the statistical base on which most performance measures rested. The spirit was willing, in other words, but the consequences of evaluations were modest.

It was not until a new government, under Prime Minister Jean Chrétien, pressed to the wall by debt and deficit, undertook an emergency program review in 1995, that much effect was felt on DIAND budgets.[5] Minor short-term cuts and personnel losses were the focus of much attention, but the real impact on Aboriginal people came through the setting of a capped rate of increase of 2 percent for all the department's social programs, most crucially education. Two decades later the cap is still mostly in place, despite inflation and rapid population growth rates. Evaluation studies have gingerly pointed out the consequences of this sweeping budgetary decision, but to little avail. The lesson seems to be that the hammer of fiscal necessity overwhelms the pinpricks of program evaluations.

In 2006, a new deputy minister and a new chief of audit and evaluation began to revamp and modernize the function in the department. With the following wind of policy statements and assistance from TBS and by its edict that all programs had to be evaluated if their funding was to continue, an expanded and methodologically better founded evaluation system was installed. Key features include risk- and materiality-based planning of evaluations, the timing of evaluations to fit the policy planning cycle, base rather than soft funding of the evaluation unit, and oversight by an Evaluation, Performance Management and Review Committee chaired by the deputy minister and salted with knowledgable external members.[6] The principal area for further work (now underway) is in the development of a sparse but robust system of performance measures covering all programs and the department as a whole – a task complicated by the disappearance of Statistics Canada's mandatory long-form census.

These admirable features are weakened, however, by directions from the centre on how evaluations should be performed and presented. Every study must conclude whether the program is still relevant to the government's goals (we cannot remember ever seeing a negative response), must examine program modalities but never question "policy," must proceed by way of a review of "relevant" regulations and administrative records, must seek the views of "key" (seems to mean a handful of) informants, and so on. These overly detailed prescriptions can turn even the most vivid and arresting conclusions to pabulum.

By 2009 the evaluation function at the department was well staffed and reported through the chief audit and evaluation executive to the deputy minister. Since April of that year, Treasury Board policy has required that all programs be evaluated on a five-year cycle, as well as in advance of periodic re-funding decisions, and that these evaluations be published on departmental web sites. Each department is given a public MAF score on its conduct of the evaluation function. Each department includes in its departmental Reports on Plans and Priorities its planned internal audits and evaluations for the next three fiscal years, which can be seen on the Treasury Board web site.[7] DIAND lists thirty-four planned evaluations ranging from evaluations of very small programs such as the Inuit Art Foundation to much larger programs such as Child and Family Services. The plan for the evaluation of these programs is coordinated with the plan for the internal audit of the same programs so as to maximize synergies and minimize duplication. The branch budget for 2010–11 was $6 million, devoted roughly evenly to salaries and for contracts with external consultants. The system is adequately resourced and fully bureaucratized.

VALUE FOR MONEY IN FEDERAL OVERSIGHT AND ASSESSMENT

In 2009–10, across the federal government, $78 million and 515 person-years were devoted to the evaluation function, an increase of more than one hundred percent since 2004–05 (Treasury Board Secretariat 2011). The companion program, internal audit, is more backward-looking, but both programs are seen as essential components of the "assurance" function. The budget for DIAND's Internal Audit function was comparable at $6 million, not including the budget of $4 million for the Assessment and Investigation Branch, which pursues allegations of malfeasance. If the balance of resources between evaluation and internal audit is approximately the same across the government, this implies an annual expenditure approaching $200 million on evaluation and internal audit. To this could be added another $100 million to operate the Management Accountability Framework (MAF) exercise and the two parliamentary reporting vehicles, the Report on Plans and Priorities (RPPs) and the Departmental Performance Reports (DPRs). We think it would be safe to almost double these numbers to include the indirect costs of other public servants who take time from their regular work to provide information for these oversight mechanisms. We estimate that the federal government spends at least half a billion dollars a year[8] on its audit, evaluation, and Parliamentary reporting functions.

AN ALTERNATIVE PERSPECTIVE

Before leaving Ottawa, Dobell had thought through and spoken about most of the conundrums and crucial distinctions needed to perform program evaluation: the purpose of the evaluation (forward-looking for purposes of improving designs and allocating resources or backward-looking for purposes of reinforcing accountability relationships), the audience for the evaluation (principal or agent),[9] and the ethical dilemmas associated with risk and decision making by public managers.[10]

The matters of purpose and audience are basic. Hartle frequently observed that asking the public service manager to subject his operations to recurrent comprehensive evaluation is like asking a dog to carry the stick with which she or he is to be beaten (Dobell and Zussman 1981), and Dobell and Zussman note that "the process of policy analysis (including policy and program appraisal, or evaluation) is subject to both procedural impediments, arising out of the fact that the work takes place in an organizational and political context, and to analytical limits arising out of the lack of analytical criteria or relevant information to guide the key choices to be faced" (404), and that there is an "extensive literature on the importance of bureaucratic games, formal and informal pay-off rules or incentive systems, procedural constraints leading to distortions in collective decision processes, and so on. The point is simply that evaluation takes place within a political and organizational context which drives analysis and analysts to an essentially adversarial role ... Within such a framework of advocacy, the bureaucratic incentives do not press in the direction of continuing searching evaluation" (Dobell and Zussman 1981, 413).

The essential distinctions between various purposes and audiences for evaluation are simply not acknowledged in the current federal evaluation and performance measurement policies, which seem to assume that the same set of measures and techniques can serve the needs of program management, resource allocation, and accountability. Indeed, the 1 April 2009 *Policy on Evaluation* holds that one flavour of evaluation is to serve all three purposes and audiences:

> 3.1 In the Government of Canada, evaluation is the systematic collection and analysis of evidence on the outcomes of programs to make judgments about their relevance, performance and alternative ways to deliver them or to achieve the same results.
> 3.2 Evaluation provides Canadians, Parliamentarians, Ministers, central agencies and deputy heads an evidence-based, neutral assessment of the value for money, i.e. relevance and performance, of federal government programs. Evaluation:
>
> a. supports accountability to Parliament and Canadians by helping the government to credibly report on the results achieved with resources invested in programs;
> b. informs government decisions on resource allocation and reallocation by:
>   i. supporting strategic reviews of existing program spending, to help Ministers understand the ongoing relevance and performance of existing programs;
>   ii. providing objective information to help Ministers understand how new spending proposals fit with existing programs, identify synergies and avoid wasteful duplication;
> c. supports deputy heads in managing for results by informing them about whether their programs are producing the outcomes that they were designed to produce, at an affordable cost; and,
> d. supports policy and program improvements by helping to identify lessons learned and best practices. (Treasury Board Secretariat 2009)

This across-the-board philosophy has been questioned by seasoned practitioners. Writing in the *Canadian Journal of Program Evaluation*, Greg Mason worries that "the federal model, as typified by what appears to be the rote methodology (consisting of document/file review, literature review, interviews, focus groups and case studies), masquerades as truth-seeking under the banner of multiple lines of evidence. It is also apparent that evaluation has drifted close to becoming a form of audit, and the standards of validity reflect a dangerous naivety" (Gauthier et al. 2009, 10).

We have noted elsewhere (Clark and Swain 2005) that the propensity of federal central agencies to ignore basic human realities in government and to resort to across-the-board, template-driven policies, frequently leads to demands that appear surreal to departmental managers. As a current example, here is the admonition in the current *Performance Reporting Guidelines* encouraging departments to include honest self-evaluations in their annual Departmental Performance Reports to Parliament:

> Balanced reporting enhances the credibility of reporting. Moreover, reporting on both the positive and negative aspects of performance meets the intention of public performance reporting – to provide the necessary information for scrutiny and decision making. Telling only half of the story is not useful.
>
> Performance information is not fairly presented when the information is limited to successes and minimizes, or even avoids, discussion of matters that did not unfold as planned. In order for reporting to be fair, key information must not be omitted. When discussing results achieved, departments should discuss what went according to plan as well as cases where things did not go according to plan but risks were mitigated. Departments should also discuss results that were not achieved, noting how and why plans were not implemented as intended. It is also important to include explanations of how the department uses both positive and negative results to make adjustments and improvements toward achieving its strategic outcomes. Findings that emerge from evaluations are important sources of information in framing these discussions. (Treasury Board Secretariat 2010, 30)

Dobell had painstakingly analyzed and then explained to his central agency colleagues forty years ago why the personal and organizational dynamics in government make balanced self-evaluation impossible. Recognizing well-researched human and bureaucratic realities, Dobell and Zussman (1981) asserted that "decision support systems for good management of an agency are different from mechanisms for political accountability to Parliament and the public. Evaluation procedures modelled on integrated financial management systems and based upon efficiency in resource use are essential for the first, and (almost) useless for the second" (Dobell and Zussman 1981, 418).

Because even a very good evaluation system cannot discharge the government's responsibility for accountability to parliament and the public, "our answer to the question 'Who should do these evaluations?' is that in the case of summative evaluation (designed to answer the question 'How well are we responding to the problem?') we should all do it – academics, journalists, parliamentary staff, the community at large – much more than we do. We should do it case-by-case, randomly, as events arise, but on the basis of full and open access to the relevant information" (Dobell and Zussman 1981, 422).

HOW EVALUATION MIGHT HAVE EVOLVED

Now for our thought experiment. If Rod Dobell had held prominent positions in the Treasury Board and Indian Affairs during the last three decades, would this half billion dollars a year be spent differently? Would the Treasury Board Secretariat, perhaps in conjunction with other central agencies, be taking a stronger role in forward-looking policy evaluations on crucial national issues such as those pertaining to the health and education of Canada's aboriginal population? Would the department's program evaluations look as they do today? Would a different approach to evaluation have caused policies and programs for aboriginal peoples to evolve in more positive ways?

We believe that if Dobell had remained in charge of the government of Canada's evaluation policy the resulting studies would be more useful and more realistic than they are today. We would have seen more of the government's evaluation resources directed to places where they could make the most difference, with some of the bigger studies godfathered by the centre, particularly where resource allocation and instrument redesign were major concerns. And we think that we would have seen more effort to engage leading scholars from universities and to make more program information public to facilitate "evaluation by all of us."

Dobell kept thinking about these issues through the 1980s and 1990s as political scientists elaborated their post-modernist theories and the analytical premises of the Planning Branch era came under intense critical scrutiny. He provided his most recent synthesis in a lengthy research paper for Ontario entitled "The Role of Government and the Government's Role in Evaluating Government: Insider Information and Outsider Beliefs." He writes:

> There are distinct approaches to project evaluation, program evaluation, performance evaluation, and policy evaluation, running from the most "factual" and amenable to uncontested characterization to least "factual" and most subject to conflicting and contested perspectives ... For the former, where facts, figures of arithmetic, and technical or engineering considerations dominate, accounting and audit can support informative reporting. For the latter, one is left with rhetoric and figures of speech, with only a process of narrative, dialogue, and deliberation to rely upon to achieve convergence within what one hopes will be accepted as a legitimate communicative forum. (Dobell 2003, 49–51)

And he closes his research report with: "The pursuit of equal opportunity for all, for the flourishing of human potential, can only be pursued, it may be argued, through the self-determination made possible within the institutions and norms of a knowledge-based democracy and an experimenting (learning) society. It is this vision, not a model of formal accountability, that should underlie the evolution of evaluation activity in Ontario over the coming decades" (Dobell 2003, 53). All this may be conceding a trifle too much to the contingent and the rhetorical, but it certainly is inconsistent with the formulaic, rules-based evaluations currently in vogue in Ottawa.

Now let us turn to how Dobell's presence might have influenced the conduct of evaluations at DIAND.

In the first place, we would not expect to see a rigid adherence to a TBS-enforced table of contents, nor the use of TBS-mandated jargon. Dobell has long argued that a narrative specific to the program and the audience lends nuance and readability. As secretary he would not have countenanced the more mindless parts of proposed central agency guidance; had he received it, as a line deputy minister, he would in the most graceful, witty but unanswerable way have ignored it. Second, in either role he would likely have insisted on a broad and forward-looking component to every evaluation. Questions of relevance, instruments, alternatives, and unspoken as well as official objectives would have always been part of the remit; narrow studies such as those reported in INAC (2008) would have been fewer and less formulaic. There would have been more weight, and more resources, devoted to a smaller number of evaluations of really important programs, rather than a lock-step, cookie-cutter approach to trivial matters just because TBS, having sunsetted most programming, requires even the smallest, most immaterial activity to be formally evaluated before new funding is granted. The crude central agency conception of "risk," as a basis for all planning and reporting, would not long survive in the domain of the author of "Social Risk, Political Rationality, and Official Responsibility: Risk Management in Context" (Dobell 2002). A much more nuanced view, not so overwhelmingly centred on financial or reputational risk to the federal government, could have been expected.

Finally, we would have expected, for those major studies that evaluated really important programs, to have seen much wider participation. Aboriginal stakeholders and critics, engaged academics, even the press and the general public, would have been urged to take part from the beginning – from the day when the scope of the study and the objectives of the program were first examined. In this respect Justice Dennis O'Connor's organization of the Walkerton Inquiry, to which Dobell was an advisor, is instructive. Part 1 had a backward-looking focus on how that particular tragedy happened. The proceedings were court-like, with evidence widely sought and subject to cross-examination by the numerous parties with standing, the legal version of an audit. Part 2 used that evidence, and much more, to make recommendations for the future. Its proceedings were entirely different except in the commissioner's insistence that all the work be done in public in both parts. Stakeholders of all sorts were invited to present and comment on all important topics: the only rule was they had to do so in public, in front of parties who might have had quite different views.[11] At DIAND, Dobell would have encountered the unwillingness of many Aboriginal stakeholders to take part in official evaluations, but to a much lesser degree than afflicts present practice, since there would have been radically fewer calls for participation, on vastly more important topics.

WHAT A DOBELL-STYLE FORWARD-LOOKING EVALUATION MIGHT LOOK LIKE

We have been impressed with how forward-looking the Dobell conception of evaluation studies was. Even in the 1970s, Cabinet evaluation studies were not primarily intended to verify whether government programs and their managers had lived up to previous commitments; they were searches for better solutions to the big policy problems at hand. This was "evaluation for improvement." It did not pretend to be "evaluation for accountability." We think that if Dobell had had his way, a substantial portion of the treasure now being spent on evaluation would be devoted to such studies. What might such evaluation studies look like in aboriginal affairs?

Below we provide a speculative example based on experience with the work of the Expert Panel on Safe Drinking Water for First Nations (INAC 2006).

Let us imagine an evaluation study of Aboriginal housing. This study would involve substantial consultation with Aboriginal communities and would include First Nations experts from outside government on the study team. The outline of the final report might look like this:

Outline for a Dobell-style Evaluation Study Entitled *Policy Options for Improving the Quality and Cost-effectiveness of Support for Aboriginal Housing*

- *The case for reform.* This section would document the sad and overcrowded state of on-reserve housing despite the considerable, often ineffective, federal investment, noting the connections to related domains such as health, education and incomes.
- *What is good housing and how is it achieved?* This section would examine good models from Canada and abroad, surveying a large literature not just on housing standards but on successful ways of financing and maintaining housing stock once constructed, taking into account the special hurdles faced by isolated small communities.
- *Challenges and complexities.* This section would examine real housing on the ground in real Canadian reserve communities. Problems and their causes, ranging from the unavailability of capital to poor maintenance practices and incentives would be

analyzed. The circular causes of poverty, poor housing, poor health, and poor education would not escape notice. Constraints on achieving good housing, ranging from the Indian Act to capital availability, would receive particular attention.

- *What we heard.* The 2006 drinking water study included public hearings in or near reserve communities in ten regions across the country as its principal means of involving the consumers and providers of drinking water on reserves. A study of housing might well adopt this technique as a means of escaping, if briefly, the clutches of distant experts and those with axes to grind. The study team, which for the reasons cited above would be composed not of public servants but supported by them, would report on insights gained in the field, reconciling them where necessary with official statistics and views.
- *What would be supported and how.* Drawing on the evidence, factors leading to better housing outcomes in small places would be isolated and commented on, with distinctions made between what governments can do and what they cannot. The section would conclude with a short list of critical elements, together with their relation to broader community factors, on which government action might have some lasting effect.
- *Program design options.* This section would package critical elements and the relaxation of constraints in several different ways. With each would be associated a probability, and the costs (not just the financial ones), of achieving a particular level of the objective of good housing for all.

This hypothetical example shows that dramatically different uses of evaluation resources are possible. This kind of evaluation would be controversial and require much greater engagement from senior officials and ministers. The effort would likely need to be led by a person of force, sophistication, and wit, someone not afraid to raise his head above the parapet of civil service anonymity. No one could be better than the writer of the 1989 masterpiece, who concluded that "even in a world of profound uncertainty and missing data, explicit and formal analysis offers the essential decision tool for informing and guiding the public manager in the often agonizingly difficult decisions that must be taken on matters of public risk. Within a framework of principle, analysis does help" (Dobell 1989, 10).

CONCLUSIONS AND SUGGESTIONS

Is it possible to draw conclusions from this review of evaluation in Aboriginal affairs and our imagination of a Dobell-driven approach to policy analysis? Are there better ways for the Canadian government to spend the $78 million per year currently devoted to evaluation-related activity? We believe so.

It is not realistic to suggest that the evaluation function be managed by people as highly trained, analytically rigorous, and intellectually curious as Rod Dobell. The world has few such people. But here are four suggestions that we believe ordinary mortals could apply.

1 The government should make explicit the distinction between "evaluation for improvement" and "evaluation for accountability" and devote the vast majority of evaluation resources to the former.
2 Senior officials should apply more judgement in selecting topics for evaluation. Rather than applying across-the-board rules such as "every program, every five years" or "before seeking renewal of any program of specific duration," the topics should be selected on the basis of *the extent to which evaluation might lead the government to make material changes in program design or funding*.
3 The central agencies that advise ministers on policy priorities and funding should become more involved in the selection and design of evaluation projects.
4 There should be fewer, but more thorough, evaluations and they should draw on the techniques of analysis employed in academic social sciences research and the techniques for engaging interested parties employed by successful public enquiries.

We think these modest suggestions are fully in the spirit of Rod Dobell.

NOTES

1 Since 2011, the government has referred to the department as Aboriginal Affairs and Northern Development (AANDC). To avoid confusion, we use the name used throughout the period under review, which remains its statutory name today.

2 In our look at the underlying theory we think of *evaluation* and *policy analysis* almost interchangeably since the fundamental skills and assumptions of high-end evaluation are so similar to those for general policy analysis.

3 An exceptional number of these recruits went on to the most senior posts in the public service in the decades to come, including Mel Cappe, Barry Carin, Ian Clark, Frank Claydon, Mark Daniels, Rod Dobell, John Edwards, Len Good, François Lacasse, Maurice Lafontaine, Paul-Henri Lapointe, Bruce Montador, Russ Robinson, Michael Wolfson, and David Zussman.

4 One of them, on industrial programs and subtitled "Giving with Both Hands," set an important but unfollowed precedent by looking at tax expenditures with the same optic as direct expenditures. To this day TBS does not require the Department of Finance to evaluate the effectiveness, costs and benefits, or economy of tax expenditures.

5 A 1991 central agency edict to cap expenditures on post-secondary education, one of the department's most successful programs, was met by nationwide protests and the shuffle of the line minister who tried but failed to defend an unthinking instruction from the centre: a good example of a decision taken in the teeth of evaluation evidence.

6 Including – full disclosure – the present authors.

7 At http://www.tbs-sct.gc.ca/rpp/2011-2012/info/ia-vi-eng.asp#ian (accessed 16 August 2011).

8 Official numbers always underestimate the hidden costs associated with these oversight functions. On the cost of the MAF, Lindquist (2009) writes: "One way to focus our attention on the implications of MAF is to consider its annualized costs. As a starter, let's consider a very conservative and 'back-of-the-envelope' estimate: 10 FTEs in the MAF directorate and its parent unit; 60 FTEs associated with the program sectors and policy centres of TBS and related central agencies (20 percent of time of around 300 full-time staff); 350 FTEs in departments and agencies (say 6 FTEs on average for the 55–60 departments and agencies covered by MAF each year, recognizing the larger departments devote more resources than smaller agencies). This leads to a conservative estimate of 420 FTEs and an annual cost of $42 million (priced at $100,000 per FTE) to run MAF. There are many officials who would argue that this grossly underestimates the cost of staff time in central agencies, departments, and agencies. While this estimate does not include the information technology and management requirements, the costs may be lower than it might seem since MAF relies on data and information already in the system, provided as part of a much

larger system of accountability and reporting." We would suggest that the cost of running the RPP and DPR processes are similar.

9 Dobell articulated this in terms of the chain of delegation between the party who has delegated, and another who has accepted, certain responsibilities (see Dobell 1975, 5–6). Today we would likely use the language of principal-agent theory.

10 Dobell later brought together these latter ideas with the then fashionable idea that public servants needed to be more entrepreneurial in a brilliant article in the *American Review of Public Administration* entitled "The Public Administrator: God? Or Entrepreneur? Or Are They the Same in the Public Service" (1989). The article opens with, "We all know that to innovate is great. But we also know that to err is human, and to forgive may be divine – but it is not customary. A tradition of entrepreneurship can only flourish in a culture in which the costs of error are not so great as to demand divine dispensation on a continuing basis." These views were further elaborated in Dobell (2002).

11 The result was interesting: a pleasing degree of civility, an unwillingness to use intemperate language, and the discovery that areas of agreement far outnumbered the others.

6

The Canada Pension Plan and Policy Reform: Shifting Spaces for Democratic Deliberation

MICHAEL J. PRINCE

INTRODUCTION

Major episodes of pension reform are opportunities for public authorities and private interests to offer advice on retirement planning, to affirm the necessity and desirability of personal responsibility for income security, to extol the virtues of financial literacy, and to promote certain standards for economic well-being of the young individual, the working family, the elderly couple, and of the overall retirement income system in Canada. Pension reforms are also exercises in some kind of democracy.

This chapter focuses on the democratic politics of pension policy reform with regard to Canada's national public pension program, the Canada Pension Plan (CPP). The CPP is a statutory plan provided by the federal and provincial governments in partnership based on earnings-related benefits.[1] Established in the 1960s, the CPP's history offers a considerable vantage point for examining developments in democratic politics in Canada and reflecting on fundamental issues of power, public participation and social citizenship.

An exploration of pension policy-making reflects Rod Dobell's abiding concerns with social policy, the values of equity and efficiency, and the significance of institutional designs and decision processes in democratic market societies. In fact, in the early 1980s Rod served as the study director to a House of Commons parliamentary task force established by the Pierre Trudeau government to examine pension policy reform. Along with a few research associates, including Michael Wolfson among others, Rod analyzed the evidence and drafted the report for that parliamentary task force (Canada 1983). The parliamentary task force is noteworthy in its attention to democratic sensibilities. Along with economic and social changes occurring in Canadian society, the task force report highlighted "public perceptions, attitudes and expectations" as an equally important contextual element in their inquiry. In respect to any reforms to pensions, this meant the necessity for "consultation, adequate notice and time to adapt." To ensure that recommendations would be feasible and acceptable to the public, the task force therefore "relied on a process of consultation rather than on an exercise of pure analysis" (Canada 1983, 5). There is here a direct engagement with politics and politicians; this was not the first nor the last interaction by Rod with Canadian policy-makers and public decision-making processes. Building on this broader perspective I wish to set public pension reform in the context of democratic values, practices, and politics.

PENSION POLICY AND REFORM POLITICS

As a mandatory, earnings-related public pension arrangement, the CPP is a social insurance plan, a transfer of tangible benefits between generations today. Further, it is an intergenerational agreement, a social contract in effect, with contributions and a legislated commitment to pay benefits well into the future. With the creation of the CPP Investment Board in the late 1990s, the CPP now has a clear mandate for the accumulation of assets sufficient to meet pension promises well into the future, adding a further dimension of security beside that of the taxing power of governments to collect revenues (Prince 2003). The CPP is also an intra-generational redistribution, apparent, in part, from the flat rate component of the CPP disability benefit and of the CPP survivor benefit, both of which are non-earnings related payments. Beside taxation and spending, the CPP is an elaborate bundle of policy instruments: legislation and regulation, constitutional powers and intergovernmental relations; public administrative delivery systems, and appellate and judicial review structures.

Information, persuasion, and exhortation are other notable governing instruments deployed in pension policy. Pensions intertwine with public, private, and personal finances, and with the activities of earnings, savings, and investments. As such, pension policies concern the way of life of individuals and the household management of budgets. Public pension programs like the CPP establish in working people's lives (and for many of those retired and disabled) values of employment, forethought and thrift, and a modicum of security. Pension reform is about manufacturing ideas and practices of risk, sustainability, balance, and responsibility, and then managing interrelationships between these and other factors, including those who pay and those who benefit. A central part in the politics of pension reform is setting the terms and conditions, the rules, structures, and procedures of a policy reform process. Pension policy-making, moreover, is about how public power is wielded as well as not exercised and about how public and private relations of power interact, constraining and/or enabling opportunities for individual and collective provisions for savings. In the case of the CPP, it is a program with national standards on certain fiscal and program matters of public pensions, developed within shared legislative powers between the federal and provincial governments. The CPP therefore involves a close interdependency between the two orders of government and democracy with regular intergovernmental interactions on the operation, review, and reform of the plan, through conferences of ministers and working groups of officials (Béland 2013).

To examine social politics and dialogue aspects of pension reform, I consider particular review processes associated with the CPP, the participants involved and their core proposals and expectations, and, in general terms, the decision outcomes. The analysis here centres on the democratic structures and processes of deliberation in three specific periods of the CPP: its policy establishment in the 1960s, the "great pension debate" in Canada of the late 1970s and early 1980s, and the CPP reforms of the mid-1990s. Taking this historical perspective, I will explore the shifting nature and scope of democratic deliberation, understood to encompass structures, processes, and mechanisms of open consultations and exchange of ideas, widespread participation, and public influence on CPP policy-making in the Canadian state.

To preview my central argument: the history of CPP policy-making and reform is not a history of continual progress along increasingly democratic lines of transparency and responsiveness. Rather, the CPP's history reveals both expansions and contractions in the democratic spaces for public participation and dialogue on pension reforms. Overall we can observe a narrowing of spaces with a shift from governance, in the 1960s and 1970s; to the government of pension reform in more recent times. The Canadian state, federal and provincial, is more than ever at the centre of this policy field, with a declining role for societal groups.

CPP POLICY DESIGN AND FORMATION: 1963–66

Interest about a contributory public pension plan among Canada's main federal political parties noticeably emerged in convention resolutions and election campaign statements (Bryden 1974). By the 1962 and 1963 federal elections, thinking within the political parties, especially the Liberals, had yielded detailed ideas and a stronger public commitment by the leader to an earnings-related public pension plan for Canadians. There was a conference of federal and provincial welfare ministers that discussed pensions, as well as three federal-provincial conferences of first ministers (Simeon 1972).

A Special Joint Committee of the House of Commons and Senate, created to examine the draft bill on the CPP, was comprised of twelve senators and twenty-four MPs. The Joint Committee held fifty-one sittings, from late 1964 to early 1965, hearing from over one hundred witnesses, as well as from officials in eight federal government departments and agencies. In the end, in addition to endorsing the principles of the CPP, the Joint Committee recommended changes in a handful of areas. One of their proposals was that a further benefit, a dependent child benefit, payable in respect of each child of a disabled contributor, be included in the CPP, and that the amount of the benefit be the same as for the orphan's benefit.

As important if not more so than the income protection goal, was the consideration given, by governments and business interests especially, to the financial affordability and economic effects of the overall CPP. At the time, concerns were raised over the effects of the CPP on investment markets, private savings, occupational pension plans, and the inflation and growth rates of the Canadian economy. Reflecting these concerns and pressures, governments limited the maximum CPP retirement benefits to 25 percent of earnings up to the average wage, adjusted automatically, while leaving considerable room for private sector pension plans, tax-assisted retirement plans, and personal savings to meet the retirement income needs of Canadians.

The original legislation contained several public reporting requirements, a feature today called transparency and accountability. At least once in every five years, the federal government's chief actuary was to prepare a report based on an actuarial examination of the legislation and the state of the CPP account, including projections for a period of at least thirty years. The legislation further stipulated that any federal action to amend the CPP must have a study done by the chief actuary, with that information placed before parliament to inform consideration of any proposed amendments. These provisions illustrate how the perspective on financial sustainability was firmly rooted in the CPP from its beginnings. They systematically placed financial concerns on political and policy agendas, conveying a message every few years about the immediate and longer-term sustainability of the CPP.

The legislation also established a CPP Advisory Committee to provide, through an annual report, policy and program advice to the Minister of National Health and Welfare. Its statutory functions were to review the operation of the legislation, the state of the CPP investment fund, and the adequacy of coverage and benefits under the plan. The committee was to comprise up to sixteen members appointed by the governor in council, with representation from employers, employees, the self-employed, and the public. In turn, the minister was to include the Advisory Committee's report in his or her own annual report to parliament on the administration, programming, and financing of the CPP. This advisory committee was one of a number formed by the federal government in the 1960s and early 1970s to foster public awareness and consumer involvement in social security in Canada, a trend called "participatory citizenship" (Guest 1998).

THE GREAT CANADIAN PENSION DEBATE AND RESULTS: 1978–87

From 1978 to 1984, there was an extensive and intensive set of consultations, discussions, and recommendations on reforming the retirement income system. Drivers behind the debate included the inadequate coverage of workers by occupational pension plans, the insufficient protection of private plans and personal savings against inflation, deficiencies in the vesting and portability of most workplace pension plans, and the continued precarious status and inequitable treatment of women, elderly and non-elderly alike, under the pension system. Limitations in the original design of the CPP also contributed to pension reform, again moving up the political agenda. The pension debate was joined by federal and provincial governments, as well as by economic, financial, and social organizations, and produced "a prolonged, animated and polarized public policy review" (Deaton 1989, 107).

The primary focus of the retirement income policy debate was on the private pension system – with its issues of coverage, inflation protection, vesting, and portability and survivors benefits. Within the public system, most political attention focused on improving tax assistance for retirement savings, addressing poverty among current elderly women, and the great unresolved issue of whether to expand significantly the earnings replacement role of the CPP; that is to say, increasing benefits above the limit of the 25 percent of average wages. During the last Liberal government of Pierre Trudeau, from 1980 to 1984, pension reform was a high social policy priority, but a social priority competing for attention and resources against a new national energy policy, intense constitutional reform efforts, and the mounting fiscal challenges associated with a serious economic recession. The minister of national health and welfare, Monique Bégin, was an active champion of pension reform, favouring a significant expansion of CPP disability benefits and the liberalization of eligibility rules.

In the spring of 1981, the federal government hosted a National Pensions Conference, the primary focus of which was private pensions for retirement. The conference, opened by Prime Minister Trudeau, examined the issues of inadequate coverage, portability, vesting, and inflation protection of occupational pension plans. A federal government position on pensions planned for July 1981 as a follow-up to the conference was delayed until December 1982, in the form of a Green Paper – a document in which a government sets out its thinking and invites reactions to its ideas. No doubt, the delay was due to the conference failing to achieve broad consensus on pension reform directions. Divisions reflected differences within the Liberal government and Cabinet itself between pro- and anti-CPP expansionists, anchored in the National Health and Welfare and Finance portfolios respectively. When the federal government's Green Paper on the retirement income system finally came out in December 1982, it cautioned that "pension reform will of necessity be a lengthy process because of the time required for consultation, negotiation, legislation and implementation" (Canada 1982, iii). The reform proposals put forward in the paper were referred to a parliamentary task force to allow for further public debate and consultations.

The Trudeau government's concluding statement on pension reform accompanied their final budget of February 1984. In their *Action Plan for Pension Reform* (Lalonde 1984), the Liberals concentrated on raising the minimum standards of private pensions, enhancing tax assistance for retirement savings, and improving public pensions in a few select ways. With respect to improving public pensions, the main action was a fifty-dollar increase in the monthly GIS for the single elderly person, introduced in two stages in June and December 1984. On the CPP, proposed Liberal reforms included splitting pension benefits upon marriage breakdown or when the younger spouse reached sixty-five; continuation of survivor benefits on remarriage; and the raising of pensionable earnings to the average *industrial* wage by 1987, a rate higher than the more general average wage rate, since it tended to include more unionized workers and thus higher wage rates.

When Bégin left office in 1984 as minister of national health and welfare, she had achieved notable successes in non-CPP policy areas for retirement and seniors but no reform of the CPP had been achieved. As the lead social policy minister, Bégin had done what she could within federal jurisdiction by convening the National Pensions Conference in 1981, co-sponsoring the 1982 Green Paper, using a parliamentary task force on pensions to hold cross-country hearings and report back by December 1983, and getting pension reform profiled in the February 1984 budget. Begin's department also conducted surveys of CPP applicants and benefit recipients to generate up-to-date information on the characteristics and unmet needs of this clientele, for use in the policy debate and Cabinet decision making. But time ran out for Bégin and the Trudeau Liberals. Public pension reform remained a work-in-progress within the ministerial and administrative committees of executive federalism.

It was under the Brian Mulroney Conservative government that an intergovernmental consensus on CPP reforms was reached by late 1985. Federal legislation on these changes was approved by June 1986, with the changes taking effect in January 1987. When the minister of national health and welfare, Jake Epp, introduced the legislation to amend the CPP, he rightly called it the culmination of several years of consultation on the subject of pension reform with the provinces, parliamentarians, and Canadians. Among the major changes to the CPP that came into effect in 1987 were a new twenty-five-year financing schedule with the first increase in the contributions rates since 1966, a review of the contribution schedule every five years by federal and provincial finance ministers, and flexible retirement benefits payable as early as age sixty and starting as late as age seventy.

THE CHRÉTIEN–MARTIN REFORMS: 1996–98

The Jean Chrétien Liberals' first budget in February 1994 set out the principles for the government's plan to reform Canada's social security system. They were to create a system "that better rewards effort and performance and offers incentives to work," while "continuing to offer security to those in need," and a social security system which was "financially sustainable" (Martin 1994, 19). In this period, pension reform lacked a great debate along the lines of the earlier reform periods. The same amount of time was not involved, nor the same broad range of issues addressed on the policy agenda. Probably because of the tighter time frame for dialogue and the political stress placed on reducing the federal deficit and public debt – a defining element of the new political climate – disputes over competing ideas for reforming the CPP were relatively muted in formal discussions and in general media coverage.

When the Liberals released their Green Paper *Improving Social Security in Canada* in October 1994, the CPP and other elderly benefits were excluded from this review. The focus instead was on education, employment, income assistance, and social services. As a consequence, pension reform was not a part of what turned out to be perhaps the widest ever public consultation exercise on federal social programs through the autumn and early winter of 1994–95. Rather, public pension reform was largely overseen by the minister of finance because of the tax implications of social insurance contributions and the intergovernmental fiscal relationship with provinces over CPP policy.

A pension debate of sorts did occur in the mid-1990s, but one more like a talk than a grand clash of contending visions and interests. The views of social policy groups were less prominent and even marginalized in the process, since they tended to argue for further enhancements to benefits and the liberalization of eligibility rules, positions regarded by government officials as out of touch with the fiscal imperatives facing governments. The Department of Human Resources Development Canada (HRDC), the successor to National Health and Welfare in 1993, also played a less prominent role than in previous pension reform cycles, while reports on the CPP by the Office of the Auditor General of Canada and the Chief Actuary to the Plan were influential in setting the tone and parameters of the pension reform discourse, as were studies by various business groups and institutes that repeated the restraint theme.

Whereas the great debate had stressed options for improving benefits and introducing new ones, discussions of pension policy in the mid-1990s, including successive federal budgets, emphasized the fiscal limits of the state and the financial distress anticipated for the CPP and other old age benefit programs. A number of suggestions were advocated for reforming the CPP, ranging from radial structural changes that included abolishing the plan to modifications of the present system that commonly called for increasing contribution rates, raising the retirement age for the full pension, removing the disability and survivor benefits from the CPP, and reducing benefits. The shift in the politics of pension reform became strongly apparent in the finance minister's May 1996 federal budget speech. That speech communicated a criticism of previous governments for not taking proper action on financing the CPP, expressed a concern for that reason about a potential crisis, and promised taking action to slow the growth rate of CPP expenditures. A central theme of this budget was securing pensions and other social programs for the next century.

Legislative reforms made to the CPP in 1998 were preceded by a two-year series of federal finance department-based policy analysis, some public consultations, intensive closed-door intergovernmental bargaining and agreement, and a parliamentary process dominated by the prime minister and Cabinet with a majority government.

In 1996, as part of the statutory review of the CPP that the federal and provincial/territorial governments must do every five years, governments agreed to a joint process of public consultations across the country. David Walker, a Liberal MP and previously parliamentary secretary to the minister of finance, co-chaired the special panel, as the chief federal representative to the consultations. Despite the title, Walker was a parliamentarian, not a member of the government – a backbencher with a special appointment. The panel was in effect a ministerial task force reporting directly to the government rather than a parliamentary committee, and as thus working more closely with the public service, especially the Department of Finance as a result. Along with Walker, ten other MPs and nineteen elected representatives from provincial and territorial governments served on a rotating basis, enabling governments to co-chair the joint hearings as they toured across the country. A secretariat was established, supported by the federal government, to maintain the consultation process. Several provinces held additional hearings of their own. The purpose of the consultations was to canvass views on a range of options for ensuring the financial sustainability of the CPP for future generations. The options presented in what was called a joint information paper, *Securing the Canada Pension Plan*, all dealt with various restraints or cuts to the CPP, combined with accelerated contribution increases to create a "steady state" contribution rate. More than information, however, was being presented in the paper. The unmistakable emphasis was on reducing costs by reducing the level of benefits and by tightening the access to benefits.

The ministerial task force held thirty-three public hearings in nineteen cities across the country. In all, it received 140 written submissions and heard 270 formal presentations, and close to 6,000 inquiries or comments were recorded on a 1-800 information line. In addition, a special one-day session on disability issues was held, led by HRDC officials. As a mid-course adjustment to the planned consultations, the task force also held roundtables with social groups, in response to their concerns about a limited process, at which civil society associations submitted their own positions and were challenged by task force members to consider broader solutions.

The consultations revealed several things: the CPP's complexity as a program; deep popularity with the public as a national social policy; low priority among most provincial governments; strong concern from organized labour that the normal retirement age for a pension under the CPP be left at age sixty-five, rather than raised to sixty-six or higher as was being proposed by some groups; and that within the CPP, the disability program was important but not very well understood.

In contrast to CPP policy reviews in the 1980s or earlier in the 1960s, the federal government went into this consultation with no social policy vision other than restraining the costs of the plan. Finance department officials effectively focused the review on the level of contributions, the stability of benefits, and the fiscal sustainability of the plan. Finance Minister Martin wanted to achieve a 10 percent reduction in the projected growth of CPP expenditures and to keep the combined contribution rate increases to less than 10 percent.

Following the consultations, federal and provincial/territorial finance ministers participated in a series of intergovernmental meetings to negotiate a consensus on changes. In February 1997, the federal finance minister announced that a federal-provincial consensus on reforming the CPP had been reached. Ottawa, eight provinces, and the Northwest Territories supported the reforms, to take effect January 1998, while the governments of British Columbia and Saskatchewan dissented. These two provinces were opposed, in principle, to any cuts to CPP benefits. The agreement on the CPP was largely based on private negotiations among governments, informed by actuarial analyses of projected costs, and partly shaped by reactions during the public consultations.

The consultations revealed something of the political limits of making direct cuts to CPP benefits and tempered the scope and depth of the cuts initially targeted by the finance minister and his senior officials. Neither raising the retirement age nor cutting retirement benefits directly or through de-indexation was popular with the public or politically risk-free, so the focus on making the CPP "financially sustainable" shifted to putting together a series of smaller changes, on the eligibility side that would generate savings. In the 1998 reforms to the CPP, retirement pensions were left virtually untouched, while disability benefits and the other supplementary benefits were restrained. In fact, changes to disability benefits and rules went well beyond the handful of options canvassed in the information paper and debated in the consultation process of 1996. Several other options were discussed and incorporated through the intergovernmental arena, led by the federal Finance Department. For people receiving benefits from 1 January 1998 onwards, the Chrétien-Martin pension reforms introduced cuts to disability benefits and death benefits, as well as to combined disability and retirement benefits and combined disability and survivor benefits.

The two most important changes overall to the CPP were as follows. First, moving from pay-as-you-go financing to fuller funding. Contribution rates were scheduled to rise from 5.85 percent to 9.9

percent of contributory earnings by 2003 (rather than the previously scheduled rise to 7.35 percent in 2003) and then remain steady, rather than follow the projected rise to 14 percent or more by 2030. And, second, investing the CPP reserve fund in a portfolio of market securities to get higher returns to grow in value from the equivalent of two years of contributions currently, to about five years of contributions.

CONCLUDING OBSERVATIONS

A child of the sixties, CPP was the offspring of constitutional reform, cooperative federalism and the Quiet Revolution in Quebec, progressive minority parliamentary governments in Ottawa under Lester Pearson, and active engagement by divergent economic and social interests in Canadian public life. It may have been a time of free love, but the CPP was no carefree social spending spree; cost considerations were a determinant in defining the plan from the outset. CPP reform processes and pension politics over the last five decades have remained fairly stable in some basic ways yet shifted in other important ways. The shared legislative stewardship of the CPP by both orders of government and its unique amending formula have not changed, nor has the fundamental architecture of the plan's design on financing and benefits, nor its place as one complementary element within the overall retirement income security system.

From this historical review of the CPP from the 1960s into the late 1990s, three general observations can be offered. The first is that pension reforms have yielded a number of changes in the CPP, most of which are relatively modest. Thus, reform in public pension policy is generally about incrementalism and the maintenance of the retirement income system (Prince 2010). Pension policy reform exercises are cultural events in which expressions of hope occur and optimistic claims that personal retirement savings will increase, that private sector pension coverage will expand. These policy exercises are also about the assertion of pessimistic beliefs and the issuance of warnings about a fragile economy, and overburdened employers.

With pension policy debate, paradoxically, there is also quiet. Policy silence is a course of non-events and inactions. It is a process where proposals for improved pensions are often simply ignored or are promised to be studied further but then with no real implementation. There are inner circles and outer circles in the pension reform community, with recurring divisions of interests and polarization of ideas concerning the place of public pensions in the retirement income security system (Béland 2013; Bryden 1974; Prince 1985). For over three decades now, a major concern about the CPP has been its built-in limited scale of income protection for retiring workers – the 25 percent replacement rate of average wages, accompanied with frequent recommendations to substantially extend this national program of income security. Most business groups, employer associations, and the financial industry regularly attack these ideas and federal governments regularly reject such recommendations for a major expansion of the plan.

The second observation is that over the period reviewed, the democratic culture and rules of the game regarding pension reform have changed, and in ways that diminish opportunities for popular involvement and policy responsiveness to public claims. A decline in political opportunity structures for civic groups and social movements appears in a series of developments: the loss of institutionalized public spaces[2] by which support or opposition to pension reform ideas can be expressed and debated with others; the outcomes from debates over CPP reforms are less favourable or responsive to social policy group interests than a generation or more ago; the organization of business interests in Canada has advanced considerably over the past thirty years, while the political status of labour and other social movements has weakened (Doern, Maslove, and Prince 2013); and the shift in major political thinking and public management practice toward mixtures of neoliberalism and neo-conservatism (Rice and Prince 2013), which have a preference "to conceptualize social security as a set of purely technical issues [which] ... allows efficiency considerations, essentially supply-side preoccupations, to be stressed and kept well separated from the down-played equity considerations" (Dixon and Kouzmin 2011, 32).

Together, these developments suggest that government reform processes do not offer broad access for and representation of societal interests as they once did. Civil society groups and popular movements for public pension reform have had success in initiating debates and in influencing agendas. But with the exception of the original adoption and design of the CPP in the 1960s and improved benefits for workers with severe disabilities in the 1980s, social groups have experienced more disappointment than satisfying impact in shaping policy developments.

A third observation is the decisive role played by the state in this policy domain. In this case, a shift can be discerned from governance in the 1960s and 1970s, in which both state and non-state organizations and actors actively participated in policy-making processes, to the government of pension reform in more recent times, in which governments dominated in relatively more closed processes. This shift in the style and process of governing is opposite to the trend that scholars of governance both promote and observe (Pal 2001). Expressed another way, the state in Canada, federal and provincial, seems more than ever at the centre of this policy field, with a declining role by societal groups to exercise democratic input. Canada's pension reform phase of the 1990s lacked important institutional forums and mechanisms for deliberation between state and social actors used in earlier reform processes. For many societal groups Canadian governments appeared in a more distant, limiting, and skeptical manner. While there may be less enabling of democratic input by the state, governments have not lost the power to manage this policy community.

The trend of participatory citizenship, optimistically regarded as a major theme in Canadian social policy-making in the 1960s and 1970s, is less robust and more uncertain today. The democratic politics of pension policy-making operates within and affects federalism as well as being shaped by federalism. Undoubtedly, the government of pension reform reflects the ongoing reality of the shared federal and provincial stewardship of the CPP, intergovernmental relations, and thus executive federalism.

Our parliamentary systems remain dominated by first ministers and cabinets, executive federalism continues as a prevalent form of intergovernmental relations, and public servants tightly manage public consultation processes and communication specialists carefully script the messages for target audiences. These long-established relations of power certainly have not dissolved under the effects of sweeping economic and social changes of late capitalism nor have they simply survived; they flourish on the Canadian political landscape. Arguably, the core political institution today for public pension policy-making is comprised of the federal, provoncial, territorial (FPT) ministers of finance, their officials, and their hired consultants.

This is a relative, though significant, change from the 1960s, 1970s, and into the 1980s, when ministers of welfare and social services and their officials played crucial roles in the development, implementation, and evaluation of public pension policy. Within the federal government, influence over the CPP has become concentrated and the effective role of HRSDC (now called Employment and Social Development Canada) in CPP reform has declined in relation to central agencies. In the Chrétien-Martin reforms to CPP, finance ministers and personnel were the dominant state actors. A similar shift has taken place in the provinces, away from social service departments to treasury portfolios. Overall, the nature of intergovernmental relations on the CPP has changed from an administrative or functional approach in the 1960s to 1980s, to more of an actuarial and financial federalism in more recent decades.

Baldwin stresses the importance of seeing contemporary pension debates "in the context of the wider swing to the political right and the positive currency that is associated with liberalizing market forces. The interest that is being shown in downsizing public pensions is hardly a stand-alone event. Public pensions are merely taking their place in the line-up of social programs, and other government programs as well, that are going through the downsizing ringer" (1996, 193). The declining role and influence of social policy groups and social departments of government commenced during the 1985–86 intergovernmental negotiations on the CPP. Essentially, the role of finance departments grew and those of social policy departments diminished at both federal and provincial levels as contributions and funding became the dominant and central issue in public pension reform, reinforced by the review cycle of contribution rates by finance ministers that gave them an increasing say over the benefits structure.

Certain policy processes and even discourses encouraging public involvement and democratic dialogue on pension reform have weakened. The Economic Council of Canada and the Ontario Economic Council, both prominent participants in earlier pension reform debates are long gone; and the capacity of other social policy institutes has diminished. The pension policy community has changed from a pattern resembling a governance network to one more government-centred today. Earlier periods of pension debate and reform, and certainly the one Rod Dobell directly engaged with in the early 1980s, involved extensive deliberation, various sources of evidence, wide consultations and negotiations, and compromises among multiple stakeholders. The design and delivery of the CPP remain within the hands of governments; the shared constitutional jurisdiction of the plan means that the core negotiations and partnerships are between the federal and provincial governments. How, then, are we to understand the democratic effect of pension policy reform exercises? In an instrumental or practical sense, it is to review and possibly change certain aspects of pension standards and rules and perhaps adjust eligibility criteria, benefit amounts, and financing. Certain tangible outputs and important resources may result for particular groups in society and interests in the economy. In another sense, a sense related to the symbolic uses of politics, consultations represent an undertaking in policy rationality, of gathering and weighing the relevant evidence, and an undertaking in representative democracy, in public authorities holding meetings and roundtables listening to community groups and stakeholders. Such events can convey reassurance to a perplexed and anxious public about the future of their pensions, public or private, and personal savings. And, with the triennial review and regularly updated seventy-five-year actuarial projections of the plan, the CPP enables political leaders an arena to be addressing long-term issues of significance to the mass population.

How policy-makers search for, and interpret evidence from experts and consultations matter a great deal. Information, ideas, and interests "remain platonic unless they are translated into politics by the means of some social instrumentality," some means of democratic deliberation (Polanyi 1944, 8). This points out the political management of knowledge as a crucial feature of pension policy consultation exercises. How policy knowledge develops, about which issues, and then is circulated, interpreted, evaluated, and applied or not is all implicated in relations of power. Evidence and policy analysis are not outside or beyond the politics of our market economy and multicultural society. In speaking truth to power, both the speaker of a truth and the decision-maker operate in a context of asymmetrical relations of power and resistance, uncertainties and calculations. As a comparative study of pension policy notes: "Despite their significance, the forms of dialogue used and the routes followed by the reform processes are generally not well known. In a way they are the hidden face of recent pension reforms." With the emphasis on technical, economic, and statistical aspects of pension systems, "decision-making aspects have largely been left in the shadows, yet they are a major factor in the implementation of reforms" (Reynaud 2000, 2). Throughout a distinguished career in public policy and administration, Rod Dobell understood the significance of dialogue and endeavoured to put into practice, in pension reform and other socio-economic policy, this fundamental fact of democratic politics.

NOTES

1 This chapter will not examine other public pension programs, such as the Old Age Security and Guaranteed Income Supplement, which are wholly federal programs, or provincial and territorial income supports for the elderly, all of which are safety net programs for current older Canadians and financed from general revenues. For recent discussions of these programs, see Prince (2010) and (2013) and Townson (2009). Moreover, for reasons of space limitations, the chapter does not examine the latest round of pension debate from 2008 to 2014, but see Béland (2013) for a useful précis.

2 There is, for example, no longer a statutory CPP advisory committee with a range of representatives to advise the responsible federal minister; it was eliminated in the late 1990s reforms.

7

Tales of Quantitative Analysis and Public Policy

MICHAEL WOLFSON

This chapter reviews several high points in the application of the tools of sophisticated quantitative analysis to public policy in Canada. It draws principally on my experience in developing, applying, and communicating the results of these tools in policy debates, mainly in the areas of social policy and taxation policy. For reasons that the narrative below will make clear, this personal slice through Canadian public policy history also serves to illuminate some of the major contributions to the conduct and understanding of public policy of my mentor Rod Dobell.

The next section briefly introduces the type of policy analytic tool with which these episodes have been mainly concerned, static and dynamic microsimulation models. The subsequent three sections then review, from a personal perspective, several of my experiences applying these modelling tools to major policy debates, in the areas of post-secondary education finance, income security, and pension policy, respectively. The final section provides some brief concluding observations.

BACKGROUND – SIMULATION MODELS

While computers today are ubiquitous and powerful, when Rod Dobell first hired me as an undergraduate research assistant in 1969 at the University of Toronto,[1] they were rare and by today's standards weak. The best we had were large mainframes controlled by punched cards, while remote access via teletype was just becoming available at ten characters per second. To my work with Rod, I brought skills in computer programming and a desire to learn what economists really did for a living. He brought a wealth of knowledge and insight, and a great set of issues and projects. While his métier was in the abstractions of optimal economic growth theory, he was also well aware of novel applied methodologies in economic and policy analysis and well connected with key players in government policy, at both the provincial and federal levels.

One of these novel methodologies was simulation modelling. Policy-oriented simulation models aim to capture, in empirically based statistical form, the main characteristics of key actors involved in a policy issue and how these characteristics evolve over time or change in response to a new policy. In any policy issue the key actors almost always include individuals, for example, in their capacities as students, workers, or taxpayers. Key actors also include other relevant institutions or programs, the particular ones depending on the issue. For example, in post-secondary education (PSE) finance, key actors include universities, governments, and student loan and grant programs. In pension policy, they include public pension programs, income tax law, and private saving through RRSP (Registered Retirement Saving Plan) contributions and home ownership. The main purpose of policy-oriented simulation models is to provide information to support decisions, usually in the form of projections of the policies' effects: What will happen if we adopt policy A, rather than policy B, or maintain the status quo?

The computer revolution enabled a vast increase in the sophistication of simulation models. The simple economic and demographic models developed using the first computers in the 1950s were virtually all aggregate models. Economic models tracked GDP and its main components – consumption, investment, government spending, taxes, imports, and exports. Demographic models tracked population counts by age, sex, and geographic region.

The computer revolution also enabled major improvements in handling the data and statistics on which the models depended. Instead of armies of clerks adding up records from households or firms to provide aggregate figures, computers allowed each record to be entered into an electronic database, then added up by software. But once the detailed data were computerized, whole new worlds of analytical possibilities opened up beyond just aggregation. For example, it became relatively easy to study distributions of population characteristics.

Not surprisingly, analysts who looked inside populations to study their distributions – people and their widely varying incomes, firms and their profitability ranging from losses to exceptional profits – found they were highly heterogeneous. While most macroeconomists ignored these Kuhnian "awkward facts" (Kuhn 1962) and continued to work with aggregate quantities and representative (i.e., average or typical) agents, other economists – both theorists and empiricists – began looking closely at the implications of heterogeneity and showing that it wreaked havoc with then standard theory. One of the pioneers in this was Guy Orcutt, to whose work Rod introduced me, as well as that of Goldman and Uzawa (1964).[2]

Orcutt is widely considered the father of one of the most powerful kinds of simulation modelling, microsimulation (Orcutt 1957; Orcutt, Caldwell, and Wertheimer 1976). Microsimulation models are often viewed as complex, and they can be computationally complex. But in conceptual terms they are much simpler than aggregated models, because their "units of analysis" – the things whose behaviour they represent – are easily recognizable entities such as individuals or firms, rather than abstract aggregations. Individuals are described by characteristics such as sex, age, family status, educational attainment, and income, which usually describe the actual population quite accurately because they are derived from a recent sample survey (subject always to sampling and measurement errors). In contrast, aggregate or semi-aggregated methods, dealing as they must with groups of individuals or of firms, must assume some abstract composite entity whose average behaviour is unlike the behaviour of any of its real-world constituent entities.

Microsimulation models can be static or dynamic. A static model focuses on characteristics of a population of interest, or a sample drawn from it, at a given time. For example, the first major policy-oriented static microsimulation model in Canada was developed in 1966 by John Bossons, a colleague of Rod's at the U of T Institute for Policy Analysis, for the Carter Royal Commission on Taxation (Canada 1966). Using a sample of real individual income tax returns, this model first computed each individual's tax under the existing system, then re-calculated the same individual's tax under various hypothetical alternative tax laws. The differences, individual by individual, could then be aggregated to estimate total revenue impacts of each proposed tax policy change or cross-tabulated by province, income level, or other characteristic, to estimate regional and redistributive impacts. The new technology was so obviously powerful and informative that the model was adopted by the federal Department of Finance, and its successors are at the core of tax policy analysis to this day.

Dynamic microsimulation models are more complex and more data hungry. They also usually start with a sample database drawn from the population of interest. But in these cases, the models "age" the sample, examining how it evolves over time under different policy scenarios. They consequently need data not just on the distribution of characteristics of interest at the starting point, but also on how each individual's characteristics evolve from year to year. Some of these data were readily available, such as demographic data on women's fertility rates at each age. Others, such as data on how different individuals' earnings change from year to year, were sparse or nonexistent, because empirical descriptions of these kinds of individual-level dynamics require longitudinal data – data that follow individuals over extended time periods.

As in other fields where theory and observation are closely coupled – e.g., in astronomy, where advances in theory drive demand for better telescopes – pressure from modellers and other social science researchers led to development of longitudinal data. The United States was an early leader in longitudinal data, with resources such as the Michigan Panel Study on Income Dynamics which launched in 1965 (Morgan et al. 1974). The United States and the United Kingdom also led in establishing early longitudinal studies for epidemiology, such as the famous Framingham Heart Study and the United Kingdom birth cohort studies, both started in 1948 (although these have only been used for health policy-oriented simulation modelling in the last decade or so). Longitudinal data suitable for policy analysis came later in Canada, with two major exceptions – federal income tax data and Manitoba administrative health-care data – that started in the 1970s.

Microsimulation modelling is closely related to another type of modelling that has become popular since the 1990s, agent-based modelling (ABM). Like microsimulation, agent-based models are computerized simulations that represent the individual-level behaviour of agents, typically heterogeneous agents, within a population. Although their origins are distinct – ABMs grew out of "toy" models of agents interacting with neighbours by extremely simple rules, usually in a spatial grid. ABMs and microsimulation models have substantial similarities. Their principal differences are that relative to the microsimulation models discussed in this chapter, ABMs tend to be simpler, more theoretical, less empirically grounded, and include richer characterization of agents' behaviour. They are often favoured by academic researchers because they are cheaper and easier to build than policy-oriented microsimulation models and because they let researchers posit and explore a wide range of rich rules for behaviour and interactions. But these same characteristics make them less useful for applied policy studies, mainly because of their weaker empirical grounding. Despite real impediments, there would be substantial benefits from further convergence between these two broad strands of microsimulation modelling.

POST-SECONDARY EDUCATION (PSE) FINANCE: THE WRIGHT COMMISSION

When I began working with Rod in 1969, student loans were a controversial policy issue. There was widespread concern that high tuition was preventing many qualified young people, especially from lower income families, from pursuing higher education. The government of Ontario established a commission on the issue headed by Doug Wright, who contracted with Rod and his colleagues at the Institute to analyze a range of policy options.

The effects of student loan policy play out over decades, from the time a student enters university or college and starts receiving loans, through graduation, then ten or more years after graduation as the loan is repaid. Models to support policy analysis thus must project choices and outcomes over this long period. The models must also be substantially disaggregated, because students in different fields accumulate different loan amounts and have different post-graduation income streams from which to repay their loans.

Rod gave me the task of writing the required simulation model and carte blanche to ask his colleagues to point me to all the relevant data. Although I was completely unaware of Orcutt's work, I was familiar with microsimulation methods from an unrelated field. I had started my undergraduate studies in physics and had spent a year working on a study of the shape of the helium nucleus. The study took a stream of pi mesons coming out of a cyclotron and bounced them off a jar of liquid helium. Unfortunately, pi mesons randomly decay into mu mesons, and the detectors around the helium jar could not tell whether a ping came from a pi or a mu meson. Because the two types have slightly different mass, this complicates the inference of the shape of the helium nucleus. The only way to resolve this conundrum was to write a simulation model of pi-mu decay as the mesons exited the cyclotron and moved through a series of magnets on their way to the helium. The model was a dynamic microsimulation model, because the units of analysis were individual mesons. I had the job of writing the model. But while the laws of motion of pi and mu mesons in magnetic fields were well known, the laws of motion of students percolating though their courses year to year then into the paid labour market were not. For this reason, Rod and I decided to develop a model that was not a full microsimulation but that was still moderately disaggregated.

In addition to considering various policy options for student loan programs, the Wright Commission was also interested in the idea of an Educational Opportunity Bank (EOB), originally proposed by Milton Friedman (Friedman 1955). The EOB resembles conventional student loans in the initial borrowing phase, but differs dramatically in the repayment phase. Instead of a fixed repayment schedule like that of a home mortgage, repayments vary year by year with the student's post-graduation earnings. Alternative designs of the EOB were described by three key parameters: the interest rate on outstanding loan balances, the tax rate on post-graduation earnings, and T, the time (typically twenty to thirty years post graduation), after which any remaining loan balance would be forgiven.

In part because the idea came from an arch conservative, student leaders opposed the EOB. They marshalled various arguments against it, including claims that it would be regressive and that any loan-based program would discourage lower-income students from seeking post-secondary education. Their alternative proposal was for free tuition and public grants to support student living expenses – a proposal they called a "living wage" for students, in hope of invoking solidarity with workers. (This was the 1960s, after all.)

Unfortunately, these progressive student leaders – including Ed Clark, now recently retired as president of TD Bank, who co-authored a key 1970 report opposing the commission's ideas – did not look closely enough at the data, including the results of our simulation model. One intriguing result of the analysis was that for certain settings of the three parameters, the EOB program could be a powerful tool for redistribution from high-income professionals (lawyers and doctors) to low-income artists and poets (English majors). Moreover, even at that time there was clear evidence that the choice to continue education was mainly determined by factors in the early to mid-teen years, several years before tuition costs or loans became salient – mainly parents' expectations and students' experience in high school. Because well-off families were more likely to assume their children would go to university and to act accordingly, most students in PSE were from well-off families – and still are. Subsidies to PSE are thus generally regressive in terms of lifetime incomes, and increasing these subsidies as the "progressive" student leaders wanted would have made them even more regressive.

Another important innovation our model could simulate was to introduce an EOB together with an increase in tuition fees. Here too, we showed there were ways to design this package of changes that would substantially increase the overall progressivity of the PSE sector – much to the consternation of student leaders at the University of Toronto and across Ontario. A related argument (not from the model) suggested that if students were asked to pay a larger share of PSE costs as tuition fees, they could rightly demand more clout in the running of the university. As a student at the time, I found this argument rather appealing. Still, the power of the student leaders – in my view, ill-informed power – overwhelmed the arguments for the innovative options and the analysis supporting it. The Wright Commission did recommend an EOB (Wright 1971), but the Ontario government never adopted the policy.

Troubles with the Canada Student Loan program have persisted, however, and the idea of financing PSE with an EOB resurfaced periodically, in the 1980s and again more seriously in the mid-1990s, when the federal ministry of Human Resources Development and the Ontario government both invested in new analytic efforts to study the issue. Their support allowed me and my staff at Statistics Canada to advance development of the LifePaths microsimulation model discussed below, and make the model available on CD to key actors in PSE finance policy, such as the Canadian Union of Students and the Canadian Bankers Association, as well as to policy analysts in the federal and provincial governments. All this effort ceased in 1998, however, when the federal Department of Finance pre-emptively and abruptly introduced the Millennium Scholarship Fund.

INCOME SECURITY

I had the good fortune to work with Rod on microsimulation and policy analysis a second time, on a new set of issues, starting in July 1974. He had moved from the University of Toronto to a senior position in the Treasury Board Secretariat (TBS) as the deputy secretary of the still quite new Planning Branch. Established in the wake of major initiatives in the US government to bring in more rational planning for large government initiatives, the Planning Branch had assembled a brain trust, most members with PhDs. While the main power of TBS lay in the Program Branch, which oversaw spending plans of all government departments, the Planning Branch was less transaction-oriented. Its role was to assemble small teams of analysts who could work for months at a time to evaluate new initiatives with large potential budgetary implications.

The Social Security Review

One of these initiatives was the Social Security Review (SSR), launched in 1973 by Marc Lalonde, minister of health and welfare and one of Prime Minister Trudeau's most trusted and powerful ministers (Canada 1973). The most novel idea considered in the SSR was to move Canada toward a guaranteed annual income (GAI). The TBS was naturally interested in this option, because it could have budgetary implications well into the billions of dollars. In addition, there was fear in the TBS that Health and Welfare, to recruit provincial support for the initiative in this major area of shared jurisdiction, might make excessively generous funding promises to the provinces. When the Planning Branch started to get involved, however, the internal bureaucratic discussions were essentially bilateral, between Health and Welfare and Finance. Beyond any intrinsic merits of the proposal, Health and Welfare wanted to champion the career of their minister and so were pushing for an expansive and generous option. Finance leaned the other way, given its mandate to protect the public purse. The TBS was not a welcome interloper.

Nevertheless, with Rod's support I proposed to write a microsimulation model to evaluate fiscal and distributional impacts of the SSR, especially the GAI proposals. This model was similar in structure to the personal income tax model developed for the Carter Commission and then adopted by Finance, with one important difference. Because the tax model was based on individuals' income tax returns, it could not analyze policy options where family structure was important. Instead, the new model was based on data from Statistics Canada's income distribution survey, which did include the required family structure information. Once our model was up and running, neither Finance nor Health and Welfare could ignore our analyses, and the TBS became a central player in the internal policy development process.

The federal government abandoned the SSR, for various reasons including the political difficulty of the major re-alignment of federal and provincial roles it implied. Some of the SSR's key ideas were retained within the federal government, however. In particular, the nascent idea of using the income tax system not just to collect revenue but also to distribute income was still alive. An inter-departmental Task Force on Tax-Transfer Integration (TTI) was established to study this concept, led by Jim Lynn (a director in Rod's Planning Branch) but located in the Department of Finance. I was seconded to this Task Force, which published its report in 1977 (Canada 1977). A key conclusion of the Task Force, that it was indeed feasible for the federal government to provide benefits through the income tax system, set the stage for a major reform of the federal Family Allowance program the following year. This long-standing program sent a monthly payment to all mothers for each child under age eighteen. Based in part on the TTI Task Force's work, when Family Allowance benefits were substantially cut in 1978, a large portion of the savings was used to fund a new refundable Child Tax Credit implemented through the income tax system. With these changes, the government was able to cut total spending on children while improving benefit levels for low-income families – an important step toward a de facto guaranteed annual income.

After the TTI Task Force, I stayed in Finance to work with Harvey Lazar's Task Force on Retirement Income Policy (discussed later) and to work in the Tax Policy Branch. In that branch, I assumed responsibility for income tax microsimulation models, including both the individual income tax model inherited from the 1966 Carter Royal Commission and building the department's first microsimulation model of corporate income tax. The individual and corporate models were used, with other data, not only for regular analyses feeding into the budget but also to produce Finance's first Tax Expenditure Account in 1978.

The Ministry of State for Social Development

The TBS experience developing its own microsimulation model for the mid-1970s Social Security Review was not forgotten. Almost a decade later, after my stint with Rod on the research staff of the Parliamentary Committee on Pension Reform (discussed later in this chapter), I joined the Ministry of State for Social Development (MSSD) in January 1984, working for Barry Carin, another former director under Rod in the Planning Branch. The branch had been abolished in 1978, but its role was partly assumed by the new MSSD "Super Ministry." The role of the MSSD minister in Cabinet was to provide in-depth evaluations of the larger social policy proposals put forward by policy ministers.

At the MSSD, it was agreed that I would concentrate on addressing a major gap in the MSSD's analytical capacity, the evaluation of social policies that cut across departmental and program lines, e.g., unemployment insurance, family allowances, and child tax credits, as well as other tax expenditures (benefits delivered through the tax system). With the reform of Family Allowances and their substantial replacement by the Child Tax Credit, a major portion of social policy had moved from the department of Health and Welfare to the Ministry of Finance. Yet Finance enjoyed such power and autonomy that its many social policy programs, implemented as tax expenditures, were never scrutinized by the relevant cabinet committee – in contrast to direct spending programs, which faced annual review by the TBS as well as parliament. We agreed, therefore, that the MSSD should expand its analytical capacities to include relevant tax expenditures and should be forthright in bringing these analyses, including activities within the Department of Finance, to Cabinet. To this end, I was tasked to lead development of a tax/transfer simulation model at the MSSD that could consistently and coherently evaluate both tax provisions like the Child Tax Credit and direct spending programs like Family Allowance.

By the spring of 1984, the model was up and running. Beyond using the model to analyze various Cabinet proposals, we also began to develop ideas for a more integrated Guaranteed Income/Simplified Tax (GI/ST) that would build explicitly on the now established role of the income tax system for delivering refundable tax credits. The power of the MSSD (and its sister Ministry of State for Economic Development) became too much for the established central agencies, however, and both super ministries were abolished in June 1984. There followed a diaspora of talented analysts, similar to that following the 1978 abolition of the Planning Branch in the Treasury Board Secretariat.

Statistics Canada and the SPSD/M

I moved from the MSSD to a dream job at Statistics Canada. Barry Carin became assistant deputy minister for policy at the Ministry of Employment and Immigration, but remained keen to continue work on both the simulation model we had just completed at the MSSD and the study of GI/ST options.[3] He therefore arranged for his department to provide two years of funding to my new group at Statistics Canada to develop a much improved Social Policy Simulation Database and Model, the SPSD/M, which Statistics Canada began publishing in 1986.

Taking advantage of the advent of personal computers, which could run software as powerful as I had formerly run on mainframe computers, Statistics Canada made the software and data available on floppy disk, in open form that could run on an ordinary PC. We thereby made widely available a policy analysis tool with the same power and credibility as the tax models used in the federal Department of Finance. While we made the tool available to anyone willing to pay the license fee, we understood realistically that few members of the general public were likely to learn to use the model effectively, and that the major effect would be to empower provincial and other federal departments, think tanks, and other policy organizations. Still, this was enough to break Finance's long-standing monopoly on this crucial information. A former colleague from the TTI Task Force, who had moved to the Social Policy Division of Finance, phoned me when he learned of our plans to make the SPSD/M publicly available. He said, in essence, "You may not have pulled the trigger, but you have given them a loaded gun" – and went on to threaten that the minister of finance would, in the House, discredit any lobby group or other analysis presenting results based on the SPSD/M. Since I had been responsible for the Finance tax models myself, however, I was able to suggest that such a statement might equally embarrass the minister himself, since the SPSD/M was demonstrably of similar quality to their own models. There was no further comment of this kind from Finance officials.

One of the higher-profile applications of the SPSD/M was in the 1992 introduction of the Goods and Services Tax (GST), a national value-added tax adopted to replace the previous, narrowly based Manufacturers Sales Tax. The Department of Finance initially proposed the GST at a 9 percent rate. But based in part on SPSD/M simulations conducted by Library of Parliament staff for the House Finance Committee, the GST rate was set at 7 percent, and different levels were set for a new refundable Sales Tax Credit (designed to offset the otherwise regressive redistributional impacts of the GST). After a few years, Finance itself began to use the SPSD/M internally and to welcome policy proponents who themselves had used the model. As a result, the level of policy discussion was significantly improved, because less effort could be spent arguing about the numbers, so that discussion could instead focus on basic ideas and principles.

PENSION REFORM: THE GREAT PENSION DEBATE

A third major policy area to which microsimulation models have made significant contributions is pension policy. The year 1966 was a watershed year in the history of Canada's public pension system, with the introduction of both the Canada and Quebec Pension Plans (C/QPP), and the Guaranteed Income Supplement (GIS) to the Old Age Security (OAS) Pension. But by the mid-1970s, high inflation was eroding private pension benefits, and pressure was mounting for further large-scale pension reforms. The several-year period of intense and repeated examination of pension policy that followed became known as The Great Pension Debate. Over this period, the federal government undertook several initiatives: a 1979 officials' Task Force on Retirement Income Policy, led by Harvey Lazar (Canada 1979), a 1981 Pensions Summit that gathered leading government and private sector authorities nationwide, and a Green Paper, "Better Pensions for Canadians" in 1982 (Canada 1982), that set out the government's view of the main issues and options, although without specific recommendations. Many other groups also published pension studies at the time, including several provincial governments, and the Economic Council of Canada.

The 1982 federal Green Paper identified several major issues with Canada's retirement income system: "Reform of the pension system is important because there are serious deficiencies relating to coverage, inflation protection, portability, and the treatment of women," said Monique Begin, minister of health and welfare. "As a result, many Canadians face a significant decline in living standards on retirement due to inadequate pension incomes."[4] With a majority in Parliament, the Liberals could have enacted new legislation, but reforms to the CPP would require provincial legislation as well, and they regarded pension issues as so important and contentious that they required broader consultation. The government referred the Green Paper and its options to a special House of Commons Task Force, which was mandated to hold hearings and report to Parliament by the end of 1983 with recommendations for government action. I served on the research staff of the 1979 Lazar Task Force, the 1982 Green Paper, and the 1983 Parliamentary Task Force. In this section I discuss several major issues in the pension debate that were addressed in these bodies, with particular attention to the 1983 Parliamentary Task Force.

The Special Parliamentary Task Force on Pension Reform

Following the 1982 Green Paper, the Parliamentary Task Force on pension reform was established and began work in early 1983. Although staffing for Parliamentary committees was usually provided by the Library of Parliament, organizers realized that the technical complexity of this task required more expert staff. As a result, the unusual decision was taken to contract out the research staff, with the result that Rod and I had the opportunity to work together again. Rod was appointed head of the research staff, and I was seconded from Finance to join his staff. The staff also included one researcher from each of the three major political parties (Liberal, Progressive Conservative, and NDP) and one person from the Library of Parliament.

Although many people perceive statistical and economic analyses as a black box, these analyses are central to understanding pension policy, as the prominence of the actuarial profession in pensions indicates. Given Rod's and my shared experience over nearly fifteen years of building, using, and communicating complex simulation models for applied economic and policy analysis, it was natural that we would draw on these powerful tools. But communicating these potentially inscrutable tools in this new setting posed significant challenges. In our previous experiences in Treasury Board and

Finance, there was a familiarity amongst senior staff with microsimulation models in policy formulation dating back to Bosson's tax model for the Carter Royal Commission in the 1960s. There was also an established set of organizational units, reporting relationships, and recruiting processes that helped give senior officials and ministers confidence that the quantitative results in their briefing notes and budget documents were reliable.

In the Parliamentary Task Force, however, this confidence and trust had to be built from scratch, both among the members of parliament on the task force, and between them and the research staff. Members were initially wary about their fellow members' views and agendas and had little familiarity or confidence in the analytic tools the research staff favored. The first step in this trust-building process was persuading the members to start their work with a series of *in camera* background and educational briefings on pension basics. The members, especially those from opposition parties, were naturally somewhat nervous about having some "technocrats" of uncertain political leanings steering their initial thinking in ways they might not want. But having a staff person from their own party on the research team helped assuage these concerns. It was particularly helpful that the party research staff were comfortable and knowledgeable in quantitative analysis, especially the PC representative Michael Hatfield. An additional helpful factor was that the models developed the previous year for the Green Paper had been intensively reviewed by an actuary from Mercer, Canada's largest actuarial consulting firm. In effect, the models had already passed stringent peer review.

The introductory in camera briefings were fundamental to providing members with a shared understanding of the task force's domain. Under Rod's leadership and with the clear support of chair Doug Frith, the briefings took members through all the components of the retirement income system and the current issues. As they proceeded, members' comfort levels improved. The briefings also helped members get to know each other, both personally and in terms of their political and ideological perspectives. While there were clear differences in members' political views, they were able to develop respect for each other in these early closed-door sessions and subsequently work together collegially, both in camera and in public hearings.

There were several issues in the task force's mandate for which economic or other quantitative analysis would be essential.

- The cost-implications for private workplace pensions of more stringent regulation, especially of inflation protection, survivor benefits, vesting, and portability.
- The distributive implications of a novel and contentious proposal for homemaker pensions.
- The requirements for long-term sustainability of public pensions.

Computer simulation models were used for the first two of these issues. For the first issue, I had developed models in working on the Green Paper the year before. For the homemaker pension proposal, a new model was constructed.

Inflation Protection in Workplace Pension Plans

One of the top issues in the pension debate was protecting retirement incomes against inflation, especially in private-sector workplace pensions. In the high inflation of the late 1970s, many retirees' pensions had dropped by more than half in purchasing power since they had retired. Addressing this question, the 1979 Lazar Task Force (Canada 1979) had developed a proposal to require inflation adjustment based on the concept of "excess interest." The proposal was based on the observation that real interest rates (i.e., the difference between nominal interest rates and the inflation rate) tend to be fairly stable and positive, even in periods of high inflation. Thus, if pension plans were required to apply investment returns above some prescribed real rate to increase pension payouts, these extra payments would generally be large enough to offset most of the erosive effects of inflation.

The proposal was technically complex, because it had to consider the wide variation in pension plan terms, as well as the behaviour of plan sponsors and their actuarial advisors. How much an employer must pay into a pension plan each year depends on an actuarial valuation of the plan's assets and liabilities (current and future payout obligations), with liability valuation in turn depending on assumptions about future wages, inflation rates, and returns on plan assets. Assuming high future rates of return makes liabilities appear smaller, reducing current required contributions to the plan. But high rates of return are associated with high inflation rates, so plans that make aggressive high interest rate actuarial assumptions are, in effect, promising their workers and retirees pensions that will rapidly erode in real purchasing power. Other plans made somewhat more conservative actuarial assumptions, but these tended to build up large surpluses which in some cases were used to benefit current workers. In these cases, erosion of future retirees' pensions was being used to finance increased benefit promises for current workers, possibly enabling employers to offset worker demands for higher current wages.

The 1979 Lazar Task Force and 1982 Green Paper both suggested regulation to require some minimal updating of pension payouts based on a formula related to "excess interest." This would force plans to use less aggressive actuarial assumptions, raising the current cost of pensions. Business, unsurprisingly, opposed the proposal, but pension supervisory authorities, including the Canadian Institute of Actuaries and many others, testified that it was feasible. In the background, our analyses as members of the research staff using a simulation model of a variety of workplace pension plans, supported the actuaries' position.

The option of mandatory inflation protection for workplace pension plans was one of the major issues referred to the 1983 Parliamentary Task Force, but in the end the task force was unable to reach consensus on the proposal. They rejected mandatory full CPI inflation adjustment for pension benefits already accrued, citing the intensity of employer opposition and the unavoidable unfairness of going back to correct these past wrongs. It would not be possible to unscramble the omelette in a practical and fair manner. More broadly, the full task force also rejected, for practical purposes, the excess interest proposal. On the other hand, a majority of the task force did recommend a specific formula for excess interest updating of newly accrued workplace pensions, as opposed to benefits previously accrued, once these came into payment.

In hindsight, the government's failure to adopt the majority recommendation was highly unfortunate. Since the 2000 bursting of the dot-com bubble, and even more so following the 2008 "great recession," many workplace pension plans' assets have fallen below their liabilities, although there has been some recent improvement. This collapse is partly due to reduced asset values but also reflects a dramatic fall in current investment returns, which increase plan liabilities when they are incorporated into future projections. If plans had adopted more conservative actuarial assumptions, as the excess interest proposal would have required, such widespread deficits would not have occurred. Instead, plans would have had to increase assets through larger contributions or reduce liabilities by reducing future pension promises to their workers, all gradually over decades – a much more manageable set of changes than those now being forced on workplace pension plans by the delay and belated crisis that they have actually experienced.

The Homemaker Pension Debate

Through the 1970s, pension debates in Canada were essentially two-sided, labour versus business. Labour favoured doubling the Canada Pension Plan by raising the retirement pension from 25 percent to 50 percent of pre-retirement earnings up to the average wage. Business opposed this proposal, based on concerns about higher payroll taxes and expansion of government's role. In the late 1970s, however, a new proposal for a homemaker's pension changed the structure of the debate, making it three-sided through the addition of women's groups, led by the National Action Committee on the Status of Women. The proposed homemaker's pension would treat years when a parent (usually a woman) dropped out of the paid workforce to raise children as if they were earning half the average wage for purposes of accruing entitlement to future C/QPP pension benefits. The data certainly supported women's concerns, since older single women, particularly widows, suffered high rates of low income. But the specific proposal for a homemaker pension embedded in the C/QPP was highly contentious.

The debate over this proposal provided perhaps the most vivid illustration of the power of quantitative analysis in the deliberations of the task force. A leading proponent for the homemaker pension was Lousie Dulude, then president of the National Action Committee. One of the leading opponents was Monica Townson, a widely read financial columnist. Each cited hypothetical examples of women's life situations in which they could either suffer badly under the current pension system, or be inequitably treated under the proposed homemaker pension. For example, Dulude often cited the fact that a woman who worked in the home all her life would be left with nothing if she was divorced at age sixty-four, just before the pension age of entitlement. Townson countered by observing that the homemaker pension proposal would penalize low-income working women with children, by requiring them to make payroll tax contributions for benefits they could receive without working at all.

With all-party agreement from the members, the research staff invited both Dulude and Townson to give us the three specific life-history examples that most strongly made the case for, and against, the homemaker pension proposal. We asked that the examples specify the woman's marital and fertility history, her and her husband's incomes year by year, and any other factors they judged relevant. We also asked them to state what measures of outcomes best made their point, e.g., the difference in the woman's post-retirement disposable income under the homemaker pension proposal versus the status quo, or any other measure they chose.

We then took these six case examples and used the simulation model to calculate the wife's and husband's pension payments and benefits, taxes, and disposable incomes – pre- and post-retirement, and for the woman as a survivor after her husband's or ex-husband's death. We gave all these results to both Dulude and Townson and asked that they review them for accuracy and relevance to their arguments, then speak to the results for the task force. All members were also given the cases and results (in advance, so they could discuss them with their staffs), and a special in camera session was convened for the discussion. The session lasted all morning, first with presentations from the two protagonists (I sat between them and moderated the discussion, while Rod sat with the Chair, as had become usual), followed by questions from members – who included strong advocates on both sides of the homemaker pension idea – and further discussion. By my recollection, this was one of the best discussions of a contentious public policy issue I ever saw, in which politicians explored and advanced their diverse political aims while also taking account of high-quality evidence about consequences and costs, informed by reasonably sophisticated quantitative analysis. Yet this was nearly thirty years ago, and although the available tools and data are much better now, examples of such high-quality and well-informed political debate remain distressingly, even increasingly, rare.

In the end, the task force unanimously recommended expanding the CPP to include a retirement benefit reflecting years spent as a homemaker whenever wages were less than half the average wage. This was one of nineteen recommendations aimed at raising the incomes of poor older women, which also included improved survivor pensions and pension splitting. While the federal government never acted on the homemaker pension recommendation, the activity had important intellectual legacies. The simulation model used to evaluate the homemaker pension was fairly crude because of limits imposed by the lack of longitudinal data. In 1994, over a decade later, Statistics Canada launched a trio of longitudinal surveys – on health, children, and incomes[5] – along with enhancements to a database of longitudinal income tax records, that provided empirical foundations for much more sophisticated individual-level microsimulation models.[6] These data enabled the first detailed statistical analysis of the linked trajectories of husband's and wife's earnings over time, including patterns of marriage, separation, and divorce.

High-quality longitudinal data are a necessary condition for effective dynamic microsimulation modelling, but they are not sufficient. In addition to data limits, the relative crudeness of the task force model also reflected lack of investment in model development by federal departments. There was nothing of comparable quality to Finance's personal income tax model "on the shelf" elsewhere for us to use.[7] This situation finally changed when Statistics Canada, with the support of the Human Resources ministry and the Policy Research Initiative, launched the LifePaths model in 1996. This model subsequently produced novel and important analyses of student loans, intergenerational equity (Wolfson and Rowe 2007), and the adequacy of Canada's retirement income system (Wolfson 2011, 2013), among other issues – although recent budget cuts have put the future of the LifePaths model in serious jeopardy.

Pensions as Transfers between Generations

The most foundational issue addressed by the Parliamentary Task Force, and the most difficult, was intergenerational fairness. The discussion of intergenerational fairness, contained in the first substantive chapter of the task force's report to parliament, did not rely primarily on quantitative analysis. Yet it is one of the best reflections of Rod's intellectual insight and leadership. The topic was not in the terms of reference, and the chapter did not propose specific policy options. Moreover, there was little substantive witness discussion of this topic, although there was (in Rod's and my view) considerable vague and ill-informed rhetoric about being "fair to future generations." Many witnesses spoke of economic costs, fiscal sustainability, and the need for adequate pensions, but these comments were typically isolated and not grounded in a broader framework. The chapter resulted primarily from research staff working with members to understand and grapple with what increasingly appeared to us as the foundation of pension policy. We viewed this discussion as essential to rising above the fray of contending proposals by articulating the basic principles of a fair and sustainable public pension system.

Some members immediately understood the aim of the chapter and strongly supported it, and in the end all members and their staffs supported the chapter and its recommendations – although one called it just a bunch of academic scribbling that he would go along with only because no one would pay attention. This member's comments were prescient in at least one important way, since it appears that the chapter has indeed been forgotten and policy debate on intergenerational equity remains as ill-informed now as it was then. For example, in discussing the phased increase in OAS and GIS eligibility age from sixty-five to sixty-seven in the 2012 budget, the prime minister argued that the change was necessary because these programs are intergenerational transfers – yet so too are CPP, public education, and much of publicly funded health care, all of which were omitted from the discussion. Announcing this policy change in his speech at Davos, the prime minister also called the CPP "fully funded," when in fact its fund as currently legislated will never exceed about 20 percent of actuarial liabilities (Harper 2012). When challenged on these claims in budget hearings, the Parliamentary secretary to the minister of finance replied that the prime minister was speaking figuratively and merely meant the CPP was financially healthy (Hansard 2012, 68). Such statements reflect a serious failure to understand the meaning of pensions as intergenerational transfers, not just among political leaders but also their advisors and many others engaged in pension policy debate.

While the objecting member was also largely correct that the chapter was "academic scribbling" – the chapter was substantially Rod's thinking, which I share – in my view it stands the test of time well. In the following paragraphs I quote from it at some length, since the core messages remain so important and did in the end achieve all-party consensus.

The opening paragraphs of the chapter state some basic principles of public pensions and their sustainability.

> Pensions are promises to make a series of payments extending into the future. They may be accompanied by schemes to generate savings ... (but this is not necessary.) ... In looking at the soundness of the C/QPP and indeed the OAS/GIS – the issue is therefore the capacity and willingness of future working generations to make contributions or pay taxes adequate to cover promised benefits (House of Commons 1983, 12).
>
> But no rules or legislation made today can formally bind future governments or future generations of workers. The matter rests on a sense of commitment and reciprocity. The central issue of pension policy is thus to establish a secure base for agreements about intergenerational transfers in such a way as to ensure that they are both clearly understood and likely to be honoured ... What then renders a public pension system sound, stable and sustainable? ... it is not strictly a question of funding, as is implied by a comparison with private sector pensions. Instead it is a clear understanding of a social commitment that past participation in production entitles retirees to a reasonable share of current consumption opportunities. A (sustainable) public pension system ... flows from a view of the community as an extended family ... (with pensioners sharing both the risks and general prosperity) ... To do otherwise is to invite the repudiation of pension promises by future governments representing working generations. (14)

This is all well and good but what, one might ask, is its practical import? The answer lies in the task force's proposal on how public pensions, as well as tax expenditures for retirement income saving, should be indexed. The crucial idea was that to be sustainable, public pensions must be seen as fair, not only today but also over time. Because pension legislation can always be amended, a sustainable system should be structured on principles that make the emergence of a future "blocking coalition" – a majority who find it in their interest to change the rules – unlikely. Among other conditions, this requires that in tough economic times, retirees cannot expect their pensions to keep increasing when the economic circumstances of others, in particular people of working age who are funding the transfers, are declining.

The idea that government pension payments to the elderly might ever actually have to decline was a very tough pill for members to swallow. There were lengthy in camera discussions. But in the end, one member articulated the issue using the metaphor of a nineteenth-century farm family: When the harvest was good, everyone around the table shared in the bounty, including the grandparents who were no longer actively working the farm. But when harvests were poor, everyone had to pull in their belts.

With this metaphor in mind, the task force got a little more specific.

> We have concluded that something along the lines of wage indexing is necessary for public pensions. However, we are not sure that the AIW (Statistics Canada's average industrial wage) is the best indexing factor. An appropriate adjustment factor should be simple and easy to understand. It should also have characteristics such that benefits would be higher when
>
> - real average wage growth is higher,
> - labour force participation is higher,
> - unemployment is lower, or
> - the old-age dependency ratio is lower,
>
> and would be lower when the opposite circumstances prevailed … The Task Force recommends that (an index of this sort) be used to adjust benefit levels and program elements under OAS, the GIS, and the C/QPP as well as the comprehensive income tax limits (for RRSPs and RPPs). (17)

Underlying these recommendations, the research staff provided members with various actual historical data series, as well as key projections such as population and life expectancy, so that they could understand their likely implications.

This was indeed a radical proposal, which was not followed by the government of the day. Something similar was adopted by Sweden in the early 1990s, however, by which public pensions coming into pay are adjusted downward as life expectancy increases. The furor over the recent increase in OAS/GIS eligibility age could arguably have been avoided, had the Parliamentary Task Force's proposal been implemented decades ago.

The task force was also highly sensitive to the fact that intergenerational transfers to the elderly come not just from public pensions, but also from other programs like health care. As a result, they recommended "that the Minister of Finance table in the House of Commons every five years ... a comprehensive set of cost projections for the public pension system (and other major programs such as health care that represent significant transfers of resources to the elderly) in order to promote public debate about the extent and sustainability of current commitments" (19).

Here and on many other points the thinking of the task force, with the skilled intellectual and policy guidance of Rod Dobell, presciently anticipated current policy issues. For example, for several years the Parliamentary Budget Office was frustrated by the lack of precisely the kinds of information the task force recommended be provided to parliament almost thirty years ago. It took me almost twenty-five years to develop the LifePaths microsimulation model to the point that these ideas about intergenerational equity could be analyzed quantitatively (Wolfson and Rowe 2007). And the continuing crescendo of agonizing over the fiscal sustainability of Canada's publicly funded health care services could well have been greatly attenuated if this latter task force recommendation had been adopted.

CONCLUDING COMMENTS

Sadly, the kind of political work informed by quantitative analysis epitomized by the 1983 Parliamentary Task Force is the exception rather than the rule in today's federal government. I look back on my work with Rod Dobell, starting with the Wright Commission analysis of post-secondary education finance, then the Treasury Board Secretariat Planning Branch, and the Parliamentary Task Force on Pension Reform, as a golden age of insightful, evidence-based, and quantitatively sophisticated policy analysis in the Government of Canada.

Technically, simulation methods have continued to grow and become central in areas of science as diverse as cosmology and global climate change. Similar methods are on the verge of dramatic growth as the private sector discovers "big data" and increasingly uses these huge volumes of data to support answering "what if" questions. As policy-oriented microsimulation has continued to advance in tandem with dramatically growing computing power, parallel advances in agent-based modelling (ABM) have made these models into rich tools for exploratory research in diverse social-science fields, as well as biology and ecology. There would be substantial value from increased cross-fertilization and convergence between these two strands of modelling, since policy-oriented models could benefit from better characterization of individuals' behaviours, while ABMs could benefit from stronger empirical grounding. There are real impediments to such convergence, however, including the tendency in academic social science toward small-scale, "cottage industry" research – in stark contrast to fields such as physics and genetics – with related limitations in research funding, especially for data and model development infrastructure, and the lack of appropriate data. A further impediment in economics remains the quasi-religious status of assumptions of equilibrium and atomistic omniscient individual agents, reinforced by implicit constraints of mathematical tractability, despite the demonstration of the tremendous benefits of an evolutionary rather than an equilibrium approach over thirty years ago (Nelson and Winter 1982), if researchers can make the transition from mathematical formalisms to computer simulation. Perhaps biology and ecology are more advanced in using ABMs because they have not had to rebel against an orthodoxy based on aggregation and equilibrium.

For government, developing and maintaining a capacity for policy-relevant modelling and analysis is expensive. It requires a sustained commitment to model development and large-scale data acquisition, as well as dedicated teams of multi-skilled analysts, with expertise spanning computer science, statistics, social science, and practical policy analysis. And while the application of such modelling and analysis to policy debates carries the potential for large social benefits, this also requires leadership – from the most senior levels of government who must value evidence over ideology and from the senior ranks of the public service who must value substantive information over transactions and process. The relevant capacity takes years to build up, but only a short time to destroy. Canada, tragically, is in the process of losing much of this capacity.

NOTES

1 At the Institute for the Quantitative Analysis of Socio-Economic Policy, later the Institute for Policy Analysis.

2 The Goldman and Uzawa paper epitomizes mathematical economics of the time. Filled with theorems and lemmas, it says nothing explicit about population heterogeneity. It does, however, show formally how restricted is the class of mathematical functions for which even partial aggregation is possible. This result implies that virtually all neo-classical specifications of demand functions, and by parallel arguments production functions, are fundamentally mis-specified, and thus cannot describe any real-world process that encompasses significant underlying heterogeneity.

3 The GI/ST proposal also lived on in the work of the McDonald Royal Commission, to which it was carried by MSSD alumnus Richard Van Loon, who became the commission's research director. A similar guaranteed income emerged as one of the commission's two major recommendations, the other being free trade with the United States (Canada 1985). But while the free trade proposal took hold and was eventually adopted, the guaranteed income did not, in part because the details of the commission's proposal were not carefully designed and in particular had not benefited from detailed simulation analysis (Wolfson 1986).

4 Health and Welfare Canada news release, 9 December 1982.

5 National Population Health Survey (NPHS), National Longitudinal Survey of Children and Youth (NLSCY), and Survey of Labour and Income Dynamics (SLID).

6 Unfortunately, all three surveys ended by 2010, owing to a combination of budget cuts, technical issues, and political decisions.

7 A partial counter-example is the employment insurance (EI or UI) model, which draws on weekly earnings data of EI claimants that may extend over more than a year – a useful and relevant period for employment policy, although far short of the decades needed for pension policy analysis. For pensions, the projection models used by Canada's chief actuary have always been aggregated and are thus unable to analyze options like those considered in the Great Pension Debate.

8

Environmental Issues: Fifty Years of Change and Current Challenges

JOSEE VAN EIJNDHOVEN

INTRODUCTION

Over the past fifty years, there have been clear shifts in the character of the most prominent environmental challenges. In the 1960s the most contentious environmental issues were relatively local in scale and were driven by obvious, visible threats to human health or the natural environment. Today the most prominent environmental issues have global consequences, and even local environmental issues are often connected to global challenges. These shifts have been accompanied by shifts in the landscape of major actors participating in environmental issues, particularly in the role of science. Science has become more visible and leading, as the debate on environmental issues has become more oriented toward future risks.

This chapter reviews the major shifts in environmental challenges over this period and their consequences for the role of different actors, particularly the changing role of science and the nature of the challenges now posed to addressing these environmental issues. The next section reviews the broad shifts that have occurred in environmental challenges and in how they are addressed. The third section discusses the shifting role of science, and the fourth considers the shifts in actors involved and required responses. The final two sections offer concluding reflections on the role of science in the policy process and how it can be made more effective.

DEVELOPMENT OF ENVIRONMENTAL ISSUES OVER TIME: LOCAL TO GLOBAL, SIMPLE TO COMPLEX

Although Rachel Carson's book *Silent Spring* (1962) is often described as the start of the environmental movement, environmental issues had in fact been on the agenda and growing in public concern for several years before its publication. This early environmental concern largely targeted relatively local environmental degradation. Much concern, including concerns in Carson's book, focused on the chemical industry, which had grown rapidly in the postwar period with little attention to potential health and environmental hazards.

Over the early decades of the environmental debate, periodic disasters associated with the chemical industry and human health risks, either from routine operational pollution or from accidents, kept attention focused on chemical health risks. The impacts of these events were obvious, relatively localized, acute, and in some cases catastrophic. A prominent early example was the Japanese fishing village of Minamata, where thousands of people died and suffered neurological disease. In 1959 Japanese scientists found that the cause was eating fish contaminated with mercury from the effluent of a nearby chemical factory. Other prominent chemical-related disasters included the 1974 explosion of a chemical plant at Flixborough, England, the large dioxin release from a chemical plant near Seveso, Italy in 1976, the discovery of chemical wastes in the Love Canal neighbourhood of Niagara Falls, New York in 1976, and the large release of toxic gases from a pesticide factory in Bhopal India in 1984.

Although each of these events was mainly local in scale, their influence on policy and on public perception of risks extended over a much larger scale, even though the severity of actual health impacts varied widely – for example, the numbers of deaths ranged from probably none in Love Canal and Seveso to tens of thousands in Bhopal. Yet despite these events' extreme effect on risk perception and attitudes, the resultant policy responses tended to be incremental rather than cataclysmic (Jasanoff 1994). Learning was manifested in small advances over existing ways of doing business rather than in wholesale reformulation of earlier practice.

In the United States, the Love Canal controversy contributed to enactment of the 1980 CERCLA, or "Superfund," law regarding cleanup and payment for old hazardous waste dumps (New York

Department of Health 2008). In Europe, although the Seveso accident can be regarded in hindsight as mainly an information disaster, because no people died, it triggered huge fear that contributed to development of European regulation. On 24 June1982 the European Community (EC) passed a Council Directive on industrial accident hazards, which became known as the Seveso Directive. It was the first community law that required sharing environmental information across borders, both among governments and to the public.

Bhopal had a powerful impact on legislation and industrial behaviour in multiple nations. In addition to leaving an indelible mark on a hundred thousand Indian citizens and the firm that injured them, it also fundamentally reshaped the way people perceive the risks and benefits of the chemical industry and stimulated multiple changes in the rules by which private firms, governments and international organizations manage the risks of hazardous technologies (Jasanoff 1994). In Europe, the Seveso Directive was supposed to be fully implemented in national laws by the end of 1984, but it was only after the Bhopal disaster that uncertainties over what exactly was required were set aside, and a fierce process of implementation started (Van Eijndhoven 1994). In the US, Bhopal was instrumental in passage of the Emergency Planning and Community Right to Know Act of 1986, which required public disclosure of all releases of toxic chemicals (Hadden 1994).

These events all had in common that they did not require science to identify risks or raise concerns. Rather, they all began with observation of concrete risks in the local environment, in most cases representing direct threats to human health. The observed risks or disasters led quite directly to policy reaction, through pressure mobilized by locally affected populations and other policy actors. Science came in secondarily, to describe the character of observed effects and diagnose causes and mechanisms.

Reaction to these events notwithstanding, attention to environmental issues generally declined in the 1980s. Reasons for this decline included the management of environmental risks through legislation and resultant change in industry behaviour and also the recession that pushed public and political attention to economic issues. Yet this period also saw a continuing shift of environmental debates from a predominant local focus to increased awareness of global-scale changes and related issues of sustainable development, extending a trend whose origins can be traced back to the 1960s (Kates, Turner, and Clark 1990, 4).

A major comparative research project conducted in the 1990s, the Social Learning Project, examined the growth in awareness and management of three major global environmental risks over this period: acidification, stratospheric ozone depletion, and climate change (Social Learning Group 2001). Separate project teams examined how these issues developed in eight countries (Germany, the United Kingdom, the Netherlands, the former Soviet Union, Hungary, Japan, Mexico, and Canada), as well as the EU and at the international level between 1957 (the year of a major international scientific collaboration, the International Geophysical Year) and 1992 (the year of the Earth Summit, the United Nations Conference on Environment and Development in Rio). In this large comparative project, Dobell and his colleagues contributed the Canadian case study (Parson et al. 2001). When this project began in 1991, the term "global environmental change" was still relatively little in use.

The study showed a pattern of widespread emergence of global risks, but with significant variation across jurisdictions and complex patterns of local-global interactions (Schreurs et al. 2001). All three issues rose to prominence in all countries studied, but not at the same time. No country was a consistent leader on all issues. Every country experienced a period in which one of the issues was high on the political agenda, but only when it was seen as locally relevant.

The shift from local toward global scale was not the only major change in character of environmental challenges over this period. An additional change was in the timeline of risks and duration of their effects. The environmental risks prominent in the sixties and seventies were experienced immediately, typically by first being directly observed and only then assessed as to their causes. The debates over stratospheric ozone and climate change were much more about future risks, which were uncertain and had to be projected using models. Yet even given these issues' long durations, the possibility of their being linked to immediate events cannot be ignored, as shown by recent controversies over what can be concluded about climate change from weather-related disasters such as Katrina and Sandy.

Environmental concerns also shifted from simple separable issues toward increasingly linked complex challenges. The issues of acidification and stratospheric ozone depletion moved partway in this direction. They involved multiple emissions sources and complex chains of chemical reactions. Yet their management was still relatively simple, achievable through responses targeting a few major activities or industries. Although they crossed borders, managing these issues did not require addressing comprehensive behaviour change across society or managing impacts on multiple ecosystems. Climate change illustrates the continuing shift toward greater complexity. Even the way the issue is perceived and named has changed over time, as more sources and impacts have been recognized and the most widely used name has shifted from "the greenhouse effect" to "global warming" to "climate change." However the issue is framed, it is clear that unlike earlier issues it cannot be managed exclusively by regulations to change industry behaviour, but requires more complex and comprehensive approaches. Understandably, the Social Learning project found that management responses took longer to develop for climate change than for acidification or ozone depletion (Jaeger, Van Eijndhoven, and Clark 2001, 176).

Finally, today's environmental issues also have more complex connections to other issues, outside the scope of what has formerly been viewed as "environmental." For example, environmental issues are now viewed as essentially linked to "sustainable development," a term first used around 1980 (IUCN 1980), which gained wide currency after the report of the Brundtland Commission (WCED 1987). The term aimed to include developing countries, some of whom had previously regarded environmental issues as problems for the rich in environmental debates (Vonkeman 1991). It also broadened the environmental debate to increasing inclusion of economic, social, and ethical issues. Similarly, the so-called Belmont Challenges identified as priority issues by ICSU (2010) – coastal vulnerability, freshwater security, ecosystem services, carbon budgets, and most vulnerable societies – are all complex, interconnected societal challenges in which environmental connections are strong but are only part of the problem.

These shifts in the character of environmental issues over the past several decades imply large change in the role played by science in their management and in the identity and role of societal actors involved in addressing them. The next two sections explore these two changes in turn.

THE ROLE OF SCIENCE: FROM SUPPORTING TO LEADING

These shifts in environmental issues toward global scale, longer timelines of effects, and greater complexity and breadth of linkages, were associated with a transformation in the role of science in identifying, understanding, and responding to them. In the early issues, science mostly did not lead, but rather reacted and explained. The typical pattern of these issues was that a harmful effect was first observed. The harmful effect, whether an explosion or leak at chemical facilities or the observation of neurological illnesses in Minamata, did not require science to see or describe it. Rather, science became involved reactively, to identify and explain the cause of the harm, and thus help to identify and evaluate potential responses.

Despite its status as an early landmark of environmental concern, *Silent Spring* also represented an early step toward a more central role for science. By highlighting pollution as an insidious threat to non-human life and ecosystems rather than an acute threat to human health, Carson's book implied both an increased focus on indirect environmental effects of human activities and a more central and anticipatory role for science in identifying and describing environmental changes underway.

As environmental issues evolved, science became more prominent, more essential, and involved earlier in issue development. In this progression, acidification can be seen as an intermediate case. Its effects were observed and identified quickly, but there was lengthy debate about atmospheric transport, chemical transformation, and deposition and impact mechanisms. This extended debate had large consequences for which actors were at the root of the problem and thus had to be involved in implementing solutions. In contrast, stratospheric ozone depletion is an issue that could not have been detected without scientific research. Measurements of ozone in the stratosphere and theoretical model calculations of stratospheric chemistry were both indispensable to projecting ozone depletion risk. Acceptance of the risk as real was strongly influenced by pictures of the "ozone hole" that made it appear concrete and immediate. Even so, acceptance of accumulating scientific evidence was not straightforward but involved a long-term struggle in which various actors slowly shifted their policy positions to maintain some coherent relation to advancing science (Parson 2003).

Climate change is a much more complex story, although science also played an essential role in the development of this issue. Indeed, climate change was an issue of scientific interest and debate long before it came to policy attention. Theoretical calculations of the effects of increased atmospheric CO_2 began early, typically based on an assumed doubling of CO_2 concentration, long before the first measurements of increasing atmospheric CO_2 began in the 1950s. Even once these increases were observed, understanding their quantitative significance for climate change required complex models that taxed both scientific knowledge and computational power, which were first developed in the 1960s and are still advancing to this day. The complexity of relationships between shifts in atmospheric concentration and resultant effects on climate and climate-sensitive ecosystems and resources still admits substantial uncertainty and controversy. This complexity extends to consideration of possible mitigation or adaptation measures, which cannot be understood in terms of simple cause-effect relationships.

How did science develop to move into this leading position? The Social Learning Project identified three phases in the development of scientific capacity, and the complex process of connecting science to policy across the countries studied. These phases were identified as a build-up of scientific capacity, the rise of issues on the political agenda, and strengthening linkages between knowledge and action (Jaeger, Van Eijndhoven, and Clark 2001). In the first phase there was a gradual build-up of scientific and analytical capacity through research, monitoring, and assessment activities. This build-up of capacity was not necessarily linked to already recognized risks, but it meant that when potential risks were identified more research and monitoring capacity was available to help characterize and understand it and identify potential directions for managing it. In this phase, it was typical that multiple response options were promoted – often technological responses or improvement goals stated in notional, round numbers – but these tended to be only loosely connected to the scientific state of knowledge and exercised little influence on the eventual course of action. To emerge on the policy agenda the framing of the issue also played an important role: the processes by which features of a problem area are singled out for attention by particular actors or communities (Hajer 1995). The frames in the policy debate were inspired, but not determined, by science. Instead new knowledge was generally fit into frames derived from existing problems and policy programs.

In the second phase, goal statements began to appear more strongly on the political agenda, typically with a period of high media attention. Goal statements were underpinned by continuing research, monitoring, and assessment activities. Goal statements were often widely shared across countries and arenas, functioning as de facto common framings of the issue. They were generally simple, rigid calls for action on emission reduction, e.g., for emission reductions of 20 or 30 percent or a cap on the production capacity of some chemical. Such simple goals often had a galvanizing impact on the subsequent issue debate.

In the third phase, following this initial surge of public attention, linkages between knowledge and action increased in frequency and ran in both directions: knowledge influenced action and vice versa. This was the period in which international agreements in response to the three studied global environmental risks began to be implemented. These agreements in turn set in motion continuing processes of monitoring, assessment, and evaluation of progress in dealing with the risks, which in turn influenced further goal-setting and action.

For the complex risks that dominate environmental debate today these three phases do not make up a simple, linear process. The route from knowledge to action may be a long one, and may be punctuated by cycles in public and political attention. Initial steps of action and implementation may not represent concrete measures to reduce risks but may instead set up institutions that increase capacity to do so in the future (Jaeger, Van Eijndhoven, and Clark 2001). Moreover, science is increasingly implicated in multiple aspects of environmental issues, not just in the physical characterization of risks but also in impacts and response options – the three basic elements represented in the three separate Working Group assessments of the Inter-governmental Panel on Climate Change. With this broader understanding of the role of science in informing environmental issues, the role of the social sciences (in addition to the physical and biological sciences) is becoming increasingly important.

SHIFTS IN ACTORS INVOLVED AND RESPONSES NEEDED

In addition to these changes in the role of science, the changes in character of environmental issues also brought changes in the nature of responses required to manage them and thus in the types of actors involved and their roles. For chemical risks and other early environmental issues, the simple structure of the issues – involving immediate and localized effects, and relatively direct coupling of single causes to clearly identifiable harms – carried clear implications for what responses were relevant and which actors would be involved. Citizens who perceived threats to their health or surrounding environment mobilized, first through local action and then, with the rise of the environmental movement, increasingly with larger-scale organization. Citizen mobilization targeted identified industry polluters, based on the clear and widely shared belief that industry was causing the problems and solving the problems required changes in industry behaviour and technology. Industry actors, who initially did not acknowledge, and in some cases did not realize the risks their activities were imposing on people and the environment, resisted these calls. Over time, however, they slowly shifted their behaviour, partly voluntarily and partly stimulated by regulation or dwindling public trust. Policy-makers and politicians acted mainly as brokers between citizens and industry. Like industry, they may also not have initially realized the potential negative impacts of chemicals in the environment, they but slowly shifted their perspectives and crafted laws and regulations that brought industry behaviour into line with environmental needs as channelled by citizen demands. Although the initial approach to regulating chemicals developed in major economies in the 1970s tended to be reactive, policy-makers have slowly shifted to a more precautionary stance. This direction is still developing, e.g., in the recent REACH directive that regulates hazardous chemicals in Europe (Registration, Evaluation, Authorization and Restriction of Chemicals, EC regulation 1907/2006).

As global environmental risks became more prominent, the pattern of actor involvement also shifted. As science came to play a stronger role in early identification and framing of issues and bringing them onto the policy agenda, this implied a lesser role in these functions for grassroots citizen initiative. Governments became involved early, but a global scale implies that multiple governments must be involved, so substantial differences are possible between government views, both scientific and regulatory. Ozone depletion is a case in point. While some observers may suggest that ozone science developed first to the point that the risk was beyond dispute, governments were in fact involved from an early date in a sustained process of linked scientific and regulatory dispute. Barely a year before the 1987 conference that adopted the treaty, stark differences persisted between groups of countries advocating sectoral controls (e.g., a ban on the nonessential use of CFCs in aerosol spray cans), comprehensive controls, and no controls – each putatively supported by science (Schreurs et al. 2001, 356).

Scholars differ in their accounts of the most significant factors contributing to the shift that enabled policy agreement. Grundman (2006) emphasizes the leadership of the United States, while Parson (2003) credits the availability of a trusted assessment. My view is that more research is needed to clarify which factors lead to policy or political tipping points and how these factors interact.

Although the ozone issue is often considered a model for how to address global environmental issues, in the complexity of required responses and actor adjustments, ozone depletion, like acidification, represents only a partial movement toward the complexity of current issues. Although these issues differed in scale and duration from earlier concerns about chemical risks, they could still be managed by fairly narrowly targeted changes in industry behaviour and technology. Required changes in consumer behaviour were at most minor. In this sense, ozone and acidification can be seen as intermediate cases between "old and new" risks, while climate change is the first prominent example of the "new" risks.

For the climate issue, simple solutions that can be taken up by one actor are not available. Nor can responses be limited to any single industry sector, not even to the energy sector, which is most obviously implicated in greenhouse gas emissions. Linkages among major resources and sectors must be considered, such as food, energy, and water. Responses cannot be limited to the production side of the economy, since consumption and decisions driven by consumption must also be considered – perhaps also the possibility of aggregate environmentally determined limits on consumption itself.

In addition, the long timeline of possible effects in these complex environmental issues complicates responses because it affects how committed different actors are to managing the risks. People facing urgent short-term problems are less likely to worry about risks that will develop over decades. Scientifically, an issue may gain attention when it represents only a potential future risk, but as the second section above discussed, issues are taken up for concrete action only when they are seen as locally relevant, and framed in ways that make this local relevance clear (Schreurs et al. 2001). Thus, climate change has been taken up earliest and most forcefully where its risks are seen as most immediate, e.g., in the small island states where inundation is an immediate risk, and in the Netherlands where safe management of flood risks is a national priority not open for debate. Democratically chosen politicians will act on a risk when they think it is real, when it has grassroots support, and when it does not threaten other political goals such as economic growth or the interests of their major supporters. Various conditions may contribute to this state, e.g., long-standing public and media attention to the issue, a disaster that is perceived as related to the issue, or widespread belief in a feasible and effective course of action.

For climate change and for other complexly linked environmental challenges such as the Belmont challenges mentioned above (ICSU 2010) or loss of biodiversity (Hulme et al. 2011), integrative responses will be required involving multiple actors across society. There is a growing recognition of a need for imaginative breakthroughs that harness the best engagement between science and those in society responsible for designing and implementing solutions, including civil society, industry, and policy-makers (Stafford-Smith et al. 2012). While some scientists and activists point out that the required shifts are technically feasible (Brown 2008; Stafford-Smith et al. 2012), comparison with past experience suggests that the climate issue has not developed to the stage where knowledge and action are effectively linked. Rather, the current situation more closely resembles the first phase discussed in the third section above, in which multiple technological management options are promoted with only loose connections to the state of scientific knowledge. For climate and other complex environmental challenges, the search for a smooth road to effective responses and their implementation is still going on. Among other challenges on this road will be that of connecting science to knowledge of ways to influence human behaviour (Thaler and Sunstein 2008; Moser and Dilling 2007).

ENHANCING THE ROLE OF SCIENCE IN THE POLICY LANDSCAPE

As the major environmental debates have become more global and more complex, the role of science has become leading, and the type and disciplinary breadth of expert knowledge involved has increased, often including social sciences and even humanities. Systematic assessments have become an integral part of global governance, advocating and often leading to policy action. In contrast to earlier issues, on which local risks were assessed in response to demands of local actors, this shift to systematic, pro-active assessment raises new challenges for science in the policy landscape. When there is a large divide perceived between the urgency of an issue and the short-term viability of potential responses, there is more room for debate about the reality of the risk and whether it is worthwhile to address it in the first place. Differences in perspective can also be driven by the stakes involved (Oreskes and Conway 2010). When the scientific knowledge supporting an issue has little meaning to ordinary people this tendency will be even stronger. It is a challenge to develop ways to diminish the divide.

Various studies have examined how environmental assessments or other efforts to mobilize science and technology for sustainable development can be made effective (e.g., Cash et al. 2003; Jaeger and Farrell 2006). They conclude that scientific information is likely to be effective in influencing social responses to the extent that relevant stakeholders perceive it to be not just credible but also salient and legitimate. In this scheme, credibility concerns the scientific adequacy of the technical evidence and arguments. Salience concerns the relevance of the assessment to the needs of decision makers. Legitimacy reflects whether the process of generating information has been respectful of stakeholders' divergent values and beliefs, unbiased in its conduct, and fair in its treatment of opposing views and interests. Cash et al. (2003, 8086) conclude that these three attributes are tightly coupled, so that efforts to enhance one attribute may incur a cost to the others.

Because issues related to global environmental change are difficult to see with the naked eye, science-driven modelling plays an important role in getting a hold of them. The choice of wording in assessment reports is also mainly science-driven, although the summaries for policy-makers in the Intergovernmental Panel on Climate Change (IPCC) process use a different process that aims to heighten the saliency for policy-makers. Controversies over the wording of these summaries show how such attempts to enhance saliency can pose challenges for scientific credibility.

Similar challenges arise in attempts to enhance legitimacy. The International Academy Council (InterAcademy Council 2010) evaluated the IPCC process and concluded that it should become more transparent and provide more direct responses to opposing views. But while this approach may enhance scientific credibility, it may not help legitimacy. Van der Sluijs, Van Est, and Riphagen (2010) note that the scientific consensus approach of the IPCC can hinder a full-blown political debate, while a more open approach that highlights diverse views and deep uncertainty in knowledge may represent a more democratic organization of the interface between climate politics and science, thereby enhancing legitimacy.

Jasanoff (2010) argues that current practice of climate science seems to render obsolete important prior categories of solidarity and experience. The challenge is to address issues in a way that has local meaning to people, as a precondition for them to support action. Diminishing the divide between scientific and local framings of issues will support implementation of policies. Perhaps by taking local meaning as the starting point, the road to action may be made shorter and less windy. In the Netherlands, for example, sea level rise was long not considered a climate issue but simply a challenge that had always been there. When climate adaptation appeared on the agenda, all that was required was a shift in framing, with little in the way of new institutions or legislation.

A related requirement is for more effective integration of science with local knowledge. There is sometimes a tendency to dismiss local knowledge as less rigorous and systematic than scientific knowledge. Yet if environmental changes shift the relationship of people and communities to their surroundings or require changes in behaviour to manage risks, local knowledge can be essential to motivate and guide responses. Local knowledge can also provide crucial inputs to scientific understanding, as Hulme et al. (2011) argue for biodiversity loss, e.g., by providing early signals of larger-scale trends or information about processes that depend on fine-scale variation. To motivate and guide effective responses, the challenge is to narrow the divide between scientific description of how the world works and the experience and perceptions of citizens. As Jasanoff (2010, 238) argues, "Living creatively with climate change will require re-linking larger scales of scientific representation with smaller scales of social meaning. How at the levels of community, space and time, will scientists' impersonal knowledge of the climate be synchronized with the mundane rhythms of lived lives and the specificity of human experience?"

A similar integration of global and local is required in science-based institutions. Although there is a shift from local to global institutions, effective institutions require trust, which develops slowly and depends on local experience. Dobell (2002) discusses the Mad Cow controversy in the United Kingdom to illustrate the challenges of developing and sustaining trust in institutions. He identifies four challenges: "how shall we find the balance between individual responsibility and collective decision in the face of uncertainties and risk? For those risks that we choose to address through collective decision making, how shall we find the balance among risks and benefits directly imposed or promised on the one hand, or assumed by default through economic returns on the other? How shall the individual consumer be assured that this balance has been found in the right place with respect to individual outcomes? And finally, how shall we ensure that the community finds acceptable and will continue to support the procedures and decision processes that yield these outcomes?" (Dobell 2002, 25).

As the previous example of climate in the Netherlands shows, institutions develop over time yet can become activated quickly when a change in perspective happens. Yet to be effective institutions have to be seen as meriting trust. Institutions for global environmental change are at an early stage of development and have only begun to surmount the challenge of connecting the global with the local to build trust.

CONCLUSION

Major shifts have occurred over the past several decades in the environmental risks that are debated and seek policy attention. The local risks prominent in the sixties have not been entirely resolved, but there are institutions, laws, and regulations to address them. Science has a key role in assessing and responding to the newer, more complex risks we now face, but the road to serious implementation of risk-avoiding activities may still be long. I see four major challenges for all actors involved: searching for solutions with meaning for people, working on building new connections between actors, diminishing the divide between expert and local knowledge, and building trusted institutions. For science specifically, the challenge is not primarily to develop better knowledge of risks and response options, but to develop ways to enhance the link between credibility, salience, and the legitimacy of findings and effective ways to communicate them.

9

Climate Engineering: New Challenges for Scientific Assessment and Global Governance

EDWARD A. PARSON AND LIA N. ERNST

INTRODUCTION: CLIMATE CHANGE, GOVERNANCE SCALE, AND EXPERTISE

Global climate change poses governance challenges that speak to two of the themes of this volume: the relationship between expertise and democracy and the multiple shifting and overlapping spatial scales of governance authority. Because climate change is driven by worldwide emissions of carbon dioxide (CO_2) and other greenhouse gases no matter where they occur, limiting climate change requires global action to cut emissions. But because every state has incentives to avoid costly emission-cutting efforts, global action requires a program of effective monitoring and enforcement of commitments, linking national and international levels, to overcome these incentives and provide mutual assurance of shared, reciprocated, and effective efforts.

Moreover, because the gravest risks of climate change lie decades in the future – notwithstanding increasingly clear present changes – effectively managing climate change requires marshalling real but uncertain scientific knowledge, including model-based calculations, to inform decisions. Effectively linking scientific evidence of environmental risks with democratic decision processes always poses challenges, but in the current climate-change debate these challenges have been magnified by political attacks on scientific knowledge and institutions.

While these challenges of climate governance are familiar, climate engineering (CE) – a form of potential response that has recently risen to prominence – presents them in modified, novel, and more acute ways. Climate engineering interventions would actively modify global-scale properties of the atmosphere and climate system, to offset some of the heating and climate disruption caused by elevated greenhouse gases. These interventions are often called "geoengineering," but we call them climate engineering to highlight their purpose of offsetting anthropogenic climate change (Asilomar Scientific Organizing Committee 2010; Royal Society 2009; Bipartisan Policy Center 2011).

These interventions are not new ideas, having been discussed as early as the 1950s (PSAC 1965; Budyko 1974; Fleming 2010). They faded from prominence as climate came onto policy agendas in the l980s (Keith 2000; Schelling 1983), then gained renewed attention after 2000 in response to growing alarm over mounting signs of climate change and continuing failure to cut emissions (Bodansky 1996; Schneider 1996; Lawrence 2006; Crutzen 2006). They have seen high interest and controversy over the past five years.

This chapter discusses the novel challenges to governance posed by the potential availability of CE interventions. In particular, it examines how the prospect of CE and potential future proposals to deploy it challenge the distribution of governance authority between national and international levels and the relationship of expertise and evidence-based knowledge with democratic decision processes.

CLIMATE ENGINEERING METHODS AND CHARACTERISTICS

Many specific forms of CE intervention have been proposed that fall into two broad types distinguished by where they intervene in the climate system. One type alters the global carbon cycle to remove CO_2 from the atmosphere, offsetting increased concentrations from burning carbon-based fuels (Parson and Keith 1998; Lackner 2002). The other type decreases the amount of sunlight absorbed at the Earth's surface, altering the Earth's radiation balance to offset the heating and climate effects of elevated atmospheric greenhouse gases.

Carbon-cycle interventions may be valuable tools to manage climate change, but they do not pose novel governance challenges. Rather, the challenges they do pose – how to motivate and coordinate costly national efforts in pursuit of a shared global goal – resemble those posed by cutting emissions. Moreover, because these methods remove CO_2 that has already been released to the atmosphere, they have low leverage over the climate: that is, making a non-trivial climate effect would require massive efforts, processing vast amounts of material over decades (Bickel and Lane 2009; Morgan and Ricke 2010). By contrast, sunlight-based interventions pose distinct and novel governance challenges because they can alter the climate with high leverage. The approach now gaining most attention, spraying a fine mist of reflective droplets in the stratosphere, illustrates their leverage: initial calculations suggest the global heating effect of a ton of atmospheric CO_2 can be offset by a few grams of reflective sulfur-based aerosols in the stratosphere (Rasch et al. 2008). In concrete terms, these interventions would make the sun's direct beam a little dimmer (by 1 percent or so), and the rest of the sky a little brighter and whiter. Because the particles would stay in the stratosphere for a year or so, a large effect can be achieved with a small injection rate. We focus on this approach because it is known to work even with present knowledge and methods and because it illustrates the acute governance challenges posed by any high-leverage CE intervention.

Such interventions have three basic characteristics that shape their governance challenges: they are fast, cheap, and imperfect (Keith, Parson, and Morgan 2010). These methods can cool the global climate a degree or so within months, whereas achieving the same cooling by either cutting emissions or removing CO_2 from the atmosphere would take decades. We know these methods act fast because volcanic eruptions that inject large plumes of sulfur into the stratosphere provide natural analogues. The most recent of these, the 1991 eruption of Mount Pinatubo in the Philippines, cooled the Earth about half a degree Celsius over the following year or so (Soden et al. 2002). Fast impact is the strongest reason to develop CE capability, because it would enable interventions to limit or reverse severe climate change and some impacts once they have already become obvious enough to motivate a response. This would represent a major advance in the human ability to manage risks of climate change.

CE interventions are also cheap. Initial estimates of the direct cost of offsetting the average heating projected this century are a few billion dollars a year – roughly a thousand times cheaper than achieving the same cooling by cutting emissions (Barrett 2008; Aurora Flight Sciences 2010). Low cost might first seem a clear advantage of CE, but it also poses problems. It has moved some observers to an ill-advised stance of naïve cheerleading for CE, based on a belief that it provides a complete and easy solution to climate change – which it does not, as we outline below. Low cost also puts CE within financial reach of many actors, posing challenges of control and risking unregulated or reckless use and associated international conflict.

CE interventions are, however, highly imperfect corrections for the diverse climatic and other environmental effects of elevated greenhouse gases. This imperfection is not mainly the result of harmful impacts of CE interventions themselves – they are real and require careful assessment, of course, although initial signs suggest they may be moderate. Rather, CE interventions are imperfect because they cannot fully reverse the harms done by greenhouse gases. They are imperfect even considering only global-average climate, because they offset heating that occurs aloft with cooling at the surface. They thus change the atmosphere's vertical temperature profile, which drives the global water cycle. As a result, CE controls precipitation more strongly than temperature: a world heated by greenhouse gases and cooled an equal amount by CE will be the same average temperature as the world at the starting point, but drier. This imperfect climate correction translates into more divergence at regional and seasonal scales. Moreover, CE does nothing to correct the non-climatic effects of greenhouse gases, which include making the oceans more acidic (by CO_2 dissolving to form carbonic acid) and disrupting competitive relationships among plants using different chemical processes for photosynthesis, which differ in how well they can take advantage of higher atmospheric CO_2.

CE GOVERNANCE CHALLENGES: THEIR ORIGIN AND CHARACTER

Because these three characteristics – fast, cheap, and imperfect – arise from the basic structure of how CE interventions work and gain high leverage, they are likely robust for future scientific and technological progress. Together they pose an acute dilemma for governance. Like many technological advances, CE offers a dual prospect, ranging from great benefits to great harms, depending on how it is used. Used prudently, competently, and benevolently, it can greatly reduce climate-change risks, whether they come from continued failure to cut emissions or from the unlucky resolution of scientific uncertainties. Rapid response in some future climate crisis is the most obvious such beneficial use, but not the only one. CE could also be used sooner and at lower intensity as part of a comprehensive climate response including emission cuts. Used in this way, a little CE could shave the peak of near-term climate heating and avoid the most severe impacts, while allowing emission cuts to proceed more gradually and cheaply as part of a long-term transition to a non-carbon world energy economy. CE could also be used to counteract specific regional effects of high global significance, for example, to slow summer loss of Arctic sea ice, cool regional heat waves, or cool tropical ocean surfaces to weaken hurricane formation. On the other hand, excessive reliance on CE could undercut already limp political will for emission cuts or lead to its being used to suppress so much heating that stopping it would be dangerous. And if CE is deployed incompetently, recklessly, or maliciously, it could bring climate disruptions far worse than projected from greenhouse gases alone or provoke new international conflicts. This sharp tension between potential benefits and risks of CE implies the need for governance to keep the capability under competent, prudent, and legitimate control and thereby gain the benefits while limiting the associated harms and risks. This section and the next aim to sharpen this generic observation by identifying specific governance functions likely to be needed for CE and potential near-term steps to start building them.

First, however, we must note that virtually no governance capacity for CE exists at present and that most forms of CE are virtually uncontrolled under present international law. For sunlight-based methods in particular, any state is free to conduct CE, for research or even operational climate modification over its own territory, over other consenting states, and over the high seas. Other states may object, but such conduct would violate no controlling international law (Parson et al. 2011; Blackstock and Gosh 2010). Yet states will face the need to make various decisions about CE, possibly soon: decisions about whether and how to pursue research, development, and possible future deployment of CE and decisions about how to respond to proposals to do so by other states or to claims and suspicions that others are doing them. On these matters, the structure of states' interests will be broadly similar to that on many international issues. They will want strong controls on CE by others that might impose risks on them, but they will also want discretion to do what they judge beneficial or necessary to reduce their own climate risks. The structure of CE suggests, however, that even powerful states probably cannot achieve such a highly asymmetric outcome. Even for these states, gaining the benefits and limiting the risks of CE is likely to require collective action and mutual accommodation to develop international governance, because of the large spatial scale of CE's effects and the strength of states' likely interests in these effects. Absent unlikely advances that would allow sharp regional targeting of effects, interventions strong enough to offset climate change in one region would change climate at a hemispheric to a global scale. If any state seriously proposes to undertake CE, all states are likely to perceive acute interests to be implicated, both in whether it is done and in how it is done.

How effectively can states advance and defend these interests? Assuming states are able to form well-founded judgments of how particular interventions will benefit or harm them, this is a question of states' operational capabilities: what can they do and what can they prevent others from doing without their consent? On the first question, what states can do alone, some early commentary has stressed CE's low cost to draw colourful scenarios of widely dispersed unilateral capability, including virtually all states and many non-state actors. More careful consideration of the requirements for sustaining a climate intervention in the face of strong opposition, however, suggests that non-trivial unilateral capability is likely limited to a few major states that are powerful enough to make it hard for others to stop them – roughly a dozen states, perhaps fewer, depending on the intensity of other states' opposition. But while this reasoning implies that CE is less catastrophically destabilizing than has been suggested, it also implies that no state is dominant enough both to preserve its ability to act and to limit others' ability to do so unilaterally. Rather, even powerful states must trade off their own discretion to conduct CE as they choose against their willingness to tolerate the risks of others doing so. In view of the multiple risks of unregulated action, or worse, of multiple uncoordinated interventions, powerful states are likely to accept, indeed demand, some form of collective international control over CE.

GLOBAL DECISION NEEDS: AUTHORIZATION, OPERATIONS, AND RESPONSE

While it is speculative to predict the shape of future international CE governance, certain requirements for effective international control of CE are evident. At a minimum, some legitimate governance authority will be required that can make and implement decisions about proposed interventions of several distinct types. The most obvious need will be for decisions of a regulatory character to authorize or not to authorize proposed CE projects: who may make what intervention, where and when, under what conditions, under whose control, and with what restrictions, including provisions for risk assessment, monitoring, and oversight? This need for international decisions is particularly clear for operational-scale interventions, but even smaller research projects may raise enough international concern that other states demand a say in their authorization. Indeed, defining the threshold of project scale or anticipated risk that requires international authorization will itself require international decisions, which may be contentious. Other states may, for example, demand a say in projects whose proponents view them as small enough to be purely domestic matters, perhaps because they represent a modest expansion of long-practised regional weather modification activities.

Given the intensity of state interests involved, these authorization decisions will require some process of political-level negotiation. The potential for conflict in these decisions will be strongly influenced by the degree of alignment or opposition in states' interests over available CE interventions. Although little that is concrete is presently known about this alignment of interests, it could in principle range from strongly aligned to strongly opposed, depending on several factors. For example, interest alignment will depend on the regional distribution of climate harms and the regional uniformity with which known CE options would mitigate these. The more closely climate harms and CE's ability to reduce them are uniform across regions, the more closely states' interests in whether and how to do CE are likely to be aligned. Interest alignment will also depend, perhaps crucially, on the regional controllability of CE interventions. If technical advances should make it possible to separately control the climate effects of CE in different regions, it would have two effects: it would increase the ability to optimize CE interventions for global benefit, and it would also increase the opportunities for inter-regional tradeoffs and conflicts. In the extreme, a state that developed precise control of regional climate or even short-term weather could use CE to inflict or threaten harms on others, greatly elevating every state's stake in how CE is controlled and creating many possibilities for heightened international tensions.

Under these conditions, deciding the details of how states share control in these political-level decisions is likely to be contentious and difficult. Although no state can control the issue unilaterally, powerful states are likely to seek to maximize their control by limiting others' control as much as possible. Because the minimum set of participants in these decisions will be states capable of sustaining unilateral action, it is most likely that the practical configuration of decision authority will privilege these states, even if nominal participation is broader.

Authorizing projects will not be the only decisions required nor the end of the acute challenges to governance. Any project that is authorized must also be implemented, and the political body that makes authorization decisions is unlikely to have the required operational capability for implementation. Rather, implementation will have to be delegated to some other body – e.g., a government agency, a firm, or an NGO – which will in turn require oversight to ensure it does what was authorized. This oversight function will be complicated by the unavoidable uncertainty of any intervention. Even with a successful research program, the effects of any novel or expanded intervention will not be known with full confidence until it is implemented. Oversight and control of projects must thus include monitoring of environmental effects to identify anomalies and modify or stop a project if signs of unexpected effects are observed, particularly harmful impacts. This process will require technically competent judgments and decisions on short time scales as an intervention proceeds, over days or even hours.

The political body that authorizes interventions might be able to specify the broad outlines of this monitoring and adaptation function. Authorization decisions might, for example, include statements of the range of expected effects, perhaps based on model projections or risk assessments required as part of proposals. But the political body will not be able to maintain complete control over operations, because the range of surprises that might be observed and appropriate responses cannot be fully specified in advance. Nor can the required real-time response decisions be made subject to the clumsiness and delay of the political decision process. Rather, these functions will require an operational body that has both the technical capability and the delegated discretionary authority to make rapid, competent decisions to limit risks in real time.

Still more decisions will be required after projects are completed or stopped, including how to respond to projects that fail or cause harms or are alleged to do so. Even with ideal procedures for advance risk assessment and project approval, such bad outcomes will sometimes occur and must be prepared for. The governance system will need to respond to project failures, adjudicate claims of harm, assign liability and provide compensation as appropriate, and incorporate learning from failures into future project design and authorization decisions. In addition, to the extent states come to perceive strong opposed interests at stake in CE interventions, they may *in extremis* be prepared to fight over them. A CE governance system must thus be able to limit and manage security threats by preventing unauthorized interventions, limiting harms from authorized interventions, enforcing decisions (both approvals and rejections), and limiting the most severe conflicts that may follow, backed by a credible threat of force when necessary. As with authorization and oversight, each of these types of decision has distinct requirements for the expertise, competency, and authority of the body making them.

Considering these decision requirements together, the challenge they pose to international governance is extreme. The high risks of uncoordinated national action suggest the need to develop international governance capacity, yet no current body has the authority, membership, and technical and administrative capacity to discharge these tasks. One can plausibly imagine existing bodies' mandates and capabilities being expanded to embrace some of these functions, but the weak fit with current institutions and the acute difficulties of effectively coordinating international bodies suggest this approach is unpromising. While many aspects of these decision needs pose severe challenges to governance capabilities, the two challenges likely to be most acute will be deciding on the configuration of state control over authorization decisions and delegating an effective degree of real-time operational authority to some project management body.

NEW CHALLENGES FOR SCIENCE-POLICY INTERACTIONS

In addition to the challenges CE poses for international governance in general, it will also impose novel demands on the ability to integrate scientific knowledge with political decision making in both international and national settings. Thus far, we have glossed over these difficulties by assuming that states are able to form judgments of how particular proposed interventions are likely to benefit or harm them and agree on collective decisions based on these judgments. But how will states make those judgments and reach those agreements? Probably based on conjectures about the feasibility and effects of specific interventions, including, crucially, the distribution of effects over the regional and seasonal scales where climate is actually experienced. These are all matters of scientific judgment on which there is some present knowledge – e.g., from general atmospheric science, natural analogues, and early modelling studies – but which also carry substantial uncertainty and on which states cannot form rational judgments without drawing on science.

Learning more about CE effectiveness and impacts will first require a program of scientific research and technology development (Parson and Keith 2013). An effective research program will need to include field studies that make small but real environmental manipulations and should be developed with international cooperation from the outset. As a result, the CE governance questions most urgent to address concern governance of research: e.g., how to cooperatively identify research priorities; provide support; evaluate, approve, and oversee projects; and share and disseminate what is learned about methods, effects, and risks to support informed decisions. Developing governance of CE research is a less daunting problem than developing governance to handle potential future proposals for operational interventions, but still not an easy one (SRMGI 2011).

Even assuming these near-term challenges are surmounted, however, and a well-designed and successful international research program is conducted, uncertainty will not disappear. Despite advancing knowledge from prior research, the effects of any new or expanded intervention will remain uncertain until it is actually done – possibly even after it is done, since its effects will be hard to separate from the confounding effects of natural climate variability and ongoing greenhouse-gas heating. Decisions about proposed interventions – whether to intervene, and how – will thus have to be made under uncertainty, balancing the uncertain risks of specific proposed CE interventions against the anticipated climate-change harms they seek to avoid.

Under these conditions, demanding certainty about effects as a pre-condition of approving any intervention, while superficially attractive, will not be a prudent response to climate risks. This stance would be equivalent to deciding never to conduct CE under any conditions, regardless of the severity of climate impacts. Rather, rational and prudent decisions about CE will have to be based on some form of adaptive management. There are many conceptions of adaptive management that differ in details, but they all include three major elements: continuing research to inform decisions; mechanisms to integrate available knowledge into decisions made under uncertainty; and methods to use the results of prior research and experience to adjust decisions and manage risks over time.

While adaptive management is a framework for rational decisions under uncertain but advancing knowledge, real political decision making is not an abstract, rational process. Rather, the interaction in practice between uncertain scientific knowledge and decision making can exhibit several well-known pathologies. Policy actors select scientific claims to support their pre-existing positions, so policy dissent tends to highlight extreme scientific claims, even when they do not represent the state of relevant knowledge. Decision processes that must produce a decisive outcome and policy actors who want the outcome to go their way attribute more certainty and more warrant for action to scientific knowledge than the knowledge actually supports. Scientists usually resist demands to exaggerate confidence as a basis for action, but determined policy actors can usually find some who are willing to play. Moreover, even fair-minded policy actors usually cannot make their own judgments about scientific disagreements or even distinguish real controversies from fabricated ones. They must thus rely on trust and can decide who to trust – what scientific body or process or what individual scientist – only based on factors that are observable to non-experts. For understandable reasons, they often do so based on non-scientific signs of identity and affiliation – i.e., tending to trust "their own" scientists and mistrust those on the "other side," however they define them.

In decisions over CE, these familiar pathologies in the use of science in policy could be magnified. CE interventions are more likely to be proposed under conditions that at least some states perceive as a crisis than by any orderly and incremental process. Decision makers may favor or oppose particular proposals based on non-scientific affinities or partisan interest, or persist in supporting some course of action (whether a rejection of CE or a favoured intervention) despite new knowledge or shifting evidence of associated risks. Particularly in crisis decisions, debate over CE could readily deteriorate to a contest between extreme proposals and their biased supporting claims. Depending on what state representatives know (or think they know) about regional climate impacts and effects of available interventions, they may perceive strongly opposed interests and thus have strong incentives to select or manipulate scientific claims in favor of their preferred actions. Worse, decisions might not be based on rational assessment of interests at all but instead reflect panic, contending ideologies, or religious views evoked by the environmental changes under way or maneuvering for political advantage. If decision makers do not have shared norms for attending to scientific evidence, conflicts over CE – over what to do, or attributing effects – could be prone to escalation, with the worst prospects as dangerous as any envisioned during the nuclear arms race of the Cold War (Dyson 2011, 158–74; quoting John Von Neumann).

These decision requirements call to mind the metaphor of Spaceship Earth, an enduring image from the early days of modern environmentalism (Ward 1966). Advanced to illustrate the limits of the Earth's environment and the need to protect it, the image also conveyed the complexity of the Earth system and the resultant need, as the global impact of human activities grew, to exercise this new control with skill and prudence. The prospect of CE brings the spaceship metaphor closer to reality than any environmental issues of the 1960s actually did – particularly in the need for operational control of interventions, i.e., recognizing when the ship is going off-course and making appropriate adjustments promptly and competently. Yet while the metaphor vividly portrays some aspects of the governance challenges of CE (and, for that matter, of climate change), there are also two respects in which it may mislead by failing to capture all the difficulties. First, the metaphor ignores uncertainty. While piloting a spaceship will no doubt require great skill, if it is an operating, production-model spaceship then presumably the envelope of its acceptable operating conditions will be well known. But given the unavoidable uncertainty about CE interventions, controlling them will be more like test-piloting a new prototype spaceship whose performance limits are imperfectly known from previous simulations than an actual production spaceship. Like real test flights of new aircraft, this would presumably call for more caution in operations – if it is even clear what "caution" means in balancing the novel risks of CE against novel risks of climate change. Second, controlling a spaceship makes no allowance for democratic decisions or political negotiations. While one purpose of the metaphor was to exhort political interests to yield to the compelling need to keep the spaceship habitable, subsequent experience makes this longing appear naïve or even dangerous. In real political decisions we value democracy as well as sustainability, and real spaceships, like ocean ships, presumably cannot be democracies. The metaphor is thus two-edged, reminding us that while we focus mainly here on the pathologies of too little science in decisions, there can also be too much, if expert bodies that lack political legitimacy take, or are given, too broad authority over risk-management decisions.

How might CE governance navigate these perils – between dangerously uninformed decisions and escalating conflict from too little reliance on scientific expertise on the one hand and loss of legitimate democratic control on the other? Part of the answer is that the power of expert bodies must be delimited by democratic authority, by either keeping them in advisory roles or giving them delegated operational authority within limits subject to political accountability. But this can be only part of the answer, because there is much latitude in the design of precise terms of advisory roles and delegated authority.

In the early steps, key decisions concern governance of CE research. Decisions here would seem to call for substantial delegation of authority to expert bodies based on scientific criteria, since assessing the scientific merit of proposed projects and how well they squeeze the most new knowledge out of small, low-risk interventions, are matters of scientific judgment. Yet even early research decisions can set perceptions or precedents that influence larger-scale future decisions and thus require consideration of their broader significance that encompasses more than scientific concerns. Early research programs will need linked, parallel initiatives in assessment in order to synthesize what is learned and communicate its significance for risks and decisions clearly and credibly. These processes need scientific inputs, but broader consultations on research scale, the design of risk assessment procedures, and interpretation of results and their significance must also involve governments and other stakeholders – people and institutions who are perceived as legitimate, who bring additional relevant criteria to the discussions, and who are skilled at communicating.

These early steps in international research cooperation, information sharing, assessment, and public consultation aim at several contributions to the development of effective longer-term governance. In addition to building knowledge, they aim to build habits and norms of transparency and cooperation and associated trust, in the hope that they can over time reinforce themselves and grow robust enough to bear the stress of future decision needs. While the precise trajectory by which this happy outcome might be achieved cannot be pre-specified, a few positive developments can be envisioned. For example, such a strong process of norm development might allow the strengthening of the role for scientific advice in future governance processes, e.g., by allowing certain factual bases for decisions or reference points to be specified by expert advisory bodies, providing a default for subsequent political decisions. Alternatively, early consultations over collaborative research might help anticipate trends in CE capabilities, and direct developments in directions likely to avoid the sharpest risks of international conflict and destabilization – at least until there are norms or institutions in place able to handle the resultant decision challenges. While these specific prospects remain plausible but hopeful speculation, they suggest the long potential future shadow of early CE research and research governance decisions and the value of early steps to build transparency, cooperation, and trust.

CONCLUSION

The requirements for a governance capability that can gain the potential benefits of CE technologies while limiting risks of dangerous or destructive use or associated conflict pose acute challenges. Effective CE governance will have to combine elements of regulatory, scientific, and security decision making: controlling the authorizing, conduct, and impacts of projects; assessing scientific knowledge to inform these decisions while also managing research to strengthen that knowledge and interpret its results; and avoiding and managing resultant international conflicts. Even considered separately, these functions appear to require a substantial increase in governance capability at the international level. To the extent that effectively managing risks requires coherent integration of these functions, the required expansion and innovation in governance authority and the associated challenges, grow even greater. These governance needs may pose particular stresses to democratic input to decisions. The two shifts in practical authority that appear to be required by CE, toward the international level and toward expert-based processes, both move further from the meaningful participation of citizens and so increase the democratic deficit that already characterizes international decision making.

The starkest view of CE's governance challenges may suggest that these technologies demand a choice between world government and catastrophe. Yet there are grounds for hope that states can develop governance processes that tame the worst risks, while staying consistent with democratic governance. The starkest requirements might not actually apply, in that a fully implemented governance system able to handle all these functions is not required immediately and a system able to discharge all required functions under the worst case of strongly opposed interests may not be required at all. Many early steps that can build knowledge, confidence, and cooperative norms are evident now, mainly through international cooperation on CE research and risk assessment. Though these target easier problems, they can still represent small steps toward building a more robust governance capacity able to handle harder issues that may arise later.

It may also be that early steps toward building norms and capacity for CE governance yield broader governance benefits. Such steps may also aid development of an integrated climate response – including emission cuts, adaptation, and CE – that can limit climate-change risks effectively at low cost. For example, negotiating integrated governance of these elements might promote development of conditional agreements and linkages, particularly between CE and mitigation cuts, to make these elements complementary and so let CE strengthen rather than weaken incentives for emission cuts. It is even plausible that the benefits of such early steps may extend beyond the climate-change issue, by creating new governance structures, capabilities, and authorities that are available to address other acute global challenges.

10

Seeing Like a Sound? Resource Management and Property Rights in Clayoquot Sound

MARTIN BUNTON

INTRODUCTION

Clayoquot Sound is a region of renowned natural beauty, cultural significance, and resource wealth. Forests constitute over 90 percent of the land base and comprise provincial Crown land and, simultaneously, the traditional territory of the Nuu-chah-nulth communities. Given continued logging in temperate rainforests worldwide, the region's remaining undisturbed valleys represent a valuable commodity, but they are also of global ecological importance. "A place of wonder," was how Canadian prime minister Jean Chrétien described the region in May 2000, adding, "It fills you with a sense of our sacred responsibility as stewards of this very special place."

In 1993 Clayoquot Sound became a symbolic battleground over the controversy of clear-cutting – a logging practice in which an area is stripped of all its trees. The area witnessed one of the largest acts of civil disobedience in Canadian history. By the end of the decade, however, First Nations, local communities, environmental groups, corporate interests, and governments sought ways to build mutual respect and trust and to tackle problems in a more participatory manner. General wariness with the roles hitherto played by outside forces spurred the creation of new community-based strategies, which recognized the experiences, practices, and knowledge embedded in the local community.

The purpose of this paper is to consider the recent shifts in resource management in Clayoquot Sound in light of the lessons learned from a growing interdisciplinary body of literature on common property regimes. Much of this literature is itself based on case studies from around the world (Hanna, Folke, and Maler 1996; Ostrom et al. 2002). This literature stresses the resilience of property rights institutions that are built to accommodate social and natural diversity and at the same time recognize the complexity and fluidity of those social and natural environments. In the case of forestry in Clayoquot Sound, these questions are made all the more complicated both by the multiple number of conflicting interests that need balancing in our increasingly globalized world and by the positions and assertions invoked by an ongoing treaty settlement process that addresses political rights and social justice issues.

But first, this paper aims to provide some clarification of the prevailing notions of private and common property and of the tragedies commonly associated with them. The failures in natural resource management evident in the last few decades of the twentieth century prompted closer analysis of the underlying reasoning about property systems. As David Bromley has observed, it is only once "we have a better understanding of different property regimes [that] we can begin to comprehend the richer tapestry that is environment policy" (Bromley 1991, 3). The first step towards this better understanding emerged from critiques of simplistic taxonomies that were based either on the ability of an *individual* to manage rights to natural resources or of the *state* to regulate.

A CONTESTED FIELD

The frequently cited starting point for researchers of common property is Garret Hardin's metaphoric thesis on "the tragedy of the commons" (1968). Hardin argued that degradation of natural resources necessarily emerges when they are open to everyone. This warning has often been used to argue that in the absence of regulation by a centralized authority, resources need to be privatized: only when rights to resources are either regulated by the state or privatized by market forces will individual users feel confident enough that they will capture the benefits of conservation and investment. In providing alternatives to both the state and the market prescriptions to resource management, the common property literature brings these categories, and the epistemologies that support them, into question.

In her discussion of the genealogy of private property (and the rhetoric supporting it), Carol Rose usefully historicizes the discussion to include the larger Enlightenment project. "The doctrines of fixed promise-keeping and fixed property entitlements," observes Rose, "developed more or less contemporaneously with an Enlightenment-era social theory that envisioned a radical separateness among human beings" (1994, 222). Arguments for private property tend to suppose a world populated by strangers acting in predictable ways. There is scant regard for a collective or for context or background or for the embeddedness of individuals in society or culture. Just as importantly, the attempt to secure fixed entitlements to individual allotments presupposes a fundamental separation between people and the environment.

The reductive tendency to view natural resources as a storehouse of divisible units of property waiting to be put to use (and transformed through wealth generation into ownership) played a prominent role in the expansion of European colonial control over large parts of the world. In many instances, the liberal view of property became inseparable from the vocabulary of European imperialism. The representation of nature as external to individual rights was key: natural resources were something to be measured, allocated and traded, because in this way nature could be "improved," "bettered," and "advanced." John Weaver has shown how fundamentally linked a settler community's interpretations of indigenous societies were to its claims to their resources, observing that "improvement and property rights have had a reciprocal relationship since the Enlightenment. People who improved land deserved property rights; property rights improved societies" (2003, 28). To the extent that colonial officials drew only on classical economic perspectives or well-defined property lines in individual plots of land, they failed to acquire a sense of the embedded knowledge of lived-in places. Cole Harris' description of the official demarcation of reserves in British Columbia as "abstract geometrical space devoid of content except that which their own data collections and predilections inclined them to place there" is relevant to many other parts of the colonized world (2002, 235).

As dominant as free market beliefs became to the structuring of institutions to address externalities from common pool resources, the role of state governments also came to hold a dominant position in the understandings that framed resource management policies during the twentieth century (Agrawal 2002, 43). In *Seeing Like a State: How Certain Schemes to Improve the Human Condition Have Failed*, James Scott notes the extent to which processes of abstraction and simplification, as described above, have been as inherent to regulatory statist management plans as they are to private property, market-driven forces. Scott describes the schematized processes that characterize the attempts by state bureaucracies to understand complex sets of environmental relationships. Central planning exercises, he observes, tend to enhance the power of resolution by treating the subject (person or tree) as consisting of standardized units. Just like the "unmarked citizens of liberal theory," what is striking about the subjects of government planning exercises is that they have "no gender, no tastes, no history, no values, no opinions or original ideas, no traditions, and no distinctive personalities to contribute to the enterprise. They have none of the particular, situated, and contextual attributes that one would expect of any population" (1998, 346).

In Scott's analysis, what might be gained in the capacity to formulate general policy for large segments of a population at a time risks being lost in its realization for local communities and the ecosystems in which they live.

Clearly, complex balancing issues are at stake here: how does one maintain, when necessary, the capacity to formulate and work with simplified abstract models while recognizing the complexity and uncertainty of social and environmental contexts. This concern of course also raises the important question of the perceived legitimacy of a policy and compliance to it. The important point here is to emphasize the extent to which both profit-maximizing individuals subject to market forces and large-scale planning processes have in many cases lacked a contextualized notion of rights to resources, one that recognizes where necessary the pervasive and profound uncertainty of the management of ecosystems and the experiences, practices, and knowledges embedded in local communities that interact with them.

GOVERNING THE COMMONS: "A WORLD OF NUANCES"

By the turn of the twenty-first century, a growing body of literature was effectively contesting the reduction of property to canonical categories as a general prescription for environmental policy. As noted above, this literature zeroed in on Hardin's metaphoric commons. Particular concerns were raised about the extent to which Hardin's thesis had unduly restricted the full spectrum of rights in land. As Berkes and Folke put it, "Western resource management often assumes a very limited set of property rights: state property (regimes based on government regulation), private property (market-based regimes) or else a 'tragedy of the commons'" (1998, 18). Or, in the words of Van Laerhoven and Ostrom, "In spite of Hardin's persistent metaphor, today many people, ranging from policy makers, donors, practitioners, and citizen activists, to scientists from different disciplines, have begun to appreciate that there is a world of nuances between the State and the Market" (2007, 19). In their attempts to reveal the much broader range of institutional mechanisms actually available in the governance of natural resources, scholars considered property in terms of the entitlements and obligations of persons and of groups of persons that are inseparable from their relations to each other and to the environment in which they live.

Elinor Ostrom's *Governing the Commons* took the lead in exposing Hardin's ambiguous use of the term "commons" (1990). She argued that common property arrangements should not be confused with the concept of "open access" resources – those characterized by no property rights, which as a result do tend to generate conflict and degrade the environment. Common property is better understood as access that is limited, not open: a specific group of users holding a specific set of rights in common. Although the common property literature argues that property does not have to be individually owned in order to be efficient or productive, it nonetheless clearly accepts that well-established rights are necessary to create incentives and allow for credible commitments to be made. The literature rejects, however, the supposition that such systems refer only to rights that are *individual* and *transferable*. In addition to exclusion, the allocation of rights of access, management, and withdrawal are emphasized as critical to the successful governance of natural resources. These bundles of rights are viewed as social constructs reflecting diverse social, historical, cultural contexts – where categories and assumptions are fluid and continually struggled over. Common-property scholars focus attention on change and adaptation. By emphasizing the specific conditions, defined by time and place, under which rights are constructed and legitimated, scholars attribute voice and agency to the local community.

From this starting point, increasing numbers of scholars began to study how surviving, traditional common pool resources in fact have been managed and governed in sustainable ways over long periods of time by groups of people exercising joint proprietorship rights. Even the classic example of the medieval common fields came to be viewed no longer as a tragic land-use policy but rather as part of a sustainable agricultural practice "which succeeded admirably at its time" (Cox 1985). Rose describes the "burst" of interest in the property rights regimes of traditional communities as a release from collective myopia, as well as driven by the need to find alternatives to resource management practices that represented only governments and individuals.

"Systems of property rights and rules defined, implemented, monitored, and enforced by resource users themselves," write Elinor Ostrom and Edella Schlager "are likely to perform better than systems of property rights and rules defined, implemented and enforced by an external authority" (1996, 145). Why exactly is this so? Though some explanations have already, if indirectly, been put forth, it is worth spelling out in greater detail the underlying assumptions and observations, particularly those to do with efficiency and sustainability.

ADVANTAGES OF COMMUNITY BASED MANAGEMENT

Efficiency

Property rights systems based on locally agreed upon rules economize on monitoring and enforcement costs. This cost is, in effect, transferred to the resource users themselves, where – according to most understandings of how property regimes are established – it belongs. As Bromley observes, "if the core of property is the external acknowledgement (that is, 'social recognition') of the legitimacy of that particular claim by the 'owner,' then it follows ineluctably that property claims failing to win this external acknowledgement will not be recognized as legitimate by those forced to forswear interest in the benefit stream" (1991, 5).

Where local communities depend on the management of adjacent resources, a "socially unrecognized" transfer into other hands of their presumed rights would require intensive, difficult, and costly monitoring. If the transfer of rights from traditional, adjacent users simply "converts owner occupiers into poachers," it in fact then likely brings about the sort of commons tragedy it was originally intended to prevent. Locally devised rules are the easiest to acknowledge and monitor. There are efficiencies simply waiting to be captured. Consider the following description of a locally managed fishery:

> Gear used on a boat can be determined by looking at the boat or examining its harvest activities. Whether a boat is using gear in the appropriate zone can be determined by viewing its harvesting activities, and the gear it is using. Whether a boat is harvesting from its assigned spot can be easily determined by looking at the boat's locations. Also it is difficult for fishers to hide or cloak rule infractions. Either a boat is on its assigned spot or not. Thus, monitoring can be engaged in as fishers go about their business ... Enforcement is also likely to be effective. Fishers face relatively powerful incentives to report and or sanction rule breakers ... The victims of rule breakers face strong incentives to take action to enforce the rules. (Ostrom and Shlager 1996, 146)

External authorities, in contrast, are hard-pressed to devise systems of rights and rules that are as effective, efficient, and legitimate as local institutions. Put simply, "while the livelihoods of resource users depend upon such institutions, the livelihoods of external bureaucrats depend on numerous other considerations."

If one thinks of common property regimes as privatizing the rights to goods without dividing the goods into pieces (as discussed above) then such arrangements offer "a way of parceling the *flow* of skimmable or harvestable 'income' (the interest) from an interactive resource system without parceling the *stock* or the principal itself" (McKean 2000, 36). Environmental resources (such as watersheds, forests, and other ecosystems) have to be managed in a way that takes into account how extractions and interventions in one area will negatively affect the use and value (e.g., in protecting water, soil, vistas, etc.) in adjacent areas. If an area is parcelled into individual allotments that are managed separately, the potential for negative impacts on each other's use can be alleviated only through endless bilateral negotiations (if left in the hands of markets and states). The common property regime offers the potentially more efficient alternative of managing decisions jointly, "acknowledging and internalizing the multiple negative externalities that are implicit in resource use." In this way, collective management tries to reap the benefits of an economy of scale, promising that collective management and collective decision making will reap lower transaction costs than bilateral exchanges that seek recourse to external authorities: "Sharing the ownership of the resource base is simply a way of institutionalizing the already obvious need to make Coaseian deals to control what are externalities for a parceled system and internalities for a co-owned system" (McKean 2000, 42). Ostrom and Schlager agree: many of the negative externalities that unregulated use of these systems would produce can be controlled as a result of the rules crafted by users in their own collective-choice arenas (1996, 139).

Sustainability

Much of the common property literature starts from the recognition that the social patterns of human interaction with the natural environment are as complex and embedded as are relationships in the natural world. "It has never been more important," write C.S. Holling and Steven Sanderson "to understand the conjunction of human and natural systems, and the nature of their interactions" (1996, 57). Everything is connected to everything else. Resource management, as a result, is being rethought in ways that recognize the natural world of which we are a part as one of inherent uncertainty, complexity, surprise, constant fluctuations, and limited ability to control. Ecosystems are considered a moving target, and any intervention on the part of resource managers must be recognized as resulting in yet more unpredictable changes. As mechanistic views of nature are replaced by a view of ecosystems as nested in time and place, this has necessarily drawn attention to the social and institutional structures in which they are embedded.

As discussed above, the modernist paradigm of environmental management – with its emphasis on either private ownership of resources or government bureaucratic regulation – has tended to assume that natural resources are characterized by linear relationships. More recent conceptual work has embraced the adaptive management approach. Adaptive management offers an attempt to deal with the unpredictable interactions within an ecosystem and between ecosystems and people. Often summarized as a process of "learning as you go," adaptive management can be seen as an alternative to the deterministic management models of the past: with the incorporation of a direct feedback loop, both scientific information and local experience is used to modify, adapt, and generally improve resource management plans (Halbert 1993). Given this integrated approach, some scholars of adaptive management have emphasized the significant role that can potentially be played by traditional ecological knowledge, practices, and institutions that are based in local community systems (and thus situated in immediate experience and direct engagement).

Locally constituted property regimes fit neatly, it has been argued, with the complex, changing physical environments of the adjacent resources. In this sense, common property regimes can be considered a practical necessity. First, the spatial and temporal scales relied upon by the community of local practitioners can often be the most appropriate for adaptive management techniques. Second, local or traditional bodies are most consciously attuned to the human impact on adjacent resources and thus best able – when these occur nearby in time and space and are observable with the tools or skills local observers have available – to recognize the feedbacks that signal disturbance (Palsson 1998, 5). Conversely, where natural resource management is overly centralized, valuable feedback information may be unavailable (Folke, Berkes, and Colding 1998, 432). Government biologists in their big city offices may be cut off from the daily reality of engaged fishers or, perhaps more accurately, the complete elimination of biologists and "gumboot" scientists as resources may be reallocated in increasingly bureaucratized negotiations. The general conclusion is that common property regimes show greater flexibility and responsiveness to the dynamics of natural resources than private, individual holders, with their interest in security and alienability, or than resource management institutions of government agencies. Ostrom and Schlager make this point very clearly: "External authorities would be hard pressed to devise such institutions because they lack the information and the understanding to devise such institutions, and because they lack the commitment to ensuring their viability and longevity" (1996, 146).

FROM THEORY TO PRACTICE: THE CASE OF IISAAK

Iisaak Forest Company, which has been operating in Clayoquot Sound for the last dozen years, offers an interesting case with which to compare innovative community-based management practices with the institutions that preceded them. It also shows how the development of such practices necessarily raises complex issues specific to a particular case.

The trigger for the development of new institutions was the massive environmental protest against the plans of the main forest company operating in Clayoquot Sound – MacMillan Bloedel (later Weyerhaeuser) – for large-scale clear-cuts. In what was widely known as "the war in the woods," the five main environmental organizations in the area – Greenpeace, Sierra Club, the Natural Resources Defense Council, the Western Canada Wilderness Committee, and the Friends of Clayoquot Sound – allied with the First Nations of Clayoquot Sound, the Ahousaht, Tla-o-qui-aht, Hesquiaht, Toquaht, and Ucluelet First Nations, to bring international attention to corporate logging operations in what remained of the region's old-growth valleys. Consequently, in October 1993 the provincial government established the innovative Scientific Panel for Sustainable Forest Practices in Clayoquot Sound, a panel of experts from the Nuu-chah-nulth communities, along with academics from a number of disciplines. They were tasked to review the existing forest management standards for Clayoquot Sound and to make recommendations for improvements and changes (Clayoquot Sound Scientific Panel 1995). The goal of the Scientific Panel was to develop world-class standards for sustainable forest management by combining traditional and scientific knowledge. Its protocols, or procedures by which it reached a decision, largely reflected the Nuu-chah-nulth approach to group processes, characterized "by a demonstrable and inclusive respect for one another, for different values, and for data founded both in science and 'lived experience.'" Under the panel's recommendations, the annual cut in Clayoquot Sound was reduced to 200,000 cubic metres. It should be noted, however, that given the challenging circumstances under which forest practices had to be reconstituted, less than 17,000 cubic metres was taken out in 1998 (Yakabuski 2008).

The lumber companies were forced to take stock of their position. Under the glare of the international spotlight, MacMillan Bloedel / Weyerhaeuser decided that a new model was necessary for the management of their Tree Farm License, an area-based forest tenure covering approximately 87,000 hectares. In 1998, the company negotiated a partnership with Ma-Mook Natural Resources

Limited, a corporation formed in 1997 to represent the economic interests of the five Nuu-chah-nulth nations. The partnership was called Iisaak (Nuu-chah-nulth for "respect") Forest Resources Ltd. Initially Ma-Mook held 51 percent ownership of Iisaak, but in 2005 they purchased the remaining 49 percent share from Weyerhauser, thus making Iisaak a 100 percent privately owned First Nations forest company. Konrad Yakabuski (2008) explains the break in terms of differing objectives: "Weyerhaeuser focused only on profitability. After all, its shareholders demanded nothing less. Iisaak also wanted to make money, but it had broader social and environmental objectives as well." As Yakabuski also notes, it would be a difficult circle for Iisaak to square, particularly given the debt burdens it now shouldered as a result of the purchase, and the higher timber prices required to sustain their aspirations.

Iisaak's business objectives were "to reduce the risk and uncertainty previously associated with harvesting operations in Clayoquot Sound by reconciling the long standing conflict over logging in the area through the leadership and initiative of First Nations" (British Columbia Ministry of Forests 1999). Iisaak states as a guiding principle the Nuu-chah-nulth philosophy *hishuk ish ts'awalk* or "everything is one." This concept describes fundamental relationships within the environment: "It connotes both the sacredness of the natural world and respect for all life ... These principles have shaped Nuu-chah-nulth land and resource use practices for centuries, and they continue to guide management decisions in the area today" (UNESCO 1999). "We understand that we cannot manage nature," explained Frank Roman, a councillor of the Ahousaht First Nations: "We can only manage ourselves."

Although the huge challenge of implementing these aspirations still lay ahead, the sincerity of the commitment to proceed differently from past practices was evident to all: the immediate results of this shift in ownership rights were, at least in the domains of perception, reputation and politics, remarkable. Business leaders welcomed, after years of controversy and confrontation under the glare of the international media, the progress towards certainty and stability. At least at the start, the provincial government weighed in by subsidizing (through lower stumpage payments) the cost of logging being conducted by Iisaak. In 1999, most of the major environmental groups signed a memorandum of understanding with Iisaak, backed Iisaak's application for eco-certification through the Forest

Stewardship Council (achieved in July 2001), offered their help to internationally market the wood as a niche, premium product, and pledged to "support First Nations in their aspirations to fully participate in a diversified and sustainable community economy and in their aspirations for ecologically sound governance and management over their traditional territories." When in the summer of 2000, following a traditional prayer ceremony, Iisaak felled an old growth red cedar, company representatives, First Nations leaders, and environmentalists together clapped and cheered.

Iisaak committed itself to making Clayoquot Sound a leading global example of ecologically sensitive forest management. Part of their strategy was to start measuring the value of the forest in terms other than simply timber (for example, in terms of ecotourism, undervalued species, and carbon storage). Trees would be selected with an emphasis on leaving forest ecosystems intact: for example, "variable-retention" techniques aimed at ensuring that the trees left standing reflect the pre-logging composition; a lighter footprint would be achieved by removing the timber by helicopter instead of by road; and the annual harvest would be determined by what a local planning process thought the forest ecosystem can handle, not what an outside government official decided.

Until 2009, this local planning process involved an administrative body positioned at the community-government interface known as the Central Region Board (CRB). The CRB had been created in 1994 as part of the treaty negotiations between the province and the five First Nations. The Nuu-chah-nulth had been demanding that the government acknowledge, pending the signing of a final treaty, that the hereditary chiefs were the ones responsible for protecting and preserving their traditional territories for succeeding generations. In response, the CRB was charged with implementing new collaborative management processes. The CRB was composed of five Nuu-chah-nulth representatives (one from each of the five Central Region First Nations) and five local, non-native representatives appointed by the provincial government. For several years, logging operations were mostly held in abeyance while the board continued to review the detailed forest stewardship plans forward to it by Iisaak. In practice, CRB decision making aimed to operate on the basis of consensus. But divisions appeared in 2001 when consideration of a land use question was forced to an explicit vote in which environmental concerns seemed clearly isolated (Dobell and Bunton 2001). When the

CRB approved watershed development plans in 2006 that endorsed logging in untouched old growth areas, for the first time, environmental groups angrily denounced the decision. For its part, the CRB confirmed that the watershed plans met the principles, recommendations, and restrictions set out by the Scientific Panel for Sustainable Forest Practices in Clayoquot Sound. However, whereas the board saw its task as balancing economic activity with environmental protection, opponents to the plans saw all pristine, old growth valleys as sacrosanct.

Although the breadth of community support and joint action was unprecedented, not all groups had been equally supportive. Friends of Clayoquot Sound (FOCS) focused attention on the global importance, given the imminent threats posed to what remained of the world's intact temperate rain forests, of the old growth valleys. FOCS remained officially opposed to the logging of old growth under any circumstances and, wanting to maintain an independent advocacy role, it did not join the consensus reached by the other four main environmental groups. Although FOCS nonetheless promised to avoid serious conflict with Iisaak's forest practices, it did continue to protest the logging operations of the other main logging operation in the region, Interfor (International Forest Products, the other big tenure holder), arguing that it had not gained the same degree of community support. In 2007, Interfor sold their holdings in the area to Ma-Mook Natural Resources Limited (which also owns Iisaak), thereby giving the privately owned First Nations company full control of forest tenure in Clayoquot Sound.

Before harvesting in a particular region, a framework would be put in place to identify culturally significant places. Unlike other logging companies, Iisaak would not operate in any traditional territory without consulting with the ha'wih (hereditary chiefs) in whose territory they planned to work. In the eyes of the First Nations communities, acquiring control over the management of their adjacent natural resources was seen as an essential step toward autonomy. The shift in the logging industry out of corporate hands and into the local community was about self-governance: "we are not fighting logging," explained Cliff Atleo, head of the Nuu-chah-nulth Tribal Council: "We were fighting how they were doing it." Accordingly, resource management in Clayoquot Sound was expected to generate economic and social benefits for the First Nations communities reeling from the death of the fishing industry, suffering high unemployment rates, and grappling with unresolved land claims. Still, as a privately owned company Iisaak also needed to turn a profit. Ideally, the profits would then be reinvested in local sawmills, which could process raw logs into the high-end finished wood products that could capture premium prices from environmentally sensitive customers. All in all, it was a tough circle to square, especially considering the competition coming from plantation forests in southern America and South America, which showed less concern for the triple bottom line. With the acquisition of the region's tree forest licenses at the cost of millions of dollars, on top of annual rent and license fees, by the end of 2007 Iisaak was struggling just to pay off debt.

The most significant – and problematic – issue in the Clayoquot Sound context was Iisaak's original commitment to set aside and protect undeveloped areas that were deemed "eehmiis" (Nuu-chah-nulth for "very, very precious"). As the harsh realities of operating a profitable logging practice according to stricter and more costly requirements became clearer, more attention was focused on the development of a marketing strategy that would ensure that Iisaak's logs could sell for a premium in the emerging market for environmentally audited products. One of the still remaining big unknowns has been the question of whether global consumers, whose pressure had done so much to bring the shifts in resource management in Clayoquot Sound, are prepared to pay a premium for the labour- and capital-intensive operations. The readiest niche available for Iisaak was cedar, a high-value species less vulnerable to the collapse of timber prices. Only a limited amount of second-growth was ready for harvest. So in 2008–09, as noted above, the company began targeting old growth cedar in specific intact ancient valleys. Before then, the cutting of old growth timber had occurred in previously developed areas of Clayoquot Sound (that is, not in areas considered pristine, or untouched by industrial logging).

With the available old growth trees running out, access to untouched watersheds (such as Hesquiaht creek and Flores Island) was considered a matter of viability for the financially strapped company. It could not meet its profitability targets without such access. However, environmental groups had assumed that the only activities allowed in the untouched watersheds would be eco-tourism and the harvest of non-timber products. They say that since these areas are pristine they meet the definition of "eehmis." Thus, they are areas in which no cutting whatsoever should take place. But the original agreement failed to specify who in fact would make this determination. As long as environmental groups and the First Nations were allied together against industrial logging practices, there was little need to parse the difference between pristine and precious. But when the alliance began to fray, Iisaak's main response was to say that the determination of where to log lay in the hands of the First Nations. Though well aware of the consequences of losing the environmental groups' approval, the First Nations nonetheless maintain that logging in these areas has the approval of the ha'wih (hereditary chiefs).

Ten years after First Nations and environmental groups joined forces in celebrating the loss of control by corporate giants, the stage is now being set, however reluctantly, for a new round of confrontation between these former allies. Previous successes in reconciling community perspectives on the social and ecological dimensions of sustainability with the imperatives of economic development were now being questioned. "I never go to the Queen and tell her how to be in her territory. What gives the right of any other society to come here and say that to me and my chiefs?" asks Frank Roman. "Give us a chance to do what we need to do on our own." To which the FOCS responds, "The entire situation here is opaque, muddy. Everything has changed in the last few years because First Nations are suddenly coming into their own as players on the territory they claim."

CONCLUSIONS

The fact that Clayoquot Sound's transformation to community-based management is clearly a work still in progress vastly complicates the challenge of drawing the right lessons. Nonetheless, as a case study in how contextualized are rights to local resources, and how difficult it can be to create recognized legitimate spaces for inclusive deliberations, resource management in Clayoquot Sound in the 1990s and 2000s can offer some limited insights.

In Clayoquot Sound, the development of participatory mechanisms raises especially complex questions of legitimacy and agency amongst the various groups claiming places at the table. Which groups speak for whom? Who speaks for the old growth cedars? Which group can claim to be representative, accountable, and eligible to participate in the contested interpretations of sustainable management? Much of the scholarly literature on community-based management tends in fact to avoid the question of how to create the conditions for communicative action, instead assuming that such conditions already exist onto which new adaptive management practices can be grafted. The literature tends to be geared more towards emphasizing the benefits of retrieving and legitimating traditional common property regimes (and their patterns of negotiation and cooperation) than in actively prescribing the crafting of new institutions.

According to Ostrom and Schlager, the full enjoyment of common property entitlements requires homogeneity of preferences, common understandings, norms of reciprocity and trust, and shared rules of collective choice among a relatively small and stable population. So what then happens when community structures, to the extent that they pre-exist, are fluid and highly contested? In Clayoquot Sound, the most significant challenges and ambiguities concern the diversity of scales: from those representing a small village's unemployed youth to those representing Earth's endangered old growth rainforests. The emergence of the Central Region Board provided the potential for an institutional presence. But the CRB was a creation of the Interim Measures Agreement between the government and the First Nations, and its efforts in developing effective ways to reconcile differing community perspectives evidently required a longer time horizon than was allowed by the twists and turns of the treaty process.

Everyone cheered when the first tree forest license was transferred to Iisaak, the first wholly owned First Nations company. Guided by First Nations values such as "everything is one" Iisaak's approach offered a fundamentally different approach from that of its predecessors. But questions remain. Are their resources any better equipped to take on new notions of adaptive management with an allegiance to precautionary approaches? While on the one hand the creation of Iisaak was part of a process of recognizing local rights and traditional knowledges, Iisaak is also a modern corporation. At what point does an indigenous knowledge or experience count as traditional for the purpose of being included in the community authorized to manage the local resources? While it is true that external management institutions are often cut off from the daily reality of engaged ecologically based forestry, as is argued by the common property literature cited above, it can similarly be true that knowledge of complex large-scale systems depends on a greater capacity for the integration of data and models than is held in the local community. Is the capacity there to enter into complex financial and commercial relations in a globalized market and persuade investors and consumers to support viable and sustainable forestry operations?

The 1993 "war in the woods" proved to many that the old industrial model of logging was no longer working in Clayoquot Sound. Had they acted sooner, or been given more time, perhaps the big companies could have developed their own technical solutions to the challenges of ecologically-based forest management in the region. What is nonetheless clear is that, to paraphrase Bromley as quoted above, the resource claims of outside corporations were no longer acknowledged or recognized as legitimate by "those forced to forswear interest in the benefit stream." In sharp contrast, the promotion of local control of resource management brought immediate returns in terms of the peace and stability required to manage the forest economy. But who exactly are the ones with the interest? What exactly is the community when one speaks of community-based management in Clayoquot Sound?

Recognition of the problems of the old resource management model and the necessary shape of the new remain highly contested. At stake in this process are the very mechanisms of participation: whose frameworks and interests ought to be recognized in the management of a community's adjacent natural resources? Why, exactly, and to what end? And at the heart of this process lies the widely accepted need to build local decision-making capacity. As Rod has underlined, however, when the legitimacy of learning processes and consensus seeking is at stake, the concern can never be solely with single decisions or particular outcomes: "It is on relationships, not individual transactions; it is on building a track record, not recording individual victories; it is on a social context where mutual gains from continuing cooperation, not concentrated winnings from competitive victories, are the goal" (Dobell and Bunton 2001).

11

Profits v. Purpose: Hybrid Companies and the Charitable Dollar

RACHEL CULLEY AND JILL R. HORWITZ

INTRODUCTION

Government programs and regulations are not the only means of advancing public purposes. Laws that enable people to organize to pursue diverse goals also advance the public interest. For-profit corporations raise capital for profitable commerce; charities and other nonprofits dedicate themselves to missions in the public interest, whether through support by voluntary contributions, government grants, or fees for services. In each case, the presumption – often valid – is that organizations pursuing their own purposes, whether the protection of birds or the sale of pizza, advance the general public welfare.

Social entrepreneurs have frequently attempted to have the best of both worlds and blur the boundaries between nonprofit and for-profit organizational ownership types. They have introduced structures and incentives typical of profit-seeking businesses into organizations with charitable goals, assuming that an institutional setting focused on profits will outperform one focused on charity. They have encouraged for-profits to donate to charities, create affiliated foundations, and, with the blessing of state stake-holder legislation, attend to social goals aside from profit maximization. Some have created nonprofit/for-profit joint ventures and public-private partnerships and endorsed the privatization of traditional government functions and activities.

Attracted by the benefits of such blurring, several jurisdictions in the United States, Great Britain, and Canada have allowed social entrepreneurs to take a significant further step in combining legal elements from nonprofit and for-profit forms. They have authorized several types of hybrid corporations but have gained the most experience with a particular variant of the limited liability company. In 2005, the United Kingdom introduced the Community Interest Company into its Company Act. In the US, the Low-Profit Limited Liability Company (L3C) is rapidly proliferating across state business codes. In Canada, British Columbia adopted an analogous hybrid structure, the Community Contribution Company (C3) through an amendment to the Business Corporations Act in 2012, and Nova Scotia is following suit.

The idea underlying hybrids is that by drawing both on the for-profit motive to seek profits and the nonprofit motive to advance the public good, they will serve public purposes in a new, maybe better, way than traditional forms. This view has some plausibility. After all, as Professor Rod Dobell has observed, "people interact differently in different institutional settings, with their different reward systems or incentive structures."[1] Indeed, proponents have made expansive claims for hybrids – claims related to the benefits of leveraging charitable dollars for social purposes, marketing to potential investors, establishing credibility with the public, harnessing the superior efficiency of for-profit organization and market-based practices, providing historical continuity, and enhancing the ability for donors/investors to control social purpose organizations – all of which we address in this chapter. In addition to these broad justifications for hybrids, we also address the narrow, legal justification for the American L3C, because it highlights the difficulty of blending forms.

In evaluating the claims in favor of hybrids, we highlight the potential costs of blending nonprofit and for-profit goals into one entity. In particular, we conclude that the American L3C is, at a minimum, unnecessary and may be undesirable. In doing so, we identify four types of problems raised by the L3C, and to at least some extent by other hybrid models: (1) their internal, legal incoherence; (2) the risk to charitable assets and the potential for inappropriate use of tax subsidies; (3) the problematic assumption that for-profits are more efficient than nonprofit or government alternatives; and (4) the potentially inappropriate use of government imprimatur. We recognize, however, the increasing and unyielding limits on the ability of nonprofits to raise capital. L3Cs may well offer a new method for accessing capital while avoiding conversions to fully for-profit ownership. Yet despite the potential benefits, we argue that the risks to charitable dollars and purposes likely outweigh the benefits of hybrid entities.

FOR-PROFIT MEANS FOR NONPROFIT ENDS

To establish a new private organization, its founders must choose a legal structure. A social entrepreneur may use her own person as the legal entity, providing labour or personal assets to advance her goals. Founders more typically establish a separate organization. For centuries, such private organizations have come in two broad forms, for-profit and nonprofit, each believed to advance general welfare but in different ways. For-profits typically benefit society by selling goods or services for which people are willing to pay, competing with each other in doing so, thereby both serving public benefit and making a profit. Nonprofits typically dedicate their assets to a specific purpose that benefits society, such as an educational, scientific, or charitable purpose. These two forms sometimes engage in similar or even identical activities. In the United States, for example, nonprofit and for-profit hospitals compete for patients and fees in the same markets.

Nonprofits and for-profits, however, operate with different legal opportunities and constraints. For-profits raise private capital and typically pay taxes on profits. They are expected to return profits to investors; indeed, it is sometimes difficult for for-profits to embrace social ends, their expansive statements about stakeholder rights notwithstanding. Nonprofits embrace a broader set of purposes. Although they may make profits, they are forbidden to distribute them to private shareholders. They may also benefit from various tax advantages.

The current enthusiasm for hybrids reflects the judgment that this division of the organizational world into for-profit and nonprofit entities is too stark, that it does not appropriately reflect the diverse mixtures of private benefits and public ones that organizations can provide. Seeking novel ways to structure organizations and the incentives that operate within them, social entrepreneurs have sought to combine some of the strengths and advantages of each form of organizations.

The L3C

The L3C is a relatively new US for-profit/nonprofit hybrid based on the limited liability company form, which allows partners to benefit from both limited liability (in which a person's liability is capped at their investment in the company) and pass-through taxation (in which the partners are taxed individually, but the partnership is not directly taxed). Early L3C proponents sought to design an entity that would attract charitable and equity capital by removing legal barriers to for-profit enterprises receiving loans or capital investments from a particular form of charitable entity known as a "private foundation." These advocates have persisted, unsuccessfully, in pressing federal legislation to ease the flow of private foundation funds to L3Cs. Other proponents of the form have focused more generally on the need for private capital to advance various laudable goals.

State law governs L3Cs. Vermont enacted the first L3C statute in 2008, and since then at least nine other states have passed such statutes. Several others have similar legislation pending. After passing a statute in June 2013 and incorporating over one hundred L3Cs, North Carolina eliminated the form in January 2014.[2] Statutes typically require that L3Cs be formed to significantly further "one or more charitable or educational purposes."[3] Although the precise number of L3Cs is unknown, as of 2012 there were over 170 registered L3Cs in Vermont[4] and in 2014, over 200 in Michigan.[5]

Benefit and Flexible Purpose Corporations

Some US states have authorized other hybrid forms than the L3C. In 2009, Maryland was the first state authorizing benefit corporations, and by 2014 almost half the states had passed laws authorizing benefit corporations.[6] Co-drafted by the Maryland legislature and B Lab – a nonprofit, charitable corporation that offers certification to businesses that amend their governing documents to reflect the goal of seeking to "solve social and environmental problems"[7] – the legislation requires benefit corporations to "have the purpose of creating a general public benefit," defined as "a material, positive impact on society and the environment, as measured by a third–party standard, through activities that promote a combination of specific public benefits."[8] The statute explicitly enables directors to consider environmental and social concerns in their corporate decision making, in addition to the interests of shareholders.[9] Unlike L3Cs, benefit corporations are not required to pursue charitable social purposes.

California, which also allows Benefit Corporations, was the first state to permit Flexible Purpose Corporations, entities that have the primary purpose of profit-making but also include a "special purpose" in their articles of incorporation. In addition to the charitable purposes permitted by the benefit corporation form, special purposes include charitable activities that minimize the adverse effects of a corporation's activities on its employees, suppliers, customers, and creditors, community, or environment.[10] The form is meant to protect directors from liability if they consider social or environmental goals, instead of profits, in their decision making.

Community Interest Companies

Developed in the United Kingdom through its Company Law and currently available in England, Wales, Scotland, and Northern Ireland, Community Interest Companies (CICs) were developed for entrepreneurs wishing to benefit the community, broadly defined, rather than company owners. A corporation can satisfy this requirement according to a reasonable-person standard that protects against a narrow definition of the community such as "my family," "my friends," or "regular drinkers of ABC beer."[11] The requirements include an "asset lock," in which both profits and any assets that exist upon dissolution cannot be distributed, except as permitted by legislation or by transfer to another CIC or a charity. The United Kingdom government, unlike US states, created a new regulatory structure to oversee the hybrid organizations. An independent public office holder known as the CIC regulator serves as a "light touch regulator" who encourages the "development of the CIC brand and provide[s] guidance and assistance on matters relating to CICs."[12] When developed there were stringent limits on the percentage of profits that a CIC may distribute to investors.[13] As of October 2014 the laws were loosened to allow CICs to pay individual shareholders an unlimited amount in annual dividends subject to a cap of 35 percent of distributable profits on total dividend payments.

CICs are required to register their existence, include the CIC designation in their name, and apply to the Regulator for special community interest status. Recent tallies have identified over 6,000 registered CICs in the United Kingdom.[14]

British Columbia and Social Entrepreneurship

British Columbia has been at the forefront of Canadian efforts to embrace social entrepreneurship.[15] It created Canada's first parliamentary secretary for social entrepreneurship in 2010, an Advisory Council on Social Entrepreneurship with the mandate to increase social innovation, and an Assistant Deputy Ministers' Committee on Social Entrepreneurship organized to maximize social innovation within government. After extensive consultations about adding a new hybrid corporate form based on the British CIC model,[16] in 2012 the province amended the BC Business Corporations Act to allow a new social enterprise company known as a Community Contribution Company (C3).

A for-profit company registered in BC may apply its profits to charitable endeavors or attempt to attract investors with promises that those profits will be used, in part or full, for charitable purposes. Short of private contracting between the company and its investors, however, there is no way for a for-profit to make restrictions on its purposes or shareholder payouts binding or enforceable. The province intended the new hybrid company form to address this gap.

A C3 must adopt a statement of its status in its notice of articles and include the term "community contribution company" in its name. The companies exist with several restrictions. C3s must (1) cap dividends at 40 percent of annual profits plus any unused dividend amount for any previous financial year, (2) restrict transfers to qualified entities (i.e., a registered charity, a community service cooperative, or a prescribed entity or class of entities as defined in section 149.1(1) of the Income Tax Act), and (3) produce an annual community contribution report.[17] Moreover, C3s are subject to an asset lock, meaning that upon dissolution the C3 may distribute up to 60 percent of its assets to shareholders and the rest must go to a qualified organization. Unlike the British model and a recent analogue in Nova Scotia, which has a community interest company regulator,[18] there is no C3 oversight body. C3s are taxable entities and are subject to securities law.

JUSTIFICATIONS FOR HYBRIDS

Proponents of L3Cs have advanced several more or less convincing justifications for L3Cs that apply to hybrid organizations more generally. Some social entrepreneurs argue that hybrids will address the concern that nonprofits, unlike for-profits, are either unduly constrained by regulation or inherently inefficient. Others ground their support for hybrids in historical practice, arguing that government has always relied on for-profits to provide public goods; the L3C merely signals a return to America's colonial corporate practices. Finally, and perhaps most convincingly, observers contend that the new legal designation will help market a company's social commitment to potential philanthropists, thereby bringing much-needed capital to social ends. Before turning to these justifications, we examine the initial goal of L3C proponents in the United States, one that involves relieving perceived legal restrictions on certain types of nonprofit foundations on making investments in for-profit enterprises.

Program Related Investments

Understanding the primary legal justification for L3Cs in the United States – and its inherent contradictions – requires background regarding regulation of a nonprofit form called a private foundation. Like public charities, private foundations are legal entities meant to advance philanthropic purposes, but they typically do so through making grants rather than operating programs, and their funding comes from a family or small number of people rather than from donations by the public. Although ordinarily exempt from income taxes, they enjoy fewer tax benefits than public charities. In the United States, federal law also requires that they make annual distributions of at least 5 percent of the previous year's assets in furtherance of their charitable purpose – typically as grants to operating charities – and imposes sizeable fines if they fail to make these payouts within a two-year period.[19] If they further the foundation's purposes, some or all of the 5 percent may be in the form of Program Related Investments (PRIS), for example below-market rate loans to for-profit businesses (once repaid, the annual payout requirement is increased by the amount of the principal repayment).[20] In the canonical example, the Gates Foundation invested in a private company to accelerate the discovery, development, and adoption of health interventions designed to reduce disease in developing countries.[21] The IRS has recently issued proposed regulations providing other examples of qualifying PRIs, including combating environmental deterioration and building a child-care facility in a low-income neighbourhood.[22]

PRIs are uncommon, less than 1 percent of private foundation distributions. L3C advocates believe this is because foundations find them too risky.[23] The IRS may disallow a PRI if the investment does not advance a foundation's particular purpose. Having disallowed a PRI, the IRS may impose large excise taxes on the foundation and, in rare cases, personal liability on its managers.[24] Although such risks are small for the many foundations with very broadly worded purposes, foundations typically draft PRI agreements carefully. Some seek advance approval from the IRS by requesting a private-letter ruling, a time-consuming and expensive process – lawyers' fees and IRS filing fees are approximately ten thousand dollars.[25]

Some hybrid proponents and many state legislators believe that L3Cs will make the PRI process easier or even obviate the need for it altogether.[26] The memorandum introducing the New York L3C legislation, for example, explained, "The business entity form and legislation were drafted with the goal of complying with federal IRS regulations relevant to PRIs by foundations. Such compliance is anticipated to make L3Cs useful vehicles for PRI investment – and ... [hopefully to] obviate the need for individual IRS private letter rulings."[27]

With this goal in mind, state legislatures drafted L3C statutes to mirror the relevant regulations. Although L3C statutes may appear in amendments to corporations, LLC, or other sections of state statutes, the key provisions all use the same language as the federal regulations. They require an L3C to meet the following conditions: it must significantly advance one or more charitable or educational purposes;[28] it would not have formed but for the company's relationship to the accomplishment of charitable or educational purposes; and "no significant purpose of the company is the production of income or the appreciation of property; provided, however, that the fact that a person produces significant income or capital appreciation shall not, in the absence of other factors, be conclusive evidence of a significant purpose involving the production of income or the appreciation of property."[29] The L3C also may not advance political or legislative purposes as defined by the tax code.

Nonetheless, these statutes are unlikely to address the inherent challenges to raising PRI funding.[30] Regardless of the applicants' legal form, private foundations considering making a PRI request must engage in an organization-specific determination for each PRI "that carefully takes into account the foundation's mission, the purpose of the organization receiving the investment, the relationship of the receiving organization's purpose to the foundation's mission, and how the governance and financial structure of the receiving organization ensures that the receiving organization will operate within the PRI requirements. At a minimum, the last-mentioned issue requires the foundation to carefully monitor the activities of the receiving organization."[31]

The IRS could loosen its standards for PRIs, but it is unlikely that the L3C form will affect "federal tax authority approval of an unduly risky, low-return, private-foundation investment ... being characterized as a ... PRI."[32] It also is possible that federal L3C legislation could be drafted to provide for the rebuttable presumption of a valid PRI investment, but even that would still require individualized analysis.[33] In fact, in 2013, Congress did not move on legislation – the Philanthropic Facilitation Act – that would streamline the PRI process.[34]

To date, neither the IRS nor Congress has demonstrated any intention to streamline the process for approving PRIs or eliminate the institution-specific review process.[35] In fact, the IRS has issued little advice on PRIs at all: it has issued a revenue ruling allowing a private foundation to offer low interest rate loans, otherwise unavailable, to blind people to allow them to establish their own businesses[36] and a private letter ruling permitting a foundation to make an investment in a for-profit limited liability company under terms that involved substantial ongoing control by the investing foundation to ensure the appropriate use of the funds.[37] Moreover, Congress has increasingly policed nonprofit organizations for abuses related to funneling nonprofit dollars to private parties, and it is unlikely that legislators are willing to loosen nonprofit tax rules.[38]

Recognizing the limitations of L3Cs, a committee of the American Bar Association Business Section registered strong opposition to the new form.[39] It issued a resolution stating that "the promotion of L3C legislation has led to the incorrect assumptions that ...

using the L3C structure somehow facilitates the PRI process; and ... structuring an enterprise to receive PRIs can and should be simple and straightforward."[40] It also emphasized the organization-specific nature of PRI letter rulings and urged "all state legislatures not to adopt L3C legislation."[41] As the ABA Committee recognized, the new L3C statutes will not and cannot address the specific federal tax problem that was the ostensible reason for their creation. Because valid PRIs require a match between a funder and a recipient, one cannot award any organizational type or even any particular organization something akin to a PRI license or a generally applicable PRI seal of approval.

Marketing

Hybrid companies are generally required to include their status in their name. The requirement also helps the hybrid publicize its social purpose and credibly market its intentions to potential philanthropically minded investors.[42] Indeed, early L3Cs identified the "halo-effect" as their motivation for adoption of the form.[43] Other marketing methods, such as obtaining B-Corp status, may be less effective branding methods than hybrid status because they are purely voluntary and are unrecognized or regulated by the state.[44]

Nonetheless, the form itself may mislead investors and the public. Investments in PRIs, and other hybrids "raise a host of complicated non-tax issues, including ... potential conflicts of fiduciary duty for the foundation trustees, securities law concerns, and 'exit rights' for the foundation."[45] Moreover, unlike nonprofit law, which grants oversight powers to attorneys general and tax authorities, current L3C statutes in US states do not charge any regulatory body with monitoring the missions of hybrids. Although the government imprimatur may be useful to the enterprise in raising funds, it may also mislead the public – and even regulators – into thinking that the government guarantees the for-profit's social mission or that the entity is exempt from rules governing for-profit investing, such as securities and solicitation rules.

Although the same challenges can be made to PRI processes, private foundations must ensure that the grantee remains qualified for the PRI, and they will risk excise taxes, or even loss of tax-exempt status, if they do not monitor their grantees sufficiently. Moreover, it would be difficult for even a conscientious private foundation to certify that the grantee L3C is pursuing appropriate non-pecuniary goals if the purpose of foundation investment is to subsidize private investors.

Of course one could simply treat L3Cs as charities, as the Illinois attorney general has done. This is not possible in some jurisdictions; British CICs may not obtain charitable status, although charities may establish CICs as charitable subsidiaries.[46] But even where it is possible, treating hybrids as charities comes with another set of risks, such as setting precedent for regulation of other legal forms such as charitable remainder and lead trusts that have traditionally, and for good reason, remained outside the aegis of the attorney general. Unlike for-profits and nonprofits, for which people roughly understand the risks of investments or donations, the public and others are quite likely to misunderstand the degree to which their interests in hybrids and their activities are being monitored and protected.

For-Profit v. Nonprofit Efficiency

Social entrepreneurs commonly claim that for-profits are more efficient than nonprofits. They blame the relative inefficiency of nonprofits on, for example, charities law, which forbids nonprofits from primarily seeking profits and distributing them to private owners, being unduly constraining;[47] the lack of competition they face;[48] and rules forbidding nonprofits from making profits or rules requiring nonprofits to operate at a deficit.[49] Legislators have similarly seen L3Cs as the way to apply hard-headed business methods to social problems. As New York legislators explained, "L3Cs share the operating efficiencies of a for-profit along with a reduced regulatory structure, and the social purposes of a nonprofit organization."[50]

These claims are largely wrong. The over two million nonprofits in the United States operate in robust markets.[51] Many compete with other nonprofits (e.g., for limited charitable donations), or even with for-profit or government entities, to sell goods and services. Moreover, they are permitted to make profits, and they do. Although Harvard University has lost money over the past few years, its revenues have typically been considerably greater than its expenses, and it reported a 2009 fund balance (net assets) of almost 31 billion dollars.[52] On a smaller scale, the Girl Scouts of Southeastern Michigan earned a $56,103 profit and held a fund balance of approximately $21 million dollars in 2009.[53]

One should also not accept on faith the view, as some do,[54] that for-profits are more efficient than nonprofits. Nonprofits are permitted to use some of the management methods typical of for-profits. For example, nonprofits may use financial incentives – including salary incentives and, in some cases salary incentives tied to profits – to motivate employees to reach goals.[55]

Conclusions about relative efficiency depend, at least, on comparing organizations with the same goal. No doubt Goldman Sachs generates profits more efficiently than does the Grameen Bank, but it is likely less efficient at microlending. Where nonprofits and for-profits compete head-to-head to provide the same goods in the same market, evidence about relative efficiency is mixed, with many studies finding that nonprofits are superior or that there is no difference in efficiency.[56]

Historical Arguments

Scholars have argued that government has never been able to solve social problems alone and that reliance on for-profits has an admirable historical pedigree. According to Professor Linda Smiddy, "social enterprise is simply the newest manifestation of historically recurring efforts to use business forms and methods to achieve public goals. For example, during the post-colonial period of the United States, privately-owned enterprises built many of the country's turnpikes and bridges – projects too large to be financed by the fledgling country's economy."[57]

Although social enterprise is an old concept, the historical argument has been short on critical details. Discussing public-private governance in colonial America, Professor Bill Novak explained: "A classic example of early American public-private governance was the use of waterlot grants to develop New York City's waterfront. While many have seen only private interests and perhaps more than a bit of private speculation and public corruption in the distribution of the city's waterfront property to private entities, Hartog portrays the waterlot system as a creative mode of public-private development and regulation. The city marshaled private energies and equity for development through the granting of private property rights while at the same time maintaining public control and regulatory oversight."[58]

The key point here is that the for-profit entities were under the tight control of the government. Indeed, the very use of the corporate form was understood historically not as a right held by private, profit-seeking activities but rather a privilege granted by the sovereign.

Access to Capital and the Case for Hybrids

Perhaps the most convincing justification for a new form is that it will attract new capital for social needs. Some L3C proponents have advanced a particular example of how this might happen – leveraging PRIs to reduce risk for private investors. They have proposed an investment structure with three tranches. In the lowest level, foundations would demand the lowest returns, allowing profits to subsidize the other levels of investments. In the middle level, socially conscious investors would accept below-market returns as the cost of investing in a market-based enterprise with social goals. At the top level, ordinary, profit-maximizing investors would demand market rates (or higher), which would be available through subsidies from the other levels of investments.[59] These investors could receive a higher rate of return than they would typically earn in a similarly risky investment. More intuitively, imagine an analogous home mortgage: "the foundation would obtain a higher-risk second mortgage while the commercial investors obtain a first mortgage."[60] The loan structure makes the second riskier than the first, despite the investment in the same property.

On its face, the proposal seems like a winner for investors and society. What's the problem? The problem is that the structure eases restrictions on charitable assets – tax-exempt foundation dollars that are subsidized by the government (in the United States and elsewhere) – to increase returns for private investors, an impermissible, non-charitable purpose. Since it likely involves more than incidental profit-making, it may well violate prohibitions on private inurement in charities.

Some experts disagree. Several prominent nonprofit scholars and lawyers, including a former director of the IRS Exempt Organizations Division counter that

> Private benefit depends on all of the facts and circumstances in a given situation. In fact, a PRI ... always involves some level of private benefit, but rather than a disqualifying private benefit, it is deemed incidental to the accomplishment of charitable purposes. One example in the Treasury regulations involves a

> foundation making a below-market-rate loan to a "business enterprise which is financially secure and the stock of which is listed and traded on a national exchange," in order to encourage the enterprise to establish a factory in a depressed urban area. In this example, there is clearly private benefit, since the corporation receives a below-market-rate loan from charity – but the private benefit is incidental.[61]

This rejoinder – that although these arrangements are not inherently about serving a private benefit, some degree of private inurement exists with conventional PRIs – is true. But that inurement exists in one situation is not a good reason to allow it in others. PRIs are a rare exception to stringent regulations because policy-makers have concluded that their benefits outweigh their risks. And, unlike hybrids, the IRS closely monitors them and requires strict supervision by granting foundations. Legal forms designed to make the PRIs more commonplace will only lead to more risk of using charitable dollars to pursue profits.

Finally, there are alternatives available to profit-minded entrepreneurs and the government.[62] Social entrepreneurs may form for-profit companies and donate their profits to charities. Those that do not like the limitation that corporations may only deduct up to 10 percent of profits donated to charities annually[63] can use the S corporation form used by other charitably minded for-profits, such as Newman's Own, and avoid this stringent limit. The government may subsidize social entrepreneurs through direct grants or through the tax exemptions and deductions they already supply. It is unclear whether there is additional benefit to allowing further, unregulated tax expenditures.

Regardless of the particular forms of corporations and subsidies, the underlying argument of L3C proponents is that current legal forms are insufficient to channel adequate funding to business-minded people who want to advance the public interest. We agree that raising money is hard, and having more of it makes it more likely that founders will achieve their private and social goals. As one law review note recently observed, "The main obstacle to operating a social enterprise as a for-profit entity is the difficulty of raising capital."[64]

But this is how the market works. Using L3Cs to save failing businesses may simply be an end run around market competition. Consider, for example, that the Maine milk cooperative, MooMilk, converted to an L3C when it was unable to survive in the competitive market after it lost an important contract with Hood Milk.[65] As Rush Limbaugh remarked, "So this is social engineering in the private sector. We're going to now reward businesses that do not make a profit if someone approves of their social mission."[66] Limbaugh might be correct: the failure of the cooperative is bad for some farmers in Maine, but might be good for social welfare. After all, Hood had cancelled its contract with MooMilk because it found cheaper organic milk suppliers closer to its plants in Connecticut.[67]

Yet some states want to use this form to prop up failing industries. The North Carolina bill was entitled An Act to Provide Enhanced Economic Development Incentives to Endangered Manufacturers and to Clarify That a Low-Profit Limited Liability Company Is a Limited Liability Company under State Law, and the preamble to the bill included the statement, "Whereas, the State of North Carolina is and should be actively engaged in economic development efforts to attract and stimulate private sector job creation and capital investors; and whereas, the furniture industry in North Carolina has been damaged by overseas competition and has now become an endangered industry in North Carolina … "[68] Even more explicitly, another advocate wrote: "An effort is underway in North Carolina to codify the L3C form and use it for furniture companies that are on the verge of going under or leaving the state. As L3Cs, these companies would be able to accept investments from private (nonprofit) foundations, which would not demand as high a return on investment as would traditional for-profit investors. And as L3Cs they would qualify as PRIs, which in turn would likely open the deep pockets of the foundations wishing to promote the community interest of a thriving furniture industry in the state."[69]

US manufacturing is suffering and communities are failing because of the attendant problems. But should the government subsidize L3Cs to prop up their favorite failing industry? Alternatives, such as grants for displaced workers, industrial development bonds, or tax-exempt nonprofit community development organizations, can do the job. It is unclear why the L3C form is superior and whether using the form to protect failing industry is welfare enhancing. Although sometimes industry subsidies may be appropriate as a method to achieve the charitable goal of community development, not all industry subsidies do so. As John Tyler explains, although creating jobs and similar activities are beneficial for society, such "social ends" alone are not appropriately deemed charitable in the exempt organizations context.[70]

Much of this essay has focused on the inappropriateness of tax-subsidized dollars lining private pockets. But what about hybrids that do not draw on government or tax-subsidized funds? Is there anything wrong, for example, with a hybrid based entirely in the realm of taxable investments, as operates in the United Kingdom and British Columbia?

First, keeping tax exemptions from applying to hybrids may not be so easy. Advocacy for exempting hybrid companies from taxation followed closely behind calls for allowing the form. [71] The Canadian Task Force on Social Finance has encouraged pension fund investing, implementation of tax incentives for social investment, and "government incentives to kick-start the flow of private capital."[72] The Parliamentary Secretary for Social Entrepreneurship Gordon Hogg has also called for tax support for social entrepreneurship.[73] And in some states, such as California, LLCs may be eligible for property tax exemptions if they are organized and operated for one of a list of particular purposes (e.g., a hospital) even if they are not charities.[74]

Regardless, suppose that no government dollars would find their way to these new entities either directly or through preferred tax status. On the one hand, one still might worry that new hybrids will crowd out private donations to fully charitable organizations, a question that is ripe for study. On the other hand, some investors might support social endeavors with low-return investments but not zero-return investments (or, rather, a return equal to the tax deduction they would get from a charitable deduction). Maybe hybrids will add new capital to socially beneficial projects, rather than crowding out nonprofits, by attracting those who believe in the relative efficiency of for-profits.[75]

Proponents think there are many such investors, as well as investors who won't donate to nonprofits because they cannot control their donations to their satisfaction but may donate to L3Cs if they can ensure that they remain a single dominant investor. But the restriction on managers' control of assets goes to the central purpose of a nonprofit. This restraint provides independence from the greed or motivations of individual persons (and the state). Autonomy is the genius of the nonprofit form.

This explanation exposes the deep incoherence of the hybrid form. Proponents often talk about a blending or balancing of profit-making and social purpose goals. Balancing is the better metaphor, because conflicts inevitably arise between charitable and personal goals. Although Professor Brakman-Reiser favours encouraging hybrids, she recognizes this difficulty and does not think they should be designated as nonprofit charities.[76] She helpfully characterizes the CIC as a model in which "other-regarding and self-regarding modes are intentionally blended. On the one hand, the CIC must provide its benefits to some relatively large class and some core of a CIC's assets must be irrevocably dedicated to community interest or charitable purposes. On the other hand, the CIC entails a kind of equity investment where the shareholders are permitted to engage in profit-taking."[77]

John Tyler has argued that a correct understanding of the L3C form resolves the tension of fiduciaries having two masters – the potentially conflicting duties to shareholders and to the charitable goal. Tyler addresses the tension arguing that "profit and value as ultimate purpose give way to charitable, exempt purposes," thereby clarifying which duty comes first.[78] Although statutes typically forbid L3Cs from adopting the production of income or the appreciation of property as a primary purpose, few states require L3Cs to pursue exclusively charitable purposes.

Moreover, even if Tyler's understanding is correct, it is not the typical understanding of how L3Cs will work. Nor is it clear how fiduciaries will interpret potential conflicts when push comes to shove. The example of the Grameen Bank is instructive. In his op-ed, "Sacrificing Microcredit for Megaprofits," bank founder Muhammed Yunus explained that "microcredit ... [gave] ... rise to its own breed of loan sharks," when profit-seeking dominated social ends.[79] The L3C similarly creates an irresolvable conflict between the necessary objective of the organization – profit – and what is espoused as the primary goal – mission. How this conflict will be resolved depends on how managerial decision making takes place. Who will decide what specific activities to undertake? At what price? How will public purposes be balanced when all these decisions are made? The schematic L3C statutes do not address how L3Cs will answer these inevitable questions.

CONCLUSION: IS THERE A ROLE FOR HYBRID ENTITIES?

The nonprofit legal form is often criticized for being "outdated."[80] Charities law is certainly old. The common law of charities derives from the Statute of Elizabeth of 1601, and lawyers in the United

States, the United Kingdom, and Canada rely on centuries-old case law when interpreting charities law. The Canada Corporations Act has not been substantially updated since it was enacted in 1917, and the UK Charities Act of 2006 signalled the first significant change to the legal definition of charitable purposes since the sixteenth century. Social entrepreneurs have embraced hybrid organizations as the next new thing that will modernize this ancient law.

But change for change's sake is seldom a good idea, and most arguments advanced in support of hybrids are unpersuasive. It is unlikely that the L3C form will increase the use of PRIs in the United States and even less clear that such a change would be desirable. Automating the PRI process by relying on the hybrid legal structure, particularly if the PRI is used to undergird a tranched funding model, would increase the risk that charitable assets will be used for impermissible or non-charitable purposes, allowing L3Cs to benefit either directly or indirectly in tax advantages meant only for nonprofit charities. Moreover, it might be difficult for charitable fiduciaries to attend to their nonprofit organizational duties rather than their for-profit goals.

Nonetheless, the increasing and unyielding difficulty of raising charitable capital must be addressed, and hybrids may provide one answer. Although the form has largely been limited to small organizations in the United States, they offer an intriguing option for large nonprofits. For example, American nonprofit hospitals that are struggling to raise capital may fruitfully incorporate as a hybrid rather than convert to for-profit form.

However, we shouldn't gamble on hybrids without answering several questions. Some of them are empirical: Will hybrids attract new entrepreneurs and new capital to social causes, thereby increasing the total capital available for social enterprise? Or will hybrids merely crowd out either charitable or public spending? Some questions are legal: When profit-making and charitable goals conflict, which should and will prevail? To whom do directors owe their fiduciary duties? Since corporate law is largely designed to enable corporate activity, does it make sense to create a new legal form for substantive ends? Other questions are political, for example, what is the appropriate role of government in terms of facilitating private exchange in the public interest?

To assess the promise of hybrids, we need more information and analysis about the overall effects of a new form on social welfare. Unfortunately, government can be ill-suited to engage in that type of analysis. In this case, the departments that regulate business organizations such as hybrids – typically the corporations or finance departments – focus on enabling the creation of new entities. They do not regulate the tax or charities implications of those entities. It is not their job to do so. To assess hybrids, however, the analyst needs to consider the interactions among legal forms, tax law, and charities law.

Perhaps policy-makers can learn from another of Professor Dobell's lessons: "One of the well-known problems of collective action [is] that apparently rational individual agents acting in their own interest can be led to conduct that leaves everybody worse off."[81] In the case of hybrids, there are large benefits to be had with interdepartmental cooperation. Policy-makers may well decide that the benefits of encouraging social entrepreneurship, particularly the benefit of directing more money towards charitable endeavours, are worth the considerable costs of weakening the wall between the for-profit and nonprofit form (not the least of which will likely including crowding some traditional philanthropy). If they do, such a decision should be guided by comprehensive analysis that has been missing from the debate so far.

NOTES

1 A.R. Dobell, "Holarchy, Panarchy, Coyote and Raven: Creation Myths for a Research Program" (31 March 2009), http://web.uvic.ca/~rdobell/assets/papers/myths.pdf.

2 Anne Field, "North Carolina Officially Abolishes the L3C," *Forbes* (11 January 2014), http://www.forbes.com/sites/annefield/2014/01/11/north-carolina-officially-abolishes-the-l3c/.

3 *Vt. Stat. Ann.* tit. 11, § 3001 (27)(B); (A)(i); (A)(ii) (1996).

4 Vermont Secretary of State, Corporations Database, Search for "L3C," http://www.sec.state.vt.us/seek/keysrch.htm (last visited 19 Dec., 2012).

5 Michigan Department of Licensing and Regulatory Affairs, Corporation Division Business Entity Search Results, http://www.dleg.state.mi.us/bcs_corp/rs_corp.asp?s_button= sword&v_search=L3C&hiddenField=&search=Search (last visited February 3, 2012).

6 Many states, such as New York, New Jersey, Virginia, Hawaii, and California passed similar legislation as of 2014 (Marc Lifsher, *Businesses Seek State's New Benefit Corporation Status*, L.A. Times, 4 January 2012,

http://articles.latimes.com/2012/jan/04/business/la-fi-benefit-corporations-20120104; CAL. *Corp. Code* § 14600 (West 2006 & Supp. 2014); *Haw. Rev. Stat. Ann.* § 414D–253 (LexisNexis 2010); *N.Y. Bus. Corp. Law* § 1707 (McKinney 2003 & Supp. 2014); *N.J. St. Ann.* § 14A:18–1 (West 2003 & Supp. 2014); *V.A. Code Ann.* § 13.1–782 (West 2011 & Supp. 2013)). Legislation is pending in Michigan, Idaho, Montana, Florida, New Hampshire, Kansas, Minnesota, Iowa, Alaska, Kentucky, Georgia, Alabama, Ohio, and Indiana. *see Passing Legislation*, Certified B Corporation, http://www.bcorporation.net/what-are-b-corps/legislation (last visited 16 2014).

7 *What Are B Corps?* Certified B Corporation, http://www.bcorporation.net/about (last visited 16 July 2014).

8 *Md. Code Ann., Corps & Ass'ns* § 5–6C–01 (*LexisNexis* 2007 & Supp. 2013).

9 *Md Code Ann., Corps & Ass'ns* § 5–6C–07 (*LexisNexis* 2007 & Supp. 2013).

10 *Cal. Corp. Code* §§2500 – 2503 (West 2014).

11 Department of Business and Innovation Skills, chapter 2: "Preliminary Considerations," Office of the Regulator of Community Interest Companies: Information and Guidance Notes 6 (November 2012) (U.K.), https://www.gov.uk/government/uploads/system/uploads/attachment_data/file/211742/12-1334-community-interest-companies-guidance-chapter-2-preliminary-considerations.pdf.

12 Department of Business and Innovation Skills, Chapter 11*: The Regulator*, Office of the Regulator of Community Interest Companies: Information and Guidance Notes 9 (March 2013) (U.K.), https://www.gov.uk/government/uploads/system/uploads/attachment_data/file/%20211751/13-714-community-interest-companies-guidance-chapter-11-the-regulator.pdf.

13 The dividend cap has three elements: (1) a maximum dividend per share, which started at 5 percent above the Bank of England base lending rate of the paid-up value of a share and now is 20 percent of the paid-up value of a share; (2) a maximum aggregate dividend limited to the total dividend declared in terms of the profits available for distribution (currently 35 percent of the distributable profits); and (3) a limited ability to carry forward unused dividends (now five years). *See* Sara Burgess, chapter 6, *The Asset Lock*, Department for Business, Innovation and Skills (2013) (U.K.), http://webarchive.nationalarchives.gov.uk/20121021151233/http://www.bis.gov.uk/assets/cicregulator/docs/guidance/12-1149-community-interest-companies-guidance-chapter-6-the-asset-lock.pdf.

14 Regulator of Community Interest Companies, Guidance: CIC Business Activities: Forms and Step-by-Step Guidelines (16 June 2014) (U.K.), https://www.gov.uk/government/publications/community-interest-companies-business-activities/cic-business-activites-step-by-step-guidelines.

15 At this writing, Nova Scotia was the only other province to have passed hybrid legislation. There have been calls for reform in Ontario, but they have largely involved proposals to loosen restrictions on nonprofit tax law rather than broader reforms to corporate law. See, e.g., Elizabeth Mulholland, Matthew Mendelsohn, and Negin Shamshiri, *Strengthening the Third Pillar of the Canadian Union* (2011), http://mowatcentre.ca/strengthening-the-third-pillar-of-the-canadian-union/.

16 Interview with Jill Sinkwich, manager, and Tona Hetherington, policy advisor, Financial and Corporate Sector Policy Branch, Ministry of Finance, Province of British Columbia (19 July 2011).

17 *Business Corporations Act*, S.B.C. 2002, c. B–57, s. 2.2, (2014) (Can.).

18 *Community Interest Companies Act*, S.N.S. 2012 c. C–38 (Can.) (enacted but not proclaimed in force), available at http://nslegislature.ca/legc/bills/61st_4th/3rd_read/b153.htm.

19 I.R.C. §4942(a)-(e)(B) (2007).

20 I.R.C. § 4942 (i)(1) (2007).

21 I.R.S Priv. Ltr. Rul. 200603031 (Jan. 20, 2006).

22 Examples of Program-Related Investments, 77 Fed. Reg. 23, 429 (2012).

23 Malika Zouhali-Worrall, "For L3C Companies, Profit Isn't the Point," CNN Money (9 Feb., 2010), http://money.cnn.com/2010/02/08/smallbusiness/l3c_low_profit_companies.

24 I.R.C. §4944(c) (2006).

25 Rev. Proc. 2011–8, 2011-1 I.R.B. 237, § 6.01(14).

26 Robert Lang, *The For Profit with a Nonprofit Soul: PRIs and Private Letter Rulings*, Americans for Community Development, http://www.americansforcommunitydevelopment.org/downloads/PRIs andPrivate LetterRulings.pdf (last visited June 19, 2014).

27 S. S3011–2011, 2011–2012 S. Reg. Sess. (memo) (N.Y. 2011).

28 The statutes define "charitable" by referring to the definition found in the Internal Revenue Code sections dealing with the deductibility of individual charitable donations, i.e., gifts to "A corporation, trust, or . . . or foundation . . . originated and operated exclusively for religious, charitable, scientific, literary, or educational purposes, or to foster national or international amateur sports competition ... or for the prevention of cruelty to children or animals." I.R.C. §170(b)(2)(A) (2007).

29 Vt. Stat. Ann. tit. 11, § 3001 (27)(B); (A)(i); (A)(ii) (1996).

30 Sherri Begin Welch, "As L3Cs Form, Lack of Clear Criteria Leaves Room for Confusion," *Crain's Detroit Business*, 11 October 2009, http://www.crainsdetroit.com/article/20091011/SUB01/310119965/as-l3cs-form-lack-of-clear-criteria-leaves-room-for-confusion#.

31 Daniel S. Kleinberger, "A Myth Deconstructed: The Emperor's New Clothes on the Low-Profit Limited Liability Company," 35 *Del. J. Corp. L.* 879 (2010).

32 Carter G. Bishop, "The Low-Profit LLC (L3C): Program Related Investment by Proxy or Perversion?" 63 *Ark. L. Rev.* 243, 265–6 (2010).

33 J. William Callison and Allan W. Vestal, "The L3C Illusion: Why Low-Profit Limited Liability Companies Will Not Stimulate Socially Optimal Private Foundation Investment in Entrepreneurial Ventures," 35 *Vt. L. Rev.* 273 (2010).

34 *Philanthropic Facilitation Act*, H.R. 2832, 113th Cong. (2013).

35 Bishop, *The Low-Profit* LLC.

36 Rev. Rul. 78–90, 1978–1 C.B. 380.

37 I.R.S. Priv. Ltr. Rul. 200610020 (13 June 2005).

38 Senator Chuck Grassley, "Grassley Outlines Goals for Charitable Governance, Transparency: Prepared Remarks of Sen. Chuck Grassley," United States Senate Committee on Finance (10 March 2009), available at http://finance.senate.gov/newsroom/ranking/release/?id= =08fee686-8575-4bd6-9147-5c1656e52aac.

39 G. Ann Baker, "Did You Know? Flexibility for Entities Providing Medical Services," 30 *Mich. Bus. L.J.* 5 (2010).

40 ABA Committee on Limited Liability Companies, Partnerships, and Unincorporated Entities, "Resolution of the Committee on Limited Liability Companies, Partnerships, and Unincorporated Entities, Section of Business Law, American Bar Association: To Be Considered at the Committee's Meeting on April 23, 2010 (2010)," *available at* http://web.archive.org/web/20111208234828/http://meetings.abanet.org/webupload/commupload/RP519000/relatedresources/ABA_LLC_Committee-L3C_Resolution_and_explanation-2-17-10.pdf.

41 *Id.*

42 Elizabeth Carrott Minnigh, "Low-Profit Limited Liability Companies: An Unlikely Marriage of For-Profit Entities and Private Foundations," 34 *Tax Mgm't, Est., Gifts & Tr. J.* 209 (2009).

43 Elizabeth Schmidt, "Vermont's Social Hybrid Pioneers: Early Observations and Questions to Ponder," 35 *Vt. L. Rev.* 163 (2010).

44 Richard Bridge, "More Reflections on Legal Structures for Community Enterprise," BC Centre for Social Enterprise (April 2010), http://www.

centreforsocialenterprise.com/f/More_Reflections_on_Legal_ Structure_for_Community_Enterprise_April_2010.pdf.

45 Kleinberger, "A Myth Deconstructed."

46 Department of Business and Innovation Skills, chapter 1, "Introduction," Office of the Regulator of Community Interest Companies: Information and Guidance Notes 9 (Nov. 2012) (U.K.), https://www.gov.uk/government/uploads/system/uploads/attachment_data/file/211741/12-1333-community-interest-companies-guidance-chapter-1-introduction.pdf.

47 Linda O. Smiddy, "Introduction, Symposium: Corporate Creativity: The Vermont L3C & Other Developments in Social Entrepreneurship," 35 *Vt. L. Rev.* 3 (2010).

48 Anup Malani and Eric A. Posner, "The Case for For-Profit Charities," 93 *Va. L. Rev.* 2017 (2007).

49 Robert Lang and Elizabeth C. Minnigh, "The L3C, History, Basic Construct, and Legal Framework," 35 *Vt. L. Rev.* 15 (2010).

50 S. S3011–2011, 2011–2012 S. Reg. Sess. (memo) (N.Y. 2011).

51 James R. Hines, Jr., Jill R. Horwitz, and Austin Nichols, "The Attack on Nonprofit Status: A Charitable Assessment," 108 *Mich. L. Rev.* 1179 (2009).

52 Presidents and Fellows of Harvard College, IRS Form 990 (2009).

53 Girl Scouts of Macomb County, Otsikita Council, Return of Organization Exempt from Income Tax, Form 990 OMB No. 1545–0047 (2009).

54 Malani and Posner, "For-Profit Charities."

55 Hines et al., "The Attack on Nonprofit Status."

56 *Id.*

57 Smiddy, "Corporate Creativity."

58 William J. Novak, "Public-Private Governance," in *Government by Contract: Outsourcing and American Democracy* 29, 29–30 (Jody Freeman and Martha Minow eds.) (2009).

59 Lang and Minnigh, "The LC3."

60 Bishop, "The Low-Profit LLC."

61 Letter from Marcus S. Owens et al. to Willard Willard L. Boyd, III ("Letter Regarding L3C") (13 July 2011), available at http://www.intersectorl3c.com/goopages/pages_downloadgallery/downloadget.php?filename=16680.pdf&orig_name=attorney_letter_-_l3c_7-13-2011.pdf.

62 See Hines et al., "The Attack on Nonprofit Staus."

63 I.R.C. §170(b)(2)(A) (2007).

64 Matthew F. Doeringer, "Fostering Social Enterprise: A Historical and International Analysis," 20 *Duke J. Comp. & Int'l L.* 291 (2010).

65 See Nancy Artz and John Sutherland, 2010. "Low-Profit Limited Liability Companies (L3Cs): Competitiveness Implications." *Competition Forum* 8 (2): 4–5 (2010); Malika Zouhali-Worrall, "For L3C Companies, Profit Isn't the Point," CNN *Money*, Feb. 9, 2010, http://money.cnn.com/2010/02/08/smallbusiness/l3c_low_profit_companies.

66 Rush Limbaugh, "Caller Asks: Should I Take a Grant?" The Rush Limbaugh Show (8 February 2010), http://www.rushlimbaugh.com/home/daily/site_020810/content/01125112.guest.html.

67 Zouhali-Worrall, "For L3C Companies."

68 *North Carolina Endangered Manufacturing and Jobs Act*, H.R. 769, Sess. 2009. (N.C. 2009).

69 Bruce Collins, "Low-Profits," *Inside Counsel* (2 January 2008), http://www.insidecounsel.com/2008/01/02/lowprofits.

70 John Tyler, "Negating the Legal Problem of Having Two Masters: A Framework for L3C Fiduciary Duties and Accountability," 35 *Vt. L. Rev.* 117, 124 (2010).

71 For a review of tax emption issues as applied to hybrids, *see* Lloyd Hitoshi Mayer and Joseph R. Ganahl, Taxing Social Enterprise, 66 *Stan. L. Rev.* 387 (2014).

72 Canadian Task Force on Social Finance, Mobilizing Private Capital for Public Good 3 (2010), http://www.mcconnellfoundation.ca/assets/Media%20Library/Reports/FinalReport_MobilizingPrivateCapitalforPublicGood_30Nov10.pdf.

73 *Id.*

74 *Cal. Rev. & Tax. Code* § 214 (West 2009 & Supp. 2014).

75 Although the article does not address this issue explicitly, a new working paper argues that some entrepreneurs who want to pursue both profits and public purposes will be able to use the new forms to do so through building public purposes into the organizing documents and thereby protecting them. See Joseph W. Yockey, *Does Social Enterprise Law Matter?* 66 *Ala. L. Rev.* (forthcoming 2014). The article does not, however, address how the form will resolve conflicts between public benefit goals and profit-making goals when these arise, since corporate documents can simply be amended.

76 Dana Brakman Reiser, "Governing and Financing Blended Enterprise," 85 *Chi.-Kent L. Rev.* 619, 647 (2010).

77 Dana Brackman Reiser, "Charity Law's Essentials," 86 *Notre Dame L. Rev.* 1 (2011).

78 Tyler, "Negating the Legal Problem," at 139.

79 Muhammad Yunus, "Sacrificing Microcredit for Megaprofits," *New York Times*, 14 January 2011, at A23.

80 Fraser Valley Centre for Social Enterprise, "Analysis of CIC and L3C Social Enterprise Forms" (2008), http://www.centreforsocialenterprise.com/f/L3C_and_CIC_social_enterprise_models_Oct_2008.doc.

81 Dobell, "Creation Myths."

12

The Future of Computer-Supported Policy Analysis: Collaboration, Openness, Collective Intelligence, and Competition

JUSTIN LONGO

The application of computer technology in support of policy analysis in Western governments over the post-World War II period reflects both advances in the networked digital computer space and the changing nature of how policy analysis has been conceptualized and practised over that period. This chapter is an attempt to sketch the relationship between the development and adoption of computer technology and the evolution of policy analysis over the post-war period and to begin to map out possible future implications for policy analysis arising from changing organizational expectations and norms, continuing advances in the ongoing diffusion of technology innovation, and shifting approaches to governance.

Advances in information and communications technology (ICT) over the past half century have generally been viewed as positive for the practice of public administration and policy analysis, but the record of their impact has been mixed. With every significant increase in hardware power, software functionality, system reliability, and affordability, renewed enthusiasm for the ability of computer technology to transform the process of policy analysis seems to have followed. When the dust of each technological upheaval has settled, however, questions are invariably raised about whether the practice of public administration and policy analysis has been fundamentally transformed by the introduction of technology innovations or whether all that has changed are the tools by which public policy analysts carry out their traditional tasks (Hood 2008).

The question this chapter explores is whether the future of computer-supported policy analysis will be so unlike its past as to represent a fundamental transformation of practice. The factors identified that, taken together, signal a possible discontinuity between the past and future of ICT-supported policy analysis include technologies and work modes that seek to flatten traditional organizational hierarchies through support for collaboration and knowledge sharing among knowledge workers within large bureaucracies (referred to here as "enterprise social collaboration"), and a growing open governance movement aimed at increasing transparency and the infiltration of external ideas from outside of government back into the policy analysis system through the open publication of government data sources and a general openness in governance processes (labelled here as "open governance").

In the next section, a brief sketch is presented of the shared sixty-year period that has witnessed the development of the field of policy analysis and of the digital electronic computer. These developments have produced a history of computer-supported policy analysis over the post-World War II period, from the use of the first commercially available computers as large number tabulators in support of public administration and early policy analysis to today's networked, mobile ICTs as key devices in the contemporary policy analyst's toolkit. Following that sketch, two emerging trends that flow from that history are discussed: the deployment of enterprise social collaboration platforms within large bureaucratic organizations as a means for knowledge workers to connect, collaborate, and share knowledge with their colleagues across the organization and the movement to turn open government data sources for widespread public scrutiny, manipulation, and re-purposing as an operationalization of the principles of open governance. These trends are supplemented by a discussion of their implications for the policy analysis profession: how enterprise social collaboration can expand the notion of who in the organization might legitimately and effectively contribute to policy analysis beyond the traditional class of "policy analysts" and how the open governance movement can provide opportunities for external-to-government policy analysts to infiltrate the internal policy analysis system, especially when their analysis is based on previously closed data resources and analytical skills that can rival the inside-of-government position of the policy analyst.

COMPUTERS IN SUPPORT OF POLICY ANALYSIS

With their respective births emerging from World War II and a reaction to its aftermath, both computers and policy analysis were seen at the time of their invention as instruments crucial for the enhancement of the human condition (Bush 1945). Having grown up together, the digital electronic computer and the policy analysis profession are not unlike most siblings: at times benefiting from each other's advances, the computer is often seen as the golden child and policy analysis as the introspective brother who has shown moments of brightness but whose self-doubt fuels a general perception of having failed to live up to expectations (Kirp 1992). Indeed, policy analysis has been dealing with an existential crisis for most of its later middle age (Shulock 1999). Whether the growing dominance of the computer will continue to overshadow the earlier hopes for policy analysis or give policy analysis new meaning and purpose is the question this chapter explores.

But before addressing the history of computer-supported policy analysis (and since most readers will have a shared understanding of what is meant by "computers"), I should clarify what is meant here by "policy analysis": it is a core function of government in which a particular type of public servant, often referred to as a "policy analyst," provides support for decision making with the aim of contributing to better decisions than would be made in the absence of such analysis (Quade 1975). A concept of policy analysis in support of decisions having a public or collective impact can be found from ancient civilizations through to the modern age (DeLeon and Overman 1998; Dunn 1981). But it was through the publication of Lerner and Lasswell's edited volume *The Policy Sciences* (1951) that an integrated, multidisciplinary approach to the study of public problems and the development of rational solutions based on careful analysis first took shape. Harold Lasswell is widely considered to be the founder of the policy sciences, and his postwar writings provide the field with its earliest concepts. Of particular note is Lasswell's introductory chapter in *The Policy Sciences*, where he advanced "policy analysis" as a term of art, seeking to differentiate it conceptually from the social sciences generally and political science specifically.

As practised by the individual public servant, policy analysis involves a range of activities, including the identification of public problems and the determination of their extent, the assembling of evidence and analysis of the problem, the projecting of outcomes and development of strategies for dealing with trade-offs, the construction and evaluation of options for addressing the problem, the assembling of bureaucratic and civil society coalitions necessary for later policy formulation and implementation, the communication of recommendations to support decision making, and the evaluation of previously adopted policies to determine effectiveness or value (Bardach 2000; Pal 2009; Weimer and Vining 2010). Policy analysts play many roles in the policy analysis process: as information and knowledge managers, decision-support reference sources, coordinators and collaborators, boundary agents, advocates, advisors and gatekeepers. Artefacts of the policy analyst's work – either as paper documents or, increasingly, as electronic records – may take the form of draft position papers, consultative documents and strategy statements, decision notes and briefing notes, draft ministerial orders, proposals for new or amended legislation, regulations or programs, formal Cabinet submissions, and less formal Cabinet presentations.

Lasswell's vision for the policy sciences was based on social science knowledge and quantitative methods to analyze policy choices, methods strongly influenced by economics. Positivism – the application of logical and mathematical treatment to empirical evidence as the basis for determining authoritative, scientific knowledge – dominates the discipline's intellectual infrastructure, and the policy analysis profession has been strongly influenced by the training, practice, and specialization of the academics that taught succeeding generations of policy analysts (Morçöl 2001).

During the first twenty-five years of the policy analysis movement, techniques such as modelling, quantification of data, descriptive statistics, statistical inference testing, operations research and systems analysis, cost-benefit and risk-benefit analysis, Markov analysis, linear programming, dynamic programming, stochastic modelling, Bayesian analysis, quasi-linearization, invariant embedding, and general systems theory became staples of the profession (Radin 2000). This "golden era" of the policy analysis movement in the late 1960s was a time when "policy analysis was essentially quantitative analysis" (Yang 2007, 351).

Quantitative methods in policy analysis were not deployed for the sake of demonstrating elegant technical prowess, however, but in response to real social and economic pressures: expansion of the welfare state, economic malaise, emerging awareness of environmental limits, space exploration, and continuation of the Cold War provided new challenges and opportunities for quantitative policy analysis. In response to that environment, theoretical and applied advances continued to be made into the 1980s using mathematical equations and computer programming (Quade 1980) and additional advances such as system dynamics (Forrester 1971; Meadows et al. 1972; Mesarovic and Pestel 1974), Integrated Assessment Models (IAMS) for integrating science with policy (Parson and Fisher-Vanden 1997); and increasingly sophisticated simulation tools (see Wolfson, in this volume). Overall advances made in the techniques of policy analysis led Brewer (1974, 239) to suggest that the practice – as it had completed its first quarter century – might be said to be finally "emerging as an identifiable, respectable, even desirable professional activity."

Yet despite the coming of age of policy analysis in the early 1970s, debates over the real, perceived, and proposed role of the policy analyst have coloured the profession's second quarter century. While technical policy analysis rooted in quantitative methods became increasingly sophisticated during the 1970s and 1980s, high-profile failures during this period also exposed the limits of policy analysis (May 1992). Coupled with the perceived inability of quantitative policy analysis to solve public problems during the 1970s, critics of positivism argued that the attempt to model social interactions on the natural sciences model was misguided (Amy 1984), that policy wisdom should be seen as more than the results of data impressively distilled (Prince 2007; Wildavsky 1978), and that positivism was fundamentally incapable of dealing with complex problems (Fischer 1995). At the same time, the implementation problem (i.e., the disconnect between policy-making and action required on the ground to realize the intent of the policy initiative) highlighted how autonomous human behaviour and judgment was not adequately accommodated in positivist models (Dobell et al. 2001; Pressman and Wildavsky 1973).

The post-positivist movement led to calls for a balancing of softer skills along with technical mastery (Fischer 2003) and approaches such as participatory design, stakeholder involvement, citizens' input, qualitative methods, and mixed methodology, among others, were advanced. Part of the response to the implementation problem focused on the knowledge gained through the work of the "street level bureaucrat" (Lipsky 1971) – those public servants whose experience at the interface of public service delivery and acting as agents exercising responsible discretion in the face of real-life problems, gave them a unique perspective on "how great expectations in Washington are dashed in Oakland" (Pressman and Wildavsky 1973). Based on this revised appreciation of the actual work of the policy analyst, contemporary policy analysis skills now include case study methods, interviewing and qualitative data analysis, organizational culture analysis, political feasibility analysis, stakeholder engagement, and small-group facilitation (Radin 2000). When first developed, these techniques required little in the way of computer support, though this has changed in recent years (Bicking and Wimmer 2010; Bicquelet and Weale 2011).

Whether positivism is still dominant in practice is an open question. There is a rich literature on what policy analysts *should do* (Jenkins-Smith 1982; Jennings 1987; Torgerson 1986). But in terms of how policy analysts today actually practise their "art and craft" (Wildavsky 1980) – beyond the facetious tautology of "policy analysis is what policy analysts do" (Meltsner 1976, vii) – the empirical evidence on what policy analysts *actually do* in practice is less developed (Dobuzinskis, Howlett, and Laycock 2007). Over a decade ago, Morçöl (2001) found that there was considerable support for positivism among policy professionals, especially among practitioners and professionals with educational backgrounds in economics, mathematics, and science. A recent survey of practising policy analysts in government found that when asked to rank five policy analyst archetypes ("connector," "entrepreneur," "listener," "synthesizer," "technician") in the order of how they understood and practised policy analysis, the "synthesizer" archetype (defined in part as "consulting various sources to understand how a problem is conceptualized ... develop recommended ways to deal with the problem") was overwhelmingly identified with, and the "technician" archetype (defined in part as "locating of primary raw data sources in order to undertake statistical policy research") was consistently ranked lowest (Longo 2013). That is, respondents strongly supported a post-positivist, narrative policy analytic approach over quantitative positivist techniques. As will be discussed below, this evolution in what it means to do policy analysis has transpired along with the changing nature of computer technology to affect how computers have been used as policy analytic support tools. This shift also has implications for the future practice of policy analysis, though it seems unlikely that the advance of technology will resolve the positivist/post-positivist stalemate between the rational practitioner's promise of precise answers – however inappropriate to the complexity of the situation – and the post-positivist's hand wringing over the uncertainty about unknowable outcomes.

Computer-supported policy analysis, the focus of this chapter, inhabits a sparsely populated corner of a vast e-government[1] literature. A broad definition of e-government includes all applications of ICTs deployed in service of the business of government and their use in support of public sector and civil society governance activities. Within the broad generality of e-government, a four-concept organizing framework that separates e-democracy, e-policy, e-management, and e-service delivery provides specificity for categorizing different elements, concepts, and practices involved in e-government, with computer-supported policy analysis operating as part of the e-policy category.

The immediate aftermath of World War II saw the development of working electronic digital computers, with the production of commercially available versions following soon after (Freed and Ishida 1995; for a general history). With the combined capacity of the welfare state and ongoing military Cold War needs providing the demand, large mainframe computers entered the public service in the early 1950s. This first generation of computer-supported policy analysis saw computers helping to perform complex mathematical calculations and to manage large data requirements in support of social welfare policy analysis and service delivery (Gammon 1954).[2] With the bipolar transistor replacing the vacuum tube around 1955, a second generation of commercially available computers that were smaller, cheaper, and consumed less electricity increased the presence of computer technology in government as elsewhere. The explosion of quantitative technique in the late 1960s described above was developed in large part through the hegemony of positivism and normative economic reasoning, though advances brought about by the computational power of modern computers were instrumental in making the application of these techniques feasible (Bossel 1977). With the market for the work of policy analysts growing, the tools (i.e., computing power) and techniques (i.e., quantitative methods) came together in a powerful combination that were increasingly in demand. Perhaps the zenith of the integration of computer technology with the welfare state and governance during this period came with the bold utopian Project Cybersyn, undertaken in an effort to engineer an economy and society in the service of the Chilean people during the government of President Salvador Allende (Beer 1974).

Despite the increasing adoption of ICTs, direct access to computer technology throughout the 1970s was still mediated by experts with programming capabilities, as the skills needed to interact with and control a large centralized mainframe computer were still beyond the capacity of generalists who would at best only have "dumb terminal" access. This changed with the development of third-generation computers built on the microprocessor, which led to the microcomputer and ultimately the personal computer (PCs). With the availability of desktop PCs at continually lower prices,[3] policy analysts throughout many governments were increasingly given first-hand access to computer technology for the first time. This happened over a period of years depending on the government, but a general timeline spans the early 1980s.[4]

This PC era also saw significant commercial competition in operating systems and program applications, each designed to make computers more "user-friendly" and useful to the non-expert. One development of note that occurred during the early 1980s PC era was the introduction of the graphical user interface (GUI) as a standard feature of desktop computers, starting with the introduction of the Macintosh operating system and followed by the Microsoft Windows interface. "Office productivity software" – which typically included word processing, spreadsheet, presentation, database and drawing programs – became standard elements of desktop computers at this time with the development of AppleWorks, Microsoft Office, and similar packages in the mid-1980s.

In its most prosaic respect, a central impact of advances in computer technology on the policy analyst's craft has been to move the tools necessary for producing professional-looking documents to under the direct control of the policy analyst. With the deployment of GUI-based office productivity software suites, attention quickly shifted from data analysis to the re-packaging of text into narrative policy analysis – the "synthesizer" version of policy analysis noted above. The proliferation of desktop computers represents a move from computers as corporate shared resources for information processing to computers as communication devices controlled by individual civil servants (Ottensmann 1985). Whether the PC-driven Microsoft Office hegemony and its effects – the growth in email culture (Whittaker and Sidner 1996), the shift from typists to self-production at most levels of the bureaucracy (Boreham et al. 2007), "wordsmithing" (Tracy and Ashcroft 2011), and the proliferation of briefing "decks" (Kaplan 2011) – has had a positive effect on workplace productivity is, of course, difficult to measure in such a multi-dimensional business as government. What is even more difficult to discern is whether the shift in policy analysis from "technician" to "synthesizer" is a cause or consequence of this shift in ICT use from analysis to presentation.

Against this tide of user-friendly presentation software was the increasing desktop availability of statistical analysis programs, notably SPSS (Statistical Package for the Social Sciences) and SAS (Statistical Analysis System). Both products became available on desktop PCs with a GUI and drop-down menus (as opposed to requiring syntax commands) in the 1980s, making their use more accessible to practising policy analysts undertaking quantitative analysis. Additionally, PC-based and increasingly user-friendly computer simulation tools became accessible to generalists using spreadsheets and as standalone products, allowing any computer user the opportunity to interact with computer simulations.[5] Desktop "decision support tools" and "management information systems" become increasingly available and further served to put specialized computer tools directly into the hands of decision makers (Ennals 1981; Hämäläinen 1988; Likierman 1982).

Coupled with the development of the computer as a data processing, office productivity, statistical analysis, and simulation and decision support tool in its own right, the linking together of individual computers into a communications network is the other striking feature of the development of ICTs over the postwar period. While the concept of transmitting data between two points predates the development of the digital electronic computer, the modern Internet changed fundamentally the nature of computers from being principally computing devices to information and communication devices. Starting around 1990, the connecting of government offices to the Internet began to take hold. Governments began to offer Internet-based email to their employees as early as 1989 (though distributed network email systems existed for some time before). This emergence of email as a workplace tool allowed policy analysts to communicate through email instead of through mail, telephone, fax, etc. as previously, both with internal-to-government colleagues as well as with external stakeholders. Document sharing was often constrained in this early period to plain text transmissions, though increasingly robust encoding protocols allowed for the transmission of more complex documents with their formatting and graphics intact, thus allowing policy analysts to collaborate on formatted documents. Since its widespread deployment in the early 1990s, email has become an indispensable communication and information tool in the policy analysis environment, serving as a document of record in the policy formulation process, allowing for a thoughtful and full response to inquiries from colleagues and stakeholders, and providing a template for answering similar future inquiries (Longo 2013).

With the development of the World Wide Web in 1991, a growing number of Internet-connected computer servers became easily accessible to desktop computer users. With the rollout to government employees of widespread desktop access to the growing resources available through the Internet – beginning around the time of the availability of the first graphical user interface web browser in 1993 – policy analysts had access to an increasing volume of resources for informing "synthesizer" type policy analysis. At the same time, the connecting of Internet users to government was also taking place. The early 1990s is generally seen as ushering in a new citizen engagement era with the publicizing of government email addresses (e.g., president@whitehouse.gov was made active in 1993). This was soon followed by the creation of official government websites as static, external communication mechanisms. Vice-President Al Gore unveiled the "Interactive Citizens' Handbook" – the first iteration of the WhiteHouse.gov website on 20 October 1994 – that promised "a place on the information superhighway where people can get needed information about government services and where they can provide immediate feedback to the President" (Gore 1994). The popularization of "the web" gave rise to a "fairy godmother" period when progressive politicians sought "to associate themselves with the magical effects of her wand," a period that promised to transform government and fix all manner of administrative inefficiencies (Margetts 1998, xiii). The focus of this "information superhighway" impulse was largely on improving citizen service delivery, specifically in health care and public education, though the general objective of supporting the growth of the domestic Internet was also a motivator. Following this initial enthusiasm for "digital-era governance" in the web era (Dunleavy et al. 2005) and out of the ashes of the 2001 "dot-com bubble" renewed enthusiasm for the Internet began to emerge around 2004 with an approach labelled "Web 2.0." This term connotes a second generation Internet built on the technologies of the first generation web, focused on user control, simple user-publishing of web content, social media communication, user participation, and peer-to-peer collaboration. Under a Web 2.0 model, the distinction between consumers of information and producers of content is blurred; the one-to-many broadcasting model of the early web now supports many-to-many interactions. Web 2.0 technologies – such as blogs and microblogs, reader commentary, wikis, social networking services, content sharing, collaboration and tagging – continue to grow in popularity and function.

Principally used for social activities (e.g., Facebook and Twitter continue to be cited as principle examples of Web 2.0 applications), Web 2.0 has also been deployed in a number of corporate environments in support of operations management, collaboration, and knowledge sharing. "Gov 2.0" – the application of Web 2.0 tools and approaches to public sector governance activities – has emerged in recent years as a sub-domain of the e-government literature (Morison 2010). Where governments have adopted Gov 2.0, it has generally been in support of external communication strategies (Wyld 2007), for stakeholder analysis through "social listening" (Jeffares 2014), and as a platform for citizen engagement (Chadwick 2009). In terms of the internal policy analysis function, however, Gov 2.0 technologies can be deployed to broaden policy development through corporate collaboration and knowledge sharing platforms (Longo 2013). In this context, Gov 2.0 are web-based applications designed for use in a corporate context (as opposed to open access social tools like Facebook and Twitter) that facilitate collaboration without relying on existing formal work-flows or predefined hierarchical structures. The tool might be a wiki (a document that any user can change or add to), a blog (a statement, paragraph, or longer document that any authorized user can comment on) or a discussion forum or other collaborative platform. These workspaces can be used to pose questions, connect to knowledge sources, initiate discussions, or co-create and collaborate on documents (Fyfe and Crookall 2010). The key is that users can easily start conversations across their entire network, and other users within the organization can join that conversation whether they are known to the originator or not, without the need for corporate approval or technical web support (McAfee 2006).

Not only the tools themselves have changed; the means by which new tools are adopted and innovation is diffused across the bureaucracy have also changed. Mergel and Bretschneider (2013) make an important observation about the adoption and implementation of social media applications inside government organizations in this Web 2.0 era: what distinguishes these new applications from previous ICT advances is the degree to which adoption and experimentation can be initiated by intrapreneurs throughout the organization, rather than requiring a management decision, system administrator authority, or funding allocation. With new technologies available using existing infrastructure (e.g., downloading a software program via the Internet or using a cloud-based software service) or when "bring your own device" became a feasible option for most people, new technologies can now be initiated autonomously by individuals to enhance their own productivity or that of their organizational subunit.

Finally, the recent rise of access to email and the Internet via handheld mobile devices such as a smartphone or tablet computer connected wirelessly to a network is significant. From the early 1990s, access to the web and email was generally limited to desktop or laptop computers with fixed-line Internet service. With the release of the Blackberry smartphone in 2003, governments rapidly adopted these mobile email devices as a way of keeping senior knowledge workers in constant contact regardless of their location. Additional smartphone platforms were released in 2007, and touchscreen tablet computers became mainstream in 2010. Available to consumers at lower prices than traditional PCs, movement towards the mobile Internet has accelerated. With employees now having mobile access to the Internet on privately owned devices that rival in power their workplace-supplied computers, governments are now recognizing that prohibiting the use of personal mobile devices in the workplace is both difficult to enforce and counter-productive. Instead, some governments are adopting "bring your own device" (BYOD) strategies that seek to accommodate the variety of ways that knowledge workers use ICTs, while also ensuring the security and confidentiality of that work (British Columbia 2013; United States 2012).

The impact of wireless email and web access on computer-supported policy analysis is mixed: in many respects, mobile technology has not changed the methods or substance of policy analysis but has simply served to increase the speed with which information is communicated between colleagues, increased expectations of how quickly requests will be responded to, and extended the expectations of what reasonably constitutes "working hours" and "the workplace" (Longo 2013). However, mobile technology does represent a continuation of the general trend in ICTs over the past sixty years as continually smaller, increasingly powerful, ubiquitous, and invisible devices integrated into everyday work and life. Throughout this evolution of the modern computer from room-sized installations in which expert operators would manage complex calculations, to handheld wireless devices at the disposal of any user, the use of ICTs in support of the practice of policy analysis has also evolved.

The foregoing was intended as a high-level survey of the sweep of history that Rod Dobell has experienced firsthand, in which both ICTs and the practice of policy analysis in government have evolved. Over the past sixty years, many ICTs have been introduced into the business of government and the practice of policy analysis. Has each new technology leap enabled emerging trends in government or driven them? The technological determinism perspective holds that new institutional forms and practices are not simply enabled by the new technology; rather the new technology shapes the institutions. While the shared histories of the modern computer and the policy analysis function are strongly entwined, the dominant social construction of technology interpretation since the 1980s has been that technology has not so much driven public sector organizational change (including the practice of policy analysis) as facilitated the implementation of intended new directions (Mergel and Bretschneider 2011; Wynne 2010). Over time, a more nuanced approach has become dominant: while new technology facilitates new forms and even provokes them, every new technology is mitigated by existing structures and any potential change is constrained by the environment it is deployed into. Whether the widespread ubiquitous infiltration of the Internet and the emergence of new technology-enabled governance models might represent developments sufficiently transformative to cause us to reappraise the social-constructivist perspective will be addressed in the second part of this chapter.

TOWARDS A RENEWAL OF COMPUTER-SUPPORTED POLICY ANALYSIS

Today, the emergence of a second-generation Internet built upon an architecture of user participation, coupled with ubiquitous cloud computing, advances in data analytic capacity and massive data availability, and movement towards powerful mobile platforms, all portend a transformation in computer-supported policy analysis. This section is an attempt to briefly consider the possible future implications for practising policy analysts as a consequence of two emerging phenomena: enterprise social collaboration (the "inside government" policy analysis process) and the open governance movement (the "outside government" policy process).

ENTERPRISE SOCIAL COLLABORATION

The policy analysis process in large government bureaucracies has evolved over its sixty-year history to suit the information needs of those organizations and the hierarchical structures they are built on. Traditionally, governments have dealt with policy problems by breaking the organization up into distinct units, taking a quasi-military hierarchical approach with ministries, divisions, and branches, in order to make sense of the breadth of policy issues governments are responsible for and to coordinate the work of their employees. In order to respond to the decision-support needs of ministers and senior executives, policy analysis assignments cascade through this hierarchy from superiors to subordinates until they become the responsibility of a special class of public servant called "policy analysts." Under the "synthesizer" model of policy analysis that now appears dominant, the individual policy analyst then draws on the resources at her disposal within the organization and beyond (using, likely, resources accessed over the Internet) to assemble the information necessary to produce an output such as a briefing note. This document then flows back up through the hierarchy, increasingly communicated through either emailed documents or cloud storage, with each successive management layer modifying and approving the work of its subordinate, seeking to add value to what was done before and serving as an information filtering mechanism. Once the document has worked its way back through the hierarchy, the information is then available to the individual it was intended for. This process for policy analysis reflects current practice (Longo 2013) and is reinforced through the training of policy analysts (Bardach 2000). The current technology configuration sketched in the previous section seems purpose-built to facilitate this process: email (whether via a mobile device or not) provides the mechanism for communicating the assignment; an Internet-connected PC with a web browser and office productivity software provides the platform upon which the analyst can acquire the material on which to base her analysis and manipulate that information into a presentable synthesis document; and the organization's network technology provides the means for transmitting the finished product back up through the hierarchy.

While this system works in many respects, the contemporary policy analysis and briefing process, as revealed in practice – assigning and drafting briefing notes based on hierarchical management and having policy analysts work in isolation on particular assignments – shows some weaknesses, especially in the context of complex public policy challenges that require a coordinated cross-governmental response drawing on the input of multiple actors. Complex policy problems rarely fall entirely within the organizational divisions established in a government, and individual policy analysts within government are unlikely to have access to the full breadth of relevant intelligence necessary to fully comprehend and address a policy problem, even with access to the resources available through the Internet.[6] One approach to dealing with complexity in a public policy context is horizontality, the act of working across the various ministries and divisions of a government in order to harness the organization's capacity and resources and direct them towards an appropriate response to the complex problem (Parsons 2004; 6 2004). One prominent mechanism for addressing the horizontality challenge is the promotion of greater organization-wide collaboration, knowledge sharing, and active knowledge seeking among a network of knowledge workers.

Enterprise collaboration platforms have emerged in recent years as a platform for collaboration and knowledge sharing and as a possible technology solution for addressing some of the problems that modern knowledge organizations like government face. Examples of the use of enterprise collaboration systems in government continue to grow, including leading work among government agencies in Canada and the United States (Akerley, Cowan, and Belanger 2008; Wigand 2010). Such tools allow knowledge workers within organizations to connect with each other over a social networking platform and, building on those connections, share knowledge and collaborate to greater effect than if they were to work in isolation. By augmenting the organizational social network with a technology-based social networking platform, the knowledge worker is better positioned to access more of the knowledge resources embodied in an organization. Enterprise collaboration tools also propose to help solve the email problem that has come to plague many organizations by moving electronic communications and document sharing into a shared collaborative space.

In some respects, enterprise collaboration systems represent a minor advance over previous knowledge management systems, which were found to have limited effect on corporate performance (Grudin 1988). Modern enterprise collaboration systems in contemporary practice also face challenges in adoption, among them employee uncertainty about whether they have the authority to share knowledge across their organization and the possible reluctance of women to proactively share knowledge in male-dominated organization settings (Longo 2013). However, in the context of the policy analysis system, these tools can have a potentially profound impact. Collaboration systems build on social networks and embodying principles of openness across the organization can serve to flatten traditional hierarchies by providing a platform for bringing all knowledge workers at all levels in an organization into a collaborative space and taking advantage of the collective intelligence of an organization (Lévy and Bonomo 1999).

In the modern government organization, in the age of the "street level bureaucrat," it is hard to imagine a public servant who is not a knowledge worker. Building on that premise, under an enterprise collaboration system every workplace interaction, every meeting with a stakeholder group, every transaction with a citizen (subject to privacy protections), every experience in a worker's personal knowledge base, and every new bit of information collected adds to the knowledge resources of the organization and is more likely to be discoverable. Whereas in the past, knowledge management systems sought to capture those information collection moments and organize them into a knowledge repository that other knowledge workers could draw on, enterprise collaboration systems are built on the understanding that knowledge resides in people, not machines (Hinds and Bailey 2003). The goal of enterprise collaboration systems, as opposed to knowledge management systems, is to engineer them so that someone that can benefit from some existing knowledge resource can be connected to someone in the organization who has that knowledge. If that can be accomplished, a profound transformation of the organization can occur (McAfee 2006).

In the realm of complex policy problems requiring horizontal solutions, organizations can ill afford to waste the knowledge that currently exists, untapped, throughout their organizations. For anyone who doubts that open collaboration systems can effectively solve knowledge and workflow coordination problems, we need look no further than the number of successful open source software products and collaborative projects. Examples such as the Linux operating system or even open collaborative projects such as the Wikipedia show that such platforms can allow many previously unconnected contributors to come together to collaborate on a large complex problem (Benkler 2006; Shirky 2008). The challenge for the policy analysis system will be in developing a comparable collaboration infrastructure that can efficiently evaluate policy contributions from across government, but from non-policy analysts working outside the traditional policy process.

THE OPEN GOVERNANCE MOVEMENT

In recent years, a confluence of events, perceptions, and technology has given rise to an open governance movement[7] that derives from at least four facets: as a response to frustration with political and institutional failure; in a search for greater public accountability and transparency; as flowing from earlier public participation movements; and as seeking to take advantage of Web 2.0 technology that provides the platform for tapping into collective intelligence. The perception that social challenges are not only increasingly complex but have become intractable to government solutions, coupled with frustration at growing political polarization, has fuelled the belief that government is "broken" and the solution is not to fix government but to look to the broader concept of governance to address the root causes of these failures. Transparency flows from a decline in trust of public institutions and calls for public decision makers to be held to higher accountability standards for the use of public resources. The open governance agenda also flows from a desire to increase avenues for citizen participation, following from a general decline in deference to authority and spurred on by populist demand for more meaningful public involvement in government decision making beyond periodic elections. Finally, open governance rests on a belief that complex problems cannot be solved using the knowledge resources within government alone but also require access to specific expertise and collective intelligence in society; Web 2.0 platforms provide the mechanism by which collective intelligence, crowd wisdom, and expertise (regardless of the expert's location) can be brought together to help solve complex problems. The focus here is primarily on this latter objective of the open governance movement and on the implications that this opening of the policy analysis process to those outside of government has for the practice of policy analysis inside of government.

Before turning to mechanisms for engaging external to government policy expertise, less targeted approaches such as the "wisdom of crowds," government-organized challenge platforms and the potential role of crowdsourcing in the public policy process are worth mentioning as alternative routes by which collective intelligence in society can contribute to the policy process. Crowd wisdom is based on the idea that, under the right circumstances – i.e., if there is diversity of opinion, independence in deciding, decentralization, and aggregation – groups are remarkably intelligent, even smarter than the smartest people in them, and that even if most of the people within a group are not well informed and rational, the group can still reach a collectively wise decision (Page 2008; Surowiecki 2005). Challenge platforms use contests with prizes and other incentives, broadcast in an open call to encourage firms and individuals to respond to the challenge posed and submit potential solutions; the objective is to generate ideas from unlikely sources with the hope that a major breakthrough will emerge (Mergel and Desouza 2013). And Web 2.0 has given new life to the practice of citizen science, providing opportunities for millions of volunteers around the world to contribute to scientific research projects and public policy challenges that use crowdsourcing to harness human computation abilities for completing classification, reasoning, and evaluation tasks (Dickinson, Zuckerberg, and Bonter 2010; Dobell, Longo, and Walsh 2011).

The central mechanism deployed thus far in the opening governance movement – having primarily a transparency objective but also aimed at fuelling the external generation of analysis and subsequent transference back into the policy analysis system – has been the open publication of government data for widespread public scrutiny, manipulation and re-purposing. By providing opportunities for external-to-government policy analysts to infiltrate the internal policy analysis system with analysis based on previously closed data resources, governments can take advantage of collective intelligence and specific expertise through processes of distributed innovation (Lakhani and Panetta 2007; Lampel, Jha, and Bhalla 2012).

Governments collect, generate, and compile vast amounts of digitized data continually as a consequence of the business of governing. Traditionally used by government for its exclusive purposes (if used at all) or occasionally treated as a resource with revenue-generating potential (Klinkenberg 2003), the masses of data held by governments has become the object of an open data movement calling for governments to provide free Internet-based access to these databases (Gurin 2014) – with appropriate action taken to ensure the protection of personal privacy and information of a confidential or proprietary nature (Weitzner 2007). Calls for greater openness in government-held data have generated significant momentum in a short period, a movement driven by advances in technology and fuelled by the access-to-information expectations that web users have (Ginsberg 2011). That open data has been embraced by governments appears to be motivated by three considerations: that application developers will use government data to enhance citizen services; that government transparency and accountability will be enhanced; and that outside-of-government policy capacity will be strengthened (Longo 2011). The focus here is on this third motivation.

Whereas the movement towards inside government enterprise collaboration systems seeks to broaden the notion of who inside the organization can contribute policy relevant knowledge to the closed policy process, the strengthening policy networks motivation of the open governance movement rests on the idea that "policy analysts" operating outside government will be better positioned to reveal new public policy relevant insights if given access to open government data. By providing channels for this specific expertise and collective intelligence to enter the inside-government closed policy process, the limited policy analytical capacity in government can be substantially increased (Bertot et al. 2010; Eaves 2010).

There is currently little empirical evidence on who these non-government analysts are, though some preliminary research has found them working as researchers in organized policy-oriented think tanks, civil society organizations, and private sector firms as academics, data journalists, data entrepreneurs, computer developers, hackers, and citizen hobbyists (Harris, Vaisman, and Murphy 2012). Working independently or connected through collaborative tools, using powerful data analysis software and traditional quantitative techniques, assessing multiple data sets in previously unconsidered ways, part of the open governance movement seeks previously unrevealed insights emerging from a collective policy capacity (Napoli and Karaganis 2010). A related stream focuses on advances in data visualization techniques and increasingly geotagged data, expanding the possibilities for drawing inferences from the spatial and visual representation of data (Viégas and Wattenberg 2010; Lindquist 2015).

CONCLUDING THOUGHTS

Computer technology and policy analysis share an intertwined history, both marked by a democratizing trend of user-orientation and accessibility. As technology development continues, and governance expectations change, there is a potential for a reconfiguration of policy analysis. Enterprise social collaboration can serve to flatten the organizational hierarchy endemic to most governments and expand the notion of who in the organization might contribute to policy analysis. The open governance movement can serve to open the policy analysis process to external-to-government public policy advocates, informed by previously closed government data resources. This movement holds the promise of a dramatic expansion of policy analysis capacity, albeit a capacity not under the traditional control of governments.

Will the future of computer-supported policy analysis be so unlike its past as to represent a fundamental transformation of practice? Will enterprise social collaboration and the open governance movement lead to a fundamental reconfiguration of policy analysis? My assessment is cautiously mixed: the inside-government policy analysis system seems unlikely to voluntarily and proactively abandon its traditional privileged position and closed approach to policy analysis to take full advantage of the new technology opportunities. The early experimentation with enterprise social collaboration in government indicates that the culture of the public sector policy analysis environment may be ill suited to the potential disruption that openness may bring (Longo 2013). Without a push by their political and executive leaders to change – a push that seems unlikely given the lack of interest political leaders have for in-house policy analysis of the Lasswellian variety (Shulock 1999; Wellstead and Stedman 2010) – a self-reflexive, internal-to-government transformation of the policy analysis process seems unlikely. So while new technology will continue to be applied to the practice of policy analysis in government, that practice will look much as it did before the recent technology advances.

It is also not clear that this data-fuelled, externally generated approach to divining policy truth should be accepted uncritically. Just as concerns over the appropriateness of quantitative techniques for investigating social behaviour and conditions gave rise to the post-positivist critique of the policy sciences, questions regarding the competency and epistemological clarity of independent public policy advocates must be considered. While policy analysts and decision makers inside government do not have an unassailable right to control policy debates or a monopoly on the truth, there is a potential downside to the rise of policy advocates armed with massive data and impressive analytical tools: responding to erroneous, tendentious, or self-serving claims by policy advocates already occupies a fair amount of time in the contemporary world of the policy analyst (Longo 2013). If such claims are made more persuasive by being fuelled by data and analytics, the challenge to the inside-government policy analyst will be increased. This is not meant to argue against transparency, since policy analysis based on open data can serve to increase the competitiveness of alternative policy analysis perspectives in the marketplace of ideas, leading ultimately to better solutions (Dobell and Zussman 1981). However, in order to compete effectively in that arena and appropriately evaluate solutions emanating from analytic work conducted outside government, the public sector policy analyst should take note of the growth in big data analytics. Despite the lack of affinity for the policy "technician" archetype noted above, a revival of policy analysis skills from the discipline's golden age, updated to account for advances in analytical techniques and tools, seems timely if for no other reason than to ensure competence in being able to critically evaluate the methods and assertions contained in externally generated analysis.

The inside-government policy analysis system should see this open governance movement not simply as a challenge to its hegemony but as a prompt to consider re-embracing its quantitative roots. As big data policy analysis is promoted outside government, the potential for it to influence how policy analysis is done inside government is profound. In some ways, the decline of quantitative methods that typified the policy analysis profession following the rise of post-positivism is a reflection of limitations in the tools of analysis and the lack of data availability. In the big data analytics era, we are now in a situation where policy ideas can become subject to continual micro-experimentation in order to propose, pilot, test, evaluate, and redesign policy interventions (Haynes et al. 2012). With a sense of inquisitiveness and openness on the part of the policy analyst profession, the massive-data era might serve to re-establish positivist policy traditions and the use of quantitative techniques inside government and lead to a new generation of computer-supported policy analysis, moving beyond prospective policy analysis (Rose 1991) to embrace emerging approaches such as real-time policy experimentation (Paquet 2009), robust adaptive planning (Lempert, Popper, and Bankes 2002) and massive scenario generation (Davis, Bankes, and Egner, 2003). With an appreciation of the lessons of history embodied in the post-positivist perspective, a renewed policy analysis profession, more analytically diverse and data-supported, could emerge.

Open governance is an important development, one that has the potential to significantly disrupt our traditional notions of governance and lead to a new era of social organization and decision making. An analytically rigorous policy analysis capacity, developing outside government but fuelled by newly opened government data sources, can potentially change the nature of public policy advocacy and evidence-based argumentation. Before the emerging paradigm of open government, external analysts were limited in the evidence and authority they could bring to the assessment of a public policy problem. While the position of the outsider always came with the freedom to speak *its truth* to power, it was handicapped by questions about whether *its truth* was the same as *the truth* (or, indeed, *the government's truth*), owing to its partially obstructed view of the field and a lack of clearance to view certain datasets. As these limits become obsolete, open governance – based on the ability of diverse expertise and the analysis of evidence originating from anywhere in the policy environment to influence deliberation and decision making – becomes increasingly viable.

What will be especially interesting is the reaction of the internal-to-government policy system to this growing external capacity that open governance potentially gives rise to. If we take at face value the open governance movement, an attempt by the policy analysis priesthood to revert to a position of privileged authority as the insiders to the process will not be a tenable strategy. If open governance is to mean more than just data transparency, to instead extend to openness in deliberation and decision making, the traditional position of the civil service as the guardians of the policy process becomes anachronistic. In an environment where they can no longer project their hegemony through their position, the inside policy analyst must learn to compete with these new colleagues, to use data, analysis, and "the unforced force of the better argument" (Habermas 1998, 306) if they hope to prevail in policy debates.

In the short term, the competition that open governance will pose may prompt the policy analysis profession to reconsider its drift away from quantitative methods while simultaneously continuing its post-positivist efforts to democratize policy analysis. These two directions should not be seen as antithetical; Fischer's (1980) proposal for a post-positive policy analysis never denied the need for rigorous analysis but instead called for an appreciation of the presence of normative judgement in the policy analysis process. Both enterprise collaboration systems and the open governance movement further respond to the post-positivist policy analysis impulse to democratize policy analysis, dispersing the ability to provide policy-relevant insights through governing organizations and to those outside of government. In following both routes, policy analysis will be better for it.

NOTES

1 E-government is also rendered as e-governance, with e-gov a convenient amalgam of the two terms (Marche and McNiven 2003).

2 Gammon's 1954 article would have likely remained hidden from any survey of e-government literature, since it made no use of the term e-government (being written some forty years before the term emerged) and was cited only once in the academic literature. This early publication was brought to light recently when Richard Heeks suggested through his blog that it could be identified as "the first research paper about e-government" (Heeks 2011).

3 IBM priced the PC XT at $7,500 in 1983, and Apple introduced the Macintosh in 1984 at $2,400. In 2014 prices, the PC XT would cost approximately $17,600 and the Macintosh approximately $5,400. Over the subsequent thirty-year history of the personal computer, cost has fallen even as performance has multiplied. Today, a policy analyst performing "synthesizer" work as described above can be provided with a desktop computer for about $2,000, assuming the network infrastructure necessary to connect to the Internet. As Moore's Law – which holds that the number of transistors on an integrated circuit doubles about every two years – shows no sign of abating, we can anticipate continued reductions in the cost, size, and power consumption of computer devices.

4 During this period, in 1982, *Time* magazine selected the personal computer as its "Machine of the Year."

5 *SimHealth* was a simulation tool for US health-care system policy analysis (Corbeil 1994); *QUEST* was a computer-based integrated assessment model and deliberation support tool designed to facilitate discussion about regional sustainability (Longo 2003); *PolicyMaker* was a tool for comparing the implications of various policy choices (Seeman 2000).

6 Another problem with the current policy analysis process lies in the ICT approach by which policy analysis is currently coordinated – corporate email systems, individual PCs, and network shared disk drives – which are typified by a large volume of email, recipients' difficulty distinguishing important from unimportant emails, inaccessibility of email contents to non-recipients, and uncertainty regarding the location of the most current and authoritative version of a document (Nairn 2011; Thompson 2011).

7 My research has benefitted directly from this movement through my appointment as "post-doctoral fellow in open governance" at Arizona State University (http://cpi.asu.edu), and my affiliation with the MacArthur Foundation Research Network on Opening Governance (http://www.opening-governance.org).

13

It's Not My Problem: Personal Moral Responsibility for Policy Advice

JOHN LANGFORD

[H]alf the battle is won once we learn to recognize that there is an ethical problem in a course of action we're contemplating.

Joel Fleishman

Not long after I came to the School of Public Administration in 1979, Rod Dobell, then the director of the school, encouraged me to begin teaching a course on responsible administrative behaviour. This led me off in many directions, one of which was the organization of a conference "Responsibility in the Senior Public Service" with colleagues Bill Neilson and Mervyn Brockett at which I gave the opening address (Langford 1985).

In that lecture, exploring the theme of administrative responsibility, I argued the point that senior public servants exercised much more power and influence in the making of policy (both at the development and implementation stages) than the bromide of the policy-administration dichotomy suggested. This led to an examination of the pressures on a senior public servant in the mid-1980s to be more political, to be more accessible and less anonymous, to connect more openly with stakeholders and the wider public, to explain and defend policy initiatives, and to deal with more demands for accountability. All of this was intended to stimulate two days of discussion of the evolving role of the senior public servant in a Westminster model government and the uncertainty surrounding the question of what responsible behaviour looked like in this changing environment.

Summarizing the discussion at the end of the conference, Rod Dobell observed that the considerable power and influence of senior public servants was not matched by any coherent sense that with this power and influence came responsibility. He notes that the meeting seemed to "develop a consensus" that Cabinet "had a right to appoint officials from whom they could expect enthusiastic implementation of their policies and loyal expression of their underlying philosophy" and that political matters and management responsibility could remain separate despite "the sense of impatience, frustration, even rage, as one delegate expressed it, that public servants in Canada have to swallow if they are to remain in a position to influence policy over the long term" (1985, 623). He reinforced this point by recounting the "increasing nervousness" of one participant that "that any action (even responsible comment on policy) might lead to a cabinet order rescinding his appointment" (622).

In my memory, Rod Dobell accurately reflected the sense of the meeting. In the discussion with senior public officials and academics over the two days of the conference there were plenty of illustrations of a disconnect between the power that senior public servants exercise and any sense of personal moral responsibility, i.e., of a willingness to accept blame or praise for involvement in the creation of government actions or inactions. To be fair, a few practitioner participants provided illustrations of a modus operandi that reflected some sense of moral responsibility for outcomes: questioning the rationale for new policy initiatives, proactively pushing political masters through reports and briefings to recognize the potential harm to clients, employees, and the wider public associated with policy options being discussed. But many more demonstrated a wide zone of indifference or acceptance as Chester Barnard and colleagues characterized it (Roe 1989), appearing willing to embrace without much deliberation any policy goal proposed by their superiors, put forward any and all policy options that would forward their superior's agenda, and then oversee the implementation of whatever option was chosen regardless of the negative impacts that might flow from that policy. They took little personal moral responsibility for the impacts of policies that they had been involved in developing and implementing – deferential to directions from above and happy to use the prevailing constitutional mythology to pass all responsibility for benefits and harms on to the minister. In his paper for the conference, Ken Kernaghan stated that "in the final analysis each bureaucrat is responsible for the morality of his or her actions" (1985). Regrettably, this notion did not appear to be widely embraced by the participants.

SERVICE DELIVERERS SEEM MORE INCLINED TO ACCEPT PERSONAL RESPONSIBILITY

Under the influence of the New Public Management philosophy, public servants dealing more directly with the public seem to have increasingly accepted the notion that they have some personal responsibility for the impacts of their actions (or inactions) on clients and the wider public. For example, social workers and their supervisors now seem to recognize that they cannot pass responsibility for a child's death on to a minister or a policy direction from above. Individual police and custodial officers and their managers are increasingly held to account for the way they treat the public. It is now common practice for ombudspersons, commissions of inquiry, client advocates, and courts to seek to detail how individual service delivery or regulatory decisions were made, who did what to whom and who asked whom to do what, knowing the risks and the potential for harm to those affected. One might argue, therefore, that the responsibility issue has been to some degree been worked out for public servants providing services directly to the public.

BUT NOT POLICY ADVISORS OR ANALYSTS

I see no evidence that policy analysts and advisors have accepted a parallel personal moral responsibility for the impacts of government policies that they have helped to create and implement. In fact, Canadian administrative history is replete with illustrations of the continuing strength of this disconnect between public servants' policy-making power and their acceptance of personal moral responsibility for outcomes to which they have contributed.

One alarming example is the interning of Japanese Canadians during World War II. Prime Minister Mackenzie King wanted a policy that would placate racist British Columbia politicians, and some of his advisors responded with proposals for the relocation of all people of Japanese descent from coastal British Columbia to internment and work camps in the British Columbia interior and other provinces (Robertson 2000, 40). Hugh Keenleyside and another advisor who showed less enthusiasm for the prime minister's approach were shunted to other positions (Keenleyside 1982; Sunahara 1981). Towards the end of the war, senior advisors to the prime minister in the Department of External Affairs dutifully set out options for dealing with more than twenty thousand interned Japanese Canadians (75 percent of whom were British subjects)[1] when the war was over, including the development of proposals (Library and Archives of Canada; Canadian Human Rights Museum 2008) that led to individuals and families being pressured to accept deportation to an impoverished and destroyed postwar Japan (Robertson 2000; Roy et al. 1990; Sunahara 1981; Timmons 2004). In his memoir, Gordon Robertson is dismissive of Hugh Keenleyside's efforts to persuade the prime minister that internment was "unnecessary and unjust" (Robertson 2000, 42). When interviewed by the CBC many years later about his involvement in the development of the deportation scheme, Robertson refused to accept any personal responsibility for the fate of the almost four thousand Japanese Canadians (Miki 2004,101) who were sent to Japan, arguing that the final decision on the deportation strategy was made by political superiors (*CBC Fifth Estate* 1995).

But one doesn't have to go so far back in history to find excellent examples of public servants who adopt an essentially amoral approach to their work, distancing themselves from any personal moral responsibility for their actions or inactions. Think of Industry Canada advisors who put forward marketing and funding proposals in support of the federal government's policy of exporting asbestos to countries ill-equipped to ensure that these products will be handled safely by the end users (Rennie 2011). Or Health Canada advisors who create plans for a drug approval process that will be dominated by the pharmaceutical industry (Lexchin 2010). Or the federal Department of Fisheries and Oceans employees who develop a departmental reorganization proposal knowing it will gut the government's capacity to enforce the water quality sections of the Fisheries Act (Hume 2011). Or advisors from the Canadian Corrections Service and the Department of Justice who provide analytical cover for more draconian approaches to criminal offenders despite the fact that many of these measures have been demonstrated to be ineffective (Jackson and Stewart 2009).

This lack of personal moral engagement with policy outcomes is evident in every ethics workshop and class I teach – which means that it is shared not just by senior policy analysts and advisors but by junior and mid-level policy analysts and students who aspire to policy analyst positions in the public service. There is widespread acceptance of the notion that the primary obligation of a policy analyst or advisor is to provide support for any initiative that an administrative superior or political master wants to pursue, including the development and presentation of options and plans that the analyst knows from the outset would harm some or all of those who would be affected by their implementation. My classroom and workshop evidence also supports the hypothesis that this sense of obligation extends beyond the development and presentation of potentially harmful options to include the writing of policy briefs "to order"; the doctoring and suppression of data that would undermine the perceived effectiveness of a policy initiative; the contracting out of data collection and legal advice to firms "friendly" to the client; the removal from policy teams of participants deemed unfriendly by political masters; and willing participation in "spin" – the development of communications instruments concerning proposed policy initiatives designed to destroy the credibility of opponents of the policy proposal and to mislead readers or watchers and distract them from shortcomings in the analysis, the policy, or the implementation plans. Contemporary examples of all of these activities are easily located throughout Westminster model jurisdictions (Savoie 2008). For a recent exploration of the flight from responsibility in Australia, for instance, see *Whatever Happened to Frank and Fearless?* (Macdermott 2010).

Christopher Hood argues that far from taking responsibility for actions and policy proposals, the focus of most public officials – elected and appointed – is on "blame avoidance." In *The Blame Game*, Hood analyzes a wide array of strategies – including a number of "presentational" strategies like those noted above – that are used to ensure that negative risks associated with government actions or inactions are dissipated or deflected on to others (Hood 2011). He argues further that common bureaucratic activities such as delegating responsibility, reorganization, partnering, and outsourcing are really just "opportunities for blame-shifting, buck-passing, and risk transfer to others who can be placed in the front line of blame when things go wrong" (Hood 2011, 67).

How do we account for this continuing rejection of a strong sense of personal moral responsibility for outcomes and impacts among contemporary policy analysts and advisors? To explain this phenomenon I think we have to look beyond the environment of blame avoidance in which many policy advisors operate and explore closely intertwined arguments about moral *responsibility* and *role* that legitimize this position.

RESPONSIBILITY LIES IN THE MINISTER'S HANDS

As the analysis to this point suggests, policy advisors begin by arguing that they are not moral agents because they are ultimately advising political masters on how to achieve ends that they as elected office holders declare to be in the public interest (Finer 1941; Thompson 1985; Amy 1984). The minister (or the members of the town council) are therefore the sole moral agents in these circumstances, and the advisor bears no moral responsibility for efforts to help them reach the goals that have been endorsed by successful election, legislation, or simply the positional authority of the political executive. As Amy notes, "Value decisions, in this view, are best left up to policymakers, and need not or should not be the subject of policy analysis" (1984, 576). This general "ethic of neutrality" is reinforced at the Canadian federal and provincial levels by the Westminster model convention of political neutrality to which senior public servants in Canada stubbornly cling (Savoie 2008). The ethic of neutrality simply denies the legitimacy of a policy advisor bringing any ethical considerations to bear on the development of a policy proposal, with the exception of loyalty to the moral principles of the political master. As Thompson puts it, "The ethic of neutrality portrays the ideal administrator as a completely reliable instrument of the goals of the organization, never injecting personal values into the process of furthering these goals" (1985, 556). Contemporary attempts to model the policy-making process still lean heavily on the notion that policy analysis is to be construed as an activity entirely in support of translating the vision of political masters into programs and actions to deliver outcomes (Parsons 2001). The personal moral responsibility of advisors is not a significant feature of the neutrality model. Within this model, responsible behaviour is what is allowed by law, responsive to hierarchical demands, and within the boundaries of the specific mandate of one's office.

Thompson (1985) raises a potentially moderating feature of the neutrality model that calls for the policy advisor to use her expertise to provide "frank and fearless" advice at least up to the point at which a decision has been made. But particularly in a period in which political agendas are more polarized, this element of the neutrality package has lost its salience. In contemporary government departments, political executives do everything they can to encourage the loyalty elements of the ethic of neutrality. A team culture is created in which the public servant is a member of a departmental or wider government team. Policy proposals responding to political executive direction are developed not in isolation from the political leadership but in close collaboration with policy and communications operatives from the politician's personal staff and – at the federal and provincial levels – the premier or prime minister's office. Anyone who challenges the team direction can be shunned, reassigned, or fired. This team culture does not encourage public servants to provide "frank and fearless" advice. Rather, a premium is placed on the provision of evidence and options designed to forward the prevailing political agenda (Walter 2006). This advice is proffered within the limits set down by the political executive's problem definition, standards of evidence, policy criteria, anticipated breadth of options, and acceptable tradeoffs (Bardach 2008). In more recent times loyalty seems to trump every other possible obligation and the distance between the agenda and vision of the political executive and the work of the policy analyst has been significantly reduced (Mulgan 2007). As one of Jane Jacob's characters in *Systems of Survival* puts it when explaining the ethical culture of the public sector, "If any single precept can be called key or central in guardian morality, it is *Be Loyal*" (Jacobs 1992, 67).

In such circumstances, it is something of a shock when policy analysts "step up" and actually insist on putting forward "frank and fearless" advice. Seymour Hersch recently recounted the story of the production of the US government's 2011 National Intelligence Estimate (NIE) on Iran's nuclear threat in which the analysts, humiliated by the way in which earlier NIEs on Iraq's and Iran's nuclear program had been manipulated by pressure from political leaders, balked this time. He quotes retired army intelligence officer, Patrick Lang, who said, "Analysts in the intelligence community are refusing to sign up this time for a lot of baloney ... These guys are not drinking the Kool-Aid," Lang said. "They stopped the NIE cold" (Hersch 2011, 31).

THE "MANY HANDS" EXCUSE

The team culture provides the lead in to another common objection to the notion that a policy advisor is a moral agent. This is often referred to as the *ethic of structure* and it rationalizes the refusal of the policy advisor to accept responsibility for policy outcomes and impacts by stressing the fact that "many hands" are at work. As Thompson again puts it: "The ethic of structure asserts that, even if administrators may have some scope for independent moral judgment, they cannot be held morally responsible for most of the decisions and policies of government. Their personal moral responsibility extends only to the specific duties of their own office for which they are legally liable" (Thompson 1985, 559).

Policy advising within government has moved a long way from the mythical model of a small group of officials packaging the results of internally generated systematic evaluation of policy options and monopolizing the attention of their political master. Contemporary policy proposals are developed through complex webs of interaction involving relations with many units within a department, with the political executives' hired guns, and with other departments, as well as with affected interest groups, industry associations, think tanks, other knowledge generators, and possibly other levels of government. Policy analysis is increasingly portrayed as a network management function, encouraging, clarifying, and brokering the views of many players, and is thus about as far as you can get from a simple one-to-one service encounter between a service deliverer and a client in which the former can see what his decision will do to the latter (McArthur 2007; Savoie 2008, 292). Hood argues that other ways to diffuse responsibility include "partnership working, multi-agency arrangements, or institutional machinery so complex that blame can be shuffled about or made to disappear ... organizations also engage in processes of defensive reorganization and revolving-door movement of officeholders so that by the time blame comes home to roost, the organizational structure that produced the perceived harm has long been superseded and the relevant individuals have all moved out or on" (Hood 2011, 19).

In these cluttered and rapidly changing organizational circumstances, the argument runs, it makes no sense to insist that any one of the players holds enough power or influence to be praised or blamed for the outcome and thus establish a significant degree of personal moral responsibility. It is noteworthy that in virtually all the public inquiries held in recent years in Canada to examine government scandals, I can recall only one public official – Monique Bégin, federal health minister during the tainted blood affair – who considered it her duty to take her share of the responsibility (Picard 1996). But Ms. Bégin's acceptance of responsibility was tempered by her assertion that the health department in general was "blameless" (Shafer 1999, 7). Eventually, however, Health Canada public servants and officials in the Canadian Red Cross Society and a pharmaceutical company involved in managing the safety of the blood supply were charged with criminal negligence causing bodily harm under the Criminal Code.

THE POLICY ADVISORY ROLE ALLOWS FOR "DIRTY HANDS"

Some readers would have been influenced in an earlier era by texts like Morgenthau's *Politics among Nations*, which argues the "realist" position that morality should never intrude into public policy-making especially in the foreign policy field (Morgenthau 2006). This apparently Machiavellian position, which gives considerable comfort to policy analysts who want to fully reject moral agency, has been overcome in recent years by more modest conceptions of the significance of role that allow for "dirty hands" – rather than blanket amorality – in some circumstances. "Dirty hands" in this paper refers to taking an action or providing advice designed to forward the public interest which would be considered to be morally unacceptable in private life (Coady 2011). After reviewing the ethic of neutrality and the ethic of structure, this final argument might be seen as the ethic of necessity. For example, Jane Jacobs' "guardian moral syndrome" establishes what appears to be a special role morality – a distinctive set of professional standards for public officials (e.g., be obedient and disciplined, respect hierarchy, be loyal, deceive for the sake of the task, be fatalistic, etc.), which could be seen to considerably extend the scope of acceptable behaviour for the policy advisor (Jacobs 1992).

Jacobs' reference to the obligation to deceive opens up a wider discussion of the concept of dirty hands. Michael Walzer talks about circumstances (e.g., a "supreme emergency") in which normal moral reasoning would give way to the necessity to do whatever is required to forward or preserve the public interest (Walzer 2004). Thomas Nagel does not advocate suspending morality, but instead he argues that public morality is more impersonal than private morality, focusing more attention on reaching the government's goals and allowing the policy advisor more latitude with respect to the options recommended to achieve those goals. Restrictions on means will be weaker, "permitting the employment of coercive, manipulative or obstructive methods that would not be allowable for individuals" (1979). But in the Nagel model, decisions about using such methods would all be made within the bounds of moral reasoning, and there would be no hiding the fact that one was advocating an evil action to avoid an even more evil outcome. The ultimate expression of this "inside the wire of morality" position is the argument that consequential calculus may at any time support the taking of action that would harm some in the name of enhancing the position of others. Fully adopted, this position effectively negates the concept of dirty hands. You just do what you have to do within the bounds of consequential moral calculus to get a demonstrably better outcome or avoid a greater evil (Nielson 2000).

PROBLEMS WITH THE MINISTER'S HANDS, MANY HANDS, AND DIRTY HANDS ARGUMENTS

To many outside observers, these arguments designed to deny the existence of moral agency, to severely limit the personal moral responsibility of policy advisors, or to provide cover for engaging in moral calculus that would shock the public are bogus and self-serving. They obscure the fact that the individual actions of policy analysts and advisors – however dictated by role or subsumed in the powers and influences of other actors – easily meet widely accepted causal and *volitional* criteria for personal moral responsibility (Thompson 1987, 40–1, 47–8). These criteria hold persons responsible for an outcome insofar as their actions or omissions make an identifiable contribution to it, and they do not act or fail to act in excusable ignorance (i.e., they either knew or should have known what the risks of doing harm were) or under compulsion – or as Thompson puts it, "they could have done otherwise."

The *ethic of neutrality* argument denies moral culpability for policy advisors by focusing on the notion that to "step up" is to illegitimately force one's personal views of the public interest on administrative superiors and political leaders. In reality the focus of this discussion should be not on foisting one's personal views but rather on the obligation to clearly signal when a policy initiative or specific approach to achieving the policy objective would visit significant harm on individuals or groups affected by the resulting actions or inactions of government. This strategy for avoiding responsibility also masks the degree of discretion available to policy advisors in vaguely defined policy analysis circumstances, underplaying the opportunity they have to identify potential harm associated with certain options and make that harm known to decision makers. Policy analysts often argue that the potential harm reveals itself only in later stages of the policy development process after the advisor has already made initial recommendations and initial actions have been taken. In such circumstances, it is argued, the advisor has already helped to move the proposal forward, and it is now too late to object to the course on which the government has embarked. Staying the course in the face of new evidence looks self-serving to the public and to inquiry commissioners who rightly insist that late is better than never when it comes to identifying harmful consequences. Politicians do ultimately make the tough choices, but they would do a better job of it if policy advisors felt obliged to rehearse the ethical dimension of these choices with them as they reveal themselves and make it clear when an option may lack moral credibility whatever calculus one uses.

The *ethic of structure* or complexity argument is equally shaky. It contends that being one of many hands at work in a networking or partnership context makes it unreasonable for any one individual to assume any significant degree of personal responsibility for harm caused. But we don't accept the fact of group action to stop us from ascribing responsibility in other contexts. Thompson uses the example of the gang of thugs beating an old man to death to argue that we don't allow the existence of a group of assailants or our inability to determine which one made the fatal kick to stop us from attributing responsibility and blame to all the gang (1985, 559–60). Being part of the gang and contributing to the death of the old man by striking him or failing to try to stop other gang members from doing so is enough to establish responsibility. Civil, criminal, and administrative law all offer multiple examples of attributing responsibility jointly and severally. Parfit (1986) makes a related case, arguing that we often make mistakes calculating the effect of a personal action, minimizing its impact (and therefore our moral responsibility) by viewing it discreetly rather than as part of a collection of actions that in aggregation do have a substantial impact. In cases of shared responsibility, omissions are often as important as commissions. Commenting on what might appear a troubling notion of "negative responsibility," Thompson contends that "in the context of organizations we can more often point to specific omissions that made a significant difference in the outcome and are ascribable to specific persons" (1985, 560).

Finally, the attempt to limit personal responsibility by arguing that policy advising is a role that provides licence to recommend harmful options (dirty hands) may not provide the latitude for irresponsible behaviour that its proponents first suggest. Jacobs argues that standards of behaviour for most public officials involved in domestic policy-making would be more restrictive than the standards for those engaged in police, military, or foreign policy fields. Referring, for example, to the prerogative of public officials to "deceive for the sake of the task," one of her characters insists that "most guardian tasks in modern democratic societies carry no legitimate reasons for deception ... The job of most bureaucrats is to serve the public openly and aboveboard. Deceiving it is thus disloyal" (1992, 76). Similarly, Applbaum, at the end of his lengthy analysis of the power of role to excuse "the violations of persons in ways that would otherwise be wrong," concludes, "This argument, despite its appearance of sophistication and its pose of knowing worldliness, is much weaker than supposed. The truth is simpler: institutions and the roles they create ordinarily cannot mint moral permissions to do what would otherwise be prohibited" (1999, 257).

Nagel, by contrast, does not attempt to draw such a hard line in the sand. He is not embracing amorality but leaving open the need in some circumstances to adjust the moral calculus to place more emphasis on impartiality. The important point in Nagel's case is that moral agency is not discarded. The policy analyst may be able to justify acting differently but is still personally responsible for harmful actions or omissions and must bear the moral cost, the potential regret and the more temporal consequences for contributing to them.

The precise latitude to be allowed to policy advisors to recommend or provide plans for actions or inactions that would harm some to improve the lot of others remains a contestable issue that we cannot solve in this paper. What is significant from the perspective of this discussion is the demand of the more compelling of these dirty hands discussants that public officials accept the ethical dimension of such situations and concede the need to be able to justify their hard choices to those affected by their advice in ethical terms that the affected can understand. Public policy-making may require a change in the moral calculus in some circumstances, but it does not provide an unrestricted ticket to ride away from personal moral responsibility or more widely recognized standards of behaviour.

WHERE DO WE GO FROM HERE?

This short paper should not be interpreted as a plea for moral perfection. It is simply an attempt to open up the question of the nature of the personal moral responsibility of policy analysts and advisors. Academic books and articles on the ethics of policy analysis generally pass over this question, assuming the acceptance of a high degree of personal moral responsibility and providing practitioners with often wildly idealistic ethical frameworks to guide them in the provision of policy advice (Benveniste 1984; Kraft and Furlong 2007; Boston, Bradstock, and Eng 2010). It is my contention that policy professionals on the whole just don't subscribe to this assumption and generally reject moral agency. One interesting form of evidence for this contention is the absence of widely accepted professional codes of conduct for policy analysts and advisors laying out standards of behaviour relating to the client, colleagues, and stakeholders affected by their work.

I also see no sign that policy analysts feel engaged as a professional group by the opportunities or obligations being placed on public servants more generally by "whistle blowing" or "disclosure" regimes. The major focus of such regimes seems to be on the work of administrators and service deliverers who might be breaking the law, misusing public resources, or endangering public health and safety. In the prevailing administrative culture, the problem of contributing to policy proposals that would allow for such activities in the future does not seem to be adequately covered. In fact, the Canadian federal whistle blowing regime appears to offer policy analysts and advisors an opportunity to avoid the obligations laid out in the legislation if "the subject matter of the disclosure ... relates to a matter that results from a balanced and informed decision-making process on a public policy issue."[2] Particularly in the context of today's politically charged policy development processes, such "balance" would be hard to find (Thompson 1983, 557–8). In any case, if we exclude Health Canada scientists (Hutton 2011), there are very few recorded instances in Canada in which a policy analyst or advisor has blown the whistle internally or externally on superiors who are asking them to provide or support proposals for action that, if they were approved, would in the view of the analyst or advisor cause significant harm to affected stakeholders.

Improved accountability provides the final reason for paying attention to this question. All these efforts to downplay personal responsibility create serious problems for democratic accountability. If a policy advisor doesn't feel any sense of personal responsibility for the power and influence he exercises, then he will feel completely comfortable in passing the obligation to account for the results of his work on to a superior – most likely his political master. This helps to obscure the complex process by which policy decisions are made and reinforce public cynicism about a governance system in which no policy advisor admits to playing a significant and independent enough role in an inherently "dirty" process to take any responsibility for the outcome of that process.

But there is no denying that embracing personal moral responsibility for the impact of advice offered will raise difficult questions about traditional obligations to be loyal to superiors, respect the organization's confidentiality rules, and serve the public interest. If a policy advisor feels obliged to "step up" when involved in a policy-making process that risks visiting significant and indefensible harm on some of those affected by its implementation, she confronts a cascading set of questions about what level of dissent is acceptable. Do the advisor's obligations extend beyond clarifying concerns about potential harm to immediate superiors? Should the advisor refuse to explore and set out certain harmful options in policy memoranda? Would cooperating on the policy development side and attempting to mitigate the harm levels during the implementation phase be an appropriate compromise? Should she seek the support of other members of the policy analysis community? Is it appropriate to open up lines of communication on certain policy options with stakeholders likely to be affected by them? Should she resort to more formal avenues of external disclosure available under whistleblower legislation? These examples provide just a suggestion of the difficult questions about appropriate behaviour that would arise in a world in which policy analysts and advisors take moral ownership of the advice they provide.

NOTES

1 All Canadian citizens were legally known as British subjects until passage of the Canadian Citizenship Act in 1946.

2 *Public Servants Disclosure Protection Act*, S.C. 2005, c. 46, (Can.), available at http://laws-lois.justice.gc.ca/eng/acts/P-31.9/page-1.html.

14

What is an Honest Policy Analyst to Do?

BARRY CARIN

One of the embarrassing dirty little secrets of economics is that there is no such thing as economic theory properly so-called. There is simply no set of foundational bedrock principles on which one can base calculations that illuminate situations in the real world.

Brad DeLong

To give and not to give: to be weak while appearing to be strong: to be obscure while appearing to be forthright: to be inconsistent while appearing to be infinitely reasonable. The hallmarks of a successful Memorandum to Cabinet.

Douglas G. Hartle

INTRODUCTION

This chapter reviews the difficulties that plague the process of making judgments about reality, values, and obstacles to good policy analysis and suggests some ideas for the honest policy analyst's toolbox.

By policy analyst, I have in mind Dobell's definition in which the role of the analyst is to order and organize information and distill data, to provide judgment, but not necessarily wisdom.[1] Policy analysis consists of three types of judgments (Vickers 1965):

- Judgments on reality: What is or is not the case?
- Value judgments: What ought or ought not to be the case?
- Instrumental judgments: What is the best means available to reduce the mismatch between what is and what ought to be?

In real, practical settings, policy analysts are called on to make judgments on reality, descriptions based on objective evidence. Simply selecting and arraying facts requires the policy analyst to assess and evaluate factors and considerations that should be included for analysis. The policy analyst must decide what is relevant. In real, practical settings, policy analysts are also called on to make normative decisions. In a world of competitive, if not inconsistent, claims and of distributional disagreements, policy analysts intrinsically make value judgements based on opinions and moral standards whenever they define policy and program objectives and priorities. The reporting of results implicitly assigns weights to different objectives – again a normative action.

This paper reviews the veritable train wreck of difficulties that plague the process of making judgments on reality, on values, and on instrumental means. Each of the three types of judgment is highly challenging, complicated by several specific obstacles that research reveals.

First, in making judgments about reality, the complex, sophisticated economic models available to us rest on an illusory foundation of sand. The implications of welfare economics' Theory of the Second Best (what happens when optimum conditions are not satisfied in an economic model) shake our confidence in the ability to model reality. Even if we had confidence in our models, there is no "correct" rate of discount to compute present values of streams of benefits and costs occurring over time, in order to compare options. Models require data. Policy analysts should be aware of the various measurement difficulties encountered in collecting data.

A second category of difficulties involves the inescapable need to make value judgments. For example, there is no value-free way to deal with risk in an uncertain world. To complicate matters, we cannot use opinion polls to simply ask people in order to determine their value judgments. Polling is an art, not a science, where the framing of questions and scoring of answers often forces desired results. Even if we could design an ideologically neutral poll, people do not have the intellectual capacity to make informed judgments given the complexities and uncertainties. Complicating matters, confidence in one's own personal capacity varies inversely with actual intelligence. And even the most intelligent are "predictably irrational" (Ariely 2010). If we could cope with these complications in a world with multiple options, Arrow's Impossibility (1951)

Theorem demonstrates that there would be no perfect way to aggregate voters' preferences. What is an honest policy analyst to do?

All is not lost. The paper suggests some ideas for the honest policy analyst's toolbox. Confidence can be regained if one identifies and explains the reasons that lead to disagreements, devises policies that make good use of incentives, introduces gradual changes, proposes incremental experiments with insurance and "off ramps" to minimize costs of changing policy, and exploits potential synergies between different policy sectors. The final recommendation is to recognize the significance of gender differences: the most effective policy analysis team will include a high proportion of women.

JUDGMENTS ON REALITY – WHAT IS OR IS NOT THE CASE?

Reality is merely an illusion, although a very persistent one.

Albert Einstein

This section provides a brief description of several of the most prominent challenges to forming well-founded judgments about the state of the world, the causal processes that determine its evolution, and thus the projected consequences of specified decisions. Some obstacles are simple and obvious; others more complex and unclear. The list of complications is intimidating:

- Policy analysis requires data, facts, and observations, at least to describe the current reality, yet the profession is plagued by measurement difficulties. Key variables describing the relevant state of the world may not be well defined or measured, so we may be stuck measuring highly imperfect proxies because they are more readily available, e.g., income vs. human welfare or treatment processes vs. health outcomes.
- We often measure the wrong things. It is always easier to measure irrelevant inputs or outputs than valued outcomes, e.g., school enrolment rather than learning. In the development area, key outcomes such as governance or capacity-building are even harder to measure than education and health outcomes. In many areas, we have poor statistical data to mine for baselines. All this makes attribution problematic for any policy initiative occurring in a multi-dimensional world.

- Managers who cannot measure what they want, often settle for wanting what they can measure. Policy analysts may be stuck dealing with the aftermath of what-to-measure decisions as stupid as the apocryphal example of the analyst who asked an actuary why he recommended selling more life insurance policies to ninety-eight-year-olds. The actuary replied, "According to our tables, very few of them die each year."
- Even well-defined quantities may be measured imperfectly or with bias or with inadequate time or space resolution or history (e.g., environmental monitoring).
- Causal relations may be imperfectly known.[2] We may only be able to estimate parameter values within an assumed model structure, not test model structure. Causal structure may be changing even as we try to measure it. Dobell (1974, 42) has reminded us, "many techniques of applied mathematics are available in principle to support applications in policy analysis, but in most cases data are lacking, knowledge of the causal structure is lacking, time for detailed system specification is lacking, and the whole structure is changing faster than anyone can model it." Only clairvoyants can describe the counterfactual needed to assess policy impact: comparing the world with the policy initiative to what would have happened without the policy.
- As Kenneth Boulding (1983, 21) notes, the "real world is in an endless dynamic flux; all equilibrium is a figment of the human imagination." Dominant economic models assume people optimize fixed objectives relative to specified constraints. The computational simplicity of this representation has led to its dominance in economic reasoning and much policy analysis, even as increasing evidence indicates this is not generally the case. Unfortunately, however, no similarly comprehensive and economical description of human behaviour has yet developed to take its place.
- Social processes and the human choices that comprise them may be reflexive – subject to internal feedbacks such as herd behaviour or changing in response to attempts to measure, model, or manipulate them. Paul Volcker (2010) has commented that a "basic flaw running through much of the recent financial innovation is that thinking embedded in mathematics and physics could be directly adapted to markets. A search for repetitive patterns of behaviour and computations of normal distribution curves are a big part of the physical sciences. However, financial markets are

not driven by changes in natural forces but by human phenomena, with all their implications for herd behaviour, for wide swings in emotion, and for political intervention and uncertainties."

VALUE JUDGMENTS – WHAT OUGHT OR OUGHT NOT TO BE THE CASE?

Policy analysis – forces us to confront conflicts among competing values ... Should a policy that would yield a great excess of benefits for society as a whole be selected even if it would inflict severe costs on a small group of people?

Weimer and Vining

Presume that we have done the best we can in arraying evidence and describing interactions and the consequences of our policy options. Any significant policy decision will have multiple consequences; how do we decide which ones are preferred, or how to trade off between multiple dimensions of benefit or harm to different people or places? In making normative decisions there are some obstacles that are simple and obvious, while others are more complex and unclear. In total, they are just as intimidating as the difficulties in determining what is or is not the case:

- We know it is perilous to assume market outcomes are optimal and try to approximate them as closely as possible. The theory of the second-best shows how that is not generally valid.
- We know policy consequences are distributed over time, but there is no objective basis to assign a social discount rate to aggregate and compare effects over time.
- Outcomes are uncertain, people have different attitudes to risk, and decisions may strongly distribute differential risks across people and communities.
- You might imagine you can just ask people to clarify these values, but people are irrational and survey responses are notoriously sensitive to small changes in question order and wording.

Theory of the Second Best

The belief that competitive equilibrium in markets is socially optimal is perhaps the most dominant normative assumption deployed in policy analysis. The Theory of the Second Best (Lipsey and Lancaster 1956) is a general rebuttal to many naïve uses of this presumption. The theory reminds us that the conditions necessary for optimal outcomes rarely exist and that near-optimal conditions will not necessarily produce near-optimal outcomes. Assuming two or more requirements for achieving the optimal economic outcome cannot be satisfied, then satisfying those other requirements that can be met is not necessarily the second best option and may not even be beneficial. In economic analysis, the system is optimized if prices in all product and factor markets are equal to their marginal costs. Yet by the Theory of the Second Best, if marginal costs do not equal prices in two or more markets, introducing policy to set price equal to marginal cost in one of the out-of-equilibrium markets may make matters worse. To remain sane in the profession is to suffer from anosognosia.

Treatment of Time

Assessments of policy options over time require a "time discount rate" to compute present values. There is no "correct" or positively valid discount rate. Nordhaus, defining the "time discount rate" as the relative weight given to the economic welfare of different generations over time, notes that the famous Stern Review on the Economics of Climate Change uses a discount rate of effectively zero (to be precise, 0.1 percent per year) (Stern 2006). A zero discount rate means that generations into the indefinite future are treated the same as present generations; a positive time discount rate means that the welfare of future generations is reduced or "discounted" compared to nearer generations.[3] Conclusions can differ radically, depending on the choice of a discount rate. Nordhaus (2006, 8) quotes Koopmans: "the problem of optimal growth is too complicated, or at least too unfamiliar, for one to feel comfortable in making an *entirely* a priori choice of [a time discount rate] before one knows the implications of alternative choices."

Nordhaus (2006) suggests a reasonable alternative view would be that each generation should leave at least as much total societal capital (tangible, natural, human, and technological) as it inherited. This would admit a wide array of time discount rates. A second alternative would be that societies should maximize the economic well-being of the poorest generation, the implication being that current consumption should *increase* sharply to reflect the anticipated projected future improvements in technological progress and in productivity. The honest policy analyst must present an array of sensitivity calculations.

Treatment of Uncertainty and Risk

Risk is a particularly problematic worry in making public policy.

> The conflict between protecting individuals and benefiting the collective arises in all aspects of public policy, but is particularly poignant on matters of risk. Neither extreme position is tenable. Because individuals matter, a position of social Darwinism that cavalierly dismisses individual suffering in order to maximize the welfare of the surviving members of society is clearly unacceptable. But neither is it possible for society to completely insure individuals against all losses suffered, both because true compensation for physical suffering is impossible, and because the attempt to compensate all victims may cripple the adaptive capacity of society as a whole. (Dobell and Parson 1986, 35)

Dobell points out that there are many nonmonetary and immeasurable factors that affect people's decisions and attitudes toward risk: "people respond to many facets of an outcome; monetary or other numerical measures of the magnitudes of consequences are by no means the only considerations that matter to people." In his article appropriately titled "The Public Administrator: God or Entrepreneur? Or are they the same in the Public Service?" Dobell reminds us that "Risk analysis is vulnerable to profound uncertainty, but so is every other approach. It requires the pricing of the priceless and placing monetary value on human life, but every other approach does so implicitly – Although analysis does not initially address the distribution of risks, it can be made to elucidate them – Even in a world of profound uncertainty and missing data, explicit and formal analysis offers the essential decision tool for informing and guiding the public manager in the often agonizingly difficult decisions that must be taken on matters of public risk. Within a framework of principle, analysis does help" (1989, 10).

The honest policy analyst can persuade people to make better risk decisions on their own behalf. Dobell's advice: "Individuals acting on their own account are free to risk their resources according to their own calculations. One can attempt to counsel them, and to demonstrate that, in light of their own objectives, behaviour more in accord with the theory and normative framework showing how decisions should, for best results, be made, would better serve their purposes" (2002, 8).

Irrationality

Laurence Peters has written that "some problems are so complex that you have to be highly intelligent and well informed just to be undecided about them." Most people who don't know what they want or like, or what will make them happy, follow heuristics that are known to be erroneous. Also troubling is that people are irrational. We all suffer from the illusion that our choices are rational. We don't know our preferences that well – we are susceptible to influences from external forces, default options, and decoys. Dan Ariely (2010) has written up many experiments that demonstrate the wide variety of our irrational behaviours. They include the effect of expectations, the influence of decisions made by people who design forms, and the impact of dummy options (alternatives nobody wants) on our preferred choices.

We don't know our preferences well enough to make rational choices. In tasting experiments with beer laced with vinegar, without foreknowledge of the vinegar, most people prefer the vinegary brew. Yet if they know in advance one beer is laced with vinegar, when they taste they prefer the non-vinegar brew. If you tell people in advance that something will be distasteful, the odds are good they will agree with you – not because their experience tells them so, but because of their expectations (Ariely 2010).

Opinion Polls

One common reaction in public policy is to resort to opinion polls, to ask "what do people want?" This raises two concerns: the intrinsic propensity to normative bias in polling and Arrow's Impossibility Theorem. It is very difficult to craft a value-neutral poll. The poll's vocabulary risks being value-laden. The set-up questions may predispose the respondent in ways favorable to the poll sponsor. The best example is the *Yes Minister* episode on the merits of polling the public on their attitudes towards compulsory national service.

Sir Humphrey: "Mr. Woolley, are you worried about the number of young people without jobs?"
Bernard Woolley: "Yes."
Sir Humphrey: "Are you worried about the rise in crime among teenagers?"
Bernard Woolley: "Yes."
Sir Humphrey: "Do you think there is a lack of discipline in our Comprehensive schools?"
Bernard Woolley: "Yes"
Sir Humphrey: "Do you think young people welcome some authority and leadership in their lives?"
Bernard Woolley: "Yes"
Sir Humphrey: "Do you think they respond to a challenge?"
Bernard Woolley: "Yes."
Sir Humphrey: "Would you be in favor of reintroducing National Service?"
Bernard Woolley: "Oh...well, I suppose I might be."
Sir Humphrey: "Yes or no?"
Bernard Woolley: "Yes."

And then,

Sir Humphrey: "can get the opposite result."
Bernard Woolley: "How?"
Sir Humphrey: "Mr. Woolley, are you worried about the danger of war?"
Bernard Woolley: "Yes."
Sir Humphrey: "Are you worried about the growth of armaments?"
Bernard Woolley: "Yes."
Sir Humphrey: "Do you think there is a danger in giving young people guns and teaching them how to kill?"
Bernard Woolley: "Yes"
Sir Humphrey: "Do you think it is wrong to force people to take up arms against their will?"
Bernard Woolley: "Yes."
Sir Humphrey: "Would you oppose the reintroduction of National Service?"
Bernard Woolley: "Yes"
Sir Humphrey: "There you are, you see Bernard." (Jay and Lynn 1980)

The same point is made in the comic strip *BC*:

Client to pollster: "I would like you to do a poll."
Pollster's Answer: "What results do you want?"
Client: "Why do you ask?"
Answer: "So I'll know what questions to ask.""

Another reason you cannot just ask people what they want follows from the fact that in the real world there are always several policy options. Analysts may be tempted to simplify matters by presenting three choices: an inexpensive initiative that does not solve the problem at issue, an unaffordable Mercedes Benz version, and a prudent middle course. Even if we could frame questions in a value-free way, Arrow's "Impossibility Theorem" holds that when voters have three or more options available, no voting system can convert the ranked preferences of individuals into a community-wide ranking while also meeting reasonable fairness criteria (Arrow 1951).

HOW TO BRIEF CHALLENGED MINISTERS

The problem in the world isn't ignorance, it's things people know that aren't so.

Mark Twain

How does one present material to a minister who might be a few gallons short of a full tank? One can attempt to counsel people – but one must appreciate the intellectual capacity of the audience. How can we ask them to suspend disbelief and question their prejudices? Confucius, Plato, and Oliver Cromwell all advise us to reflect and consider that we might be wrong. People have a "confirmation bias," and it gets worse when you consider heterogeneity among people. Max Planck and recent literature on expert over-confidence remind us that experts aren't exempt from inappropriate prejudice, and might even be worse.

We attribute to Confucius the aphorism "Real knowledge is to recognize the extent of one's ignorance." Lindblom (1979) advises that people cannot handle the calculations for all the values in play for any mildly complex decision. George Miller (1955) focuses on the limits of our capacity for processing information- leading to the possible conclusion never to exceed the number seven in lists of items we expect people to remember. Recall George Carlin's reminder: "Imagine the average American ... half of them are dumber than that."

The Dunning Kruger Effect adds to the handicap – unskilled people lack the skill to rate their own level of competence. Unskilled people rate themselves higher than more competent people rate themselves (Kruger and Dunning 1999). The unfortunate possibility is that Bertrand Russell appears to have been correct when he observed that "the trouble with the world is that the stupid are cocksure and the intelligent are full of doubt." Yeats expressed the same insight poetically: "The best lack all conviction, while the worst are full of passionate intensity." The policy analyst must work with political masters and must accurately take their measure. Russell (1951, 164) also said, "our great democracies still tend to think that a stupid man is more likely to be honest than a clever man, and our politicians take advantage of this prejudice by pretending to be even more stupid than nature has made them." In George Bernard Shaw's characterization (Shaw 1907, act 3), "He knows nothing and he thinks he knows everything. That clearly points to a political career."

People are generally pigheaded. The phenomenon has been characterized as the "confirmation bias." We develop an irrational loyalty to our beliefs and work hard to find evidence that supports those opinions and to discredit, discount, or avoid information that does not (Fine 2011). Note Max Planck's observation: "An important scientific innovation rarely makes its way by gradually winning over and converting its opponents: What happens is that the opponents gradually die out."

"Even though people are pigheaded, don't be too quick or arrogant in dismissing community preferences or common sense." Leslie Pal (1987) reminds us not to go overboard – one of his "ten tips for good policy analysis" (see below) is that we should "be cautiously respectful of common sense." Policy analysts should not dismiss community preferences or common sense as simplistic; "people are never as stupid as they sometimes appear."

The prescription for explaining the results of policy analysis is to accept the foregoing diagnosis of the audience. Then lay out the various problems and considerations framed with options. Given that the most effective form of flattery is to ask for advice, solicit views on which of the options should be accepted, explaining the consequences for policy decisions.

INSTRUMENTAL JUDGMENTS – WHAT IS THE BEST MEANS AVAILABLE TO REDUCE THE MISMATCH BETWEEN WHAT IS AND WHAT OUGHT TO BE?

Obstacles

In addition to the list of obstacles presented in the preceding pages, there are several barriers to marshalling policy analysis so it contributes usefully to good public decisions. One difficulty of translating policy advice into appropriate action is the propensity to duck hard choices. David Victor (2011) has written, "When society confronts really hard problems there are strong pressures on policy makers to avoid making costly decisions. The result is symbolic policies – that is policy ventures that look serious but have no real impact."

Policy analysts will confront other difficulties translating policy advice into action. In large, far-flung organizations, the individuals responsible for operations in the field will be resistant to new ideas. In presenting a new policy or program proposal based on a successful experiment, be prepared for the reaction, "your job is to get the money; our job is to decide how to spend it."

Jurisdictional jealousies are a fact of life. Large organizations are replete with bureaucratic warriors resistant to any change perceived as potentially diminishing their influence. They will resort to stalling techniques best described in another episode of *Yes, Minister*:

> Jim: Stalling technique?
> Tom: Yeah, comes in five stages. First of all he'll tell you that your administration is very new and that there's lots of things to be getting on with … Then if you still persist whatever your idea is he'll say something like, er yes Minister I quite appreciate the intention certainly something ought to be done but are you sure this is the right way to achieve it – Now if you are still unperturbed he will shift his ground, he will shift from telling you how to do, to when you should do it, you know I mean he'll say now Minister this is not the right time, for all sorts of reasons – if you don't [settle for that] he'll simply say that the policy has run into difficulties – Technical, political, legal. Now legal are the best sort because he can make these totally incomprehensible and with any luck this stalling technique will have lasted for about three years and you'll know that you're at the final stage where

he says now Minister we're getting very close to the run up to the next general election, are you sure you can get this policy through. (Jay and Lynn 1980; "Big Brother")

Time and the political election cycle can be a limiting factor. Ideally, any major research project should invest as much time to explain and promote proposals as it took to research and develop the recommended policy proposals. For example, high-level panels or commissions should not publish their final report with a press release at the end of the term – ideally they would spend several months lobbying for their findings.

The list of challenges/obstacles in the previous sections makes the problem look truly daunting. What's an honest policy analyst to do? All is not lost; there are means to navigate through the minefields and do a little good while keeping your conscience clear enough that you can sleep at night. The remainder of this paper suggests some potential ways forward in making instrumental judgments, given the intimidating list of problems in appreciating reality and in a world of ordinary people bedeviled by a wide range of inconsistent values.

The literature abounds with advice for policy analysts. Dobell and Mitchell (1996) provide a helpful aide-memoire.

Leslie Pal (1987, 251) provides a handy checklist of Ten Tips:

- Dive deep.
- Know the law.
- Count the stakes.
- Look at the big picture.
- Be cautiously skeptical of experts.
- Be cautiously respectful of common sense.
- Have a bias towards small solutions.
- Choose policy targets you have a reasonable chance of controlling.
- Structure choice into policy.
- Err on the side of diffuse interests.

The following sections present guidance to navigate the labyrinth. Ideas explored include understanding points of disagreement to highlight potential common ground, exploiting the use of incentives, doing good by stealth, exploiting synergies, and benefitting from female perspectives.

Table 14.1
Ten commandments to guide strategic action for policy analysts.

Policy formulation	*Public participation*	*Effective advocacy*
Know the real problems	Inform participants	Understand decision-makers' motivations
Forget means/ends distinction	Clarify your role	Limit priorities
Seek resilience not stability/equilibrium	Clarify your mandate	Anticipate implementation obstacles
Focus on changing behavior not reducing risk	Finesse consultation fatigue	Ensure winners compensate losers
Broaden feasible options	Encourage and inform choices	Prioritize action over analysis
Status quo not an option	Reframe positions on hypotheses	Focus on central issues
Focus on small/reversible actions	Encourage diversity	Do both opportunistic and contingency planning
Concentrate on key evidence	Monitor results/share learning	Prepares persuasive individual comparisons
Consider all potential instruments	Get incentives right	Stress entrepreneurship
Encourage competition	Encourage openness /due process	Communication is crucial

Source: Dobell and Mitchell (1986).

UNDERSTAND WHY PEOPLE DISAGREE

The honest policy analyst appreciates differences in perspectives on aggregation, time horizon, and market structure and power.

Understanding the nature of disagreements is an important prerequisite to diagnosing policy problems. You can generate surprising insights, and practical progress, by digging deeper to examine why people disagree. Sometimes they disagree because they are looking at different aspects of the same problem. For example, one cogent explanation (Kanbur 2001) is to be aware of the different prisms of technocrats (finance ministries' officials, economic analysts, policy operational managers in development banks, the financial press) compared to poverty advocates (NGO analysts, UN specialized agencies, aid ministries, social sector ministries in the South and non-economist researchers). Technocrats view the consequences of policy in highly aggregated terms, perceive markets as neutral instruments, and assess consequences in a five-to-ten-year medium-term perspective. Poverty advocates view the consequences of policy in disaggregated terms, perceive markets as riddled with power relations, which disadvantage the poor, and highlight short-term consequences (which can drive a family into starvation, or children out of school). Technocrats see the *decreasing proportion* of people below the poverty line – they are optimistic regarding the long term. Poverty advocates see the *increasing absolute number* of people below the poverty line – they worry whether growth is sustainable long-term given current rates of resource depletion and earth's limited carrying capacity. Poverty advocates are critical of the oversimplification of the technocrat's surveys, which omit the value of public services: "bus service is cancelled, health post runs out of drugs, or teacher does not turn up to teach."

The implication is that good policy analysis acknowledges different perspectives and explains recommendations in terms of the various ways problems are perceived. Successful policy analysis must convince technocrats, operational managers, and poverty advocates, as well as ministers. This requires recognition of the respective prisms, values, priorities, and vocabularies of the different audiences and constituencies.

INCENTIVES

The honest policy analyst seeks to embed incentives in the policy under consideration.

Very often, the consequences and effectiveness of policies depend fundamentally on how people react to them. So analysis should always include the questions of people will react, what incentives the policy creates, and how can these be constructed to motivate behaviour likely to help the policy succeed. The route to effectiveness for the honest policy analyst is to focus on incentive effects in the design of policy. The quintessential example is the reported approach to property tax assessment in Renaissance-era Venice. Governments need accurate assessment of property values to decide how to tax them fairly. Governments might be tempted to rely on owners to tell them, since they have better knowledge about their property than the government. But since owners prefer to be taxed less, they have an incentive to understate the value of their property. In Venice, they solved this problem by having property owners self-assess (saving the cost of officials to determine property valuations and finessing the costs of an appeal system). The incentive to report a fair value was that the state had the right to expropriate the property for the self-assessed value plus 10 percent. Problem solved. Similarly, Karlan and Appel (2011) identify seven interventions that build rational incentives into development policy: micro-savings initiatives, reminders to save, prepaid fertilizer sales, de-worming, small-group remedial education, chlorine dispensers for clean water, and commitment devices that help people make choices that advance their long-term goals.

Another example is the cure for teacher absenteeism in the state of Rajasthan in India. The solution was to take time-stamped photos of the teachers in the classroom and penalize them for absences. But a similar effort in the same region to deal with absenteeism of nurses did not work. After an initial burst of compliance, attendance deteriorated as nurses figured out just how willing their supervisors were to look away. Monitoring equipment was trashed and supervisors increased the number of excused absences for health workers. Nurse absenteeism actually got worse (Benarjee and Duflo 2011). In the latter case thought should have been given to the incentives facing the supervisors, given that the same problem did not arise for teachers.

An attractive approach was developed to deal with the problem of the disincentives facing investment in research on diseases specific to developing countries, e.g., pneumococcal. The pharmaceutical industry does not develop vaccines against such diseases, out of concern that customers in developing countries will not be able to pay the prices needed to offset high research and development costs. An Advance Market Commitment (AMC) is "a legally-binding agreement for an amount of funds to subsidize the purchase, at a given price, of an as yet unavailable vaccine against a specific disease causing high morbidity and mortality in developing countries" (Levine, Kremer, and Albright 2005). Making a commitment in advance to buy vaccines if and when they are developed creates incentives for industry to increase investment in research and development. Vaccines are bought only if they meet pre-determined standards of efficacy and safety and if developing countries ask for them. "Once this fixed number of sales or total amount has been reached, manufacturers having benefited from the subsidy would be contractually obliged to either sell to developing countries at a price affordable over the long term or to license their technology to other manufacturers" (World Health Organization 2006).

DOING GOOD BY STEALTH

The honest policy analyst, facing a polity with a short time horizon, must introduce change very gradually, if not imperceptibly.

There is merit in "going small" in order not to awaken opposition. One of Pal's Ten Tips was to have a bias towards small solutions. "A small solution may be defined as one which has narrow scope – 'Small solutions' may also be regarded as limited experiments that allow policy-makers to see whether their proposals work or not. A bias towards small solutions can thus become a willingness to try new ideas and experiment with old forms" (Pal 1987, 251). So an additional rationale for going small is to experiment, to demonstrate benefits, and thereby create support for future expansion.

Banerjee and Duflo argue that "it is possible to make very significant progress against the biggest problems in the world through the accumulation of a set of small steps, each well thought out, carefully tested, and judiciously implemented. The political constraints are real, and they make it difficult to find big solutions to big problems. But there is considerable slack to improve institutions and policy at the margin. These changes will be incremental, but they will sustain and build on themselves. They can be the start of a quiet revolution." Such small and incremental changes may also, under some conditions, serve as experiments to learn what does and does not work, including learning about what incentives are most effective.

Jeffrey Simpson (2011) has quipped that in Canada any proposal that promises "long-term gain for short-term pain" is dead on arrival. So we must find a way to forgo the short-term pain, by phasing in change imperceptibly. Doug Hartle's described public service use of the term "phasing" as a euphemism for at least delaying, and perhaps, shelving a proposal. "What is phased today need never be completed tomorrow. Fortunately for the politician and the bureaucrat the journalist's 'bring forward' filing system doesn't work well. The public is usually distracted by another issue when the magic implementation date appears on the calendar" (Hartle 1976).

However, if the changes can be legislated, postponing cost increases and obscuring negative impacts, the public's distraction works in the right direction. David Victor (2011, 12) has written, "The political viability of policies rises when the cost can be imposed on groups that are highly diffused and often unaware of what they are paying." The case below illustrates one way forward.

The honest policy analyst can introduce major changes gradually, to escape opposition. An excellent example is the late-1970s debate in Canada on universal eligibility for social-security benefits. Ministers were disturbed to learn that the impact of the universal family allowance (a monthly payment to mothers for each child introduced in 1945) combined with a child tax exemption was heavily regressive.[4] But they worried that the regressivity was necessary to get the middle class to support transfers to low-income people. The decision was made in 1978 to gradually replace the family allowance and tax exemption programs by a progressive refundable child tax credit (National Child Benefit 2006). But it was introduced so gradually over a period of years, slowly decreasing the value of the family allowance and tax exemption, that the reform escaped opposition.[5] Any tax reforms are likely to be more politically palatable if a multi-year schedule of changes is legislated, with "cuts" to benefits phased in so slowly as to be almost imperceptible.

We feel like we make decisions, but many of our decisions are made by default, by people who design forms. An excellent example is the organ-donation decision on driver license forms. In countries where you must check a box to participate, such as Denmark, the Netherlands, the United Kingdom, and Germany, participation rates are below 20 percent. In countries where you must check a box to decline to participate, such as Sweden, Belgium, and Austria, participation rates approach 100 percent. Policy analysts should be aware of this pervasive quirk and exploit it to promote progressive policies.

EXPLOITING SYNERGIES

The honest policy analyst seeks synergies between diverse policy sectors.

"We can't solve problems by using the same kind of thinking we used when we created them" is wisdom attributed to Albert Einstein. Lateral thinking is called for. Consider Joseph Hallinan's description of the candle problem. Give someone a book of matches, a box of tacks, and a candle. The task is to attach the candle to the wall. The candle is too thick to use the tacks to nail it to the wall. Melting the candle on the wall does not work. The solution is to use the box as a candleholder, tacking the box to the wall. People think of the box as a container for tacks; they do not think *outside* the box (Hallinan 2009, 182). The Walkman radio is a classic example. Sony engineers failed in the attempt to design a small, portable stereo tape recorder until an executive asked about combining headphones with the tape player, eliminating the recorder function altogether. This reversed the common assumption that a play-back machine must also record and, therefore, created something new (Michalko 2000).

Policy analysts should look for synergies between different policy areas. Sometimes a single initiative can be crafted so as to simultaneously advance two or more areas, each of which appears to be blocked if considered separately." An excellent example is Singapore's approach to pension policy and public housing. Forty years ago, there were concerns about an inadequate savings rate and prospects for long-term social security. At the same time, Singapore faced the challenge of providing public housing in a culture that disdained public or common areas: it was common for residents to simply pitch trash out of windows. The response to these seemingly independent policy problems was to initiate a mandatory defined-contribution pension plan.

Contribution rates in the 1970s were as high as 25 percent of payroll for both employers and employees. Citizens could either leave their contributions to grow in the Central Provident Fund (CPF) or use their balance to buy their flats in government-built public housing. Seeing housing values grow faster than returns in the CPF, many citizens opted to purchase their flats. This transformed public housing developments into well-maintained private condominium estates. Singapore thus achieved both satisfactory outcomes in provision for retirement and a home-ownership rate above 85 percent. A bonus feature was that annual changes in payroll contribution rates became an effective counter-cyclical macroeconomic policy instrument.

Climate change is an issue offering promising potential synergies. Changes made to mitigate carbon emissions can complement policies on air quality, public health, energy security, taxation, and fiscal policies. In all likelihood, the best prospects for political approval will be to initiate policy in areas appealing to priorities other than climate change. For example, public health policies to combat obesity will have positive effects on carbon emissions – overweight people require more energy for food and transportation (Edwards and Roberts 2009). Similarly, policies to promote secondary education for girls in developing countries, adopted to advance human rights and gender equality, will also as a by-product lower fertility rates and thus reduce climate change and other environmental burdens by decreasing future population.

THE GENDER FACTOR

In politics if you want anything said, ask a man; if you want anything done, ask a woman.

Margaret Thatcher

The honest policy analyst privileges the female perspective. Women take a different approach than men to decision making, business strategy, and risk assessment. An MIT study concluded that group intelligence increases with the proportion of women in the group (Dizikes 2010). Given that most complex policy research efforts involve group rather than individual effort, the prudent team leader will ensure a high proportion of women on the team.

In business, the proportion of women in senior management correlates positively with Fortune 500 companies' performance on several measures (McFarland 2011). In a study on the role of gender on acquisitions and mergers, when the CEO is a woman, the "bid premium paid over the pre-announcement target share price is, *ceteris paribus*, over 70 percent smaller than when the bidding company CEO is a man" (Levi, Li, and Zhang 2008, 1). The same study concluded that having a higher number of independently appointed women on a board of directors reduces the bid premium of the target company (figure 14.1).

Research demonstrates that "illusory superiority"– a factor related to the Dunning Kruger effect mentioned above – has a gender dimension. Male students tend to overestimate their performance, whilst female students tend to underestimate their performance, despite female students' performance actually being equal or superior to that of male students (Lanyon and Hubball 2008). A good example is individual investor performance, where men act on their unsubstantiated ideas more frequently than women.

Figure 14.1 "That's an excellent suggestion Miss Triggs. Perhaps one of the men here would like to make it." © Punch Limited

In areas such as finance, men are more overconfident than women and trade excessively compared to women. A study by Barber and Odean (2001) found that women achieve better investment results than men, about 1 percentage point annually. These findings were reinforced by a more recent study by Barclays Wealth and Ledbury Research, which found women were less likely to take risks and therefore more likely to make money in the market (Melnick 2011). Risk aversion is a gender difference attributed to lower levels of testosterone in women. A study by Sapienza, Zingales, and Maestripieri (2009) examined the effects of testosterone levels on decision making. The choice was between guaranteed sums of money or playing the lottery. Those with higher levels of testosterone were more likely to choose a riskier lottery with unfavourable odds.

In general, women are more likely to have less volatile portfolios, lower expectations, wear their seatbelts, floss and brush their teeth, check their blood pressure (Zweig 2009), and less likely to engage in recreational drug use (Gupta et al. 2009). However, if all of the foregoing has not convinced the reader, there is the additional point that women are more honest than men, in the United States at least. In an exhaustive national survey, the results were that the odds of shoplifting were significantly higher for men than for women (Blanco et al. 2008). The honest policy analyst, considering the above evidence, should ensure there are a good number of women on the team.

SOME MORE GUIDANCE

Careful treatment of process and effective communication are two generic critical skills to cultivate. Take consultation seriously and prepare to be surprised and/or persuaded. Process is substance. Policy analysts are often confronted by organized civil society and the general public demanding to be involved in meaningful consultation on the development of policy. The honest policy analyst resists the natural temptation of superficial consultations (many suffer from arrogance presuming we know what we will be told) and recommends constructive engagement. An excellent example is provided by UNAIDS, which adopted an uncommon approach in the constitution of its governing body – its Programme Coordinating Board (PCB). It has representatives of twenty-two governments from all geographic regions, the UNAIDS Cosponsor organizations, and five seats for non-governmental organizations (NGOs), including associations of people living with HIV. The process of identification of the non-governmental organizations is determined by the non-governmental organizations themselves (UNAIDS 2011). This out-of-the-box approach, which enhances participation, turns out to have worked very effectively for the last fifteen years.

Policy analysts should invest in perfecting strategies and techniques of effective communication. Use humour and visual aids to communicate messages. While a picture is worth a thousand words, a humorous cartoon is even more valuable. People remember funny cartoons and the ideas they present. Cartoons can be invaluable in visual presentations, by securing the audience's attention: no one likes to miss a joke. Bear in mind the cultural context, however: humour based on religion, sex, or politics may be inappropriate.

Recognize your audience's limitations and have some compassion for them. Be careful in selecting options to avoid the perception that you have included a dummy option – an alternative dissimilar to unfavored options but roughly comparable to the preferred option.

Ariely provides several examples that in complex decisions between alternatives – real estate purchases, vacation packages, subscription bundles – people are influenced by similar relatively unattractive options that bias our choice. (The message is that when you go bar hopping always bring a friend slightly less attractive than yourself).

CONCLUSION

What then is an honest policy analyst to do? By honest, I mean a set of characteristics listed by Dobell – a willingness to re-examine and challenge one's own starting points, biases, and belief systems, including

- To give up using expert knowledge to hide a value-driven agenda
- To avoid appeal to simple concepts like a uniform social threshold for "acceptable risk."
- To recognize that distributional issues and ethical dilemmas cannot be resolved or disguised as technical computations (Dobell, Barrett, and Lee 2002).

There are ways to overcome the many constraints – understanding the basis of different points of view, deploying incentives, exploiting potential synergy, calibrating phasing to the threshold of collective tolerance, and ensuring female participation. Process matters – respecting the values and vocabularies of various stakeholders. Communication is more effective if it uses humour and colourful presentations. There is a substantial reward in effective, honest policy analysis – contributing to public service by decoding the fascinating intellectual puzzles of over-constrained issues that matter.

A final observation from Rod Dobell, quoted from Drury (1975), "Analysis of public policy must be relevant: it must take into account the process of policy formation, and the nature of collective decision-making; it must emphasize the art of presentation (of complex results in meaningful ways) and the art of representation (of complex systems in simple forms preserving key features); it must marry institutional wisdom with esoteric models to yield insight."

Yes, it is not easy, but the practical advice in previous sections can really make a difference. And anyway, what is the alternative? The alternative is to give up in despair and leave the field to others less thoughtful and honest than you – so take heart, go forth, and try to be an honest policy analyst.

NOTES

1 Dobell, ghost-writing for C.M. Drury (1975). See also Dobell (2002), identifying the analyst's roles (with traits) as Agent (responsive), Double Agent (responsible), Scapegoat (silent), Communicator (consultative), Convener (deliberative), and Co-Manager (participatory).
2 See "Spurious Correlations," at www.tylervigen.com, for an amusing website on the danger of correlation being mistaken for causation.
3 The waggish observation is that it is always hard to convincingly answer the person who asks, "What has posterity ever done for me?"
4 Minister Lloyd Axworthy's reaction in a private briefing to a graph presented by Michael Wolfson that showed the after-tax effects, by income level, of the combination of transfer and tax expenditure was, "Make sure no one sees this chart."
5 Ironically, the current Canadian government re-introduced the regressive universal benefit – a taxable $100 monthly payment to families for each child under the age of six.

15

Speaking Elusive Truth to Shifting Power: Reflections on Evolving Styles, Changing Views, and New Problems

A.R. DOBELL

INTRODUCTION

In a diverse, plural world characterized by differing perceptions and conflicting interests, facing uncertainty and challenged by complexity, how can collective decisions imposing risks and consequences on others legitimately be made? More specifically, how can recommendations or comment to those who will make the decisions and exercise authority responsibly be offered by advisors who assume no accountability to those ultimately affected? Is there any proper balance between expertise and experience, reason and passion in the political setting in which policy advice is to be offered?

In retrospect, that seems to be the puzzle I have been pursuing ever since a longer-than-expected assignment in Ottawa to contribute to the rational pursuit of scientific government embraced by Prime Minister Pierre Trudeau following his election in 1968 disrupted my confident career as professor of political economy at the University of Toronto. (Though that position was still titled "political economy," my role was seen to be the application of the science of economics to policy-relevant analysis. My confidence flowed from years of study of economics and mathematics at UBC and MIT, with a post-doctoral stint as assistant professor of economics at Harvard).[1] That assignment in Ottawa thrust me unexpectedly into more basic questions as to how all that assembled scientific expertise ought to be brought to bear within the realities of large bureaucracies driven by electoral politics (machinery that owes more to passions than to reason, as Chantal Mouffe (2000), among many others, has emphasized).

With the early preconceptions and largely unexamined beliefs I carried to Ottawa, the truth seemed neater and power exercised in more orderly political processes than now seems an accurate characterization. This note sketches one idiosyncratic view of an evolution, from clear roles for experts in well-defined "inside" processes addressing well-formulated problems to much fuzzier accounts of attempts to respond to wicked messes encountered in a maze of institutional settings embedded in complex systems.

Exploring the changing balance between expertise and experience, precision and perspective, calculation and context, in the formation of public policy also entails examining the evolving roles and responsibilities of the academic and the academy in building evidence and knowledge for that purpose, and of the changing balance of inside expertise and outside experience through the stages of interpreting relevant knowledge in appropriate context.

Any component of this topic represents a vast territory; the discussion here is necessarily very sketchy, at a high level of abstraction. It is also rather whimsical, relying on a couple of figures to put many topics crossing many disciplines into some context in a small but illustrative space. The target audience is equally mixed: for the specialist in the relatively new discipline of public policy, the aim is simply to offer a reminder of the relevance of much related literature; for the academic more generally, it is to offer a sketchy survey of some issues surrounding the role of scholarship and scholarly outreach in response to social priorities. But the hope is that this discussion may also interest policy practitioners, community members active in the social economy, and citizens generally, as ideas about citizen science and participatory decision processes continue to evolve.

Much of this book addresses the classic subject of the policy analyst in the bureaucracy (Meltsner 1976), and this note starts from there. But the problems are changing dramatically, becoming more general and more global. Ultimately this sketch moves to address a few of the issues raised by the changing balance between expertise and experience in the pursuit of sustainability. Starting from a vision of well-defined problems in program design or evaluation, the ultimate goal of such work now is here taken to be to influence individual and social decisions toward social transitions in pursuit of sustainability – that is, sustained human wellbeing within a healthy and resilient biosphere.

This evolution of ideas around policy analysis and expert advice might be seen in several dimensions:

- Changing criteria for recommendations within government; and changing notions of rationality (sketched in the second section);
- Changing understandings of science, with consequent changing understandings of expert and other roles in interpretation of evidence; changing social expectations of the academy in "steering" research and the formation of graduates as carriers of knowledge into society; all perhaps leading to declining trust in the objectivity and independence of experts ("hired guns"), and growing cynicism surrounding the processes (the third section);
- Rising expectations about participation in decision processes – not just a general right to information but to voice, and indeed an expectation of influence, leading to new developments in citizen science and participatory decision processes (the fourth section);
- The challenge of sustainability in the Anthropocene era: increasing scale and changing character of problems extending to embrace challenges of global reach, with concern for justice, intergenerational equity, and ecological integrity (the fifth section);
- Changing views about possible responses, raising the need to address collective action problems, institutional frameworks and abstract languages that distance humans from awareness of aggregate consequences of, and moral responsibilities for, their individual actions (the sixth section).

This move to engagement of experts in civic science and broader "outside" community processes and the concomitant dissolution of clear dichotomies between fact and value, administration and politics, or truth and power thus leads to much fuzzier perceptions of the classic process of "speaking truth to power" (Wildavsky 1979).

ROADMAP OF THE RATIONALITIES

Over many years spent in various organizational settings, starting from clear and strong (but largely untested) convictions on the subject of rationality and responsible decision, I came to realize that one must recognize many different accounts and understandings of the notion of "rationality" for purposes of decision. I also came to appreciate some of the crucial differences between decision analysis by, or in support of, an identifiable individual agent,[2] as contrasted with decision analysis on behalf of anonymous others not present or not empowered to decide, but nevertheless bearing the risks. In the end these last features seem to lead to different concepts of democracy.

My convictions – characteristic of the era – emerged from intense study of economic theory and mathematical economics, just as economics was being transformed by the stimulus flowing from post-World War II triumphs in physical sciences, applied analysis, and operations research. For me that thrust could be seen as emerging from the seminal book *Foundations of Economic Analysis*, published in 1947 by my mentor at MIT, Paul Samuelson. When I started as an undergraduate student, I still had obligatory readings from Alfred Marshall's *Principles of Economics* (1920), and insightful scholars like Kenneth Boulding were writing texts in economics. But these were largely peripheral to the growing emphasis on scientific method, theoretical rigour, and indeed abstract elegance.

The roadmap diagram (figure 15.1) illustrates an evolution in thinking (at least in policy analysis circles in the government of Canada, but perhaps more generally) about criteria for responsible decisions in the formation of public policy. Increasingly the insistence on procedurally legitimate decisions seems to have moved us from authoritative advice based on established expertise and rigorous reasoning – away from cost-benefit analysis and formal optimization – toward changing notions of democracy, particularly more inclusive participatory political mechanisms that permit us to confront underlying contradictions and conflicts. At the same time, doctrine in the field has proclaimed the triumph of market mechanisms that were supposed to achieve the expert's abstract optimization goals in a decentralized manner in "the real world." (Excessive allegiance to these now has proved them to be inadequate in that role – indeed even antagonistic to the pursuit of human well-being – but that is a story for later.)

This vaguely chronological diagram outlines a broad sweep of changing ideas – suggestive more than precise or faithful to the vast political science literature on alternative views of democracy – around the notions of rationality that should guide public policy. I suggest a starting point in a broadly based political economy, human-oriented as distinct from the more corporate and system-oriented approach to follow. That starting point is well illustrated in the work of Alfred Marshall, to which I should have paid much more attention than I (or most of my contemporaries) did as we moved briskly on to bold analysis and scientific approaches to social issues. The relevant text is too lengthy to quote here; it will have to be represented by Marshall's own marginal notations offered in summary: "Poverty causes degradation." And "May we not outgrow the belief that poverty is necessary?" (Marshall 1920, 2–3).[3]

This emphasis is the starting point characterized in figure 15.1 as HOPE, with its pursuit of poverty alleviation and equality. As just suggested, one can see it giving way to a much more focused and hard-edged mathematically oriented discipline concerned with what Timothy Mitchell (2011) has suggested is a novel concept of the economy as a new construct centred on flows of money, a concept that he traces to the influence of Keynes in popularizing a statistically and mathematically complete dynamic macroeconomic model.

From this new emphasis in the 1960s and 1970s on economic science to guide allocation of scarce resources in pursuit of prescribed ends we saw within government the emergence in the 1980s of counterweights in two approaches to bureaucratic criteria directed more to keeping the machine running and services delivered than to broader notions of effectiveness and social purpose. One moved toward ostensibly consultative initiatives to define program merit (as "client satisfaction"), the other to management accounting. Neither emphasized substantive social science.

Subsequently one can see appeal to more inclusive processes resting on populist participation and deliberation, more sophisticated information systems serving those making decisions, or simply New Public Management driven largely by "market forces," shaping public policy on the basis of ideas (or ideology) more than on the basis of evidence or analysis, leaving decisions to be taken by individual agents outside government.

In the continuing search for reconciliation of conflicting perspectives, the road to DAMASCUS (Democracy And Markets And Socially-Construed Understandings of Science)[4] seemed to me a wonderful way to focus on "both/and" rather than "either/or." Recent events may now have called this imagery considerably into question, despite its nice biblical roots (and happy acronym). But it still seems to me that the road to DAMASCUS is the road to go, as we

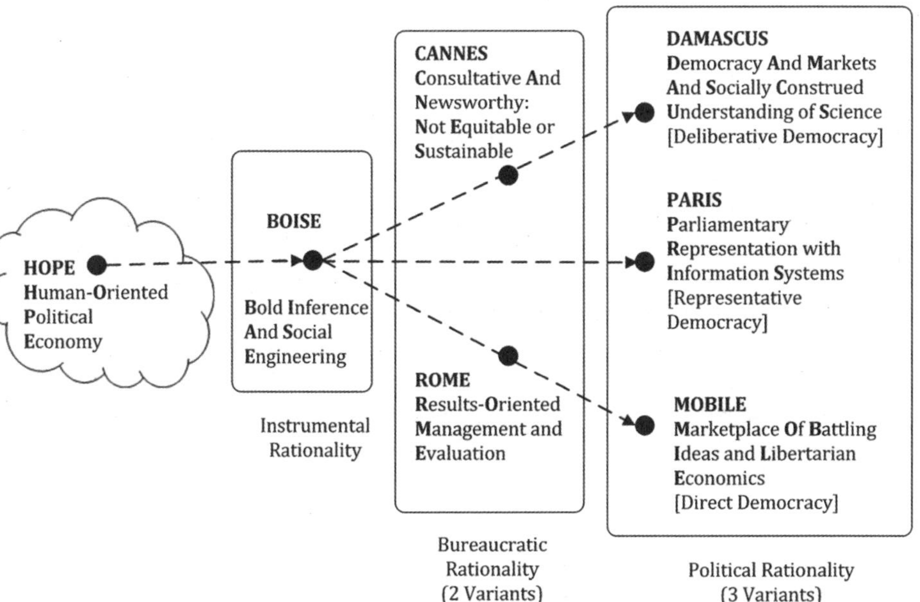

Figure 15.1 A roughly chronological progression of alternative ideas of the character and goals of democratic decision-making, and the resultant basis for policy analysis and advice

search for an effective and legitimate democracy, whether deliberative or agonistic.[5]

Unfortunately all the evidence from recent developments seems to be pointing not to any of these possible approaches to rational public policy or collective decision but to a veritable bonfire of the rationalities, with a collapse to polarized and dysfunctional democratic institutions paralyzed not by analysis but by an inability to achieve even a minimal foundation for cohesive collective action.[6]

But perhaps there is an alternative, dissolving not into paralyzing dysfunction but appealing to the dialogic democracy resting on co-creation of knowledge built in hybrid forums supporting the adaptive approach of measured action (Callon, Lascoumes, and Barthe 2009), or agonistic democracy (Mouffe 2000), as will be discussed below. We may see reason for optimism, perhaps resting on faith in the crowds of younger folks outside North America, in the evolution from the early informal hybrids of HOPE to more sophisticated web-enabled hybrids supporting DAMASCUS and bringing us back around again, toward a more web-based cosmopolitan democracy, whether in these hybrid forums or in other spaces for the development of collective intentions and public policy (figure 15.1).

A big challenge in these settings must be to disentangle cultural affiliations from cognitive capacity, to attenuate the enduring polarization that flows from "motivated reasoning," in which allegiance to affinity groups trumps persuasive evidence in policy formation (Kahan 2013; Kahan et al. 2013).[7] Might web-based platforms for collaborative work and participatory policy formation (to be mentioned below) build an experience from which a sufficient sense of unity and solidarity ("synthetic empathy"; see Krishnamurthy et al. 2012) might flow to overcome the collective action barriers that Kahan has called "the tragedy of the science communication commons"?

A further fascinating question is whether such platforms might realize the three prerequisites for legitimate deliberative democracy: inclusion, absence of exercise of power, and informed reason and persuasion. Without assurance of these conditions, Smith (2004, 2013) suggests, a community may have to resort to – and have justification for – (non-violent) civil disobedience (see also Tully 2013).

In these hybrid forums or otherwise, we still also encounter the central challenge, the performer's dilemma: the need to interpret and realize, concretely, in the changing and contested circumstances of application in particular places, the intent of abstract covenants or collective undertakings expressed in the "work" or the "text" (Taruskin 1995) or "the text in context" (Ramadan 2009), but now negotiated endlessly at many scales, from global to local (Wiener 2014).

This implementation challenge must also be an integral part of these web-based engagement platforms. It and other features of boundary objects in emerging boundary organizations within universities are examined by Parker and Crona (2012).

CHANGING UNDERSTANDINGS OF EVIDENCE, SCIENCE, AND TRUTH

New disciplines going under names such as Social Studies of Science or Science and Technology Studies all suggest that what we consider our facts are socially construed (Douglas 1995). Buzz Holling (1984) claimed that "reality is not perceived, it is conceived." This work suggests that even our values may be up for grabs, to be amended as we come to grips with what they mean in the face of the constraints they place on our exercise of discretion and freedom of action. What are we to do when the foundations of fact and evidence and sound science on which we are supposed to rely seem to shake beneath our work?

We must learn to deal collectively with paradox and contradictions, or what appear to be contradictions – to address what was and was not; what happened and did not. Jan Zwicky, in her wonderful book *Wisdom and Metaphor* (Zwicky 2003), quotes Herakleitos: "We step and do not step into the same stream; we encounter what is and what is not." Or, more scientifically, "Clarity does not reside in reduction to a single directly comprehensible model, but in the exhaustive overlay of different descriptions that incorporate apparently contradictory notions" (Holton 1988, 102).

These contradictions need not be so devastating for our ambitions to be rigorous and rational as is often claimed. Holton (1970) traces the roots of the principle of complementarity enunciated by the eminent physicist Niels Bohr, in which contradictions of the sort mentioned above need not be seen as uncomfortable but rather as essential to a full understanding of physical phenomena, or life more generally: "Bohr's proposal of 1927 was ... we should attempt not to reconcile the dichotomies [of classical physics and continuity on the one hand, and quantum physics and discontinuity on the other] but rather to realize the complementarity of the representation of events in these two quite different languages. The separateness of the accounts is merely a token of the fact that, in the normal language available to us ... it is possible to express the wholeness of nature only through a complementary mode of descriptions."

According to Holton later (in language that resonates strongly in a world where the Arab Spring confronts the Clash of Civilizations),

> The full grandeur of Bohr's ambition was to apply the complementarity point of view also to the understanding and toleration of differences between traditional cultural systems. What gave it all such urgency for him was of course his perception that the most time-honoured method of conflict between societies was chiefly the attempt by one to annihilate the other, and that in the

> atomic age this method had become a guarantee for universal catastrophe, for mutual suicide. As Bohr put it, the main obstacle to a peaceful relation between various human societies is "the deep-rooted differences of the traditional backgrounds ... which exclude any simple accommodation between such cultures. It is above all in this connection that the viewpoint of complementarity offers itself as a means of coping with the situation. (1988, 466)[8]

The point here is that a move away from formal analysis and expertise toward observation and experience is not a fall from grace. The attempt to pursue participatory community-engaged research exploiting local and traditional knowledge and other ways of knowing or seeing or other ways of believing or belonging or being is not a second-class activity inferior to "sound science."[9]

Holton cites Karl Popper as characterizing the status of science in these familiar words: "I think that we shall have to get accustomed to the idea that we must not look upon science as a body of knowledge but rather as a system of guesses or anticipations which in principle cannot be justified, but with which we work as long as they stand up to tests, and of which we are never justified in saying that we know they are true or more or less certain or even probable." Holton goes on to say, "*Our justification for these hypotheses is that they have a hold on our imagination and that they help us deal with our experience*" (1988, 20; emphasis in the original).

James C. Scott (1998), in a book now well known in the public policy literature, offered a flash of insight giving academic legitimacy to the different ways in which policy problems might be framed. He identified the inherent tension between the need for uniform, abstract, and homogeneous concepts to frame decisions at the scale of states or global aggregations, as against the need to recognize all the changing particularities of individuals in particular places. The extended research program of Elinor Ostrom and Vincent Ostrom, as described in her Nobel Prize address (Ostrom 2009), makes the case for the feasibility and sustainability of the community-based nested institutions that can forge the links and bridge the gaps. This in turn led me to argue (Dobell 2009) for integrating not just social sciences and natural sciences considerations in policy discussions but also for bringing in fully the humanities and fine arts, as the sources of insight into the perspectives, interpretations, and performance practices that ground these institutions and attempt to accommodate ongoing contradictions.[10] All of this generates major challenges for academics attempting to define what constitutes a socially responsible role for them in a changing world. And where does it all leave the expert?

The pressure is to move toward substantive involvement of those on the outside, in the agora, civic society, crowds. The goal is not simply use-inspired work in Pasteur's quadrant (Stokes 1997; Clark, Crutzen, and Schellnhuber 2005; Clark 2007) but post-academic research (Ziman 1996) more generally, engaged on the ground, in the yard outside the tower, aiming at co-production of explicit knowledge and mutual learning around culturally grounded collective tacit knowledge (Collins 2010).[11]

Thus the crucial point is that social expectations about the role of science and the post-secondary sector more generally, and the role of analysts and social actors within those processes, have changed dramatically. The original deal emerging at the end of the World War II (Bush 1945; Price 1965) was straightforward. In exchange for massive funding of basic research, essentially on faith, with little formal accountability, it promised from the academy astonishing technological miracles and consequent increase in material standards of living. And it did indeed pay off. But in the new conditions just described, that deal has been overtaken by new and in some cases overriding considerations.

Calls for the development in the post-secondary community of a new social contract with society have emerged as a result of all this (Lubchenco 1998; Samarasekara 2009). In a chapter on the new social contract, Jasanoff explores the changing social relations of science and technology with a comparative analysis of the transformation of basic university-based biological research to bio*technological* research (2005, 227). Related reference to a new social contract is found in later work, for example, Halliwell and Smith (2011) and Hessels, Van Lente, and Smits (2009). Though these discussions are all couched in terms of a new contract with science, we must understand them now as a new contract with the academy in general, the higher education sector as a whole. And the point of that contract is that the academy, along with its ongoing traditional missions, must be much more directly responsive to social needs. The faith in the ultimate social relevance of all knowledge and teaching must be supplemented in some part of the academy by a capacity and willingness to mobilize academic resources for mission-oriented research more directly responsive to social priorities as identified by civil society along with more established research sponsors.

Indeed, more strongly, a commitment to co-creation of knowledge and mutual learning through continuing inclusive interaction leads to the movement of the academy outside its traditional walls and into the messy world of the agora and agonistic democracy in which knowledge claims are never truly settled. Some of the conclusions I draw about the appropriate response within the academy are sketched in Dobell, Moore, and Taylor (2012), but are all brilliantly anticipated in the insightful review by Donald Schon (1995).

With this vision we have now moved fully "outside the lab." This is the image of the tower *in* the yard, analysis *in* the arena. It takes the academy right into the agora, with the academic in unfamiliar (perhaps inappropriate?) roles as agent, advocate, actor, even activist. We see the loss of traditional criteria to gauge academic performance. Beyond *supplementing* conventional measures, we now have a *clash* of criteria as intellectual merit or rigour are pitted against engagement with other ways of knowing, relying on local observation and knowledge built from informal experience, not formal expertise. We have moved into the territory *between* government, civil society, and business, with the mobilization of academic resources drawing those resources outside the walls and beyond the reach of conventional disciplinary criteria and metrics. More generally, we have seen the development of think tanks and foundations, for-profit analysis and advocacy, corporate presence in research and dissemination as well as lobbying, and the explosion of individual opinion offered as evidence through blogs, Twitter and all.

What happens to trust and confidence in the disinterested analytical or scientific process under these circumstances? Must the legitimacy of science be altogether replaced by the legitimacy of process, appraised against principles of deliberative democracy or other criteria of social justice – or indeed merely against the demands of current social approval?

We can in this view no longer delimit issues in a way that permits them simply to be delegated to analysis within the academy or to elite expertise in other forms, with results to be translated and delivered in appropriate fashion and diverse vehicles. At the same time, of course, we cannot give up the appeal to reason buttressed by evidence.

Thus the world of authoritative science working with clear universal constructs ("immutable mobiles" in the phrase introduced by Bruno Latour (1987)) underlying the first two visions of academic roles (teaching and research) must accommodate also the particularities of place and service to a world of individuals deeply embedded in local social and cultural networks. From abstract global perspectives or partnerships with formal civil society organizations (CSOs), we move toward informal civic society in place.[12]

Within government, policy analysis perhaps moves toward a more limited and less ambitious role. "The 'synthesizer' archetype is ranked consistently high as describing the role and orientation of policy analysts, followed closely by 'connector' and 'entrepreneur', with 'listener' and 'technician' rounding out the rankings. Across all respondents and within all groupings investigated (by gender, and by ministry type), the 'synthesizer' archetype was consistently ranked highest. The results are consistent across all analytical approaches" (Longo 2012).

In response, it becomes important to understand the impact of Web 2 (social web) and Web 3 (semantic web) capacities on the conduct of policy analysis and the role of the analyst and the scientist in the larger democratic process.

STAIRCASE OF KNOWLEDGE

Beginning in the 1980s and expanded a bit in the 1990s, there has been discussion of the so-called DIKW scheme in the briefly fashionable field of knowledge management (not to be confused with the currently very fashionable field of knowledge mobilization), building from Data and Information through Knowledge to Wisdom.

Abbreviated versions were topics of conversations and papers around 1983 (Cleveland 1982), but the idea goes back to T.S. Eliot (whom I quoted in testimony before the MacDonald Commission in 1983; Serageldin 2012 quoted this passage again in this context in a plenary lecture).[13]

Figure 15.2 suggests several distinct steps in the development of decision-relevant science or analysis leading to a platform for decision. On the right side of the diagram, one can see traditional inside processes – secluded research driving conventional policy analysis – dominated by expertise and disciplinary criteria. On the left side, one can see the knowledge that comes from observation and

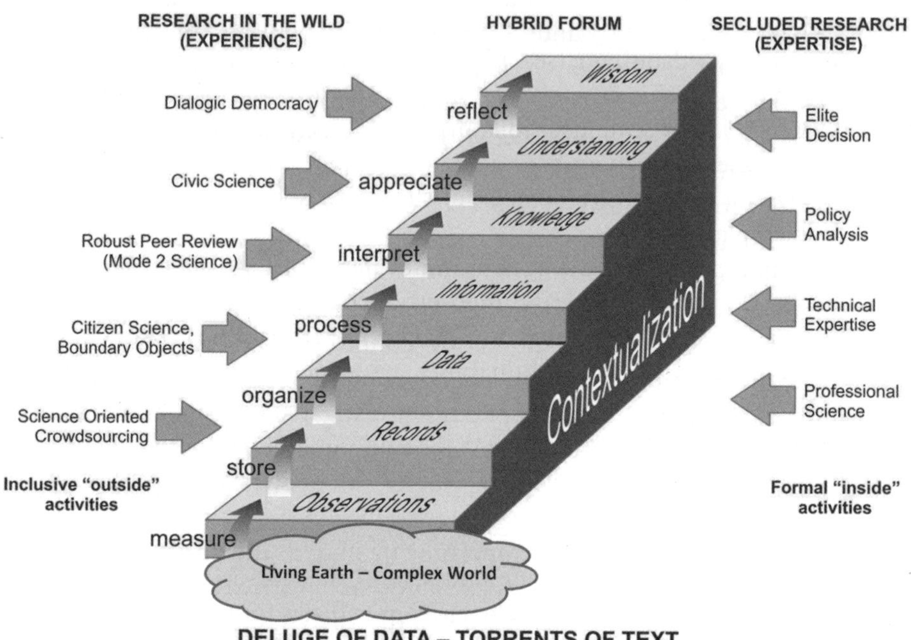

Figure 15.2 Diverse forms of knowledge, and the processes that integrate and contextualize knowledge, as viewed from the perspectives of idealized scholarly research (right side), lived experience (left side), and attempts to integrate these in support of legitimate participatory decisions (central staircase)

lived experience, with the attention to relationships and connections that Iain McGilchrist (2009) argues flows from the context-seeking right brain. (McGilchrist suggests we have gone too far, delegated too much, from the contextualized influences of the right brain to the executive drive flowing more from the analytically inclined left brain. Roscoe (2014) seems to support that argument, at least so far as economic reasoning drives us. On the other hand, Heath (2014) appeals to the resurgent rationality of Enlightenment 2.0 to restore sanity to our civic affairs, through a return to "slow politics.") In the middle, perhaps we can see the hybrid forums drawing on the work of hybrid research collectives undertaking research in the wild, bringing together the information flowing from secluded research with the perspectives flowing from the crowd to build the context in which responsible measured action can be pursued (Callon, Lascoumes, and Barthe 2009).

Here are varieties of more inclusive participation, from science-oriented crowdsourcing (see, for example, www.digitalfishers.net) to more engaged citizen science at various stages building up evidence on which larger-scale decisions must be made, leading on to forms of civic science, participatory decision making, and ultimately global dialogic or deliberative democracy driven by social media and net-enabled platforms.

European experience suggests some evidence that the science-policy interface is moving toward this co-production model (Pregernig and Bocher 2013) and some evidence that such platforms promote social learning in integrated sustainability assessment (Bohunovsky and Jager 2013).

A growing range of tools has been developing to carry out the transitions needed at each step of the staircase as one moves toward the broader context within which evidence must be interpreted and knowledge understood. This brief sketch calls attention to web platforms and associated practices (e.g., science-oriented crowdsourcing, citizen science, civic science) as vehicles for the engagement and mobilization of citizens in participatory mechanisms for social decisions and vehicles for social change. The question is whether Web 2 platforms can offer a new and hopeful answer to the question about who may be at the table in the various forums operating at different scales. Might these change the nature of the cascade from global intent or covenant, through the chain of negotiated interpretations of diverse perspectives, resulting finally in local realization or action? The growing but isolated literatures on the link from belief to behaviour obviously must be brought closer together; one might see Web 2 platforms as facilitating such integration.[14]

More specifically for this paper, Web 3 platforms and associated Big Data capacities can be seen as offering potentially new pathways for a positive contribution of expertise, either directly or through software agents, within deliberative processes and co-creation of knowledge. New developments in this direction are described – perhaps a bit optimistically – by Pentland (2014).

We may have reached the point where the reservations associated with too much context, too much democracy, lead us to turn back towards more systematic appeal to reason and analysis. But now it would be with a different role for the "expert" – as delegate not master, as described, for example, in the web-based hybrid forum Climate Co-Lab developed by Thomas Malone's Centre for Collective Intelligence at MIT (see Malone 2013) and in Pentland (2014). Here the role of the expert or policy analyst lies not so much in authoritatively generating ideas or formulating solutions as in facilitating the framing of issues by communities in the wild and in filtering or evaluating (increasingly with the help of ever-smarter software agents rather than bright graduate students) the proposals flowing from a range of outside processes.

THE CHANGING CHARACTER OF THE "PROBLEMATIQUE"

The literature behind all this is sprawling and fascinating. But the purpose in reviewing it here is in the end to explore how such co-creation of knowledge might be brought to bear to change belief systems and understandings and so to move individual and collective behaviour toward an elusive but crucial social goal. That goal we have, for shorthand purposes, come to call sustainability, pulling together pursuit of current well-being and social justice with concepts of intergenerational equity appropriate to a finite world.

In pursuit of that goal, humans must be recognized as intrinsic parts of complex earthly social-ecological systems, not as a force against Nature or in themselves inherently a threat to ecosystem integrity. But at current (increasing) levels of population, with current (increasing) global appetites for material consumption, and current (increasing) technological scales, humans represent not just a peak predator, but an invasive species with massive destructive impact on habitat globally. Unless that footprint can be dramatically reduced, the outlook for humanity does indeed seem grim.

Here we must recognize first the changing social-ecological context within which societal outcomes – and the activities of post-secondary institutions in particular – must be set. The starting point is captured in the proposal to designate the present time as part of the new Anthropocene epoch (Crutzen and Stoermer 2000; Crutzen 2002) a period in which humankind has become "a mighty geological force" (Vernadsky 1945) capable of altering, perhaps irreversibly, the complex Earth systems that form its home. The Anthropocene idea goes back at least to about 1925 (Vernadsky 1945). The basic challenge is that as a "mighty geological force," humanity is apparently out of control (Chakrabarty 2009). But humanity does not act, does not exercise agency. Humans act, and it is the unintended consequences of their action in aggregate that create the mighty geological force.[15]

To meet the challenge of climate change, or global change more generally, or sustainability perhaps more generally still, humans have somehow to be persuaded to change their individual behaviour, even though their individual actions make no significant contribution to the overall problem of climate change. This sounds like the classic problem of collective action (Olson 1965), now elaborated in a research program (Kahan et al. 2013) that highlights the ongoing tensions between passions and reason in individual decisions in this context. But might the evolution to the noosphere (maybe now supported by technologies of universal social networking) prove to be sufficient to create a self-conscious reflective humanity, in which individuals can be brought to recognize the moral responsibility to act individually in light of their contribution to an aggregate impact, and adjust their actions accordingly?[16]

CHANGING DEEP BELIEF SYSTEMS AND INSTITUTIONAL FRAMEWORKS TO PROMOTE TRANSITION TO SUSTAINABILITY

It is not unreasonable to argue that in our world of economic and social policy, we have lost our way. We are working with the wrong metrics, wrong maximand, wrong paradigm, wrong vocabulary, wrong cultural moorings, and a dysfunctional economic religion to go along with, perhaps, an increasingly dysfunctional political system. We suffer from fundamental goal displacement, and fundamental failure of agency (Dobell 2010).

At its extreme, then, we seem to have come full circle. We find that the whole institutional edifice built on reasoning about the inevitable efficiency of unguided markets is folktale – misleading, counterfactual, damaging. It has become religious doctrine of a most extreme kind, to be accepted as dogma, not on the basis of any testable claim to science or analytical coherence or empirical relevance. The agents it envisages correspond to no human attributes, and the motivations it imagines correspond to little that drives humans in their deeper lives. The "welfare" it maximizes has little to do with well-being in the world. The critical fundamental features of Earth systems are almost nowhere taken into account, nor is the deeper fabric of society and community emphasizing equality and justice reflected in the calculus.

Evidently we can and should use economic systems for social purposes. Markets and economic instruments offer the most effective signaling device and decentralization machinery imaginable – but we must be sure we have the overarching social controls and public regulation in place[17] (Dobell 1995; Dobell 1996).

We have to recognize that the market is a social contrivance for social purposes, not given from without but open to amendment, and indeed reliant on continuing social intervention for its functioning. Thus "market forces" can be challenged. Within market institutions, the corporate form is a particular social construct, intended to serve a social purpose and a public interest. Institutional arrangements that ensure it continues to serve that purpose are critical. There are many other organizational forms that exist within market systems, and there are many further organizational forms and norms that exist to serve public purposes outside market mechanisms. Market institutions based on notions of private property start from and depart from a pre-existing commons that represents a common heritage of humankind, with use possibly based on other notions of reciprocity and obligation. There are many possible arrangements for land tenure and resource stewardship; not all forms of claim need be immutable mobiles.

There are many examples we can pursue in looking to possibilities for deliberation in place of corporate calculation or "market discipline." Roundtables for land and resource use planning or watershed governance, coastal and marine spatial planning, community mapping, or ocean zoning proposals all illustrate possibilities for participatory decision processes supported by detailed local information on ecological resources and community assets, without the need for appeal to monetary valuations or speculative trading of individual property rights.[18]

With effective nested institutions, social consensus might be built on the pursuit of strong sustainability – the identification of the irreplaceable resources and overarching systems that are too valuable and too central to the interests of future generations to be the subject of commercial transactions alone – implemented simply through zoning or other community regulation governing access to those resources and ecosystems. Following Henry George (1912), one could imagine a system in which full-cost pricing to support trade-offs in rights to ecosystems is replaced by simple lease of elements of the common heritage for agreed activities during an agreed period in which returns to those activities can be claimed by the operator but speculative gains in the asset value of the resources remain with the (common) owner. Water rights, air rights, rights of way could all revert to the public owner when the rights of access or use are traded by those who currently hold them. Socially regulated creation of community quota for purposes of sustainable harvesting of renewable resources could be a component. Such activity might be governed generally by a public trust doctrine, as described by Joseph Sax (1970) and promoted in Canada by Jackson, Brandes, and Christensen (2012). This would impose on legislators as well as others a fundamental accountability for the use of the common heritage in the interests of the common owners.[19]

What concrete steps might take us toward an alternative to pushing beyond its limits the argument for free market environmentalism with economic mechanisms based on full-cost pricing and market instruments, in the attempt to make economic mechanisms serve human purposes? First we might recognize that in the construction and evolution of economic institutions, humanity has made two fundamental errors. The first is the creation of the legal fiction of the corporation as a person – a nice illustration of bifurcation in complex systems. The second is the notion of inevitable private ownership of elements of the commons, resources that make up a common heritage of humankind and play crucial roles in the dynamics and functioning of ecosystems.

The first error, the creation of the corporate person, flows from a legal fiction now endowed with almost all the fundamental rights of the person, but without moral responsibility – indeed with an overriding fiduciary responsibility to an exclusive group of owners – and with only limited legal liability, in a unique position to take advantage of the second error. There comes the problem that the corporate persons that have become the major players, exercising overwhelming financial and political power, cannot effectively participate as moral persons in any alternative discourse around the community's management of rights of access to the adjacent resources and ecosystems within which they live. The associated deployment of bureaucratic expertise to entrench corporate or investor rights at the expense of more fundamental human rights and public policy interests is perhaps one notable feature of a changing public service.

In a review of Anna Grear's book, *Redirecting Human Rights: Facing the Challenge of Corporate Legal Humanity* (2010), analyst Charlie Cray underlines the flimsy foundation on which corporate personhood rests:

> Although dominant theories of the corporation continue to assume that they are rights-bearing entities by definition, there is no convincing argument that this should be the case. Nor did such a theory always have legitimacy. During the early nineteenth century the reverse was true. Corporations were artificial entities "existing only in contemplation of law" as Justice Marshall put it. States created corporations by charter, a franchise or concession that defined their existence, usually with the public interest in mind ... A restoration of the notion that corporations are "creatures of law" established (through the process of incorporation) by governments, which in turn draw their legitimacy from a sovereign people, would be useful for challenging corporations ... Unfortunately the context for raising this challenge (outside of legal theory) is currently missing. (Cray 2011)

Perhaps the optimistic reading of the Arab Spring offered by observers such as Dabashi (2012) might be seen as opening that context? "New frameworks might be constructed to clarify the place of human beings within human rights law, as well as reshape property relations in a manner that enhances community rights and the natural resource commons" (Cray 2011).

The possibility of challenging the personhood of the corporation seems generally to have been viewed with scepticism, as a preoccupation of initiatives such as the Program on Corporations, Law and Democracy (POCLAD.org) or ReclaimDemocracy, or the Occupy movement itself, generally seen as consisting of fringe groups. But the growing body of documentation behind these and the growing credibility and influence of diverse organizational forms within the social economy are building conviction – as is the growing recognition that the current path of increasing inequality is not sustainable.

This concern with the corporate form leads to the second error, the creation and now nearly universal spread of a notion of property rights that includes, within what James Tully (2013) calls the first-tier rights of modern capitalism, property rights that defend the enclosure and privatization of the Earth itself – the resources and ecosystems that might be considered the common heritage of humankind, and crucial in the dynamics of ecosystem function.

Ideas like this take us into the many contested areas surrounding recognition of property rights as rights to exclude (Bromley 1991). Troublesome questions arise with respect to the overwhelming failures of market mechanisms in dealing with common pool resources forming parts of complex systems, thus failing to recognize the possible validity of claims to human rights stemming from common ownership of the Earth.[20] From this second error emerges the problem that paper claims to natural capital become the object of chaotic speculative trading that excludes the initial owners and fails to recognize the realities of the ecological systems within which all human activity is embedded.

We lack any consensus about how we ought to regulate human access to resources or ecological services. In many settings, this issue of property rights – rights to nature or natural systems – has not been resolved. More fundamentally we have not achieved across the many cultural gulfs any genuinely shared understandings of our obligations to others or of more general cultural norms or ecological rights – rights of Nature (Sheehan 2012).

The ultimate ecological constraints and cultural norms to be taken into account by a growing global population aspiring to rising standards of material well-being must be transmitted through social institutions that can guide and bound economic activity. Attitudes towards rights – human rights or rights of Nature as distinct from property rights understood as investor rights – must shift dramatically as part of that process. More generally we must find institutional frameworks that do not permit us to distance ourselves from appreciation of the consequences of our individual action.

Thus we might deploy economic instruments and exploit economic institutions within a social frame that sees common resources used to serve social purposes, and within an ethical frame that reflects the rights of those in other places and other times, as well, perhaps, as inherent rights of Nature. We can have social regulation driven by ethical commitments and workplace democracy and still deploy all the magic of market mechanisms and market capitalism for purposes of efficient decentralization of resource allocation decisions and as vehicles for effective realization of personal as well as societal goals.[21]

Some conceptions of democracy and some ideas about diverse economies – for example, Gibson-Graham, Cameron, and Healy (2013) – may offer hope in the face of a rather bleak outlook. They suggest avenues by which the massive virtues of market mechanisms created to serve human purposes may be once again employed for those purposes without all the instabilities and injustice associated with the casino capitalism that has emerged as the cumulative impact of a number of incremental knife-edge legal decisions, international agreements, and social developments.

As just noted, if we are to have any hope of addressing the challenges of global change, it is crucial that we reform these institutional frameworks in ways that do not distance the exercise of human agency from the moral responsibility for the consequences, as do current structures built on corporate action or remote bureaucracy. But for these purposes we must rebalance the voices in all these deliberative processes. Both the voices for human rights and the voices for rights of Nature must be vastly louder relative to the existing voice of corporate interests in land use questions and governance more generally. Proper representation of these other interests is hard to achieve; speaking either for Nature or for future generations is difficult, but it does at least keep the interests on the table – and may be perhaps no harder than the contingent valuation estimates that might otherwise be conjured up. Indeed the whole marvellous program of work pursued by Bowles and Gintis (2011) on the emergence and impact of reciprocity and cooperation in human societies is central to the story of the social economy and economic democracy that underlies much of this discussion and offers promise of an alternative path.

It is around these issues that the expert in the community, if not the policy analyst in the bureaucracy, must now find a way to work. There is neither world enough nor time to develop these topics as they deserve. We are left simply with the impression that the swing of history may be taking us back from excessive faith in both abstract decontextualized expertise and economistic fundamentalism, returning towards an earlier and more holistic vision of political economy and social responsibility as the frame within which expertise appeals to reason. Perhaps we may again see ourselves as responsible actors facing possibly tragic choices (Calabresi and Bobbitt 1978) among conflicting principles of social conduct, all of which we as a community hold dear, around which we are prepared to build continuing respectful interaction.

CONCLUSION

The fifty-year academic journey sketched here might be seen as ultimately a search for context and for some kinds of guides to resolution of inescapable tensions and seeming contradictions, encountered as we try responsibly to build evidence-informed foundations for legitimate collective decisions in diverse groups with widely differing, socially construed views and conflicting interests contending in a full world.

This evolution corresponds to a migration from decisions within well-defined structures and hierarchies of expertise, toward increasing inclusiveness and growing recognition of the relevance of experience outside the academies that build formal expertise. Such a migration features growing appeal to the wisdom of crowds – crowdsourcing, civic engagement, inclusive and open deliberative democracy, participatory decision processes. And now that process itself seems to be reaching its own limits with growing reservations about pushback stemming from the evident stalemates and dysfunction of current social processes at large scale.

In this note I have tried to sketch, in caricature fashion, four large, linked territories. The first is an evolution toward inclusive participation and transdisciplinarity in approaches to governance and to political economy – perhaps leading to the bonfire of the rationalities and dysfunctional democracy, but maybe to a return to HOPE. The second was to explore the changing role of the academic or of formal expertise more generally. The suggestion was that policy research and analysis must be less secluded, conducted iteratively and interactively in open hybrid forums. This is messy and inelegant, but mostly inevitable. Policy development is moving toward outside processes in an open source world.[22]

The staircase of knowledge illustrates the several stages and transitions in interpreting the evidence around us as a foundation for responsible decisions in procedurally legitimate ways that are now essential. More particularly, it emphasizes the potential capacities of the Web 2 and Web 3 worlds to bring those ambitious procedural goals within reach – while also noting that the same technological progress opens the possibility of massive authoritarian abuse to thwart those ambitions. And that, finally, offers perhaps some possibility – if tenuous and ambiguous – of progress toward the substantive goal of sustainability, by moving toward the persistent vision of the social economy while rolling back some elements of the two big errors in the design of economic mechanisms noted above: the personhood of the corporation and the enclosure, or capture, of the commons – as well as substantial control of governments – by those same corporations.

It seems we have to come back to limited decisions in local places, driven not just by evidence grounded in science but also by intuition, experience, heuristics, and capacity to come to resolution in some form of legitimate and inclusive consensus-building forum. Most crucially, we must count on faith in the impacts of those decisions not exceeding the adaptive capacity of resilient social systems to absorb. And in the possibility of building continuing allegiance to a system that does not always serve our immediate interest or make us momentarily happy but is better in the long run for the community as a whole than any alternative. A growing literature argues the feasibility of pursuing such goals by building the diverse social economy in parallel with our current globalized structures.

We have to recognize that as we move to put more weight socially on concerns for sustainability and justice, intergenerationally and otherwise, we move away from any hope of finding the tight numerical metrics that Lord Kelvin, Sir Richard Stone, and all their followers in economic science have sought. We cannot, for example, find adequate measures to give us objective or explicitly numerical thresholds for ecological flows respecting the needs of Nature. We cannot rely solely on the "numbers guys": we need to find forums in which we can reflect together to the point of some consensus on interim targets for flows in an ongoing adaptive management framework leading to "measured action," open to changing relationships as our physical world changes. We need reflexive governance and social innovation linking design and implementation in more integrated fashion. And the biggest challenge of all will be to devise relationships that offer adequate certainty of process – certainty of procedural fairness – in adapting contractual claims and rights to Nature about which, in complex changing ecosystems, there can be no certainty of outcome or ownership.

It is the local that counts in life, so far as adaptive management or measured action is concerned. But still we need the guiding frameworks of norms within which covenants can be effectively established and subsidiarity can be effectively pursued through all the interpretations and negotiations of implementation actions within nested institutions at various scales.

In this note I have suggested that we have seen – or at least can trace – over this past century a rather long swing from political economy (with Alfred Marshall) through economic science (with Samuelson) and now back to an attempt to achieve something like political economy again – or something broader, sustainability science – with transdisciplinary community-engaged work, now at a global scale with virtual communities, along with action at local scale within communities of place.

So the reading from all this reflection seems unclear, poised between promise and dismay. To roll back the religion of the market and the dominant corporation, to establish respect for the essential rights of Nature on which our own survival rests, may seem unlikely. The triumph of such efforts, even pursued to the point of non-violent civil disobedience, over entrenched remote authority may seem implausible. But we can only try.

Maybe I can do no better than to finish with some words of Nobel Prize winner Wislawa Szymborska, translated from Polish by Joanna Maria Trzeciak.

Reality demands
Reality demands
we also state the following:
life goes on.

Intervening stanzas list the many tragic battlefields, from ancient to modern, from Hiroshima to Sarajevo, in which lives and the trappings of life have been shattered, but something has been rebuilt … and life goes on.

On the tragic mountain passes
the wind blows hats off heads
and we cannot help – but laugh.

NOTES

1 Actually my confidence began to be shaken a bit earlier when an undergraduate research assistant, a refugee non-student from Haight-Ashbury –

he knows who he is – challenged me about the complete absence from my models of any reference to fairness, equity, or justice.

2 Such agents may be thought to be "rational" in the sense of Bayes and Raiffa, or perhaps systematically "irrational" in the ways identified by Kahneman and Tversky (see Bell, Raiffa, and Tversky (1988)) and Tversky and Kahneman (1974, 1986) for discussion of these distinctions). A somewhat different perspective is offered by Gigerenzer, Todd, and ABC Research Group (1999), who suggest simple heuristics as adaptive responses to uncertainty, not irrational.

3 Marshall also insisted on the need to see the specialized analysis of economic conduct in the overall context of humanity in organized society, a search for interdisciplinarity to which the profession is perhaps now returning.

4 Without venturing into the "science wars," I follow Mary Douglas (1995, 1997) in the belief that our knowledge of the world is certainly socially construed.

5 Setting the bar yet higher, however, we have the ideal of a democratic society based on civic engagement as outlined by Laden (2012) and on cooperative citizenship as described by Tully (2013).

6 It is interesting, in the midst of current widespread discussion of dysfunctional political systems, to recall the concerns about risks associated with the "excesses of democracy" expressed in the Task Force Report by Crozier, Huntington, and Watanuki for the Trilateral Commission in 1975. It is also interesting in light of casual conversations suggesting that a successful response to challenges like global change may demand an enlightened dictator or a determined executive authority rather than democratic deliberation. (See, for example, the suggestion of a "form of authoritarian government by experts" in Shearman and Smith (2007) or the contrary approach of Verweij et al. (2006) and Voss, Smith, and Grin (2009).

7 Of course, the existence of belief-bias and other "defects" in individual reasoning has been recognized for a long time. The retrospective discussions in a recent book (de Neys and Osman 2014) offer a succinct review, as does an earlier article "In Two Minds: Dual-process Accounts of Reasoning" (Evans 2003) and the later book of almost the same title (Evans 2013), along with the well-known work of Ariely (2009).

8 One might see these ideas as a remarkable anticipation of the pathbreaking current work of Joshua Greene (2013).

9 Indeed Gallopín et al. (2001) argue that this move is the only route by which we might hope to address what Weaver (1948) astonishingly anticipated as the challenge of "organized complexity" and the only foundation

on which to build the "sustainability science" we seek later in this paper. The important complementary role played also by Zadeh's concept of "fuzzy systems" and "soft computing" is noted by Seising (2012).

10 It is tempting to think of Scott's work as suggesting a contradiction between the abstract homogeneous model at global scale and fine-grained reality at local scale that parallels the inability to reconcile Einsteinian relativity with quantum physics. (In Part I of *The Elegant Universe*, Greene (2010) introduces that central problem of modern physics: the incompatibility of Einstein's theory of general relativity with quantum mechanics.)

11 A growing literature on boundary work and boundary objects offers possible resolution of some of the tensions arising as academic resources are mobilized to address changing social priorities and move into the contested territories of civic society. Space does not permit review here, but links to that literature include Clark et al. (2010), and Parker and Crona (2012).

12 This important distinction between formal civil society organizations and informal civic society reflects Tully (2008); see also Laden (2012).

13 "Where is the wisdom we have lost in information?
Where is the information we have lost in the data?"
Choruses from the Rock (Eliot 1934)

14 It is not possible to move past this point without some reference to a massive literature that has developed since the symposium documented in this volume. Of course the tension between reason and passion goes back centuries, to Hume and Locke and many others, if not to Plato and all. The gap between Bayes-Raiffa rules for rational decision in the face of uncertainty and Kahneman-Tversky heuristics and biases as documented in Prospect Theory has been mentioned earlier in this chapter, as has the work in the field of reasoning research on belief-bias and the influence of emotion on individual decisions. But now the work on the "dual-process brain" (Evans 2003, 2013; Kahneman 2011; Greene 2013) and motivated reasoning has brought the controversy around who might properly have an opinion and who has the expertise to judge, to a heightened pitch as the challenge of meeting expectations for political participation grows intense. Sadly, there is no opportunity to develop these questions here.

15 Note that this emphasis in the Anthropocene addresses only the physical impact or ecological footprint dimensions of sustainability, not issues of justice, equity, and well-being, except perhaps implicitly through the idea of the noosphere (Vernadsky 1945) and "resocialization" (Robinson and Tinker 1997).

16 A fascinating question is whether there may be any plausible link to First Nations traditions capturing the notion of unity: "tsawalk" as a Nuu-chah-ulth concept referring to all creation as one; "hishukish tsawalk" as a description of interdependent complex social-ecological systems that suggests "everything is one"; or "namwayut," a Coast Salish term, apparently, that can be understood as "we are all one" (for human purpose at this time and place). Is there perhaps some connection with the noosphere that we approach, without knowing it?

17 Robert Reich, in his provocative 2008 book *Supercapitalism*, written before the current crisis in the globalized financial system, suggests that the required recapture of democracy in political processes may now turn out to be even much more difficult, however. Stiglitz (2003, 2012) strengthens the argument further, and current events of course continue to underline this concern.

18 All this rests on effective devolution and decentralization, however, in an increasingly globalized world. Many might question whether we are likely to see any successful creation of the nested institutions Elinor Ostrom has recommended throughout her extensive research program on "governing the commons," or elaborated more recently in her Nobel Prize address (2009), or the related suggestions in Dietz, Ostrom, and Stern (2003). The need for coordinated action in complex settings at global scale has perhaps become too great?

19 The extensive research program of Mathias Risse (2008) provides strong rationale for such an approach. That research program and the much earlier reasoning of Henry George, who said, "we must make land common property" both discussed the ownership of land and the claims on the surplus arising from its rising scarcity value. They provide a foundation for more comprehensive ideas of social regulation that could establish the boundaries around privatization of the common heritage of humankind (George 1912, 6.2.3). Such regulation could be fully consistent with the concepts of cooperative democracy and citizenship introduced by James Tully (2010), as earlier noted.

20 Crucially, they also fail to deal adequately with property rights to information assets, intellectual property that cannot readily be identified or clearly defined, and hence posing serious challenges to attempts at enclosures or privatization. The work of Sam Bowles on what he calls the "Second Property Rights Revolution" (2009) is telling here.

21 But this middle way hinges crucially on the ability to take back democratic control of political institutions and to move away from a setting in which financial power dictates the composition and conclusions of those

institutions. As Tully observes, this may entail moving away from formal representative government and toward less hierarchical cooperative democracy.

22 If government continues to move toward a role simply as operations subcommittees serving corporate cartels, and advice to government increasingly flows as proprietary information from outside consultants, treated as Cabinet confidences, this trend obviously could be reversed.

16

A Subtle Balance: Reflection and Synthesis

EDWARD A. PARSON

This closing chapter aims to highlight and synthesize the major insights from the diverse and provocative set of contributions in the volume and from commentary and discussion at the accompanying symposium. These contributions identify several prominent dimensions of change over the past half century in the nature of the challenges posed to public decision making in Canada and in how governing institutions have responded to those challenges.

The most prominent and consistent messages across the contributions concern the volume's first theme, the role of science, evidence, and analysis in policy-making and their relationship to democratic processes and institutions. On this, multiple chapters identify a rise and fall from the 1960s to the present, in the status of analysis and expertise in Canadian federal policy-making. This rise and fall is seen in several ways – in the resources devoted to analysis in the public service, the prominence of strategic planning processes, the institutionalization of these activities in such bodies as the 1970s Planning Branch and the 1980s Ministries of State (and their subsequent abolition), and the influence and status of these methods relative to traditional political bases for decision making. Beyond these relatively concrete measures, contributors also identified a parallel rise and fall in a broader attitude toward policy-making, which combined respect for formal and quantitative methods of policy analysis; confidence in the ability of these methods, plus advancing scientific knowledge, to inform and (to some degree) rationalize public decision making; and optimism that government policies, so guided, can advance public welfare and social progress. Contributors to the volume use several terms to describe this cluster of methods, institutions, and attitudes. Clark and Swain follow the critical accounts of Moran et al. (2006) and Scott (1998) in calling it "high modernism." Here, I simply call it the analytic approach to policy.

The analytic approach embraces not just formal policy analysis but also the role of scientific data and evidence in informing public decision making. It is thus closely related to recent controversies over a decline of "evidence-based policy," as marked by several trends since 1990: e.g., abolition of research and advisory bodies, cuts to government-supported research and data, limits on the professional autonomy of government scientists, and disregard for relevant research and evidence in major policy decisions – disregard increasingly flaunted as a sign of populist virtue or commitment to principle.

This long decline in analysis and evidence-based policy has occurred in parallel with several other shifts in the distribution and basis of political power in Canada. These have included shifts in the spatial scale of major policy issues and required responses, both to the international level to address global-scale linkages and to smaller scales to allow greater responsiveness to local conditions – as discussed in the contributions here by van Eijndhoven, Parson and Ernst, and Bunton. Over the same period, political polarization has increased and trust in government decreased, in Canada as in other Western democracies – a trend sometimes exploited by office-seekers running against "government." More specifically, within the Canadian federal government there has been a dramatic shift of power to the centre. Parliament, departments, ministers, and even Cabinet as a collective, have lost autonomy and influence relative to the prime minister and central agencies, while even among central agencies the Prime Minister's Office has gained relative to other offices more identified with the career public service (Savoie 1999). A final major parallel trend – noted by some scholars but more contested – is the trend from "government" to "governance," from influence over policy debates and decisions, and associated analytic capacity, being concentrated within the federal government to their being diffused throughout issue networks of multiple actors both inside and outside government (Amin and Hausner 1997; Kooiman 1993; Pal 2009). These parallel trends are all consistent with a weakening of the career public service, the place where expertise in the development, analysis, and evaluation of policies has traditionally resided.

Thus far, this account largely reaffirms an understanding of the rise and decline of the analytic approach to policy that is familiar from other scholarship and practitioners' accounts. But the contributions here add significant new insights into the character, origins, and significance of these trends, including rebutting some widely held understandings. In particular, several contributions rebut the notion of this rise and decline as a morality tale of overreach and failure by a naïve or arrogant technocratic elite. There are several aspects to this rebuttal. First, rational analysis and planning never dominated Canadian federal policy-making – or indeed, aspired to dominate it – to the extent some critiques have suggested. Even at its zenith, the analytic approach had to co-exist with, and maneuver among, other centres of bureaucratic and political power with bases other than expertise, from which it met serious and sustained opposition. As French (1984) noted, systems of analysis and planning succeed only by focusing political power. In these terms, the first wave of policy analysis appears to have had more success achieving such focusing for its rivals than for its supporters. In all the cases discussed in this volume, there is no example of a simple, decisive win for the analytic approach – i.e., an important policy choice determined as the outcome of an analytic exercise that overcame opposition and persuaded the relevant political decision makers. Moreover, the highest points of influence and institutionalization that the approach achieved – e.g., in the Cabinet evaluation studies and other comprehensive evaluation exercises of the mid-1970s and the Ministries of State of the early 1980s – mobilized such strong opposition that they were soon abandoned.

From these relatively high points, the decline of the analytic approach reflected multiple factors at work, some of them rather direct consequences of its successes. Whenever the approach or its concrete execution held up problematic, wasteful government programs to searching public evaluations; when it suggested substantial re-orientations of policies or priorities; or when it put constraints on ministers' access to the Cabinet agenda for their initiatives – i.e., when it was doing its job – it powerfully focused opposition. Over time, additional factors combined to weaken the approach. Successive reorganizations of government machinery provided a way for new governments to distinguish themselves from their predecessors. In tight times, budget cuts routinely squeezed hardest on staff functions like planning and analysis that lacked outside constituencies of support. Increased centralization of authority in the Prime Minister's Office reduced the need for processes to plan and prioritize across ministries. And political campaigns since the 1980s, particularly from the right, sought power by campaigning against government and treated the public service with suspicion and hostility once they gained it. Given all these factors, explaining the decline of the approach does not require invoking any particular failing by its proponents – whether arrogance, over-reach, or naïveté about political and bureaucratic incentives. Discussions at the symposium did suggest a few potential examples of overreach – early Cabinet evaluation studies and the aggressive tax reforms of the 1981 MacEachen budget were identified as possibilities – but these do not account for the broad and sustained decline. Moreover, many thoughtful early discussions of limits to the analytic approach were provided by its main proponents (e.g., Hartle 1973; Dobell 1975). The record is clear that early supporters of the analytic approach understood that analytic methods can't deliver unique preferred choices, certainty about consequences, or conflict-free decisions; that clean separation between the intellectual orientation of planning and analytic exercises and the political principles that motivate policy decisions is not achievable; and thus, that analysis and planning must always reside within democratically legitimate decision processes (Dobell 1989, 1999; Bird et al. 1999).[1]

Contributions here also provide more nuanced descriptions of both the value of the analytic approach and the manifestations of its decline. In contrast to the imperial ambitions often attributed to the analytic approach, its realized contributions in multiple cases recounted were often subtle, more concerned with elevating democratic debate than trying to supplant it. Rather than attempting to impose a rigid understanding of an issue or seeking a single right answer, it often instead expanded the set of options to consider, by generating new ideas or showing that ideas previously deemed implausible merited serious consideration. It gave focus and discipline to policy debate, pushing it toward real points of commonality and dispute rather than fabricated differences or duelling anecdotes. It gave context to debates, highlighting the longevity or recurrence of serious policy challenges and proposed solutions. Its strongest long-term effect may have been diffusion of analytic skills and a critical mind-set throughout the public service – at least until the recent demoralization and exodus. Such contributions do not exhibit the main faults attributed to policy analysis and indeed are hard to object to: they no doubt strengthened the case and raised the prospects for some policy proposals while lowering others, but not to the extent of dictating answers or usurping ministerial authority.

Papers here, particularly that of Clark and Swain, also enrich our understanding of the character of the decline in the analytic approach by examining in greater detail the type of activities conducted within it. Using a framework suggested by Dobell and Zussman (1981), they note how the analytic resources that remain within the public service have been re-directed toward a set of functions they call "evaluation for accountability," which tend to be backward-looking, oriented toward audit-like assurance of accountability, and deployed uniformly across policies and programs regardless of their scale and importance. The expansion of these analytic functions has reduced capacity for prospective, larger-scale analysis of needs, priorities, and plans – functions they call "evaluation for improvement," which are essential to adapt to changing conditions and needs – by even more than aggregate budget figures would suggest.

Paradoxically, the decline of the analytic approach and of analytic capacity in the public service has occurred in parallel with increases in both the evident need for such an approach and the technological capability to meet that need. Increasing complexity of policy issues, rapid technological change, increasing international linkages, and sharper competition for resources and political attention all appear to call for more, not less, rational analysis and planning in policymaking and effective connection to relevant scientific knowledge. At the same time, continuing rapid growth in modelling methods, data, and computational capacity, as well as scientific knowledge in both natural and social domains, promise large increases in the value and versatility of analytic methods. These capabilities are being developed and applied in all manner of institutions for diverse purposes – including commercial advantage, electoral advantage, military advantage, and erosion of citizen privacy by both state and private actors – i.e., in virtually every domain except the development of socially beneficial public policies.

Most authors and symposium participants argued forcefully that this decline in analytic capacity has been damaging, to the capacity for effective federal policy development and governance and thus to Canada. This view was not completely uniform, however. Some participants suggested that lamentation over the decline of analysis might simply be about loss of political power by a particular faction – in harshest terms, whining by elitist 1970s soft-left liberals that different groups, expressing different values, now hold office. This critique is not without merit, but three points weaken its persuasiveness. First, the decline of analysis and planning is of such long standing that it cannot be blamed on any one change of government: indeed, it may represent a rare area of de facto agreement among recent governments holding office. Second, to the extent that the decline of the analytic approach can be attributed to the intellectual critiques mounted against it, these came far more from the political left than from the right. Third, even the proponents of this "stop whining" view also suggested that any government, whatever its ideology and support base, should want to be as well informed about the consequences of its actions as current knowledge allows – just as Zussman suggested in his analogy to baseball teams seeking a winning advantage through data and analysis.

What then can it mean when a government, unless compelled by conditions outside its control, actively participates in weakening capacity for data and analysis to inform its decisions: how can it be that a government does not want foresight, within the limits of what is available, about its decisions? Various explanations are possible. Perhaps political leaders are committed to acting for expressive or symbolic reasons and willing to gamble that the effects of bad decisions will not be obvious enough to surmount spin. Perhaps they believe that evidence, data, and analysis merely reflect political ideology and can be made subordinate to it. Perhaps they believe providers of research, data, and analysis are political adversaries who cannot be trusted. While different in detail, these explanations all suggest that a government uninterested in objective expert input must believe the information either to be unreliable or not important enough to override their other reasons for decisions. Broader cuts to research and data in areas of potential policy concern – whether the environment, social and economic policy, or the census – and attempts to control the speech of government researchers, suggest a similar but even stronger hostility to science and reasoned argument. If expertise means anything real, then a government acting on such beliefs will sometimes, or often, turn out to be wrong – thereby putting at risk not just the welfare of the nation and its citizens, but also their own agenda and electoral prospects. Consequently, although analysis and evidence in support of public policy is not a topic to grab public attention, it should be one that gains support from all political sides. Yet the record suggests the opposite, that it has attracted nearly universal neglect or opposition, most strongly from the recent Harper governments but not only from them.

In view of this long decline and its toll, the case for a restoration of analytic capacity to inform Canadian public policy appears compelling. As Clark and Swain argue, this need is not being met by the current, substantial investment in "evaluation for accountability." Nor, as Longo and other authors argue, is it met by a diffuse analytic capacity spread among a large network of non-governmental organizations, industry groups, think tanks, political parties, journalists, bloggers, and engaged citizens outside government. While broad pluralistic engagement in policy debates can generate a rich collection of ideas, proposals, and arguments, it provides no basis for the coherent integration of knowledge and perspectives that is required to support decisions. As Longo argues, the analytic capacity needed to support this integration must be located in some institutional setting where there is the capability to assess technical quality and objectivity of arguments and data, and where conduct is subject to professional norms of impartiality, integrity, and openness – including replicability. Absent some new institution with these abilities and obligations, this means in the career public service. Policy analysis cannot all be outsourced.

But even setting aside for the moment the practical questions of how to achieve it, what would such a restoration mean? It would be both wrong-headed and futile to try to turn back the clock from today's open and pluralistic debate to a restored monopoly on policy ideas and argument inside government. But as Longo notes, the post-positivist shift in policy analysis involved two distinct directions of movement, toward broader participation and away from scientific evidence and analytic methods. These are not necessarily linked, and it is only the second that needs correction through restoring a robust analytic capacity in the public service. Indeed, the value of such a capacity is substantially increased in a pluralistic, "governance-rather-than-government" policy landscape – even if, as Prince argues, the extent and uniformity of the shift to pluralistic governance has sometimes been overstated. Maintaining an effective debate among a large number of engaged participants requires more skilful moderation. To stretch Zussman's sports metaphor, more players on the field require more, and more skilful, referees. Wolfson's detailed accounts of the use of analytic methods and models show how they can serve this function, opening up policy debate by providing common points of reference and clarity about assumptions and thereby enabling people of diverse views to communicate more effectively. The Parliamentary Task Force on Pension Reform provides the most striking example, in which strong analysis and research did not usurp effective political debate but facilitated it. This task force, with its sibling on federal-provincial fiscal arrangements, is often identified as yet another high point in the early expansion of the analytic approach that bears the fingerprints of Rod Dobell.

A re-invigorated analytic capacity in government must avoid the pitfalls that critics identified in the first wave of policy analysis, to the extent that these criticisms were correct. Several major criticisms were advanced, posing challenges that vary in their character and severity. The most general and theoretical critique of the analytic approach, discussed in several chapters, is that most prominently associated with Scott (1998). This critique holds that policy analysis, and modernism more broadly, must view the world through processes of aggregation and abstraction. They thus suppress crucial variation and cannot effectively engage or respond to the particular situations and perspectives of diverse citizens and communities. This critique pertains both to state action itself and to the analytic methods or other processes that inform state action, and it evokes long-recognized structural tensions between the interests of individuals and the collective. For example, one participant noted its resonance with the eighteenth-century Bernoulli-d'Alembert debate over individual versus collective benefits in vaccination policy (Halpern 2004), a perennially fresh problem flagged by Dobell in 1981 and that, in various forms, has fascinated him throughout his career.

Yet this critique has less reach than is often claimed for it, because it depends on the specifics of state action, and of the analytic methods and processes used to inform it, which are in fact highly variable. Granted that state action necessarily has a unitary, authoritative character and must aggregate and abstract to some degree. Not every perspective can be represented in decision processes – universal empowerment in state action is an oxymoron – and there are limits to how much state action can take account of individual variation. But these limits fall far short of requiring total uniformity of action that suppresses all variation and particularity: consider, for example, all the policies criticized for excessive complexity as they aim to advance multiple aims in widely variable individual cases. Moreover, these limits exist not just because of limited administrative and analytic capacity, but for multiple other good reasons – e.g., privacy, fairness, and avoiding corruption.

Like state action, modelling and analysis always involve some degree of abstraction. The map is not the territory. Yet current data and analytic capabilities allow great latitude in how much abstraction, along what dimensions, is introduced in any particular analytic exercise. An analytic and evidence-based approach to public policy need not homogenize citizens' diverse situations. On the contrary, when compared to other bases used to develop and decide state action – whether supporter preferences, elite interest-group bargaining, poll-following, ideology, or vivid anecdote – the analytic approach may well be better able to represent and respond to such diversity. As Wolfson's account of life in the trenches of policy analysis shows, even the tools of the 1970s allowed rich, disaggregated representation of diversity among citizens in exploring implications of proposed policies. Technical advances since then have greatly expanded the ability to represent diversity in describing the world and projecting the effects of policies. Policy analysis still requires judgments of how much detail is needed to fairly represent any given issue or decision, potential consequences, and disparities or distributional impacts. These, like all exercises of analytic judgment, must be transparent regarding choices made and reasons for them, precisely because they admit of no authoritative resolution. But the charge that analytic methods of policy development necessarily reduce diverse citizens to uniformity, if not generally false, is greatly overstated. "Personalized public policy" may be an even more distant aspiration than personalized medicine and may be precluded or undesirable for reasons unrelated to analytic limits. But if fine-grained differentiation of policy is judged a desirable goal, progress toward it is more likely to be aided than obstructed by use of increasingly fine-grained data, modelling, and analysis to support policy decisions.

Whereas this first line of post-positivist criticism of the analytic approach targets abstraction and aggregation, the second broad cluster of criticisms targets overreach and over-claiming, particularly in the ability of an analytic approach to provide an objective, value-free basis for decisions. The critique is that policy analysis maintains the pretence of being value-free, while actually giving away crucial control over framing questions and valuing outcomes to unaccountable functionaries beyond the scope of public scrutiny.

This critique comes in many forms, widely variable in their force and implications. In its extreme form it approaches caricature, targeting forms of over-claiming that are clearly not just improper but also highly infrequent. It is surely obvious that policy analysts should not claim certainty for their analyses or results. They should not claim perfect separation between ends and means of state action when real decisions about policies and programs routinely implicate both of these. They should not claim that technical expertise can provide right answers to policy problems or confer elevated standing to make judgments of importance, relevance, or value. Rather, as Dobell argues, re-empowered analysts and planners must recognize that integrating knowledge into public decisions always depends on mobilizing political will through legitimate decision channels. Avoiding these obvious failure modes should not be difficult, but as multiple authors note, should rather be judged among the basic competencies of public servants.

Yet the subtler forms of this critique are more challenging to recognize and effectively address. It is always possible that analytic methods, models, or evaluation criteria may embed some particular set of political or social values, so policy analysis does not just impose order and clarity on a debate but rather steers it in some particular direction or suppresses arguments that should be getting a forum.

To recognize and be vigilant to this risk without relinquishing the aim to inform policy through reason buttressed by evidence requires a delicate balance, which will be highly sensitive to particular contexts. The clearest way to limit this risk is transparency in policy analysis, including as much explicitness about assumptions, goals, and other elements of analysis as is feasible. This is one aspect of good practice of policy analysis that may well be facilitated by the more open and pluralistic policy environment that now exists. Dobell's own essay probes wisely and judiciously into these questions, and sketches a couple of additional directions forward. First, he suggests the need for a reconfiguration of expertise as developed and pursued within the academy, in order to take greater account of societal needs in identifying what questions are important and relevant to pursue – perhaps even to admit pluralism of knowledge sources and bases for verification in areas where traditional science is limited in its data and causal understanding (although what that would mean for the authority of empirical verification and falsification is unclear). Second, he calls for applying different legitimation conditions for knowledge as it moves by degrees from pure scientific inquiry toward deployment as a basis for collective action. Each of these proposals would require a balancing of contending aims and claims that is both subtle and difficult, and in plumbing these murky depths Dobell does not offer any simple codification of how to proceed. It is thus appropriate that his essay exhorts on the importance of embracing paradox and that his exposition shifts at certain points into the poetic.

Even absent definitive resolution of these deep problems, however, there are practical steps that can be taken to begin restoring an analytic capacity within the federal government. Rebuilding this capacity after thirty years of decline is a tall order, particularly under current budgetary and political constraints, but contributors offer several concrete suggestions that appear feasible even given these constraints. Clark and Swain find promise in shifting priorities within the function of evaluation, to allow more open-ended, forward-looking and judgment-based processes aimed at improving outcomes. They suggest such a shift could begin in individual departments with support of senior officials. Zussman notes that there has been no central office responsible for analytic and planning methods since the 1995 Program Review and proposes re-establishing one in a central agency to promote a rebuilding of analytic capacity throughout the public service. Such an office could serve as an exponent and pedagogue of relevant methods and skills and as a champion, practitioner, and modeller (in the sense of modelling behaviour) of high-quality work. These two proposals – one bottom-up or led from within individual ministries, one top-down, led from central agencies – are complementary, but restoring and defending a significant analytic capacity is likely to be a slow process, and a major impact would require serious commitment from political leaders.

These proposed reforms, indeed any initiative to strengthen analysis and evidence in policy-making, approach policy reform indirectly, by reconfiguring the processes and institutions by which decisions are made. Changing the configurations, mandates, and authorities of institutions is a frequent, indeed venerable, approach to policy reform. The power of the approach is most obvious for government organizations, but its reach extends outside government as well, because government-set laws define what forms of organizations are allowed, with their attendant missions, allowed scope of activities, available resources, and incentives influencing decision making. Institutional innovation and reform can thus be a powerful tool to advance social goals, for institutions inside government, outside, and on the boundary between government and the rest of society.

In addition to the proposed reforms to strengthen analytic capacity discussed above, four other chapters deal with issues of institutional innovation in diverse settings. Two of these – Bunton, and Culley and Horwitz – address the now-prominent topic of hybrid organizations. Proposals to allow or promote hybrid organizations are being advanced in multiple jurisdictions, in response to frustration that the three standard large-scale organizational forms presently available – government, private for-profit, and charitable not-for-profit – provide too limited a menu of means to advance diverse public purposes. Just as private firms in competitive markets advance public welfare by efficiently providing valued goods and services without government direction, proponents of novel forms of hybrid organization argue these can advance a broader set of public purposes without government having to specify the details – providing, in effect, a new invisible hand, with even broader reach than Adam Smith's original.

Both these chapters suggest caution, however, about how much can be achieved through hybrids of for-profit and not-for-profit forms. Bunton's account of the grand hopes but mixed results from the novel Iisaak institution in Clayoquot Sound highlights how institutional context – in this case, the need to service debt – limited Iisaak's ability to pursue a diverse blend of commercial and community interests, despite attempts to embed all these aims into its novel mission and governance structure. Culley and Horwitz express broader skepticism about hybrid forms, for both legal and practical reasons. They counsel against naïve or too-general assumptions about how decisions will be made in such organizations. Particularly when organizations are charged with advancing multiple goals that specific decisions may bring into tension, e.g., profitability for investors and some specified charitable or public purpose – the authors caution that one incentive may simply prevail over the other, so that the organization fails at the integration of distinct goals for which it was established. Both chapters thus counsel caution about the supposed transformative effects ascribed to these novel organizations, for distinct but complementary reasons – organizational context and constraints, and the incentives that bear on actual managerial decision making.

Two other chapters, by Longo and Dobell, speculate about the potential for novel institutional forms based on expanded data and IT capabilities to transform public decision making, to its benefit or otherwise. Both discussions are speculative and exploratory, based on rapidly developing technical capabilities plus a few small-scale process experiments rather than on any clearly emerging trends. Longo addresses the potential for expanded data and IT capability, particularly novel web-based interaction platforms, to transform processes of policy analysis, consultation, and deliberation. Identifying current trends as promising a dramatic expansion in policy analytic capacity but one that is not under the traditional control of governments, he cautions on the need for institutions that can control for quality and impartiality and so ensure these new capacities serve to strengthen, not weaken, the competency and legitimacy of the policy-making system. He argues that government analysis could benefit from interaction with outside web-enabled policy networks if inside analysts are able to exercise judgment in what contributions they engage or respond to, not reduced to reactive procedural roles.

Dobell speculates that web-based interaction platforms could facilitate an even more powerful disruption, not just facilitating the integration of knowledge and preferences to support better public decisions, but becoming vehicles for new reflective modes of interaction among citizens, officials, and experts. They might thereby not just surmount the problem of decontextualized expertise that he identifies but also influence citizen preferences and beliefs by promoting clearer recognition of the consequences of choices and surmounting the various paradoxes of collective action.

Viewed merely as a sketch of hopeful potentials, this is hard to reject, but the most optimistic variants of this vision must contend with some suggestively contrary evidence. The societal benefits of technological progress depend on the specifics of how technologies are implemented and used, and the societal effects of the recent rapid growth of web technologies thus far appear a mixed bag, more based in assertion and anecdote than impartial measurement. Moreover, the details of IT deployments thus far – other than in the open-source movement – have not been particularly driven by visions of social progress but by frenzied pursuit of leverage for commercial advantage. Indeed, to the extent that web interaction has influenced politics and policy thus far, it is as arguable that it has debased interaction as elevated it, sharpened the contradictions, polarization, and deadlocks inherent in collective action rather than helped surmount them. The more promising visions for beneficial impact of these technologies thus remain hopeful speculation, plausible but with only a few current signs favouring them.

Picking up these debates about institutional reform but offering – as he has so often done – a deeper and more radical perspective, Dobell closes his essay by looking back historically to consider two transformative institutional innovations of the past two centuries: legal personhood of corporations and private ownership of the commons. Each of these represents the combined effect of so many individual decisions made over such an extended period that they now seem part of the essential landscape of contemporary society. Yet Dobell argues each of them has now reached, or passed, the limits of its social usefulness and invites us to contemplate an alternative world in which these decisions are reversed, or at least amended. He thus provides a historical parallel to the criticisms about uncritical reliance on institutional design offered by Bunton and by Culley and Horwitz in contemporary settings, which suggests two general insights about institutional reform.

First, the consequences of major institutional changes may not be visible until long afterwards. Indeed, the juxtaposition of the critiques in these three chapters suggests that the consequences of major institutional changes may escape informed social control altogether, for reasons of a paradox similar to that identified by Collingridge (1980) for technological change: when the change is proposed or newly implemented, there is not enough information available to assess its social benefits and harms; but once it is implemented and scaled up so this information is available, strong material interests accrete around it so changes become politically obstructed. Second, major institutional changes may initially mainly bring benefits, particularly for changes intentionally enacted to address some identified social problem. But as they persist, their context (social, economic, and political) may change so much – in part owing to their own influence – that their harms come to dominate their benefits. Corporate personhood, by expanding corporate rights to contract and sue, may have been sensible and beneficial at a time when the major socio-economic problem was to expand production, but it is less so as the scale of human economic activity poses risks to global environmental constraints, and sustainability and equity emerge as the dominant societal challenges. Similarly, private ownership of the commons may have posed no serious problem so long as the relevant common resources were so abundant that private exploitation caused no harm, but it has become an increasingly severe problem as common resources became scarcer and more threatened.

While diverse in details, these critiques all stress the importance of considering not just guiding principles and objectives but also the actual incentives faced by decision makers. They show how in any proposed reform of institutions or processes, it is worth working hard to project the incentives and constraints that will shape decisions in the new setting. Yet because this projection is so difficult and prone to error, it is also important to be vigilant about what actual decisions emerge and be prepared to adapt. These are prospective warnings, but they also mirror one of the criticisms made retrospectively against proponents of policy analysis in the 1970s – that they did not attend enough to political and bureaucratic incentives. Attending carefully to these was good advice for institutional reformers then, and remains so now.

Yet one must not try to be too clever. Institutions are not automatons, and even meticulous attention to prospectively designing incentives is not enough to ensure institutions act to advance the general welfare, for several reasons. Institutional design may simply overlook important aspects of the decision environment, as in Bunton's account. Decisions may turn on nuances of incentives, information, and authority relations that are too fine-grained to capture in large-scale institutional design, as Culley and Horwitz argue, particularly in complex environments where multiple decisions interact. Time and changed conditions may reveal previously unrecognized limits to the alignment of institutional incentives with societal benefit, as Dobell's critique suggests. Perhaps most important, material interests are not the only, or even the most important, motivator of human behaviour. Effective public policy development and decision making must also take account of normative factors and aim to develop and sustain norms and principles that are aligned with the pursuit of public benefits.

Standards of honest debate in policy making, respectful disagreement, and commitment to the public interest cannot be effectively enforced or even fully codified, but require nurturing and maintenance of norms. While the papers by Langford, Carin, and Dobell all consider normative obligations explicitly and centrally, the need for norms is evident in contributions throughout the volume, including those that address the role of analysis and expertise in democratic policy-making. Officials doing policy research and analysis live within the basic role tension described by Zussman – obliged to provide both fearless advice and faithful implementation. However discouraged by being cut or ignored, they are still subject to professional and moral obligations in how they fulfill this dual role and have room to maneuver in pursuing beneficial policies while fulfilling these obligations, as Langford and Carin, respectively, point out. Indeed, as Longo argues, professional norms are a major reason that a strong analytic capacity is needed inside government, even when there is also a robust ecosystem of outside actors advancing their own policy proposals and supporting arguments and analyses.

The normative obligations of public servants advising on policy consist partly of those that promote honest, measured, substantive debate, e.g., impartiality, transparency about assumptions and goals, and good-faith exploration of differences. But good governance also depends on similar norms regulating the behaviour of political leaders who receive this and other advice, e.g., seeking input, listening, and willingness to be persuaded from one's initial impulses. In addition to these, alarm over the stifling of government-supported scientific research and data collection points to another important normative obligation of political leaders that has often been overlooked. Given the high social value of these activities and the certainty that the results of these activities will sometimes appear to lend support to government critics, leaders must be confident enough to tolerate the production and dissemination of potentially embarrassing research, data, and analysis. They must be prepared to defend their choices and reasons without seeking false certainty or unanimity of view by abandoning research and data collection, suppressing results, or attempting to prevent government scientists from speaking about their work. On this, both Canadian and American governments have recently fallen short.

In closing, what are the largest-scale messages to draw from the rich and wide-ranging contributions of this project? The insights they offer are too many and too diverse to distil into a few sharp take-away messages – indeed, they do not in every respect agree. But a few powerful points emerge concerning the challenges faced by public policy-making, the criteria and conditions for doing it well, and the most promising directions to pursue this. In his thoughtful reflection, Dobell identifies these highlights aptly as "inescapable tensions and seeming contradictions." Each of the major themes of the volume maps onto an enduring, perhaps inescapable tension. There is the enduring tension of the nature and scale of the challenges to public policy and the distribution of authority among governing institutions to respond to it. There is the enduring tension of the contending claims of participatory and representative institutions. And most prominent in this project, there is the enduring tension of the need for both expertise and legitimacy in public decisions. It seems that these two basic values can never be either fully integrated or fully separated, but must find a workable boundary for each issue at each time – a boundary whose appropriate location and form depend on contestable, and contested, judgments of the objective demands on policy, ranging from purely expressive, symbolic, or distributive decisions in which expert knowledge has little to contribute, to actually operating the controls of Spaceship Earth. On all three tensions, conditions change, specific policies and institutional responses come and go, yet the tensions endure, raising questions deep enough to admit no definitive answers. The required judgments cannot be codified or reduced to algorithm but rather require maintaining a subtle balance – a balance of the contending forces and a balance in the judgments to be made and the temperament to make them with competence, honest inquiry, civil exploration of differences, and humility. For his long body of contributions that have consistently exhibited these virtues, for the generosity with which he has shared and taught his insights, and for his enduring optimism that good sense and goodwill can bring social benefits through public policy, the participants in this project are thankful for the guidance and inspiration provided by the work of Rod Dobell.

NOTE

1 Or at least this is clear for proponents of the analytic approach within government. Dobell's "BOISE" approach in his sketched history of approaches to policy-making suggests (perhaps ironically?) it might have been otherwise among some advocates, consultants, and academics.

References

Agrawal, Arun. 2002. "Common Resources and Institutional Sustainability." In *The Drama of the Commons*, edited by Elinor Ostrom et al., 41–86. Washington, DC: National Academy Press.

Akerley, Marj, Peter Cowan, and Anna Belanger. 2008. "Collaborative Revolution." *Canadian Government Executive* 14 (8): 6–8.

Amin, Ash, and Jerzy Hausner. 1997. *Beyond Market and Hierarchy: Interactive Governance and Social Complexity*. Cheltenham: Edward Elgar.

Amy, Douglas J. 1984. "Towards a Post-Positivist Policy Analysis." *Policy Studies Journal* 13 (1): 207–11.

Applbaum, A. 1999. *Ethics for Adversaries: The Morality of Role in Public and Professional Life*. Princeton: Princeton University Press.

Ariely, Dan. 2009. *Predictably Irrational: The Hidden Forces that Shape Our Decisions*. New York: HarperCollins.

Arrow, Kenneth J. 1951. *Social Choice and Individual Values*. New Haven: Yale University Press.

Asilomar Scientific Organizing Committee. 2010. *Asilomar Conference Recommendations on Principles for Research into Climate Engineering Techniques*. Washington, DC: Climate Institute.

Aucoin, Peter. 1986. "Organizational Change in the Machinery of Canadian Government: From Rational Management to Brokerage Politics." *Canadian Journal of Political Science* 19 (1): 3–27.

Auditor-General of Canada. 1975. "Supplement to the Annual Report to the House of Commons." http://archive.org/stream/reportofauditsup7475cana/reportofauditsup7475cana_djvu.txt.

Aurora Flight Sciences. 2011. *Geoengineering Cost Analysis: Final Report*. Cambridge, MA: Aurora Flight Sciences Corp.

Ayres, Ian. 2007. *Super Crunchers: How Anything Can Be Predicted*. London: John Murray.

Baldwin, Bob. 1996. "Income Security Prospects for Older Canadians." In *Aging Workforce, Income Security, and Retirement: Policy and Practical Implications*, edited by Anju Joshi and Ellie Berger, 69–74. Hamilton: McMaster University Summer Institute on Gerontology Proceedings.

Banerjee, Abhijit, and Esther Duflo. 2011. *Poor Economics: A Radical Rethinking of the Way to Fight Global Poverty*. New York: Public Affairs.

Barber, Brad, and Terrance Odean. 2001. "Boys Will Be Boys: Gender Overconfidence and Common Stock Investment." *Quarterly Journal of Economics* 116 (1): 261–92.

Bardach, Eugene. 2000. *A Practical Guide for Policy Analysis: The Eightfold Path to More Effective Problem Solving*. Berkeley, CA: Berkeley Academic Press.

– 2008. *A Practical Guide for Policy Analysis: The Eightfold Path to More Effective Problem Solving*. 3d ed. Washington, DC: CQ Press.

Barrett, Scott. 2008. "The Incredible Economics of Geoengineering." *Environmental and Resource Economics*. 39 (1): 45–54.

Baumgartner, Frank, and Bryan Jones. 2009. *Agendas and Instability in American Politics*. Chicago: Chicago University Press.

Beer, Stafford. 1974. *Designing Freedom*. Toronto: CBC Learning Systems.

Béland, Daniel. 2013. "The Politics of the Canada Pension Plan: Private Pensions and Federal-Provincial Parallelism." In *How Ottawa Spends 2013–2014: The Harper Government: Mid-Term Blues and Long-Term Plans*, edited by Christopher Stoney and G. Bruce Doern, 76–87. Montreal and Kingston: McGill-Queen's University Press.

Bell, David, Howard Raiffa, and Amos Tversky. 1988. *Decision-Making: Descriptive, Normative and Prescriptive Interactions*. Cambridge: Cambridge University Press.

Benkler, Yochai. 2006. *The Wealth of Networks: How Social Production Transforms Markets and Freedom*. New Haven, CT: Yale.

Benveniste, Guy. 1984. "On a Code of Ethics for Policy Experts." *Journal of Policy Analysis and Management*. 3(4): 561–72.

Berkes, Fikret, and Carl Folke. 1998. "Linking Social and Ecological Systems for Resilience and Sustainability." In *Linking Social and Ecological Systems: Management Practices and Social Mechanisms for Building Resilience*, edited by Fikret Berkes and Carl Folke, 1–26. Cambridge: Cambridge University Press.

Bertot, John C., Paul T. Jaeger, Sean Munson, and Tom Glaisyer. 2010. "Engaging the Public in Open Government: Social Media Technology and Policy for Government Transparency." *Technology Mediated Social Participation Workshop Discussion Paper*. http://www.tmsp.umd.edu/TMSPreports_files/6.IEEE-Computer-TMSP-Government-Bertot-100817pdf.pdf.

Bickel, J. Eric, and Lee Lane. 2009. *An Analysis of Climate Engineering as a Response to Climate Change*. Denmark: Copenhagen Consensus Center.

Bicking, Melanie, and Maria A. Wimmer. 2010. "Need for Computer-Assisted Qualitative Data Analysis in the Strategic Planning of e-Government Research." In *Proceedings of the 11th Annual International Digital Government Research Conference on Public Administration Online: Challenges and Opportunities*, edited by Soon Ae Chun, Rodrigo Sandoval, and Andrew Philpot, 153–62. Digital Government Society of North America.

Bicquelet, Aude, and Albert Weale. 2011. "Coping with the Cornucopia: Can Text Mining Help Handle the Data Deluge in Public Policy Analysis?" *Policy & Internet* 3 (4): 1–21.

Bipartisan Policy Center. 2011. *Geoengineering: A National Strategic Plan for Research on the Potential Effectiveness, Feasibility, and Consequences of Climate Remediation Technologies*. Task Force on Climate Remediation Research.

Bird, R., M. Trebilcock, and T. Wilson, eds. 1999. *Rationality in Public Policy: Retrospect and Prospect, a Tribute to Douglas G. Hartle*, Toronto: Canadian Tax Foundation.

Blackstock, Jason J., and Arunabha Gosh. 2011. "Does Geoengineering Need a Global Response – And What Kind? International Aspects of SRM Research Governance." *Solar Radiation Management Governance Initiative*. 21 March. http://www.srmgi.org/files/2011/09/SRMGI-International-background-paper.pdf.

Blanco, Carlos, Jon Grant, Nancy M. Petry, H. Blair Simpson, Analucia Alegria, Shang-Min Liu, and Deborah Hasin. 2008. "Prevalence and Correlates of Shoplifting in the United States: Results from the National Epidemiologic Survey on Alcohol and Related Conditions (NESARC)." *American Journal of Psychiatry* 165 (7): 905–13.

Bodansky, Daniel. 1996. "May We Engineer the Climate." *Climatic Change* 33 (3): 309–21.

Bohunovsky, Lisa, and Jill Jager. 2013. "Stakeholder Integration and Social Learning in Integrated Sustainability Assessment." In *Long-term*

Governance for Social-Ecological Change, edited by Bernd Siebenhuner, Marlen Arnold, Klaus Eisenack, Klaus Jacob. New York: Routledge.

Boreham, Paul, Rachel Parker, Paul Thompson, and Richard Hall. 2007. *New Technology@Work*. Routledge.

Bossel, Hartmut. 1977. *Concepts and Tools of Computer Assisted Policy Analysis*. Basel: Birkhäuser.

Boston, Jonathan, Andrew Bradstock, and David Eng. 2011. *Public Policy: Why Ethics Matters*. Canberra: ANU Press.

Boulding, Kenneth. 1983. Foreword to *The Art of Judgment: A Study of Policy Making*, by Geoffrey Vickers. New York: Sage Publications.

Bowles, Samuel. 2009. "Information and Property Rights in the Weightless Economy." Presentation to Berkman Center for Internet and Society, Harvard Law School. 17 November. cyber.law.harvard.edu/interactive/events/luncheons/2009/11/bowles.

Bowles, Samuel, and Herbert Gintis. 2011. *A Cooperative Species: Human Reciprocity and Its Evolution*. Princeton: Princeton University Press.

Bretschneider, Stuart I., Ines Mergel. 2011. "Technology and Public Management Information Systems." In *The State of Public Administration: Issues, Challenges, and Opportunities*, edited by Donald C. Menzel and Harvey L. White, 187–203. New York: M.E. Sharpe.

Brewer, Garry D. 1974. "The Policy Sciences Emerge: To Nurture and Structure a Discipline." *Policy Sciences* 5 (3): 239–44.

British Columbia. 2013. "Information Security Program for the BC Government. Office of the Chief Information Officer." Victoria, BC: Ministry of Citizens' Services and Open Government. http://www.cio.gov.bc.ca/local/cio/informationsecurity/documents/InformationSecurityProgram.pdf.

British Columbia Ministry of Forests. 1999. "Backgrounder: MacMillan Bloedel Ltd. and Iisaak Forest Resources Ltd. Proposal for Change of Control of Clayquot Portion of TFL 44." http://web.uvic.ca/clayoquot/files/volume3/IX.7.pdf.

Bromley, Daniel W. 1991. *Environment and Economy: Property Rights and Public Policy*. Oxford: Blackwell.

Brooks, Stephen, and Marc Ménard. 2013. *Canadian Democracy: A Concise Introduction*. Toronto: Oxford University Press.

Brown, Lester. 2008. *Plan B 3.0: Mobilizing to Save Civilization*. New York: Norton.

Bryden, Kenneth. 1974. *Old Age Pensions and Policy-Making in Canada*. Kingston and Montreal: McGill-Queen's University Press.

Budyko, Mikhail I. 1974. *Climate and Life*. New York: Academic Press.

Bush, Vannevar. 1945a. "As We May Think." *Atlantic Monthly* 176 (1): 101–8.

– 1945b. *Science – The Endless Frontier: A Report to the President on a Program for Postwar Scientific Research*. Washington, DC: National Science Foundation.

Cairney, Paul. 2012. "'Public Administration in an Age of Austerity': Positive Lessons from Policy Studies." *Public Policy and Administration* 27 (3): 230–47.

Calabresi, Guido, and Philip Bobbitt. 1978. *Tragic Choices*. New York: Norton.

Calder v. British Columbia (Attorney General). 1973. S.C.R. 313.

Callon, Michel, Pierre Lascoumes, and Yannick Barthe. 2009. *Acting in an Uncertain World: An Essay on Technical Democracy*. Cambridge, MA, and London: MIT Press.

Canada. 1966. Royal Commission on Taxation (Carter Commission), *Report*. 6 Vols. Ottawa.

– 1973. Working Paper on Social Security in Canada ("Orange Paper, Social Security Review"). Ottawa: Minister of National Health and Welfare, 18 April 1973.

– 1977. Task Force on Tax / Transfer Integration (TTI Task Force), Department of Finance, Ottawa.

– 1979. Task Force on Retirement Income Policy (Lazar Report), Department of Finance, Ottawa.

– 1982. *Better Pensions for Canadians*. Ottawa: Minister of Supply and Services

– 1983. *Pension Reform: Report of the Parliamentary Task Force*. Ottawa: House of Commons Canada.

– 1985. Royal Commission on the Economic Union and Development Prospects for Canada (Macdonald Commission). Ottawa.

– 1992. *Restructuring Government: A Report to the Prime Minister*, 7 September 1992 (the de Cotret report). Ottawa.

Canadian Human Rights Museum. 2008. Memorandum from Gordon Robertson (Department of External Affairs) to Norman Robertson (Under Secretary of State for External Affairs, no relation), 20 March 1944. http://humanrightsmuseum.ca/media/imagegallery/detail/579.

Cappe, Mel. 2011. "Analysis and Evidence for Good Public Policy: The Demand and Supply Equation." Tansley Lecture, Johnson Shoyama School of Public Policy, University of Regina, Regina, Canada.

Cardinal, Harold. 1969. *Red Paper on Native Development*. Indian Chiefs of Alberta, Edmonton.

Carson, Rachel. 1962. *Silent Spring: Fortieth Anniversary Edition*. New York: Houghton Mifflin Company.

Cash, David, et al. 2003. "Knowledge Systems for Sustainable Development." *Proceedings of the National Academy of Sciences* 100 (14): 8086–91.

CBC Fifth Estate. 1995. *Throwaway Citizens: Deportation*. VHS. Toronto: Canadian Broadcasting Corporation.

Chadwick, Andrew. 2009. "The Internet and Politics in Flux." *Journal of Information Technology & Politics* 6 (3): 195–6.

Chakrabarty, Dipesh. 2009. "The Climate of History: Four Theses." *Critical Inquiry* 35 (2): 197–222.

Clark, Ian D. 2008. "Professionalizing Policy Analysis in Canada." *Canadian Public Administration* 5 (1): 171–9.

Clark, Ian D., and Harry Swain. 2005. "Distinguishing the Real from the Surreal in Management Reform: Suggestions for Beleaguered Administrators in the Government of Canada." *Canadian Public Administration* 48 (4): 453–76.

Clark, William C. 2007. "Sustainability Science: A Room of its Own." *Proceedings of the National Academy of Science (PNAS)* 104 (6): 1737–8.

Clark, William C., Paul J. Crutzen, and Hans J. Schellnhuber. 2005. *Science for Global Sustainability: Toward a New Paradigm*. Harvard University, Center for International Development, Working Paper No. 120. http://www.hks.harvard.edu/var/ezp_site/storage/fckeditor/file/pdfs/centers-programs/centers/cid/publications/faculty/wp/120.pdf.

Clark, William C., Thomas P. Tomach, Meine Van Noordwijk, Nancy M. Dickson, Delia Catacutan, David Gustan, and Elizabeth McNie. 2010. *Toward a General Theory of Boundary Work: Insights from the CGIAR's Natural Resource Management Programs*. Harvard University, Centre for International Development Working Paper No. 199.

Clayoquot Sound Scientific Panel. 1995. *Report of the Scientific Panel for Sustainable Forest Practices in Clayoquot Sound*. http://www.cortex.ca/Rep1.pdf.

Cleveland, Harland. 1982. "Information as a Resource." *The Futurist*, December, 34–9.

Coady, C.A.J. 2011."The Problem of Dirty Hands." *The Stanford Encyclopedia of Philosophy*. http://plato.stanford.edu/archives/sum2011/entries/dirty-hands.

Collingridge, David. 1980. *The Social Control of Technology*. London: Pinter.

Collins, Harry. 2010. *Tacit and Explicit Knowledge*. Chicago: The University of Chicago Press.

Corbeil, Phillippe. 1994. "Review: SIMHEALTH – A Democracy and Society Computer Simulation." *Simulation Gaming* 25 (4): 551–5.

Cox, Susan. 1985. "No Tragedy on the Commons." *Environmental Ethics* 7 (1): 49–61.

Cray, Charlie. 2011. "Anna Grear, Redirecting Human Rights: Facing the Challenge of Corporate Legal Humanity." Logos 10 (2) (spring). http://logosjournal.com/2011/anna-grear-redirecting-human-rights-facing-the-challenge-of-corporate-legal-humanity.

Crozier, Michel, Samuel P. Huntington, and Joji Watnuki. 1975. *The Crisis of Democracy: Report to the Trilateral Commission on the Governability of Democracies*. New York: New York University Press.

Crutzen, Paul J. 2002. "The 'Anthropocene.'" *Journal de Physique IV (Proceedings)* 12(10): 1–5.

– 2006. "Albedo Enhancement by Stratospheric Sulfur Injections: A Contribution to Resolve a Policy Dilemma?" *Climatic Change* 77 (3–4): 211–20.

Crutzen, Paul J., and E. Stoermer. 2000. "The Anthropocene." *Global Change Newsletter* 41 (1): 17–18.

Dabashi, Hamid. 2012. *The Arab Spring: The End of Postcolonialism*. London, New York: Zed Books.

Dahl, Robert. 1991. *Democracy and Its Critics*. New Haven: Yale University Press.

Davis, Paul K., Steven C. Bankes, and Michael Egner. 2003. *Enhancing Strategic Planning with Massive Scenario Generation: Theory and Experiments*. Santa Monica: RAND National Security Research Division.

Deaton, Richard Lee. 1989. *The Political Economy of Pensions: Power, Politics and Social Change in Canada, Britain and the United States*. Vancouver: University of British Columbia Press.

DeLeon, Peter, and E. Sam Overman. 1998. "A History of the Policy Sciences." In *Handbook of Public Administration*. 2d ed. Edited by Jack Rabin, W. Bartly Hildreth, and Gerald J. Miller, 405–42. New York: Marcel Dekker.

DeLong, Brad. 2010. "Jean-Claude Trichet Rejects the Counsels of History." 23 July. http://delong.typepad.com/sdj/2010/07/jean-claude-trichet-rejects-the-counsels-of-history.html.

De Neys, Wim, and Magda Osman, eds. 2014. *New Approaches in Reasoning Research*. New York: Psychology Press.

Dickinson, Janis L., Benjamin Zuckerberg, and David N. Bonter. 2010. "Citizen Science as an Ecological Research Tool: Challenges and Benefits." *Annual Review of Ecology, Evolution, and Systematics* 41:14972.

Dietz, Thomas, Elinor Ostrom, and Paul C. Stern. 2003. "The Struggle to Govern the Commons." *Science* 302: 1907–12.

Dixon, John, and Alexander Kouzmin. 2001. "The Market Appropriation of Statutory Social Security: Global Experiences and Governance Issues." In *The Marketization of Social Security*, edited by John Dixon and Mark Hyde, 27–42. London: Quorum Books.

Dizikes, Peter. 2010. "Groups Demonstrate Distinctive 'Collective Intelligence' When Facing Difficult Tasks." MIT *News Office*, September 23. http://mitsloan. mit.edu/newsroom/2010-malone2.php.

Dobell, A.R. 1974. "Quantitative Analysis: The Use and Abuse of Mathematics in Policy Analysis." *Science Council of Canada*, 42–9. Paper presented at Mathematics in Today's World, Ottawa, ON, 3–4 June.

– 1975. "Measure for Measure, Value for Money, or Keeping out the Elephants: Efficiency and Program Effectiveness in Government Programs." Speech to Conference of Supreme Legislative Auditors, Quebec City, 22 September, 1975.

– 1985. "Responsibility and the Senior Public Service: Some Reflections in Summary." In *Responsibility in the Senior Public Service*, edited by Mervyn Brockett, John W. Langford, and William A. Neilson, 617–27. Toronto: IPAC.

– 1989. "The Public Administrator: God? Or Entrepreneur? Or Are They the Same in the Public Service." *American Review of Public Administration* 19 (1): 1–11.

– 1995. "Environmental Degradation and the Religion of the Market". In *Population, Consumption, and the Environment: Religious and Secular Responses*, edited by Harold G. Coward, 229–50. Albany, NY: State University of New York Press.

– 1996. "The 'Dance of the Deficit' and the Real World of Wealth: Re-Thinking Economic Management for Social Purpose." *National Forum on Family Security*. http://web.uvic.ca/~rdobell/assets/papers/dance.html.

– 1999. "Evaluation and Entitlements: Hartle's Search for Rationality in Government." In *Rationality in Public Policy: Retrospect and Prospect, A Tribute to Douglas G. Hartle*, edited by Richard Bird, Michael Trebilcock, and Thomas Wilson, 79–108. Toronto: Canadian Tax Foundation.

– 2002. "Social Risk, Political Rationality and Official Responsibility: Risk Management in Context." *Commissioned Paper 13*. Report of the Walkerton Inquiry, Toronto.

– 2003. "The Role of Government and the Government's Role in Evaluating Government: Insider Information and Outsider Beliefs." Panel on the Role of Government. Research Paper. August 12, 2003. At http://www.lawlib.utoronto.ca/investing/reports/rp47.pdf.

– 2009. *Holarchy, Panarchy, Coyote and Raven: Creation Myths for a Research Program.* 31 March 31. http://web.uvic.ca/~rdobell/assets/papers/myths.pdf.

– 2010. "Managing Canada-US Economic Space: Postcards from the Fringe." *Conference on North American Futures: Canada-US Perspectives.* David Brower Center, Berkeley, California. 12 March.

Dobell, A.R., Katherine Barrett, and Stuart Lee. 2002. "Whose Knowledge Counts? How Do We Count It?" Presentation for *National Policy Research Conference*, Ottawa, ON.

Dobell, A.R., and Martin Bunton. 2001. "Sound Governance: The Emergence of Collaborative Networks and New Institutions in the Clayoquot Sound Region." Background Paper for Clayoquot Sound Regional Workshop, 25 September. http://www.clayoquotalliance.uvic.ca/PDFs/SOUND_GOV_2.pdf.

Dobell, A.R., Justin Longo, Jeannine Cavender-Bares, William C. Clark, Nancy M. Dickson, Gerda Dinkelman, Adam Fenech, Peter M. Hass, Jill Jager, Ruud Pleune, Ferenc L. Toth, Miranda A. Schreurs, and Josee van Eijndhoven. 2001. "Implementation in the Management of Global Environmental Risks." In *Learning to Manage Global Environmental Risks.* Vol. 2: *A Functional Analysis of Social Responses to Climate Change, Ozone Depletion, and Acid Rain*, part 3: *Studies of Management Functions*, edited by William C. Clark, Jill Jaeger, and Josee van Eijndhoven, 115–46. Boston: The MIT Press.

Dobell, A.R., Justin Longo, and Jodie Walsh. 2011. "Digital Fishers in the Salish Sea: Cutting Edge Science for Inclusive Public Policy." *Salish Sea Ecosystem Conference.* Vancouver, British Columbia, 25–7 October 2011.

Dobell, A.R., and Darcy Mitchell. 1996. "Three Hats for the Policy Analyst." *A Review of Theory, Method, and Practice*, Commissioned by Ministry of Environment, Lands, and Parks.

Dobell, A.R., Michelle-Lee Moore, and Martin Taylor. 2012. *Social Innovation and Civil Society: Might the Wisdom of the Crowd Improve the Metrics of the HERD?* http://rdobell.files.wordpress.com/2012/01/dobell-knowledge-synthesis-on-leveraging-investments-in-herd-final-report-may-15-2012.pdf.

Dobell, A.R., and Edward A. Parson. 1986. "Collective Decisions Involving Risk: Literature Review." *IRPP Working Paper.* Victoria: Institute for Research on Public Policy.

Dobell, A.R., and David Zussman. 1981. "An Evaluation System for Government: If Politics Is Theatre, Then Evaluation Is (Mostly) Art." *Canadian Public Administration* 24 (3): 404–27.

Dobuzinskis, Laurent, Michael Howlett, and David Laycock. 2007. *Policy Analysis in Canada: The State of the Art*. Toronto: University of Toronto Press.

Doern, G. Bruce, Allan M. Maslove, and Michael J. Prince. 2013. *Canadian Public Budgeting in the Age of Crises: Shifting Budget Domains and Temporal Budgeting*. Montreal and Kingston: McGill-Queen's University Press.

Douglas, Mary. 1995. "Acceptance." *Science, Technology and Human Values* 20 (2): 262–6.

– 1997. "The Depoliticisation of Risk." In *Culture Matters: Essays in Honor of Aaron Wildavsky*, edited by Richard J. Ellis and Michael Thompson, 121–32. Boulder: Westview.

Drummond, Don. 2011. "Personal Reflections on the State of Public Policy in Canada." In *New Directions for Intelligent Government in Canada*, edited by Fred Gorbet and Andrew Sharpe, 337–52. Ottawa: Centre for the Study of Living Standards.

Drury, C.M. 1975. "Quantitative Analysis and Public Policy Making." *Canadian Public Policy* 1 (1): 89–96.

Dunleavy, Patrick, Helen Margetts, Simon Bastow, and Jane Tinkler. 2005. "New Public Management Is Dead: Long Live Digital-Era Governance." *Journal of Public Administration Research and Theory* 16 (3): 467–94.

Dunn, William N. 1981. *Public Policy Analysis: An Introduction*. Englewood Cliffs, NJ: Prentice-Hall.

Dyson, George. 2012. *Turing's Cathedral: The Origins of the Digital Universe*. London: Allen Lane.

Eaves, David. 2010. "After the Collapse: Open Government and the Future of Civil Service." In *Open Government: Collaboration, Transparency and Participation in Practice*, edited by Daniel Lathrop and Laurel Ruma. Sebastopol, CA: O'Reilly Media, Inc.

Edwards, Phil, and Ian Roberts. 2009. "Population Adiposity and Climate Change." *International Journal of Epidemiology* 38 (4): 1137–40.

Eichbaum, Chris, and Richard Shaw. 2008. "Revisiting Politicization: Political Advisers and Public Servants in Westminster Systems." *Governance: An International Journal of Public Administration and Institutions* 28 (3): 337–63.

– 2010. *Partisan Appointees and Public Servants: An International Analysis of the Role of the Political Adviser*. London: Edward Elgar.

Eliot, T.S. 1934. Choruses from *The Rock*. London: Faber and Faber.

Ennals, Ken. 1981. "The Management Information System for Ministers in the Department of the Environment." *Local Government Studies* 7 (1): 39–46.

Evans, Jonathan S. 2003. "In Two Minds: Dual Process Accounts of Reasoning." *Trends in Cognitive Science* 7 (10): 454–9.

– 2013. *In Two Minds: Dual Processes and Beyond*. Oxford: Oxford University Press.

Fallows, James M. 1996. *Breaking the News: How the Media Undermine American Democracy*. New York: First Vintage Books.

Fine, Cordelia. 2011. "Biased but Brilliant." *New York Times*, 30 July. http://www.nytimes.com/2011/07/31/opinion/sunday/biased-but-brilliant-science-embraces-pigheadedness.html.

Finer, Herman. 1941. "Administrative Responsibility and Democratic Government." *Public Administration Review* 1 (4): 335–50.

Fischer, Frank. 1980. *Politics, Values, and Public Policy: The Problem of Methodology*. Boulder, CO: Westview Press.

– 1995. *Evaluating Public Policy*. Chicago, IL: Nelson-Hall.

– 2003. *Reframing Public Policy: Discursive Politics and Deliberative Practices*. New York: Oxford University Press.

Fleishman, Joel L. 1996–97. "The Case for Ethics." *Duke Policy News Online* 25.

Fleming, James R. 2010. *Fixing the Sky: The Checkered History of Weather and Climate Control*. New York: Columbia University Press.

Flynn, Greg. 2011. "Rethinking Policy Capacity in Canada: The Role of Parties and Election Platforms in Government Policy-Making." *Canadian Public Administration* 54 (2): 235–53.

Folke, Carl, Fikret Berkes, and Johan Colding. 1998. "Ecological Processes and Social Mechanisms for Building Resilience and Sustainability." In *Linking Social and Ecological Systems: Management Practices and Social Mechanisms for Building Resilience*, edited by Fikret Berkes and Carl Folke, 414–46. Cambridge, MA: Cambridge University Press.

Forrester, Jay W. 1971. *World Dynamics*. Cambridge, MA: Wright-Allen Press.

Freed, Les, and Sarah Ishida. 1995. *The History of Computers*. Emeryville, CA: Ziff-Davis.

French, Richard. 1984. *How Ottawa Decides: Planning and Industrial Policy Making 1968–1984*. Toronto: James Lorimer and Company.

Friedman, Milton. 1955. "The Role of Government in Higher Education." In *Economics and the Public Interest*, edited by Robert A. Solo, 135–43. Piscataway Township, NJ: Rutgers University Press.

Fyfe, Toby, and Paul Crookall. 2010. *Social Media and Public Sector Policy Dilemmas*. Toronto: Institute of Public Administration of Canada.

Gallopin, Gilberto C., Silvio Funtowicz, Martin O'Connor, and Jerry Ravetz. 2001. "Science for the Twenty-First Century: From Social Contract to the Scientific Core." *International Social Science Journal* 53 (168): 219–29.

Gammon, Howard. 1954. "The Automatic Handling of Office Paper Work." *Public Administration Review* 14 (1): 63–73.

Gauthier, Benoît, Gail V. Barrington, Sandra L. Bozzo, Kaireen Chaytor, Alice Dignard, Robert Lahey, Robert Malatest, et al. 2010. "The Lay of the Land: Evaluation Practice in Canada in 2009." *Canadian Journal of Program Evaluation* 24 (1): 1–49.

George, Henry. 1912. *Progress and Poverty: An Inquiry into the Cause of Industrial Depressions and of Increase of Want with Increase of Wealth: The Remedy.* Garden City, NY: Doubleday Page & Co.

Gibson-Graham, J.K., Jenny Cameron, and Stephen Healy. 2013. *Take Back the Economy*. Minneapolis, MN: University of Minnesota Press.

Gigerenzer, Gerd, Peter M. Todd, and the ABC Research Group. 1999. *Simple Heuristics That Make Us Smart*. Oxford: Oxford University Press.

Ginsberg, Wendy R. 2011. *The Obama Administration's Open Government Initiative: Issues for Congress*. Congressional Research Service Report R41361. Washington, DC: Library of Congress, Congressional Research Service.

Goldman, S., and H. Uzawa. 1964. "A Note on Separability in Demand Analysis." *Econometrica* 32 (3): 387–98.

Good, David. 2007. *The Politics of Public Money*. Toronto: University of Toronto Press.

Gore, Al. 1994. "Vice-President Unveils First Interactive Citizens' Handbook." The White House: Office of the Vice President, 20 October 1994. http://clinton6.nara.gov/1994/10/1994-10-20-vice-president-unveils-white-house-internet-service.html.

Grear, Anna. 2010. *Redirecting Human Rights: Facing the Challenge of Corporate Legal Humanity.* New York: Palgrave-Macmillan.

Greene, Brian. 2010. *The Elegant Universe*. New York: W.W. Norton & Company Ltd.

Greene, Joshua. 2013. *Moral Tribes: Emotion, Reason and the Gap between Us and Them*. New York: Penguin.

Gregg, Allan. 2012. "1984 in 2012 – The Assault on Reason." *Notes for Remarks to Carelton University*, 7 September.

Griffith, Andrew. 2013. *Policy Arrogance or Innocent Bias: Resetting Citizenship and Multiculturalism*. Ottawa: Anar Press.

Grudin, Jonathan. 1988. "Why CSCW Applications Fail: Problems in the Design and Evaluation of Organizational Interfaces." *Proceedings of the 1988 ACM Conference on Computer-Supported Cooperative Work*, 85–93. Austin, TX: MCC.

Grundman, Reiner. 2006. "Ozone and Climate: Scientific Consensus and Leadership." *Science, Technology and Human Values* 31(1): 73–101.

Guest, Dennis. 1998. *The Emergence of Social Security in Canada*. 3d ed. Vancouver: University of British Columbia Press.

Gupta, Vipin, Sylvia Maxfield, Mary Shapiro, and Susan Hass. 2009. "Risky Business: Busting the Myth as Women as Risk Averse." *Center for Gender in Organizations Insights, Briefing Note 28*. Boston: Simmons School of Management. www.simmons.edu/som/docs/insights_28.pdf.

Gurin, Jonathan. 2014. *Open Data Now*. New York: McGraw Hill Education.

Habermas, Jürgen. 1998. *Between Facts and Norms*. Trans. William Rehg. Cambridge, MA: MIT Press.

Hadden, Susan G. 1994. "Citizen Participation in Environmental Decision Making." In *Learning from Disaster, Risk Management after Bhopal*, edited by Sheila Jasanoff, 91–112. Philadelphia: University of Pennsylvania Press.

Hajer, Maarten. 1995. *The Politics of Environmental Discourse*. Oxford: Clarendon Press.

Halbert, C.L. 1993. "How Adaptive is Adaptive Management? Implementing Adaptive Management in Washington State and British Columbia." *Reviews in Fisheries Science*, 1 (3): 261–83.

Hallinan, Joe. 2009. *Why We Make Mistakes*. New York: Broadway Books.

Halliwell, Janet, and Willie Smith. 2011. "Paradox and Potential: Trends in Science Policy and Practice in Canada and New Zealand." *Prometheus: Critical Studies in Innovation* 29 (4): 373–91.

Hallsworth, Michael, and Jill Rutter. 2011. *Making Policy Better: Improving Whitehall's Core Business*. London: Institute for Government.

Halpern, Sydney A. 2004. *Lesser Harms: The Morality of Risk in Medical Research*. Chicago: University of Chicago Press.

Hämäläinen, Raimo P. 1988. "Computer Assisted Energy Policy Analysis in the Parliament of Finland." *Interfaces* 18 (4): 12–23.

Hanna, Susan, Carl Folke, and Karl-Goran Maler. 1996. *Rights to Nature: Ecological, Economic, Cultural and Political Principles of Institutions for the Environment*. Washington, DC: Island Press.

Hansard. 2012. "Evidence." Canada House of Commons, Standing Committee on Finance. Meeting 68, June 1, 2012. http://www.parl.gc.ca/HousePublications/Publication.aspx?Language=E&Mode=1&Parl=41&Ses=1&DocId=5633893&File=0.

Hardin, Garrett. 1968. "The Tragedy of the Commons." *Science* 162: 1243–8.

Harper, S.J. 2012. "The Wealth of Western Economies Is No More Inevitable than the Poverty of Emerging Ones." Address to the World Economic Forum, Davos, Switzerland, January 26, 2012.

Harris, Cole. 2002. *Making Native Space: Colonialism, Resistance and Reserves in British Columbia*. Vancouver: UBC Press.

Harris, Harlan, Marck Vaisman, and Sean Murphy. 2012. "Data Scientists Survey Results Teaser." *Data Community DC Blog*. http://datacommunitydc.org/blog/2012/08/data-scientists-survey-results-teaser.

Hartle, Douglas G. 1973. "A Proposed System of Program and Policy Evaluation." *Canadian Public Administration* 16 (2): 243–66

– 1976. *Draft Memorandum to Cabinet*. Toronto: Institute of Public Administration of Canada Case Study Program 1.29.

Hawthorn, H.B. 1966–67. *A Survey of the Contemporary Indians of Canada: A Report on Economic, Political, Educational Needs and Policies*. 2 vols. Ottawa: Indian Affairs Branch.

Haynes, Laura, Owain Service, Ben Goldacre, and David Torgerson. 2012. *Test, Learn, Adapt: Developing Public Policy with Randomised Controlled Trials*. UK Cabinet Office. https://www.gov.uk/government/publications/test-learn-adapt-developing-public-policy-with-randomised-controlled-trials.

Heath, Joseph. 2014 *Enlightenment 2.0: Restoring Sanity to Our Politics, Our Economy, and Our Lives*. Toronto: HarperCollins.

Heeks, Richard. 2011. "The First e-Government Research Paper." *ICTs for Development blog*. 30 April. http://ict4dblog.wordpress.com/2011/04/30/the-first-e-government-research-paper.

Heintzman, Ralph. 2013. "Establishing the Boundaries of the Public Service: Toward a New Moral Contract." In *Governing: Essays in Honour of Donald J. Savoie*. Montreal: McGill-Queen's University Press.

Hennessey, Peter. 1986. *Cabinet*. London: Basil Blackwood.

Hersch, Seymour. 2011. "Iran and the Bomb." *New Yorker*. 6 June, 30–5.

Hessels, Laurens K., Harro van Lente, and Ruud Smits. 2009. "In Search of Relevance: The Changing Contract between Science and Society." *Science and Public Policy* 36 (5): 387–401.

Hinds, Pamela J., and Diane E. Bailey. 2003. "Out of Sight, Out of Sync: Understanding Conflict in Distributed Teams." *Organization Science* 14 (6): 615–32.

Hogwood, Brian, and Lewis Gunn. 1988. *Policy Analysis for the Real World*. Oxford: Oxford Press.

Holling, C.S. 1984. "Director's Corner: Surprise!" *Options*. Laxenburg, Austria: International Institute for Applied Systems Analysis.

Holling, C.S., and Steven Sanderson. 1996. "The Dynamics of (Dis)harmony in Human and Ecological Systems." In *Rights to Nature: Ecological, Economic, Cultural and Political Principles of Institutions for the Environment*, edited by Susan Hanna, Carl Folke, Karl-Goran Mäler, and A. Jansson. Washington, DC: Island Press.

Holton, Gerald. 1970. "The Roots of Complementarity." *Daedalus*. 99 (4): 1015–55.

– 1988. *Thematic Origins of Scientific Thought: Kepler to Einstein*. Revised Ed. Cambridge, MA: Harvard University Press.

Hood, Christopher. 2008. "The Tools of Government in the Information Age." *The Oxford Handbook of Public Policy*, edited by Michael Moran, Martin Rein, and Robert E. Goodin, 469–81. Oxford: Oxford University Press.

– 2011. *The Blame Game*. Princeton: Princeton University Press.

Hulme, Mike et al. 2011. "Science-Policy Interface, Beyond Assessments." *Science* 333: 697–8.

Hume, Mark. 2011. "DFO Restructuring Caused Confusion, Hampered Fish Habitat Protection." *Globe and Mail*, 7 June.

Hutton, David. 2011. "Effectively Silencing Canada's Whistleblowers." *Toronto Star*, 13 August.

ICSU. 2010. "Regional Environmental Change: Human Action and Adaptation, What Does It Take to Meet the Belmont Challenge?" *International Council for Science*. Paris: International Council for Science.

INAC (Indian and Northern Affairs). 2006. Report of the Expert Panel on Safe Drinking Water for First Nations. Ottawa.

– 2008. *Review of Program-Led Evaluation Reports*. Ottawa.

IUCN (International Union for Conservation of Nature). 1980. "World Conservation Strategy: Living Resource Conservation for Sustainable Development." *International Union for Conservation of Nature and Natural Resources*. Gland, Switzerland.

InterAcademy Council. 2010. *Climate Change Assessments, Review of the Processes and Procedures of the* IPCC. Amsterdam: InterAcademy Council.

Jackson, Michael, and Graham Stewart. 2009. *A Flawed Compass: A Human Rights Analysis of the Roadmap to Strengthening Public Safety*. Vancouver, BC: justicebehindthewalls.net.

Jackson, Sarah, Oliver M. Brandes, and Randy Christensen. 2012. "Lessons from an Ancient Concept: How the Public Trust Doctrine Will Meet Obligations to Protect the Environment and the Public Interest in Canadian Water Management and Governance in the 21st Century." *Journal of Environmental Law and Practice* 23 (2): 175–99.

Jacobs, Jane. 1992. *Systems of Survival: A Dialogue on the Moral Foundations of Commerce and Politics*. New York: Random House.

Jaeger, Jill, Josee van Eijndhoven, and Wiliam C. Clark. 2001. "Linkages among Management Functions for Global Environmental Risks." In *Social Learning Group, Learning to Manage Global Environmental Risks*, 165–78. Cambridge, MA: MIT Press.

Jaeger, Jill, and Alexander E. Farrell. 2010. "Improving the Practice of Environmental Assessment." *In Assessments of Regional and Global Environmental Risks, Resources for the Future*, edited by Alexander E. Farrell and Jill Jaeger, 278–95. Washington, DC: Resources for the Future.

Jasanoff, Sheila S. 1994. *The Fifth Branch: Scientific Advisors as Policymakers*. Cambridge, MA: Harvard Press.

– 1994. *Learning from Disaster, Risk Management after Bhopal*. Philadelphia, PA: University of Pennsylvania Press.

– 2005. *Designs on Nature: Science and Democracy in Europe and the United States*. Princeton, NJ: Princeton University Press.

– 2010. "A New Climate for Society." *Theory, Culture and Society* 27 (2–3): 233–53.

Jay, Anthony, and Jonathan Lynn. 1980a. "The Official Visit," *Yes Minister*, season 1, episode 2, Directed by Sydney Lotterby, aired 3 March. BBC.

– 1980b. "Big Brother," *Yes Minister*, season 1, episode 4, Directed by Sydney Lotterby, aired 17 March. BBC.

Jeffares, Stephen. 2014. *Interpreting Hashtag Politics: Policy Ideas in an Era of Social Media*. Palgrave Macmillan.

Jenkins-Smith, Hank. 1982. "Professional Roles of Policy Analysts." *Journal of Policy Analysis and Management* 2 (1): 88–100.

Jennings, B. 1987. "Policy Analysis: Science, Advocacy, or Counsel?" *Research in Public Policy Analysis and Management* 4: 121–34.
John, Peter. 1998. *Analysing Public Policy*. London: Continuum.
Johnson, A.W. 1971. "The Treasury Board of Canada and the Machinery of Government of the 1970s." *Canadian Journal of Political Science* 4(3): 346–66.
– 1992. *Reflections on Administrative Reform in the Government of Canada, 1962–1991*. Ottawa: Office of the Auditor-General of Canada.
Kahan, Dan M. 2013. "Ideology, Motivated Reasoning, and Cognitive Reflection." *Judgement and Decision Making* 8 (4): 407–24.
Kahan, Dan M., Ellen Peters, Erica C. Dawson, and Paul Slovic. 2013. "Motivated Numeracy and Enlightened Self Government." *Cultural Cognition Project Working Paper 116*. http://papers.ssrn.com/sol3/papers.cfm?abstract_id=2319992.
Kahneman, Daniel. 2011. *Thinking, Fast and Slow*. Canada: Doubleday.
Kanbur, Ravi. 2001. "Economic Policy, Distribution and Poverty: The Nature of Disagreement." *World Development* 26 (6): 1083–94.
Kaplan, Sarah. 2011. "Strategy and PowerPoint: An Inquiry into the Epistemic Culture and Machinery of Strategy Making." *Organization Science* 22 (2): 320–46.
Karlan, Dean, and Jacob Appel. 2011. *More than Good Intentions: How a New Economics Is Helping Solve Global Poverty*. Boston, MA: Dutton Press.
Kates, Robert, B.L. Turner, and William C. Clark. 1990. "The Great Transformation." In *The Earth as Transformed by Human Action*, edited by B.L. Turner et al., 1–17. Cambridge, MA: Cambridge University Press.
Keenleyside, Hugh L. 1982. *Memoirs of Hugh L. Keenleyside*. Vol. 2, *On the Bridge of Time*. Toronto: McClelland and Stewart.
Keith, David W. 2000. "Geoengineering the Climate: History and Prospect." *Annual Review of Energy and the Environment* 25 (1): 245–84.
Keith, David W., Edward A. Parson, and M. Granger Morgan. 2010. "Research on Global Sun Block Needed Now." *Nature* 463: 426–7.
Kernaghan, Kenneth. 1985. "The Conscience of the Bureaucrat: Accomplice or Constraint?" In *Responsibility in the Senior Public Service*, edited by Mervyn Brockett, John W. Langford, and William A. Neilson. Toronto: Institute of Public Administration of Canada.
Kirp, David L. 1992. "The End of Policy Analysis: With Apologies to Daniel ('The End of Ideology') Bell and Francis ('The End of History') Fukiyama." *Journal of Policy Analysis and Management* 11 (4): 693–6.

Klinkenberg, Brian. 2003. "The True Cost of Spatial Data in Canada." *Canadian Geographer* 47 (1): 37–49.

Kooiman, Jan. 1993. *Modern Governance: New Government-Society Interactions*. London: Sage.

Kraft, Michael E., and Scott R. Furlong. 2007. *Public Policy: Politics, Analysis, and Alternatives*. Washington, DC: CQ Press.

Krishnamurty, Rashmi, Akshay Bhagwatar, Erik Johnston and Kevin Desouza. 2013. "A Glimpse into Policy Informatics: The Case of Participatory Platforms That Generate Synthetic Empathy." In *Communications of the Association for Information Systems* 33, Article 21. http://aisel.aisnet.org/cgi/viewcontent.cgi?article= 3713&context=cais.

Kruger, Justin, and David Dunning. 1999. "Unskilled and Unaware of It: How Difficulties in Recognizing One's Own Incompetence Lead to Inflated Self-Assessments." *Journal of Personality and Social Psychology* 77 (6): 1121–34.

Kuhn, Thomas. 1962. *The Structure of Scientific Revolutions*. Chicago: University of Chicago Press.

Lackner, Klaus S. 2002. "Carbonate Chemistry for Sequestering Fossil Carbon." *Annual Review of Energy and the Environment* 27: 195–232.

Laden, Anthony Simon. 2012. "Taking the Engagement in Civic Engagement Seriously." *University of Illinois at Chicago College of Liberal Arts and Sciences*. http://www.uic.edu/cuppa/ipce/interior/TakingCivic EngagementSeriouslyFinalFY12.pdf .

Lakhani, Karim R., and Jill A. Panetta. 2007. "The Principles of Distributed Innovation." *Innovations* 2 (3): 97112.

Lalonde, Marc. 1984. *Action Plan for Pension Reform: Building Better Pensions for Canadians*. Ottawa: Department of Finance.

Lampel, Joseph, Pushkar P. Jha, and Ajay Bhalla. 2012. "TestDriving the Future: How Design Competitions are Changing Innovation." *The Academy of Management Perspectives* 26 (2): 7185.

Langford, John. 1985. "Responsibility in the Senior Public Service; Marching to Several Drummers." In *Responsibility in the Senior Public Service*, edited by Mervyn Brockett, John W. Langford, and William A. Neilson. Toronto: IPAC.

Lanyon, Linda, and Harry Hubball. 2008. "Gender Considerations and Innovative Learning-Centered Assessment Practices." *Transformative Dialogues: Teaching and Learning* 2 (1): 1–12.

Lasswell, Harold D. 1951. "The Policy Orientation." In *The Policy Sciences*, edited by Daniel Lerner and Harold D. Lasswell, 3–15. Stanford: Stanford University Press.

Latour, Bruno. 1987. *Science in Action: How to Follow Scientists and Engineers through Society.* Cambridge, MA: Harvard University Press.
Lawrence, Mark G. 2006. "The Geoengineering Dilemma: To Speak or Not to Speak." *Climatic Change* 77 (3–4): 245–8.
Lempert, Robert, Steven Popper, and Steven Bankes. 2002. "Confronting Surprise." *Social Science Computer Review* 20 (4): 420–40.
Levi, Maurice D., Kai Li, and Feng Zhang. 2008. *Mergers and Acquisitions: The Role of Gender.*
Levine, Ruth, Michael Kremer, Alice Albright. 2005. Making Markets for Vaccines. *Centre for Global Development Working Group Report.* http://www.cgdev.org/doc/books/vaccine/MakingMarkets-complete.pdf.
Lévy, Pierre, and Robert Bonomo. 1999. *Collective Intelligence: Mankind's Emerging World in Cyberspace.* Perseus.
Lexchin, Joel. 2010. "Drug Safety and Health Canada." *International Journal of Health Services* 22 (1): 41–53.
Library and Archives Canada. 1944. RG 25, Volume 5761, File 104(s)–1–1940, 20 March. e010692346.
Lifsher, Marc. 2012. "Businesses Seek State's New 'Benefit Corporation' Status." LA *Times*, January 4. http://www.latimes.com/business/la-fi-benefit-corporations-20120104,0,552054.story.
Likierman, Aandrew. 1982. "Management Information for Ministers: The MINIS System in the Department of the Environment." *Public Administration* 60 (summer): 127–42.
Lindblom, Charles E. 1979. "Still Muddling, Not Yet Through." *Public Administration Review* 39 (6): 517–26.
Lindquist, Evert. 2009. "How Ottawa Assesses Department/Agency Performance: Treasury Board of Canada's Management Accountability Framework." *School of Public Administration.* Victoria, BC: University of Victoria.
– 2015. "Visualization Meets Policy Making: Visual Traditions, Policy Complexity, Strategic Investments." In *Governance in the Information Era: Theory and Practice of Policy Informatics*, edited by Erik W. Johnston. New York: Routledge.
Lipsey, Richard, and Kelvin Lancaster. 1956. "The General Theory of the Second Best." *Review of Economic Studies* 24 (1): 11–32.
Lipsky, Michael. 1971. "Street-Level Bureaucracy and the Analysis of Urban Reform." *Urban Affairs Review* 6 (4): 391–409.
Longo, Justin. 2003. "Reflections on the Informal User Testing of a Computer-Based Simulation Tool as a Potential Aid to Policy Analysis: Just

When You Thought People Were Really Stupid." Paper presented at the WTMC Summer School, The Netherlands. 9–12 September 2003.

– 2011. "#OpenData: Digital-Era Governance Thoroughbred or New Public Management Trojan Horse?" *Public Policy and Governance Review* 2 (2): 38–51.

– 2012. *The Archetypical Policy Analyst, Mitacs Report 6*. University of Victoria.

– 2013. *Towards Policy Analysis 2.0*. PHD diss., University of Victoria.

Lubchenco, Jane. 1998. "Entering the Century of the Environment: A New Social Contract for Science." *Science*. 279 (5350): 491–7.

Ludwig, Donald, Ray Hilborn, and Carl Walters. 1993. "Uncertainty, Resource Exploitation, and Conservation: Lessons from History." *Science* 260: 17–36.

MacDermott, Kathy. 2008. *Whatever Happened to Frank and Fearless? The Impact of New Public Management on the Australian Public Service*. Canberra: ANU Press.

Malcolmson, Patrick, and Richard Myers. 2012. *The Canadian Regime: An Introduction to the Parliamentary Government in Canada*. Toronto: University of Toronto Press.

Malone, Thomas. 2013. Center for Collective Intelligence. Accessed November 10. http://cci.mit.edu/.

Marche, Sunny, and James D. McNiven. 2003. "E-Government and E-Governance: The Future Isn't What It Used to Be." *Canadian Journal of Administrative Sciences* 20 (1): 74–86.

Margetts, Helen. 1998. *Information Technology in Government: Britain and America*. London: Routledge.

Marshall, Alfred. 1920. *Principles of Economics, an Introductory Volume*. 8th ed. New York: MacMillan.

Martin, Paul. 1994. *The Budget Speech*. 22 February. Ottawa: Department of Finance Canada.

May, Peter J. 1992. "Policy Learning and Failure." *Journal of Public Policy* 12 (4): 331–54.

McAfee, Andrew P. 2006. "Enterprise 2.0: The Dawn of Emergent Collaboration." MIT *Sloan Management Review* 47 (3): 21–8.

McArthur, Doug. 2007. "Policy Analysis in Provincial Governments in Canada: From PPBS to Network Management." In *Policy Analysis in Canada: The State of the Art*, edited by Laurent Dobuzinski, Michael Howlett, and David Laycock, 342–78. Toronto: University of Toronto Press.

McFarland, Janet. 2011. "A Woman's Touch Rewards Shareholders." *Globe and Mail*, 8 March.

McGilchrist, Iain. 2009. *The Master and His Emissary: The Divided Brain and the Making of the Western World*. New Haven: Yale University Press.

McKean, Margaret. 2000. "Common Property: What Is It, What Is It Good for, and What Makes It Work?" In *People and Forests: Communities, Institutions, and Governance*, edited by Clark C. Gibson, Margaret A. McKean, and Elinor Ostrom, 27–58. Cambridge, MA: MIT Press.

Meadows, Donella H., Dennis L. Meadows, Jorgen Randers, and William W. Behrens. 1972. *The Limits to Growth: A Report for the Club of Rome's Project on the Predicament of Mankind*. New York: Universe.

Melnick, Meredith. 2011. "Why Women Are Better at Everything," *Time*, 28 June.

Meltsner, Arnold J. 1976. *Policy Analysts in the Bureaucracy*. Berkeley, CA: University of California Press.

Mergel, Ines, and Stuart I. Bretschneider. 2013. "A Three-Stage Adoption Process for Social Media Use in Government." *Public Administration Review* 73 (3): 390–400.

Mergel, Ines, and Kevin C. Desouza. 2013. "Implementing Open Innovation in the Public Sector: The Case of Challenge.gov." *Public Administration Review* 73 (6): 882–90.

Mesarovic, Mihajlo, and Eduard Pestel. 1974. *Mankind at the Turning Point: The Second Report to the Club of Rome*. New York: EP Dutton.

Michalko, Michael. 2000. "Thinking Out of the Box." *Innovative Leader*. http://www.winstonbrill.com/bril001/html/article_index/articles/451-500/article472_body.html.

Miki, Roy. 2004. *Redress: Inside the Japanese Canadian Call for Justice*. Vancouver: Raincoast Press.

Miller, George. 1955. "The Magical Number Seven, Plus or Minus Two Some Limits on Our Capacity for Processing Information." *Psychological Review* 101 (2): 343–52.

Mitchell, Timothy. 2011. *Carbon Democracy: Political Power in the Age of Oil*. New York: Verso Books.

Moran, Michael, Martin Rein, and Robert E. Goodin. 2006. "The Public and Its Policies." In *Oxford Handbook of Public Policy*, edited by Michael Moran, Martin Rein, and Robert E. Goodin, 1–36. New York: Oxford University Press.

Morçöl, Göktug. 2001. "Positivist Beliefs among Policy Professionals: An Empirical Investigation." *Policy Sciences* 34 (3–4): 381–401.

Morgan, James N., Katherine Dickinson, Jonathan Dickinson, Jacob Benus, and Greg Duncan. 1974. *Five Thousand American Families – Patterns of Economic Progress.* Vol. 1: *An Analysis of the First Five Years of the Panel Study of Income Dynamics.* Ann Arbor: University of Michigan.

Morgan, M. Granger, and Katharine Ricke. 2010. *Cooling the Earth through Solar Radiation Management.* Geneva: International Risk Governance Council. http://www.irgc.org/IMG/pdf/SRM_Opinion_Piece_web.pdf.

Morgenthau, Hans J. 2006. *Politics among Nations: The Struggle for Power and Peace.* 7th ed. Boston, MA: McGraw-Hill Higher Education.

Morison, John. 2010. "Gov 2.0: Towards a User Generated State?" *The Modern Law Review* 73 (4): 551–77.

Moser, Susanne C., and Lisa Dilling. 2007. *Creating a Climate for Change: Communicating Climate Change and Facilitating Social Change.* Cambridge, MA: Cambridge University Press.

Mouffe, Chantal. 2000. *The Democratic Paradox.* London: Verso Books.

Mulgan, Geoff. 1998. *Connexity: Responsibility, Freedom, Business and Power in the New Century.* London: Vintage Books.

– 2009. *The Art of Public Strategy: Mobilizing Power and Knowledge for the Common Good.* Oxford: Oxford University Press.

Mulgan, Richard. 2007. "Truth in Government and the Politicisation of Public Service Advice." *Public Administration* 85 (3): 569–86.

Nagel, Thomas. 1979. *Mortal Questions.* Cambridge, UK: Cambridge University Press.

Nairn, Geoff. 2011. "The Trouble with Office Email," *Financial Times*, 17 February.

Napoli, Philip M., and Joe Karaganis. 2010. "On Making Public Policy with Publicly Available Data: The Case of U.S. Communications Policymaking." *Government Information Quarterly* 27 (4): 384–91.

National Child Benefit. 2006. *The National Child Benefit Progress Report: 2006.* Ottawa: National Child Benefit. http://www.nationalchildbenefit.ca/eng/06/chap1.shtml.

Nelson, Richard R., and Sidney G. Winter. 1982. *An Evolutionary Theory of Economic Change.* Cambridge, MA: Harvard University Press.

New York Department of Health. 2008. *Love Canal Follow-up Health Study.* State of New York, Department of Health.

Nielson, Kai. 2000. "There Is No Dilemma of Dirty Hands." In *Cruelty & Deception: The Controversy over Dirty Hands in Politics*, edited by Paul Rynard and David P. Shugarman, 139–55. Peterborough, ON: Broadview Press.

Oberlander, H. Peter, and Arthur Fallick. 1987. *The Ministry of State for Urban Affairs: A Courageous Experiment in Public Administration*. Vancouver: Centre for Human Settlements, University of British Columbia.

Olson, Mancur. 1965. *The Logic of Collective Action: Public Goods and the Theory of Groups*. Cambridge, MA: Harvard University Press.

Orcutt, Guy H. 1957. "A New Type of Socio-Economic System." *Review of Economics and Statistics* 39 (2): 116–23.

Orcutt, Guy H., Steven Caldwell, and Richard F. Wertheimer. 1976. *Policy Exploration through Microanalytic Simulation*. Washington, DC: The Urban Institute.

Oreskes, Naomi, and Erik M. Conway. 2010. *Merchants of Doubt*. New York: Bloomsbury Press.

Ostrom, Elinor. 1990. *Governing the Commons: The Evolution of Institutions for Collective Action*. Cambridge, MA: Cambridge University Press.

– 2009. "Prize Lecture: Beyond Markets and States, Polycentric Governance of Complex Economic Systems." Nobel Prize Lecture. http://www.nobelprize.org/nobel_prizes/economics/laureates/2009/ostrom_lecture.pdf.

Ostrom, Elinor, Thomas Dietz, Nives Dolsak, Paul C. Stern, Susan Stonich, and Elke U. Weber. 2002. *The Drama of the Commons: Committee on the Human Dimensions of Global Change*. Washington, DC: National Academy Press.

Ostrom, Elinor, and Edella Schlager. 1996. "The Formation of Property Rights." In *Rights to Nature: Ecological, Economic, Cultural, and Political Principles of Institutions for the Environment*, edited by Susan Hanna, Carl Folke, and Karl-Goran Maler, 127–56. Washington, DC: Island Press.

Ottensmann, J.R. 1985. *Using Personal Computers in Public Agencies*. New York: Wiley.

Page, Scott E. 2008. *The Difference: How the Power of Diversity Creates Better Groups, Firms, Schools, and Societies*. Princeton: Princeton University Press.

Pal, Leslie. 1987. *Public Policy Analysis: An Introduction*. Toronto: Methuen.

– 2009. *Beyond Policy Analysis: Public Issue Management in Turbulent Times*. Toronto: Nelson.

Palsson, Gisli. 1998. "Learning by Fishing: Practical Engagement and Environmental Concerns." In *Linking Social and Ecological Systems: Management Practices and Social Mechanisms for Building Resilience*, edited by Fikret Berkes and Carl Folke. Cambridge, MA: Cambridge University Press.

Paquet, Gilles. 2009. *Crippling Epistemologies and Governance Failures: A Plea for Experimentalism*. Ottawa: University of Ottawa Press.

Paquet, Gilles, and Robert Shepherd. 1996. "The Program Review Process: A Deconstruction." In *How Ottawa Spends 1996–97: Life under the Knife*, edited by Gene Swimmer, 39–72. Ottawa: Carleton University Press.

Parfit, Derek. 1986. *Reasons and Persons*. Oxford: Oxford University Press.

Parker, John N., and Beatrice Crona. 2012. "On Being All Things to All People: Boundary Organizations and the Contemporary Research University." *Social Studies of Science* 42 (2): 262–89.

Parson, Edward A. 2003. *Protecting the Ozone Layer: Science and Strategy*. Oxford: Oxford University Press.

Parson, Edward A., Vicente Barros, Clive Hamilton, David Keith, Jane Long, Sospeter Muhongo, Phil Rasch et al. 2011. "'Mechanics' of SRM Research Governance." *Solar Radiation Management Governance Initiative*. 31 March. http://www.srmgi.org/files/2011/09/SRMGI-Mechanics-background-paper.pdf.

Parson Edward A., A.R. Dobell, Adam French, and Donald Munton. 2001. "Leading While Keeping in Step: Management of Global Environmental Issues in Canada." In *Learning to Manage Global Environmental Risks*, 235–58. Cambridge, MA: MIT Press.

Parson, Edward A., and Karen Fisher-Vanden. 1997. "Integrated Assessment Models of Global Climate Change." *Annual Review of Energy and Environment* 22 (1): 589–628. http://www.srmgi.org/files/2011/09/SRMGI-Mechanics-background-paper.pdf.

Parson, Edward A., and David W. Keith. 1998. "Fossil Fuels without CO_2 Emissions." *Science* 282: 1053–4.

– 2013. "End the Deadlock on Governance of Geoengineering Research." *Science* 339:1278–9.

Parsons, Wayne. 2001. "Modernising Policy-making for the Twenty First Century: The Professional Model." *Public Policy and Administration* 16 (3): 93–110.

– 2004. “Not Just Steering but Weaving: Relevant Knowledge and the Craft of Building Policy Capacity and Coherence.” *Australian Journal of Public Administration* 63 (1): 43–57.

Pentland, Alex. 2014. *Social Physics: How Good Ideas Spread: The Lessons from a New Science*. New York: Penguin.

Picard, Andre. 1996. “Blame Me for Blood Scandal Bégin Says.” *Globe and Mail*, 21 August.

Polanyi, Karl. 1944. *The Great Transformation: The Political and Economic Origins of Our Times*. Boston: Beacon Press.

Pregernig, Michael, and Michael Bocher. 2013. “The Role of Expertise in Environmental Governance: Theoretical Perspectives and Empirical Evidence.” In *Long-Term Governance for Social-Ecological Change*, edited by Bernd Siebenhuner, Marlen Arnold, Klaus Eisenack, and Klaus H. Jacob, 29–46. New York: Routledge.

Pressman, Jeffery L., and Aaron Wildavsky. 1973. *Implementation: How Great Expectations in Washington Are Dashed in Oakland*. Berkeley: University of California Press.

Price, Don K. 1965. *The Scientific Estate*. Cambridge: Harvard University Press.

Prince, Michael J. 1985. “Startling Facts, Sobering Truths and Sacred Trust: Pension Policy and the Tories.” In *How Ottawa Spends 1985: Sharing the Pie*, edited by Allan M. Maslove, 114–61. Toronto: Methuen.

– 2003. “Taking Stock: Governance Practices and Portfolio Performance of the Canada Pension Plan Investment Board.” In *How Ottawa Spends 2003–2004: Regime Change and Policy Shift*, edited by G.B. Doern, 134–54. Toronto: Oxford University Press.

– 2007. “Soft Craft, Hard Choices, Altered Context: Reflections on Twenty-Five Years of Policy Advice in Canada.” In *Policy Analysis in Canada: The State of the Art*, edited by Laurent Dobuzinskis, Michael Howlett, and David Laycock, 244–71. Toronto: University of Toronto Press.

– 2010. “Avoiding Blame, Doing Good, and Claiming Credit: Reforming Canadian Income Security.” *Canadian Public Administration* 53 (3): 1–30.

– 2013. “Blue Rinse: Harper’s Treatment of Old Age Security and Other Elderly Benefits.” In *How Ottawa Spends 2013–2014: The Harper Government, Mid-Term Blues and Long-Term Plans*, edited by Christopher Stoney and G. Bruce Doern, 64–75. Montreal and Kingston: McGill-Queen’s University Press.

PSAC. 1965. *Restoring the Quality of Our Environment*. United States: Environmental Pollution Panel, President's Science Advisory Committee.

Quade, Edward S. 1975. *Analysis for Public Decisions*. New York: Elsevier.

– 1980. "Pitfalls in Formulation and Modeling." In *Pitfalls in Analysis*, edited by Giandomenico Majone and Edward S. Quade, 23–43. New York: Wiley.

Radin, Beryl A. 2000. *Beyond Machiavelli: Policy Analysis Comes of Age*. Washington, DC: Georgetown University Press.

Ramadan, Tariq. 2009. *Radical Reform: Islamic Ethics and Radical Reform*. Oxford: Oxford University Press.

Rasch, Philip J., et al. 2008. "An Overview of Geoengineering of Climate Using Stratospheric Sulphate Aerosols." *Philosophical Transactions of the Royal Society A* 366: 4007–37.

Reich, Robert B. 2008. *Supercapitalism: The Transformation of Business, Democracy, and Everyday Life*. New York: Vintage.

Rennie, Steve. 2011. "Canada Blocks Asbestos from Hazardous Chemicals List at UN Summit," *Toronto Star*, 22 June.

Reynaud, Emmanuel. 2000. "Introduction and Summary." In *Social Dialogue and Pension Reform*, edited by Emmanuel Reynaud, 1–10. Geneva: International Labour Office.

Rhodes, Rod, John Wanna, and Patrick Weller. 2009. *Comparing Westminster*. Oxford, UK: Oxford University Press.

Rice, James J., and Michael J. Prince. 2013. *Changing Politics of Canadian Social Policy*. 2d ed. Toronto: University of Toronto Press.

Risse, Mathias. 2008. "Original Ownership of the Earth: A Contemporary Approach." *HKS Faculty Research Working Paper Series, RWP08–073*. Cambridge, MA: Harvard.

Robertson, Gordon. 2000. *Memoirs of a Very Civil Servant: Mackenzie King to Pierre Trudeau*. Toronto: University of Toronto Press.

Robinson, John, and John Tinker. 1997. "Reconciling Ecological, Economic and Social Imperatives: A New Conceptual Framework." In *Surviving Globalism: Social and Environmental Dimensions*, edited by Ted Schrecker, 71–94. London, New York: Macmillan, St. Martin's Press.

Roe, Emery M. 1989. "The Zone of Acceptance in Organization Theory: An Explanation of the Challenger Disaster." *Administration and Society* 21 (2): 234–64.

Roscoe, Philip. 2014. *I Spend, Therefore I Am: How Economics Has Changed the Way We Think and Feel*. Toronto: Random House Canada.

Rose, Carol. 1994. *Property and Persuasion: Essays on the History, Theory, and Rhetoric of Ownership*. Boulder, CO: Westview Press.

Rose, Richard. 1991. "What is Lesson-Drawing?" *Journal of Public Policy*. 11 (1): 3–30.

Roy, Patricia, J.L. Granatstein, Masako Lino, and Hiroko Takamura. 1990. *Mutual Hostages: Canadians and Japanese during the Second World War*. Toronto: University of Toronto Press.

Royal Society. 2009. *Geoengineering the Climate: Science, Governance, and Uncertainty*. London: The Royal Society.

Russell, Bertrand. 1951. *New Hopes for a Changing World*. Michigan: Allen and Unwin.

Sabatier, Paul A. 2007. "The Need for Better Theories." In *Theories of the Policy Process*. 2d ed. Edited by Paul A. Sabatier, 3–18. Boulder: Westview.

Samarasekera, Indira V. 2009. "Universities Need a New Social Contract." *Nature* 462 (157): 160–1.

Samuelson, Paul A. 1947. *Foundations of Economic Analysis*. Cambridge, MA: Harvard University Press.

Sapienza, Paola, Zingales Luigi, and Dario Maestripieri. 2009. "Gender Differences in Financial Risk Aversion and Career Choices Are Affected by Testosterone." *Proceedings of the National Academy of Sciences* 106 (36): 15268–73.

Savoie, Donald. 1999. *Governing from the Centre: The Concentration of Power in Canadian Politics*. Toronto: University of Toronto Press.

– 2003. *Breaking the Bargain: Public Servants, Ministers and Parliament*. Toronto: University of Toronto Press.

– 2008. *Court Government and the Collapse of Accountability*. Toronto: University of Toronto Press.

– 2013. "Running Government like a Business Has Been a Dismal Failure," *The Globe and Mail*, 7 January.

Sax, Joseph. 1970. "The Public Trust Doctrine in Natural Resources Law: Effective Judicial Intervention." *Michigan Law Review* 68 (471): 509–46.

Schelling, Thomas C. 1983. "Climatic Change: Implications for Welfare and Policy." In *Changing Climate: Report of the Carbon Dioxide Assessment Committee*, edited by the National Research Council, Carbon Dioxide Assessment Committee, 449–82. Washington, DC: National Academy Press.

Schneider, Stephen H. 1996. "Geoengineering: Could – or Should – We Do It?" *Climatic Change* 33 (3): 291–302.

Schon, Donald A. 1995 "Knowing in Action: The New Scholarship Requires a New Epistemology." *Change* 27 (6): 27–34.

Schreurs, Miranda, William C. Clark, Nancy M. Dickson, and Jill Jäger. 2001. "Issue Attention, Framing and Actors: An Analysis of Patterns Across Arenas." In *Learning to Manage Global Environmental Risks: A Comparative History of Social Responses to Climate Change, Ozone Depletion and Acid Rain*. Vol. 1, edited by Social Learning Group, 349–64. Cambridge, MA: MIT Press.

Scott, James C. 1998. *Seeing Like a State: How Certain Schemes to Improve the Human Condition Have Failed*. New Haven: Yale University Press.

Seeman, Neil. 2000. "Software for Tyrants," *Weekly Standard*, 28 August.

Seising, Rudolf. 2012. "Warren Weaver's 'Science and Complexity' Revisited." In *Soft Computing in Humanities and Social Sciences, Studies in Fuzziness and Soft Computing*, edited by Rudolf Seising and Veronica Sanz, 55–87. Berlin: Springer-Verlag Berlin Heidelberg.

Serageldin, Ismail. 2012. *Science and Democracy*. Plenary lecture, annual meeting, American Association for the Advancement of Science (AAAS), Vancouver, BC, February 19. http://membercentral.aaas.org/multimedia/videos/plenary-lecture-ismail-serageldin-science-and-democracy.

Shafer, Arthur. 1999. "A Wink and a Nod: A Conceptual Map of Responsibility and Accountability in Bureaucratic Organizations." *Canadian Public Administration* 42 (1): 5–25.

Shaw, George Bernard. 1907. *Major Barbara*. London: Brentano.

Shearman, David, and Joseph Smith. 2007. *The Climate Change Challenge and the Failure of Democracy*. Westport, CT: Praeger.

Sheehan, Linda. 2013. "Rights of Nature." Accessed November 10. http://www.earthlawcentre.org.

Shirky, Clay. 2008. *Here Comes Everybody: The Power of Organizing without Organizations*. New York: Penguin.

Shulock, Nancy. 1999. "The Paradox of Policy Analysis: If It Is Not Used, Why Do We Produce So Much of It?" *Journal of Policy Analysis and Management* 18 (2): 226–44.

Simeon, Richard. 1972. *Federal-Provincial Diplomacy: The Making of Recent Policy in Canada*. Toronto: University of Toronto Press.

– 1976. "Studying Public Policy." *Canadian Journal of Political Science* 9 (4): 548–80.

Simpson, Jeffrey. 2001. *The Friendly Dictatorship*. Toronto: McClelland and Stewart.

– 2011. "Save Resource Money for the Future? Nah, Says Alberta." *Globe and Mail*, 25 May.

Smith, William. 2004. "Democracy, Deliberation and Disobedience." *Res Publica* 10 (4): 353–77.

– 2013. *Civil Disobedience and Deliberative Democracy*. New York: Routledge.

Snow, Charles P. 1960. *Science and Government: The Godkin Lectures*. Cambridge, MA: Harvard University Press.

Social Learning Group. 2001. *Learning to Manage Global Environmental Risks: A Comparative History of Social Responses to Climate Change, Ozone Depletion and Acid Rain*. Vol. 1. MIT Press, Cambridge.

Soden, Brian J., Richard T. Wetherald, Georgiy L. Stenchikov, and Alan Robock. 2002. "Global Cooling after the Eruption of Mt. Pinatubo: A Test of Climate Feedback by Water Vapor." *Science* 296: 727–30.

SRMGI (Solar Radiation Management Governance Initiative). 2011. *Solar Radiation Management: The Governance of Research*. http://www.srmgi.org/report.

Stafford-Smith, Mark, Owen Gaffney, Linda Brito, Elinor Ostrom, and Sybil Setzinger. 2012. "Interconnected Risks and Solutions for a Planet under Pressure." *Current Opinion in Environmental Sustainability* 4 (1): 3–6.

Stern, Howard. 2006. *Stern Review Report on the Economics of Climate Change*. Cambridge: Cambridge University Press.

Stiglitz, Joseph. 2003. *Globalization and its Discontents*. New York: Norton.

– 2012. *The Price of Inequality*. New York: Norton.

Stokes, Donald E. 1997. *Pasteur's Quadrant: Basic Science and Technological Innovation*. Washington, DC: Brookings Institution Press.

Sunahara, Ann G. 1981. *The Politics of Racism: The Uprooting of Japanese Canadians during the Second World War*. Toronto: Lorimer and Company.

Surowiecki, James. 2005. *The Wisdom of Crowds*. New York: Knopf Doubleday.

Taruskin, Richard. 1995. *Text and Act: Essays on Music and Performance*. Oxford: Oxford University Press.

Thaler, Richard, and Cass Sunstein. 2008. *Nudge: Improving Decisions about Health, Wealth and Happiness*. Princeton, NJ: Yale University Press.

Thatcher, Margaret. 1965. Speech to National Union of Townswomen's Guilds Conference. May 20.

Thompson, Dennis. 1983. "Ascribing Responsibility to Advisers in Government." *Ethics* 93 (3): 546–60.

– 1985. "The Possibility of Administrative Ethics." *Public Administration Review*. 45 (5): 555–61.

– 1987. *Political Ethics and Public Office*. Cambridge: Harvard University Press.

Thompson, Derek. 2011. "The Case for Banning Email at Work," *Atlantic Monthly*, 1 December.

Timmons, D.J. 2004. *"Evangelines of 1946": The Exile of Nikkei from Canada to Occupied Japan*. MA thesis, Department of History, University of Victoria.

Torgerson, Douglas. 1986. "Between Knowledge and Politics: Three Faces of Policy Analysis." *Policy Sciences* 19 (1): 33–59.

Townson, Monica. 2009. *A Stronger Foundation: Pension Reform and Old Age Security*. Ottawa: Canadian Centre for Policy Alternatives.

Tracy, Karen, and Catherine Ashcraft. 2001. "Crafting Policies about Controversial Values: How Wording Disputes Manage a Group Dilemma." *Journal of Applied Communication Research* 29 (4): 297–316.

Travers, Jim. 2006. "Mandarins Learning to Like Harper," *Toronto Star*, 22 August, A17.

Treasury Board Secretariat. 2009. *Policy on Evaluation*. http://www.tbs-sct.gc.ca/pol/doc-eng.aspx?evttoo=X§ion=text&id=15024.

– 2010. *Performance Reporting: Good Practices Handbook 2010*. http://www.tbs-sct.gc.ca/rma/guide/practices-pratiques-eng.pdf.

– 2011. *2010 Annual Report on the Health of the Evaluation Function*. http://www.tbs-sct.gc.ca/report/orp/2011/arhef-raefe-eng.pdf.

– 2012. *Management Accountability Framework*. http.www.tbs-sct.gc.ca/maf-crg/index-eng.

Tully, James. 2008. "On Global Citizenship." University of Victoria Distinguished Professor Lecture, Victoria, BC, 13 March.

– 2010. "A Dilemma of Democratic Citizenship." The Changing Face of Citizen Action Conference. Victoria, BC, May. http://www.hivos.nl/knowledge/Hivos-Knowledge-Programme/Themes/The-Changing-Face-of-Citizen-Action/News/A-Dilemma-of-Democratic-Citizenship.

– 2013. "Citizenship for the Love of the World." Address, Cornell University, March 2013. http://government.arts.cornell.edu/assets/events/Tully_Citizenship_for_the_Love_of_the_World.pdf.

Tversky, Amos, and Daniel Kahneman. 1974. "Judgement and Uncertainty: Heuristics and Biases." *Science* 185 (4157): 1124–31.

– 1986. "Rational Choice and the Framing of Decisions," *Journal of Business* 59 (4): S251–78.

UNAIDS. 2011. "About UN Aids." http://www.unaids.org/en/aboutunaids/unaidsprogrammecoordinatingboard.

UNESCO. 1999. *Clayoquot Biosphere Reserve Nomination*. January 25. British Columbia: UNESCO.

United States. 2012. "Bring Your Own Device: A Toolkit to Support Federal Agencies Implementing Bring Your Own Device (BYOD) Programs." Product of the Digital Services Advisory Group and Federal Chief Information Officers Council. Washington, DC: The White House. August 23. http://www.whitehouse.gov/digitalgov/bring-your-own-device.

Van der Sluijs, Jeroen P., Rinie Van Est, and Monique Riphagen. 2010. "Beyond Consensus: Reflections from a Democratic Perspective on the Interaction between Climate Politics and Science." *Current Opinion in Environmental Sustainability* 2 (5–6): 1–7.

Van Eijndhoven, Josee. 1994. "Disaster Prevention in Europe." In *Learning from Disaster: Risk Management after Bhopal*, edited by Jasanoff, Sheila, 113–32. Philadelphia, PA: University of Pennsylvania Press.

Van Laerhoven, Frank, and Elinor Ostrom. 2007. "Traditions and Trends in the Study of the Commons." *International Journal of the Commons* 1 (1): 3–28.

Van Loon, Richard. 1981. "Stop the Music: The Current Policy and Expenditure Management System in Ottawa." *Canadian Public Administration* 24 (2): 175–99.

Vernadsky, Vladmir I. 1945. "The Biosphere and the Nöosphere." *American Scientist* 33 (1): 1–12.

Verweij, Marco, Mary Douglas, Richard Ellis, Christoph Engel, Frank Hendriks, Susanne Lohmann, Steven Ney, Steve Raynor, and Michael Thompson. 2006. "Clumsy Solutions for a Complex World: The Case of Climate Change." *Public Administration* 84 (4): 817–43.

Viégas, Fernanda, and Martin Wattenberg. 2010. "Case Study: Many Eyes." In *Open Government: Collaboration, Transparency and Participation in Practice*, edited by Daniel Lathrop and Laurel Ruma, 249–56. Sebastopol, CA: O'Reilly Media, Inc.

Vickers, Geoffrey. 1965. *The Art of Judgement: A Study of Policy Making*. London: Chapman & Hall.

Victor, David. 2011. *Global Warming Gridlock: Creating More Effective Strategies for Protecting the Planet*. Cambridge: University Press.

Volcker, Paul. 2010. "The Time We Have Is Growing Short." *New York Review of Books, 25* May. http://www.nybooks.com/articles/archives/2010/jun/24/time-we-have-growing-short.

Vonkeman, Gerrit, and Graham Bennett. 1991. *Highlights from the Environment: Ideas for the 21st Century*. The Hague: Dutch Committee for Long Term Environmental Policy.

Voss, Jan-Peter, Adrian Smith, and John Grin. 2009. "Designing Long-Term Policy: Rethinking Transition Management." *Policy Sciences* 42 (4): 275–302.

Walter, James. 2006. "Ministers, Minders and Public Servants: Changing Parameters of Responsibility in Australia." *Australian Journal of Public Administration* 65 (3): 22–7.

Walzer, Michael. 2004. "Emergency Ethics." In *Arguing about War*, 33–50. New Haven: Yale University Press.

Ward, Barbara. 1966. *Spaceship Earth: The George B. Pegram Lectures*. New York: Columbia University Press.

WCED (World Commission on Environment and Development). 1987. *Our Common Future*. Oxford: Oxford University Press.

Weaver, John C. 2003. *The Great Land Rush and the Making of the Modern World: 1650–1900*. Montreal and Kingston: McGill-Queen's University Press.

Weaver, Warren. 1948. "Science and Complexity." *American Scientist* 36: 536.

Weimer, David, and Aidan R. Vining. 2010. *Policy Analysis: Concepts and Practice*. 5th ed. London: Longman.

Weitzner, Daniel. 2007. "Beyond Secrecy: New Privacy Protection Strategies for Open Information Spaces." *IEEE Internet Computing* 11 (5): 94–6.

Wellstead, Adam, and Richard Stedman. 2010. "Policy Capacity and Incapacity in Canada's Federal Government: The Intersection of Policy Analysis and Street-Level Bureaucracy." *Public Management Review* 12 (6): 893–910.

Whittaker, Steve, and Candice Sidner. 1996. "Email Overload: Exploring Personal Information Management of Email." In *Proceedings of the ACM SIGCHI Conference on Human Factors in Computing Systems*, 276–83.

Wiener, Antje. 2014. *A Theory of Contestation*. Berlin: Springer.

Wigand, F. Dianne Lux. 2010. "Twitter in Government: Building Relationships One Tweet at a Time." In *Information Technology: New Generations (ITNG), 2010 Seventh International Conference on Information Technology*, 563–7. IEEE.

Wildavsky, Aaron. 1978. "Policy Analysis Is What Information Systems Are Not." *Accounting, Organizations and Society* 3 (1): 77–88.

– 1979. *Speaking Truth to Power: The Art and Craft of Policy Analysis.* Boston, MA: Little, Brown.

– 1980. *The Art and Craft of Policy Analysis.* London: Macmillan.

Wolfson, Michael. 1986. "Guaranteed Incomes for Canadians." *Policy Options* January: 35–45.

– 2011. "Projecting the Adequacy of Canada's Retirement Income System." IRPP *Study* No. 17, April. http://irpp.org/wp-content/uploads/assets/research/faces-of-aging/projecting-the-adequacy-of-canadians-retirement-incomes/IRPP-Study-no17.pdf.

– 2013. "Not So Modest Options for Expanding the CPP/QPP." IRPP *Study* No. 41, May. http://www.irpp.org/assets/research/faces-of-aging/not-so-modest-reforms/Wolfson-No41.pdf.

Wolfson, Michael, and Geoff Rowe. 2007. "Aging and Inter-Generational Fairness: A Canadian Analysis." In *Equity Research on Economic Inequality*, edited by Peter J. Lambert, 197–231. Bingley, UK: Emerald Group Publishing.

World Health Organization. 2006. *Advanced Market Commitments for Vaccines.* http://www.who.int/immunization/newsroom/amcs/en/index.html.

Wright, Douglas T. 1971. *Post-Secondary Education in Ontario: A Statement of Issues.* Toronto: Commission on Post-secondary Education in Ontario.

Wyld, David C. 2007. *The Blogging Revolution: Government in the Age of Web 2.0.* Washington, DC: IBM Center for the Business of Government.

Wynne, Brian. 2010. "Foreword." In *Between Reason and Experience: Essays in Technology and Modernity*, edited by Andrew Feenberg, ix–xvi. Cambridge, MA: MIT Press.

Yakabuski, Konrad. 2008. "Woods War II." *Globe and Mail*, 26 September.

Yang, K. 2007. "Quantitative Methods for Policy Analysis." In *Handbook of Public Policy Analysis: Theory, Politics, and Methods,* edited by Frank Fischer, Gerald J. Miller, and Mara S. Sidney, 349–68. Boca Raton, FL: CRC Press.

Ziman, John. 1996. "Post-Academic Science: Constructing Knowledge with Networks and Norms." *Science Studies* 9(1): 67–80.

Zussman, David. 1986. "Walking the Tightrope: The Mulroney Government and the Public Service." In *How Ottawa Spends 1986–87*, edited by Michael J. Prince, Toronto: Methuen.

– 1987. *Confidence in Canadian Government Institution*, Montreal: The Institute for Research on Public Policy.

– 2009. *Political Advisors*. Expert Group on Conflict of Interest, Public Governance Committee, Public Governance and Territorial Development Directorate, OECD. Paris: OECD.

– 2010. "The Precarious State of the Federal Public Service." In *How Ottawa Spends*. Montreal: McGill-Queen's University Press.

Zweig, Jason. 2009. "For Mother's Day, Give Her Reins to the Portfolio." *Wall Street Journal*, 9 May.

Zwicky, Jan. 2003. *Wisdom and Metaphor*. Kentville, NS: Gaspereau Press.

6, Perri. 2004. *E-Governance: Styles of Political Judgment in the Information Age Polity.* London: Palgrave Macmillan.

Contributors

MARTIN BUNTON is associate professor of history at the University of Victoria.

BARRY CARIN is senior fellow at the Centre for International Governance Innovation.

IAN D. CLARK is professor of public policy at the University of Toronto.

RACHEL CULLEY is a law clerk at the United States District Court for the Eastern District of New York.

A.R. (ROD) DOBELL is professor emeritus of public policy at the University of Victoria.

JOSEE VAN EIJNDHOVEN is professor of sustainability management at Erasmus University, Rotterdam.

LIA N. ERNST is a law clerk at the United States Court of Appeals for the First Circuit.

JILL R. HORWITZ is professor of law at UCLA and adjunct professor of economics at the University of Victoria.

JOHN LANGFORD is professor emeritus in the School of Public Administration of the University of Victoria.

JUSTIN LONGO is a postdoctoral fellow in open governance at the Center for Policy Informatics, Arizona State University.

EDWARD A. PARSON is Dan and Rae Emmett Professor of Environmental Law and faculty co-director of the Emmett Institute for Climate Change and the Environment at UCLA, and senior research associate at the Centre for Global Studies, University of Victoria.

MICHAEL J. PRINCE is Lansdowne Professor of Social Policy at the University of Victoria.

HARRY SWAIN is senior research associate at the Centre for Global Studies, University of Victoria.

CHARLES UNGERLEIDER is professor of the sociology of education at the University of British Columbia and managing partner and director of research at Directions Evidence and Policy Research Group, LLP.

MICHAEL WOLFSON is Canada Research Chair in Population Health Modelling at the Faculty of Medicine, University of Ottawa.

DAVID ZUSSMAN is Jarislowsky Chair in Public Sector Management at the Graduate School of Public and International Affairs, University of Ottawa.

Index